Women Healers

EARLY AMERICAN STUDIES

Series Editors
Kathleen M. Brown, Roquinaldo Ferreira, Emma Hart, and Daniel K. Richter

Exploring neglected aspects of our colonial, revolutionary, and early
national history and culture, Early American Studies reinterprets
familiar themes and events in fresh ways. Interdisciplinary in character,
and with a special emphasis on the period from about 1600 to 1850,
the series is published in partnership with the McNeil Center for
Early American Studies.

A complete list of books in the series is available from the publisher.

WOMEN HEALERS

Gender, Authority, and Medicine
in Early Philadelphia

Susan H. Brandt

PENN

UNIVERSITY OF PENNSYLVANIA PRESS

PHILADELPHIA

Published by
University of Pennsylvania Press
Philadelphia, Pennsylvania 19104-4112
www.upenn.edu/pennpress

Printed in the United States of America on acid-free paper
10 9 8 7 6 5 4 3 2 1

Hardcover ISBN: 978-0-8122-5386-3
Ebook ISBN: 978-0-8122-9847-5

Library of Congress Cataloging-in-Publication Data

Names: Brandt, Susan Hanket, author.
Title: Women healers : gender, authority, and medicine in early
Philadelphia / Susan H. Brandt.
Other titles: Early American studies.
Description: 1st edition. | Philadelphia : University of Pennsylvania
Press, [2022] | Series: Early American studies | Includes
bibliographical references and index.
Identifiers: LCCN 2021039334 | ISBN 978-0-8122-5386-3 (hardcover)
Subjects: LCSH: Women in medicine—Pennsylvania—Philadelphia—
History—18th century. | Women healers—Pennsylvania—
Philadelphia—History—18th century. | Minorities in medicine—
Pennsylvania—Philadelphia—History—18th century. | Medicine—
Pennsylvania—Philadelphia—History—18th century.
Classification: LCC R692 .B743 2022 | DDC 610.8209748/11—dc23
LC record available at https://lccn.loc.gov/2021039334

Cures and remedies described in this book are presented
for historical purposes only and should not be used
as medical treatments.

To Sam

CONTENTS

Figure 1. *Plan of the City and Environs of Philadelphia*, Nicholas Scull and George Heap, surveyors, engraved by William Faden, 1777 (revision of Scull and Heaps's 1752 map).

INTRODUCTION

In 1855, Dr. Ann Preston addressed the incoming class at the first women's medical school in the United States, the Female Medical College of Pennsylvania. Preston had received her medical degree from the college in 1851. She now offered encouragement to women medical students embarking on a "new and untried course" of professional medical education. The history of women physicians in the United States often begins with the 1850 founding of the college in Philadelphia, and the battles that women like Preston faced as male doctors attempted to impede their medical training and marginalize their practices. However, the narrative of women as medical practitioners has much deeper roots. Preston and other mid-nineteenth-century women physicians continued the legacies of women healers who had played a central role in the provision of health care for centuries. While historians have described the contributions of medieval and early modern European women healers, there are few scholarly works on female practitioners in early America. This book recovers the medical activities of early Philadelphia-area women and demonstrates that Female Medical College professors and students stood on the shoulders of numerous women who had practiced medicine, nursing, and pharmacy. It was no accident that the first women's medical school was founded in Philadelphia. Rather, it was the result of unique circumstances that supported a robust culture of women's public health care work in the region for almost two hundred years. In fact, Preston's "new and untried course" was merely one signpost on a well-trodden path populated with medically skilled women.[1]

Although women healers were ubiquitous in early modern society, they are relatively invisible in historical archives. One way to catch glimpses of them is to follow the transmission of the depictions of skilled practitioners in popular culture from Britain to Philadelphia. A well-known example is the character of Lady Bountiful, an elite woman healer in George Farquhar's play *The Beaux-Stratagem*, a popular Restoration comedy that the Murray

Figure 2. Frontispiece from George Farquhar, *The Beaux-Stratagem: A Comedy* (London: printed for Bernard Lintott, 1711). The healer Lady Bountiful (front left) administers a stimulant to Aimwell (center) after his feigned fainting spell.

and Keane theatrical troupe introduced to Philadelphia audiences in 1749. According to the playwright, Lady Bountiful was "an old, civil, country gentlewoman that cures all her neighbors of all distempers [diseases]."[2]

The Beaux-Stratagem is comedy of hidden identities that features a down-on-his-luck rake named Aimwell, who pretends to be a viscount to win the hand of Lady Bountiful's daughter, Dorinda. The local tavern keeper toasts Lady Bountiful and informs Aimwell that along with spending half her fortune on charity for her poor neighbors, the benevolent lady also "cures rheumatisms, ruptures, and broken shins in men; green-sickness, obstructions, and fits of the mother in women; the king's evil, chincough, and chilblains, in children." "In short," quips the tavern keeper, "she has cured more people in and about Litchfield within ten years than the doctors have killed in twenty." Nonetheless, Lady Bountiful's skills fail her when Aimwell appears at her door in the throes of a feigned fainting spell. The good lady prescribes "Hartshorne drops" and "Hungary Water," when the real cure for Aimwell's malady is the heart and fortune of the lovely Dorinda. When asked if her medicines have "cured anybody," Lady Bountiful staunchly defends her practice: "Though you laugh, I have done miracles about the country here with my receipts [medical recipes]." *The Beaux-Stratagem* was staged frequently in Britain and Anglo North America throughout the eighteenth and early nineteenth centuries, solidifying the Lady Bountiful caricature in the public's imagination. Catharine Maria Charke and other leading lights of the Georgian theater portrayed this character. The printed play was published and sold on both sides of the Atlantic, widening Bountiful's renown.[3]

Lady Bountiful's literary antithesis in Anglo-American popular culture was the stereotyped image of the village "wise woman" healer, derisively called "old wife." This pejorative connoted a woman from the lower social orders whose remedies were at best folk medicine or at worst, harmful superstition. Unlike the wealthy Bountiful, old wives charged or bartered for their services, which placed them in direct economic competition with male physicians, apothecaries, and surgeons. This negative, gendered image has deep roots. In his authoritative 1597 *Herball*, the surgeon John Gerard disparaged "Old Wives" as "that beggarly rabble of witches, charmers, & such like couseners [deceivers], that regarde more to get money than to helpe for charitie." Gerard argued that old wives should be "cast out" of both "books and memory." Village healers were also called "cunning-women," and their remedies might include occult charms or potions. The term "old wives" situated lower-class women healers as illiterate imposters, in contrast to educated male practitioners whose ideas were grounded in evidence-based inquiry and validated by scholarly writings.

The caricatures of old wives and Ladies Bountiful raise questions regarding women healers. Are they best understood as unappreciated miracle workers or laughable frauds? Were they authoritative providers of care or merely deceitful quacks? These powerful representations have obscured the actual lives and practices of early British North American women healers.[4] This book looks beyond these stereotypes to recover women practitioners' lived experiences and health care work. Women's vernacular healing cultures were often transmitted through oral rather than written networks, leaving behind only shadowy traces in historical archives. Apart from a few foundational studies, women's roles, practices, authority, and contributions to the health care labor force remain understudied. Standard historical narratives often depict these women as "amateurs" and emphasize their declining influence. By contrast, this book constructs case studies from the greater Philadelphia area to demonstrate that Euro-American, Native American, and African American women continued to play a central role in health care well into the nineteenth century. Women healers were not inflexible traditional practitioners destined to fall victim to Enlightenment science, capitalism, and medical professionalization. Instead, women practitioners adapted their practices as they found new sources of health care authority through medical information networks, manuscript authorship, female education in the sciences, health reform, and access to medical print media. Female doctors, herbalists, and apothecaries of various classes and ethnicities also participated in an unregulated consumer health care marketplace and created new arenas to assert their expertise. University-educated professional women physicians, pharmacists, and nurses would later build on this foundation.[5]

It is not surprising that images of Ladies Bountiful and old wives resonated with eighteenth-century readers and theatergoers because these satires included elements of actual women healers' diagnoses, remedies, and practices in British and Anglo-American communities. Diseases such as chincough (whooping cough) and king's evil (scrofula), as well as popular medicines like hartshorn drops extracted from deer horns, would have been familiar to audiences. Indeed, Catharine Maria Charke, who popularized Lady Bountiful on American stages, had a personal interest in female practitioners. Her mother, the actress Charlotte Cibber Charke, called herself "a young lady Bountiful" in her 1755 autobiography. As Charlotte Charke divulged, before embarking on a stage career, she "grew passionately fond of the study of physic [medicine]" and visited an apothecary's widow "to furnish" herself with drugs. When her father refused to pay the apothecary's bill, Charke compounded her own ointments for patients in her home "Dispensary." She consulted popular medical manuals by the botanist Nicholas Culpeper and the self-styled "Professor of Physick" William Salmon. Charke's autobiography went through multiple editions and appeared in serial form in the *Gentleman's Magazine*. Literate women in the Philadelphia area avidly read this periodical and they likely knew of Charke's medical accomplishments.[6]

Although Charlotte Charke is best known for her flamboyant theatrical lifestyle characterized by cross-dressing, her foray into medicine was consistent with traditional feminine gender norms. Elite British and European women had long provided health care for people in their communities, often passing down medical knowledge to female kin. As Charke noted, she was inspired by her grandmother, another Lady Bountiful, who "took particular delight in visiting the old, the indigent and the infirm . . . and in preparing such medicines as were useful to the maladies of the peasantry." According to Charke, her grandmother was devoted to "botanic study," served as "the village doctress," and "seldom passed a day without exemplifying the benevolence of her nature." Charke's grandmother was influenced by her godmother, Lady Tynt, who was the "lady Bountiful of the surrounding villages." For elite women, health care practices satisfied their intellectual curiosity, enacted their religious devotion, and enhanced their social capital.[7]

Charlotte Charke's autobiography demonstrates that women's paid and unpaid health care work was far more complicated than the simple binary of Ladies Bountiful and old wives. This was also true in eighteenth-century Philadelphia. The healer Anna Dalemoa Bellamy was described as "a woman of education" and "the black doctor." She charged for her specialized services in bone setting, dentistry, and wound care. By contrast, Elizabeth Coates Paschall, a Philadelphia Quaker shopkeeper and healer, diagnosed and treated patients gratis with medicines that she compounded herself. Her confidence in her practice is reflected in the phrase "cured when the doctors failed," which repeats like a refrain in her medical recipe book. Like Charlotte Charke, Paschall consulted medical texts containing up-to-date medical and natural philosophical theories that she applied to her practice.[8]

Although women's roles as vendors of medicines are poorly documented in the historical record, Charke's visit to a female apothecary reflects their presence in the health care marketplace. Female entrepreneurs in Philadelphia took advantage of an emerging culture of medical consumerism accompanied by increased demand for printed health care information, therapeutic advice, and pharmaceuticals. In an unregulated marketplace with no licensure requirements, there were few legal barriers to prevent women such as Paschall's cousin, Margaret Hill Morris, from setting up shop as apothecaries and physicians. Women healers of various social orders, including women of color, participated in an emerging capitalist marketplace by preparing and selling popular patent medicines and by peddling pharmaceuticals door-to-door.

Elizabeth Paschall and other Ladies Bountiful solicited medical information from healers of the lower social orders who male practitioners might categorize as "old wives." In their manuscripts, Paschall and Morris identified servants and "country women" with respected healing practices as "creditable" sources for remedies. The Lenape healer Hannah Freeman and the African American doctor Anna Bellamy were recognized practitioners in their communities. However, these healers' knowledge of herbs and poisons gave them the power to harm as well as to heal, which kindled misgivings among some of their Euro-American patients. Despite important healing work provided by women of color, the denigrating epithets of "squaw" and "wench" joined the lexicon of "old wife" healers to undermine these practitioners' medical authority. Nonetheless, racialized discourses only underscored the contradictions between Delaware Valley colonists' desires for successful cures and their anxieties regarding women healers' power.[9]

The greater Philadelphia area, encompassing the Delaware Valley regions of eastern Pennsylvania, western New Jersey, and Delaware, had an important role in early American health care history. Philadelphia was British North America's premier city of medicine and science. The city housed the colonies' first hospital, medical school, medical society, and philosophical society. These institutions' reputations reached far beyond the mid-Atlantic region. The Delaware Valley's diverse population comprised voluntary and coerced immigrants from the British Isles, Africa, the Caribbean, the German states, and other European countries. Health care practitioners of various ethnicities and religious persuasions contributed a rich array of health practices and differing medical worldviews to the healing milieu. In this diverse medical landscape women healers found common ground in their desire to exchange health information and to discover innovative cures for illnesses.[10]

The expansive term "women healers" construes healing in its broadest sense to encompass a spectrum of paid and unpaid healing work, including diagnostic, prescriptive, therapeutic, pharmaceutical, obstetric, and nursing services. In the early twenty-first century, we place these roles in rigid categories regulated by the state licensure of physicians, nurses, nurse practitioners, nurse midwives, nurses' aides, physicians' assistants, and pharmacists. By contrast, eighteenth- and early nineteenth-century women healers practiced in an unregulated medical marketplace, and their healing work could incorporate any combination of these categories at various stages of their lives. Early modern patients frequently identified a female practitioner as a woman "skilled in physic [medicine]" and/or "chirurgery [surgery]." Other common terms included doctress, doctoress, midwife, wise woman, nurse, and occasionally village healer. Although the title "doctress" may sound patronizing to a twenty-first-century reader, it was the feminine gendering of the noun *doctor*, much like the term *actress* denoted a female actor and *heiress* a female heir. Seventeenth- and eighteenth-century dictionaries defined *doctress* as a "female doctor," "she-doctor," or "woman that practices Physic," which implied diagnostic and prescriptive capabilities. Whatever moniker was used to describe them, their contemporaries understood that women practitioners provided the preponderance of health care services for people of all social classes in their communities. When historians disregard women healers, they also overlook the care provided to populations that were not served by male physicians. However, uncovering the history of women healers poses challenges for scholars.[11]

Recovering Hidden Histories

"Why is it," asked the Puritan divine Jared Eliot, "that the troublers of others Peace have been Celebrated in History," while "real worth has been disregarded?" In his 1739 eulogy, Eliot praised the midwife and healer Elizabeth Smithson as a "person of Superior Skill and Capacity" who provided "relief of those that were Afflicted." The historian Laurel Thatcher Ulrich quotes Eliot in her pathbreaking 1991 book *A Midwife's Tale*, which explores the life of Maine midwife Martha Moore Ballard. Ulrich shatters negative stereotypes of incompetent "old wives" to reveal a skilled midwife who was the "most important practitioner in her town." In addition to midwifery, Ballard provided general medical care for the women, men, and children in her community. Historical interest in female health care providers emerged out of the women's health movement during the 1970s, as feminist historians broke new ground in the study of women and gender and social historians challenged traditional medical histories that vaunted the purported "victory" of enlightened physicians over the superstitions of women healers, "quacks," and midwives. These studies argued that male obstetricians' eighteenth-century takeover of the female ritual of childbirth and their suppression of female healers obscured women's historical contributions to the healing arts.[12]

Surprisingly, Ulrich's Pulitzer Prize–winning book generated only a few additional monographs on eighteenth- and early nineteenth-century North American female healers. Scholarly interest dissipated as the women's health movement progressed from radical grassroots activism to the health care mainstream. This book complements and expands on foundational research on women practitioners by Ulrich, Rebecca Tannenbaum, and Susan Klepp. However, due to the dearth of Anglo-American studies, this work also builds on research by historians of early modern Europe. Additional scholars have discovered that medical recipe books are invaluable sources for understanding the wide-ranging circulation of medical knowledge and the relationship between gender and healing authority. Although gender operated through healing practices to create and sustain power hierarchies, this study complicates earlier narratives in which physicians were the oppressors and women healers the heroic victims doomed to failure. Physicians were unable to monopolize medical practice, and the victim role does not characterize the successful practices of many Philadelphia-area women who often collaborated with doctors. Setting aside this dated framework, I analyze how the emerging consumer-oriented medical marketplace challenged physicians' exclusive claims to medical knowledge and practice.[13]

To understand women's roles in the health care marketplace, this study mines medical recipe books, papers, and objects alongside newspapers, legal documents, published herbals, dispensatories, city directories, scholarly medical books, and popular self-help manuals. By revealing the extent of women's medical practices, this book adds a new dimension to research on women's roles as economic actors in the development of market capitalism by scholars such as Ellen Hartigan-O'Connor. It highlights women's participation in health care commerce, pharmaceutical advertising, and the development of patent medicines. Works by Roy Porter and Harold Cook chart the outlines of an unregulated medical marketplace during England's long eighteenth century that offered consumers a myriad of choices in health care providers. This research revised previous medical historians' assertions of a fixed and regulated tripartite hierarchy of physicians, surgeons and apothecaries, whose societies and guilds controlled nonphysicians' practices. Historians have documented a similar consumer-oriented marketplace in the early nineteenth-century United States, which featured a self-help print market peddling literature that proclaimed "Every Man His Own Doctor" and "Every Woman her Own Doctress." An unregulated market of medical knowledge, products, and practices placed healing authority in the hands of patients and nonphysician practitioners. This study demonstrates the continuities between women's medical work in the early modern English marketplace and their participation in the early nineteenth-century popular health movement in the United States.[14]

Analyzing healing in a period before the era of professional medicine requires that we consider how contemporaries understood the meaning of authority. Samuel Johnson's influential *Dictionary of the English Language*, published in 1755 and reprinted into the nineteenth century, provides crucial insights. Johnson used four phrases to define *authority*: legal power, influence, credibility, and testimony. Other popular dictionaries provided similar definitions. Coercive legal medical authority could be enforced for men in the military, for enslaved people, and for those in public institutions such as hospitals and almshouses. In these spaces, punitive medical procedures could be used as technologies of terror and control. In certain domestic contexts, white female healers could exert coercive medical power over children, servants, and enslaved people. Nonetheless, influence, credibility, and testimony were the salient meanings for most female healers and physicians in private practice. In an unregulated medical marketplace, both male and female health care practitioners had to use their influence to win patients' hearts and minds and to convince sufferers that their medical knowledge, judgment, and remedies were superior to those of other healers.[15]

It was in this context that a rancorous printed discourse emerged in the mid-eighteenth-century Delaware Valley, in which participants debated whether practitioners and their remedies were authentic or counterfeit. These controversies reflected Johnson's definition of authority and authenticity as synonymous. In his popular *Dictionarium Anglo-Britannicum*, John Kersey also acknowledged the power of print by describing authority as "a Testimony, or Passage of an Author, quoted to make good what one says." The printed word became self-authenticating. To enhance their credibility, healers shared a language of testimonials found in printed works and recipe manuscripts, including the phrases "approved," "cured to admiration," and "given to me by a person of credit." Healers' trustworthiness, credibility, and authority were closely linked with those of their medical prescriptions, often advertised in print. Women and men practitioners, whether trained or self-taught, constructed their medical reputations on a foundation of healing successes within wide-ranging interpersonal and intertextual networks.[16]

Entering the World of Early Modern Healing

Although it is tempting to evaluate historical healing practices on the basis of twenty-first-century medical ideologies, historians strive to appreciate the internal logic of early modern theories and therapies that originated in Europe, Africa, and North America. Ideas and beliefs about wellness, illness, and pain are socially constructed and vary across time and cultures. The women healers in this book used the concepts and therapeutics available to them in their attempts to alleviate their patients' suffering and to promote wellness. Their perceptions of a successful cure might differ from our personal views, which are also mediated by our own cultural contexts.

Most Euro-American women healers and formally trained physicians, surgeons, and apothecaries shared the same standard theoretical framework based on the humoral medical theories established by the second-century Roman physician Galen. According to Galenic principles, the four humors—phlegm, black bile, yellow bile, and blood—were linked to the corresponding elements of water, earth, fire, and air, as well as qualities of warmth, wetness, coolness, and dryness. To treat a patient appropriately, a doctor or practitioner had to "read" the patient's dominant bodily constitution, categorizing the person as phlegmatic, melancholic, choleric, or sanguine. Treatments were individualized on the basis of the patient's foremost bodily humor, his or her age, symptoms, activity level, the season of the year, the temperature and humidity level, the physical environment, and astrological birth signs. In addition to prescribing medical therapies, simple herbs, and compounded pharmaceuticals in an effort to balance the humors, practitioners also prescribed changes in health-related behaviors. Despite the longevity of Galenic practice, new discoveries in the seventeenth and early eighteenth centuries generated innovative theories regarding bodily physiology. Isaac Newton's principles of matter, William Harvey's description of the circulation of the blood, and Albrecht von Haller's experiments with the nervous system modified Galen's precepts by introducing the concept of the body as an organized machine. However, these new theories did little to change actual therapies and medications. Women healers, along with most physicians, continued to practice Galenic humoral medicine with some modifications.[17]

Nonetheless, Galenic practices faced a serious challenge from the follow-ers of the Swiss-born Renaissance physician and philosopher Paracelsus. Paracelsus and his prominent seventeenth-century acolyte Jan Baptiste van Helmont argued that three essences (mercury, sulfur, and salt) were con-nected to three spiritual principles (spirit, body, and soul). They linked bodily disease to chemical imbalances, which could be cured by mineral-based remedies targeting particular symptoms and diseases. Paracelsus's para-digm argued that specific remedies for distinct illnesses could be general-ized across populations, as opposed to an individualized Galenic analysis of a patient's bodily constitution. Despite rancorous debates between followers of these therapeutic models, both Galenic humoral theories and Paracelsian chemical therapies became intermixed as part of the standard healing prac-tices of trained physicians and women healers.[18]

Religious beliefs were also closely intertwined with healing practices for Europeans, Africans, and Native Americans in the Philadelphia region. Spir-itual power could be as significant as practical remedies for sufferers seeking wellness. Scholars describe a holistic healing milieu encompassing spiritual and community wholeness, which characterized African American and Na-tive American concepts of well-being. Europeans invoked their god's heal-ing power through prayers or the intervention of priests and ministers. The boundaries between what we might call science, medicine, religion, and mys-ticism were indistinct. The early Delaware Valley provided women healers with a rich environment to share medical knowledge.[19]

Following in Their Footsteps

As they settled the greater Philadelphia area, Euro-American women heal-ers built on the legacies of their foremothers and fashioned medical author-ity within mutually affirming networks of medical information exchanges. Gulielma Springett Penn, the wife of Pennsylvania's founder, William Penn, exemplifies Englishwomen who practiced as "Lady Bountiful" healers in the late seventeenth century. Penn's medical recipe manuscript maps her expert knowledge of what we would recognize as medicine, surgery, ophthalmology, pharmacy, and nursing. Her medical remedies demonstrate literate women's participation in the production of healing knowledge and their engagement with early modern science. Along with her husband, Gulielma Penn was instrumental in establishing a radical sect called the Society of Friends, or Quakers. Friends' emphasis on female literacy and spiritual equality allowed Quaker women to enter the public sphere to a greater degree than their non-Quaker counterparts. Quaker women conveyed these controversial values and contested gender roles to the colonies of Pennsylvania and New Jersey. Beulah Jacques Coates was one of these first Quaker settlers who passed down her healing and literacy skills to her daughter Elizabeth Coates Paschall.

Paschall was a widowed Philadelphia merchant who kept a detailed medical recipe book that documents her healing practice. Her uniquely discursive manuscript describes her remedy ingredients, consultations with patients, medical experiments, and webs of health information exchanges that crossed lines of gender, class, and race. Within empowering local and transatlantic healing networks, women such as Paschall claimed medical legitimacy as skilled and respected practitioners. Paschall's recipe exchanges with local Lenape healers also demonstrate how healing could be a site of intercultural collaboration as well as conflict between European settlers and resident Native American groups.

Although Indigenous women's healing work is difficult to recover, Hannah Freeman's medical practice exemplifies how Lenape healers garnered healing authority on the basis of their knowledge of local botanicals and their reputations for successful cures that were valued within their communities and among Pennsylvania's colonists. By selling herbs, healing advice, and baskets, along with paid domestic work, Freeman earned income that allowed her to spend the majority of her life in the places of her Lenape ancestors. Healing facilitated Freeman's cultural and geographic persistence amid the dislocations and violence caused by European colonization and the Seven Years' War. Like Paschall, European "men of science" and university-trained physicians acknowledged the healing expertise of Native American women such as Freeman even as they erased medical remedies' Indigenous origins and appropriated the knowledge. The emerging prestige of European Enlightenment science and the influence of the printed word could be used to denigrate the healing expertise of both Native American and Euro-American women.

Nonetheless, literate women healers learned to wield the new power of Enlightenment science to maintain their healing authority. Despite the disruptions of warfare in the mid-eighteenth-century Delaware Valley, Quakers' promotion of gender equality and women's education in the sciences provided new opportunities for women healers. The rise of empirical science challenged the long-standing preeminence of university degrees and ancient experts. Undeterred by male natural philosophers' contentions that women were innately too "irrational" to contribute to the medical sciences, literate women such as Paschall read medical texts, engaged in experimentation, participated in natural philosophical societies, and authorized their healing practices as recognized producers of scientific knowledge.

Along with the misogynistic discourses of Enlightenment science, the emergence of a male culture of market capitalism posed potential barriers to women's traditional healing legitimacy. Nonetheless, both elite and working-class women healers navigated the economic downturns of the American Revolutionary period by harnessing a flourishing market in pharmaceuticals to develop profitable entrepreneurial medical practices. Medical consumerism along with a profusion of self-help printed works weakened physicians' hegemony and empowered women healers. Their economic successes attest to these women's ongoing medical authority.

The growth of a self-interested capitalist marketplace was accompanied by a popular culture of humanitarian sensibility that lauded those who exhibited deeply felt, self-sacrificing benevolence. Some women deployed sensibility to legitimize their practices as nurses and healers and to deflect defamatory stereotypes of paid caregivers as inebriates and prostitutes. However, when Philadelphia's African American women, such as Sarah Bass, risked their lives to provide vital nursing care for white Philadelphians during the devastating 1793 yellow fever epidemic, a popular publisher used racialized imagery to denounce them in the press. At the insistence of Bass and the Black nurses, their ministers Richard Allen and Absalom Jones wrote a pamphlet that affirmed the nurses' authority as self-sacrificing humanitarian activist-healers who demonstrated African Americans' worthiness for civil equality. However, as Bass and her colleagues discovered, an emerging culture of domesticity created new challenges for women of all ethnicities who attempted to practice humanitarian healing while engaging in public activist reform movements and participating as economic actors in the capitalist marketplace.

Women healers' achievements in the early decades of the nineteenth century were obscured by a powerful discourse of domesticity that sought to relegate women to the private household sphere, safe from the perils of the business domain. Nonetheless, Euro-American and African American women continued to embrace medical entrepreneurship and deploy the culture of humanitarian sensibility to counteract both the constraining bonds of domesticity and physicians' attempts to marginalize them. In the Quaker-influenced Delaware Valley, some women healers appropriated the authority of health reform movements to bring their traditional domestic healing power into the public arena, while leveraging the economic potential of an increasingly mainstream popular health movement. In addition, the rise of female educational institutions countered notions of women's mental inferiority and provided women with skills in oratory and organization that allowed them to become activist leaders in health reform and women's rights organizations. As part of this impulse for social improvement, women healers embraced nontraditional medical movements and became practitioners in hydropathy, homeopathy, and Thomsonianism, which challenged "regular" physicians' authority. By 1830, Philadelphia-area women were poised to take full advantage of this next wave of the popular health movement. Within a few decades, Quakers' endeavors as women's rights and health reform activists would pave the way for women like Ann Preston to establish medical and nursing schools in Philadelphia and to enter the health care professions.

As one of George Farquhar's characters quips in *The Beaux' Stratagem*, "in a comedy . . . the ending of the play is never in doubt. The only question is how we get there." Knowing the ending of a story can erase the complex narratives that tell "how we got here." Recognizing that male medical professionals ultimately sidelined women practitioners by the early twentieth century can make the decline of women's healing authority seem inevitable. This book rewrites that narrative and demonstrates that women in the Philadelphia region played critical roles in the delivery of health care from the late seventeenth century through the mid-nineteenth century.[20]

CHAPTER 1

Healing Legacies

In October 1702, the household at Warminghurst Manor in West Sussex was in a flurry. William Penn Jr. was scheduled to set sail from England for Philadelphia in a mere fortnight. He was the eldest surviving son of his late mother, Gulielma Springett Penn, and the namesake of his father, the founder of the colony of Pennsylvania. Although Philadelphia had developed into a commercial town since Penn Senior had founded it in 1681, packing for this expedition to the colonial outpost of Pennsylvania still required planning. Amid the bustle of servants sorting and packing provisions and clothing, William Junior decided at the last minute that he wanted to bring his mother's culinary and medical recipe book. He had claimed ownership of this keepsake by writing on the fly page, "My Mother's Recaipts [receipts or recipes] for Cookerys Presarving and Cyrurgery [Surgery]—William Penn." But young Penn realized suddenly that this treasure trove of information might be lost or damaged during the voyage. He prevailed on the family clerk to waste no time in making a copy. In an apparent apology for his poor penmanship, the clerk noted, "Here ends the book of Coockary in great hast [haste] transcribed by Edward Blackfan the 25th of October 1702." However, Blackfan might have taken the time to make a more legible copy, because young William Penn's journey was delayed for a year. Penn Junior and the recipe book arrived in Philadelphia around the turn of the New Year in 1704. Gulielma Penn never came to Pennsylvania, but her family preserved the memory of her medical acumen as documented in her recipe manuscript.[1]

The Penn manuscript embodies the written and oral transmission of a foundational culture of authoritative women healers from Britain to its mid-Atlantic North American colonies. As one peruses the Penn manuscript, it is evident that healers such as Gulielma Penn were models for George Farquhar's character Lady Bountiful in his 1707 play *The Beaux-Stratagem*. Like

Figure 3. *Gulielma Springett Penn* (1644–94), by William Miller, line engraving, date unknown. Courtesy Religious Society of Friends (Quakers) in Britain. Signed "Thy trully Lo[ved] & affectionate friend Guli Penn."

Lady Bountiful, Gulielma Penn compounded hartshorn jelly to treat dysentery and distilled a syrup to thwart a life-threatening case of chincough (whooping cough). However, Penn was clearly not a farcical character in a Restoration comedy. Her leather-bound manuscript charts her expert knowledge of what we would recognize as medicine, surgery, ophthalmology, pharmacy, and nursing. Like many aristocratic or gentry families' domestic manuals, it contained cooking, medical, and home maintenance recipes collected over the years and passed down through generations. The manuscript included treatments for fevers, wounds, sprains, scurvy, kidney stones, and childbirth-related problems. In a new colony that offered few trained physicians, the book would have been a critical resource. A close reading of Penn's remedy book and those of her contemporaries demonstrates literate Englishwomen's participation in healing knowledge production, their engagement with early modern science, and their use of innovative medical theories.[2]

Gulielma Penn's religious background informed her healing practice. Along with her husband, William, Gulielma helped to establish a radical sect called the Society of Friends, or Quakers. The Friends' emphasis on spiritual equality allowed Quaker women to enter the public sphere in roles as ministers, preachers, and healers to a greater extent than non-Quaker women. The Friends' emphasis on literacy gave Quaker women access to printed medical and scientific texts that they could apply to their healing work. Some women Friends also published books that publicly asserted the legitimacy of their controversial lives and beliefs. When Quaker women immigrated to the mid-Atlantic colonies, they introduced expanded gender roles that conflicted with Englishwomen's traditional social norms. Along with his mother's medical recipe manuscript, William Penn Jr. conveyed a legacy of outspoken, literate, and accomplished Quaker women healers to Pennsylvania.[3]

Founding Quaker Mother and Skilled Healer

Gulielma Springett Penn's recipe book is an important source of information about her life and healing practice. The only surviving documents attributed to her are the recipe manuscript and a few letters. Narratives and letters written by her contemporaries provide additional biographical details. Like her husband, Gulielma Penn came from a family of the upper gentry class. Gulielma's father, Sir William Springett, died while fighting with the Puritan Parliamentarians in the English Civil War. Shortly after traveling to attend him on his deathbed in early 1644, Lady Mary Proude Springett gave birth to a daughter, Gulielma Maria Posthuma. Saddled with her husband's war-related debts, the widowed Mary Springett went to live in Kent with her husband's widowed mother, Lady Catherine Partridge Springett, who was recognized as a skilled physician, surgeon, and oculist. Along with their healing expertise, Gulielma's mother and grandmother were adept at managing their estates and tenants. Under English common law, a married woman's legal rights and identity were subsumed under that of her husband. However, as widows, Catherine Springett and Mary Penington were considered feme sole and could engage in legal contracts and business. Gulielma inherited her grandmother's medical recipe book and was influenced by these self-sufficient women.[4]

In 1654, Mary Springett married Isaac Penington, and Gulielma moved to her stepfather's house in Sussex. In the late 1650s, Gulielma's mother and stepfather converted to a new radical sect called the Society of Friends. To the consternation of her neighbors and extended family, Gulielma joined the Friends at age fourteen. Under the influence of the movement's founders, George Fox and Margaret Fell, Gulielma and her family became devout converts and leaders of a religious group that dissented from the Church of England's tenets. The Friends were just one of numerous mid-seventeenth-century antiauthoritarian religious movements that emerged during the turbulence of the English Civil War. The shocking 1649 execution of King Charles I by Parliamentarians exemplified the period's profound challenges to monarchical and patriarchal authority. Radical dissenting religious groups such as the Anabaptists, Levellers, Ranters, Diggers, Muggletonians, and Friends challenged political, social, and gender hierarchies as well as the theological status quo. The destabilizing effects of these new religious groups reverberated from the mid-century Puritan interregnum under Oliver Cromwell to the restoration of the English monarchy in 1660.[5]

Within this context of social ferment, the Quakers developed religious tenets with subversive potential for women such as Gulielma Springett. Friends asserted that every person had an indwelling "inner light" of God. They were called Quakers by their detractors because of their ecstatic movements when under the influence of God's spirit. Over time, the epithet stuck, and even Friends accepted the term "Quaker." Friends sought lives that testified to their equality, simplicity, and integrity. Their assertions of equality prompted them to eschew norms of social deference, and they also refused to swear allegiance to the government or pay Church of England taxes. Their practices threatened the basic structures of English society. Moreover, women Friends challenged gender hierarchies by speaking in Quaker religious meetings and preaching to crowds of men and women. Female Quakers held leadership positions in separate Women's Meetings, which granted them the authority to guide and discipline male Friends. Gulielma was acquainted with numerous women called "Public Friends" who traveled without their husbands throughout England and the Atlantic world preaching to Quakers and non-Quakers. Women Friends' behavior was far outside the norms for Englishwomen, who, according to Biblical precepts, should remain silent in church, avoid public roles, and never "usurp authority over the man."[6]

The Friends also promoted basic education and literacy for both women and men so they could interpret the Bible for themselves. As entries in the Penn manuscript suggest, literacy allowed elite Quaker women such as Gulielma and her grandmother to access medical works and apply the information to their practices. Some literate women Friends claimed the authority of authorship that was generally reserved for men. Gulielma's friend and fellow Quaker founder Margaret Fell (later Fox) wrote a tract titled *Women's Speaking Justified, Proved, and Allowed by the Scriptures*, in which she affirmed women's spiritual equality and promoted women preaching in public by "the Spirit and Power of the Lord Jesus." Fell Fox was a prolific writer, authoring twenty-three controversial religious pamphlets. More than two hundred Quaker women ministers would publish popular tracts and spiritual biographies. Gulielma Springett was a founder of a religious sect that transgressed gender norms and created new spaces for women to assert their religious authority in print and in public settings that were considered men's purview. Women healers could appropriate their religious authority to bolster their legitimacy as benevolent medical practitioners.[7]

The radicalism of Quaker women's attempts to expand gender roles is reflected in the magnitude of the backlash against them. Anti-Quaker tracts targeted outspoken women preachers, and English town officials punished them with public humiliations and whippings. Devices called branks or "scold's bridles" illustrate graphically the use of torture to silence Quaker women's public speech. A brank was a cage-like iron device that encircled the head. It featured a bridle bit that projected into the victim's mouth and pressed down on the tongue, interfering with speaking, eating, and drinking. A more vicious version included spikes that speared the tongue. Gulielma would have been familiar with the Quaker preachers Dorothy Waugh and Anne Robinson, who in 1655 were led through the town of Carlisle wearing branks "to the Scorn and Derision of the Rabble" and then imprisoned. In the British North American colonies, New England Puritan officials also persecuted Quaker women preachers with whippings, banishment, or executions. Gulielma experienced this anti-Quaker backlash firsthand when her friends and family members were imprisoned for their religious beliefs. Margaret Fell wrote *Women Speaking Justified* during one of her incarcerations. Isaac Penington was jailed six times, leaving Mary and Gulielma to oversee the family's property and business matters.[8]

Managing the family's estates provided Gulielma with opportunities to enact the role of Lady Bountiful by visiting the sick, providing free health care, and offering provisions to her tenants and dependent poor. The remedies in Gulielma's medical manuscript for minor injuries as well as life-threatening illnesses confirm a contemporary biographer's description of her "great skill in physic [medicine] and surgery." In his autobiography, a family friend named Thomas Ellwood also noted the "endowments of her [Gulielma's] mind." Ellwood described escorting Gulielma on horseback to collect rents on an estate inherited from her father. Tenants and cottage dwellers reciprocated the ministrations of Ladies Bountiful such as Gulielma with their rent payments and by displaying deference to their social "betters." Gentry women healers' generosity to social inferiors bolstered their social capital and reinforced class differences. Because the Quakers' equality testimony conflicted with social hierarchies, Gulielma likely viewed her healing work as religious service and Quaker benevolence.[9]

While visiting English Quaker congregations in 1668, Gulielma met her future husband, William Penn, who was the scion of a gentry family. However, William's father, Admiral William Penn, had disowned him for joining the radical Quakers. During their courtship, Gulielma corresponded with William while he was imprisoned in the Tower of London for publishing inflammatory Quaker pamphlets. Remedies for coughs and colds in Gulielma's medical manuscript that cite "my husband William Penn" reflect William's respiratory ailments and chronic ill health related to his frequent incarcerations. Gulielma and William's 1672 wedding illustrates the Friends' unconventional gender norms, which emphasized the spouses' spiritual equality. Unlike the Church of England's rituals, in which the bride was given by the father to the husband to symbolize women's dependency on male kin, Quaker marriage partners entered the meeting house together and stood among the congregation. The bride and groom exchanged vows without a presiding minister, often omitting the promise that the wife would obey the husband. Gulielma was William's social as well as spiritual equal. She brought a dowry of ten thousand pounds and valuable estates into the marriage. The Penns settled on an estate in Hertfordshire, but sadly, their first three children died in infancy. In 1676, the Penns sought a fresh start amid their grief, and they borrowed heavily to purchase an estate called Warminghurst Manor in West Sussex, which became a center of the Quaker movement.[10]

In the face of Quaker persecutions in England, William Penn envisioned a utopian colony in British North America that would be a haven of religious tolerance for god-fearing people. King Charles II had issued William a proprietary charter in 1681 for extensive land tracts in the Delaware Valley region to repay a debt owed to William's father. William also hoped that profits from this new colony, called Pennsylvania, would help clear his own family's debts. In the summer of 1682, as the Penn family prepared to sail to Pennsylvania, Gulielma's mother fell dangerously ill. Gulielma was herself "in delicate health" in the early stages of her seventh pregnancy. Instead of joining the expedition, Gulielma stayed behind to nurse her mother. The Penn's three surviving children also remained at Warminghurst. Recognizing the dangers of the Atlantic crossing, William wrote to Gulielma that "neither sea nor land, nor death itself" could extinguish his devotion.[11]

William left Gulielma in charge of the children's education, but he added, "Let it be useful knowledge" since "ingenuity mixed with industry is good for the body and mind." In his writings on education, Penn asserted that children should study gardening, botany, and healing skills, so they could "know simples [healing remedies with minimal herbal ingredients], and to learn to make [medicinal] oils and ointments." According to Penn, nature "should be the Subject of the Education of our Youth." As a literate healer, Gulielma was well suited to provide her children with a "useful" education. Gulielma also assisted in managing the estates, which was a challenge in the face of the Penns' extensive debts. William charged Gulielma to live "low and sparingly, till my debts are paid." Nonetheless, he advised her to "help the poor and needy." Gulielma's healing acumen and her provision of health care for the estate would have helped her to balance her role as a thrifty lady of the manor with an impetus toward Quaker benevolence.[12]

The documentary fragments of Gulielma Penn's biography reflect the importance of women's supportive healing networks at a time when maternal and infant mortality rates were high and when a person's sudden illness could result in death. Despite Gulielma's ministrations, her mother died two weeks after William's departure to America. Amid her grief, Gulielma gave birth to a sickly daughter in March 1683. As Gulielma explained in a letter to her "affectionate friend" Margaret Fell Fox, "the infant was neer [near] dead when it was born" and it "pleased the Lord to take away my little on [one] which it was about 3 weeks old." Her confidante Fell Fox was an experienced mother of eight living children who had also lost an infant. Gulielma suffered from a common postpartum illness that she called "St. Antony's fire," or erysipelas, which often caused maternal and infant deaths. We now understand that this disease is caused by a virulent strain of streptococcus, and it may have infected the Penns' infant daughter. Gulielma suffered from the disabling effects of St. Antony's fire through late August, which prevented her from joining William in Pennsylvania. Although Gulielma carried eight pregnancies to term, only three children survived infancy. Estimates from rural English parish records suggest that infant mortality in the late seventeenth century averaged approximately 140 deaths per 1,000 live births, but it could be as high as 245 per 1,000 in unhealthy lowland areas such as West Sussex. Maternal deaths during childbirth and throughout the postpartum period were also high. In addition to relying on the services of female midwives, Gulielma Penn and other childbearing women depended on the encouragement and healing advice of experienced women to allay their well-founded anxieties.[13]

During the next decade, William returned to England, where he and Gulielma were embroiled in shifting Crown politics and apprised of bitter controversies across the Atlantic in Pennsylvania. Although William had constructed a home called Pennsbury Manor for his wife and family, Gulielma never traveled to America. In 1694, at age fifty, Gulielma succumbed to a final illness. Aptly, on her deathbed, the healer reassured her family, "I have cast my care upon the Lord, he is the Physician of Value." In his eulogy, William remembered his wife as an exemplary Lady Bountiful and "a good Neighbor, especially to the poor." She was "one of ten thousand, wise, chaste, humble, plain, modest, industrious, constant and undaunted." While biographers remember her as a model of steadfast Quaker womanhood, Gulielma's recipe manuscript sheds additional light on her "great skill in physic [medicine] and surgery." The recipe book also reflects the authoritative healing practices of other Quaker women who immigrated to the greater Philadelphia area in the late seventeenth and early eighteenth centuries.[14]

Exploring the Evidence in Women's Medical Manuscripts

Like many seventeenth-century Englishwomen's domestic recipe books, Gulielma Springett Penn's manuscript provides invaluable insights into the ways that medical knowledge was collected, recorded, annotated, and passed down through generations of family members. On brief examination, recipe books seem to offer only a straightforward record of ingredients, their preparation, and prescriptions. However, in the past few decades, scholars have recognized household books as rich repositories that document women's literacy, authorship, medical knowledge production, and engagement with early modern science. The Penn manuscript exemplifies hundreds of eighteenth-century English recipe books extant in archives in the United States and the United Kingdom, but these sources represent only a fraction of the domestic manuals and family recipe books that were produced during the period. Unfortunately, until recently, many historical archives considered household manuscripts mere antiquarian trivia and only rarely acquired them for their collections. It is impossible to know how many recipe books were rejected by archives or simply thrown away by descendants, thus erasing innumerable women's accumulated medical knowledge. In addition, manuscript recipe books focus mainly on the practices of literate women practitioners. Although nonliterate women healers of the lower and middling social orders also developed authoritative healing practices, the lack of documentation makes it difficult to recover their work. Nonetheless, manuscripts written by women of the nobility or gentry classes describe extensive healing networks that crossed the lines of social class, and they provide glimpses into a vibrant oral culture of nonliterate as well as literate practitioners.[15]

In some cases, historians can compare a woman's medical recipe manuscript with the same writer's diaries, memoirs, and letters. However, even literate women's letters are often not extant or were destroyed purposely to protect the writer's privacy. Indeed, only a few of Penn's letters survive. In other instances, a recipe book may be the sole evidence of a woman's healing work. To corroborate the information in existing medical recipe books, scholars can look to other sources such as public records, contemporaries' letters and biographies, or even epitaphs on gravestones. In his gossipy memoirs of his prominent acquaintances titled *Brief Lives*, John Aubrey confirmed Gulielma Penn's medical and surgical skills in a few sentences amid his more extensive biography of William Penn. In another biographical account of King Charles II, Aubrey also mentioned the medical and surgical accomplishments of the Penns' acquaintance Susanna Wren Holder, the sister of the prominent architect and anatomist Sir Christopher Wren. As Aubrey explained, when Charles II sustained a hand injury that his surgeons were unable to treat, he sent for "Mrs. Holder," "a rare shee-surgeon" with a "sagacity as to curing wounds" by her "owne excogitancy [careful deliberation], considering the causes, effects, and circumstances." Despite the putrefaction extending into the king's shoulder, Holder's treatment effected the cure, to the "great griefe" of the jealous male surgeons. Another biographer of her brother Christopher Wren noted that "thousands were happily healed" by Holder. These brief references to Penn's and Holder's medical skills demonstrate that the accomplishments of women healers renowned in their own time can be overshadowed by their celebrated male kin or lost to the historical record altogether.[16]

This potential erasure of women's lives is even more acute for healers who did not leave a written record. For these women, inscriptions on gravestones may be the only trace of their medical practices. Although Gulielma Penn's headstone records only her name and date of death, the epitaph of another late seventeenth-century English healer provides clues to her practice. According to her gravestone, Margaret Colfe, the wife of the vicar of Lewisham, served for forty years as a "nurse, midwife, surgeon, and in part physician to all both rich and poore; without expecting reward." Similarly, Prudence Potter, a Devon rector's wife, spent her life "in the industrious and successful practice of physick, chirugery [surgery] and midwifery." London hospital archives also record that some women were paid for medical and minor surgical work. The shortage of sources documenting women's medical practices underscores the importance of close analyses of the contents and organization of surviving medical recipe manuscripts.[17]

The structure of the Penn manuscript is typical of many recipe books and provides information regarding its authors. Most recipe books began with a page indicating the original compiler, sometimes followed by the names of additional writers or owners, which reflected the collaborative nature of manuscript authorship. Blank manuscripts were an expensive privilege of the elite. Women signaled their pride in book ownership with their signature on the fly page and occasionally the phrase "Her Book." This notation emphasized a woman's awareness of her accomplishments in the complex skills of reading, writing, and organizing information, which were learned and reinforced through the production of recipe books. However, recipe manuscripts were also bequeathed to male kin such as William Penn Jr., demonstrating the porousness of a domestic sphere where men could be as avid recipe collectors as women. In other instances, a male clerk or scribe such as Edward Black-fan might copy a recipe book to create a duplicate or to produce an elegantly transcribed manuscript that could be given as a gift, often as a wedding present for a woman setting up housekeeping. A 1669 manuscript titled "My Lady Frescheville's Receipt Book," owned by an English baron's wife, exemplifies an aristocratic woman's household manual, bound in gold-embossed Moroccan leather and written in flowery calligraphy. By contrast, Gulielma's grandmother Catherine Springett recorded her remedies in a simple leather book in a clear but less elegant hand, reflecting both her writing literacy and a religious dissenter's disdain for ostentation.[18]

Manuscripts such as Penn's attest to women's participation in extensive webs of healing information exchanges that expanded their skills, created new knowledge, and conferred medical authority. Health care was considered a culturally "natural" part of women's domestic work, and women frequently provided diagnostic and prescriptive medicine for themselves or family members. In early modern England, public hospitals served only impoverished patients, and most people received care from physicians or lay healers within the household. However, rather than being circumscribed spheres, households were outward-facing nodes in extensive medical information networks. Recipe books were collective experimental enterprises, and compilers often cited reputable sources for their remedies and therapeutic practices.[19]

Springett's and Penn's healing networks included family, friends, neighbors, lay healers, servants, men of science, physicians, ocular specialists, and printed sources. In the manuscript, Penn recorded a fortifying pudding endorsed by her sister-in-law Margaret Lowther, as well as "A Plaister for the Sciatica, approved by Mrs. Church." "A Recaipt [recipe] out of Jane Bullock's Book" suggests that Penn perused and transcribed recipes from other women's manuscripts. Remedy books often contain recipes written on slips of paper by the compiler's medical sources and inserted between the pages, which offer additional glimpses into the circulation of medical knowledge. Penn appropriated medical recipes from both physicians and male lay practitioners. She cited "Doctor Butler's Receipt for the hearing" and "An approved

Medicine to cure the Reins [kidneys] of gravell [stones]" from "Mr. Green the Empirick [nonphysician healer]." The sources for Penn's recipes are recorded similarly, and the remedies from a physician appear to carry a comparable authoritative weight as those from nonphysicians. By naming her contributors, Penn provided testimonials to the efficacy of the recipes. Like other recipe book authors, Penn and Springett created collaborative manuscripts that evinced their accumulated medical knowledge within broad circles of kin and community.[20]

Manuscript entries underscore the blurry boundaries between women's work as medical experts within their immediate households and as healers, such as Springett and Penn, whose practices extended beyond domestic spaces. When a household book was handed down among female descendants, a woman's preferences for medicine or cookery were indicated in the choice of recipes that she added to those of her forebears. For example, in her "Book of Cookery and Medical Receipts" begun in 1690, an Englishwoman named Mary Chantrell recorded detailed recipes that demonstrate her intense fascination with medicine and a possible health care practice. In her one-and-a-half-page recipe for "The Green Oyntment" to treat bruises, wounds, dropsy, and pain in the spleen, Chantrell even included instructions on how and when to harvest the herbs to maximize their efficacy. Chantrell touted her confidence in the remedy by noting, "It hath cured when the ablest dockters in London hath left of dead persons" and "it never fails." Both women healers and physicians accrued authority on the basis of the successes of their therapies, and lay healers felt free to besmirch a doctor's reputation. Despite Chantrell's healing acumen, the second manuscript section written by one of Chantrell's descendants concentrates on cooking rather than medicine. The interest in medicine skipped down to the third generation and another kinswoman whose entries focused on healing. Chantrell may have fostered her granddaughter's interest in medicine, just as Catherine Springett inspired Gulielma Springett Penn's healing practice. The evidence from multigenerational manuscript compilers speaks to the importance of kinship networks in the hands-on education and development of a young healer's skills.[21]

The Penn manuscript reflects this intergenerational transmission, along with common organizational styles. Like many recipe books, it is subdivided into sections with general topical headings. Within these sections, some recipes appear to be recorded in real time, reflecting an encounter with another healer or the results of a successful pharmaceutical experiment. The first section of the 158-page Penn manuscript contains 29 pages of ophthalmologic, neurologic, and ear, nose, and throat remedies that originated with Gulielma's grandmother Catherine Springett and is written in Springett's hand. The second section, transcribed by Blackfan, consists mainly of cooking recipes interspersed with cordials, oils, and "waters" with medical uses. The third and fourth sections of the manuscript, also in Blackfan's spidery scrawl, speak to Penn's extensive healing practice, which included wound care, nursing, pharmaceutical production, minor surgery, and the treatment of acute and chronic illnesses. William Penn Jr. titled these last sections "Recaipts [receipts or recipes] of Physick [Medicine] and such things and [medicinal] waters out of my Mothers Book" and "Recaipts of oyntments and salves and such Like of my Mothers." Catherine Springett likely initiated the manuscript book and handed it down to her family members. Blackfan later transcribed Gulielma Penn's recipe entries in the blank pages of her grandmother's book.[22]

The manuscript's first section highlights Catherine Springett's general medical and surgical work as well as her ophthalmic specialty practice. Her daughter-in-law Mary Penington described Springett as an accomplished healer, who had "admirable success" because of her "eminent judgement" in medical matters. Penington grew up in Springett's household before her marriage to Springett's son and thus had firsthand knowledge of her mother-in-law's practice. According to Penington, Springett spent her time "in a bountiful manner" and "bestowed [a] great part of her jointure [widow's settlement] yearly upon the poor, in providing physic and surgery." Springett often saw twenty patients "in a morning—men, women, and children," and cared for long-term invalids at no charge. She cured serious lacerations, sores, and the "king's evil," an infection of the lymph nodes in the neck that presented as gaping, festering wounds. Springett was an innovative practitioner who developed her own therapies. Penington recalled that her mother-in-law healed a child with a severely burned skull by protecting the blackened head wound with her own invention, a "pan of beaten silver covered with a bladder to preserve the head in case of a knock or fall." Springett's extensive practice suggests that patients acknowledged her healing acumen.[23]

Patients from distant counties also sought Springett's skills in treating eye diseases. According to her daughter-in-law, Springett was so proficient in cataract surgery "that Stephens the great oculist sent many to her house when there was difficulty of a cure." It was not unusual for women to become ocular experts who prescribed medicines and "couched" cataracts using a flat needle to displace the cloudy diseased lens. The surgical procedure required the same fine motor skills developed by elite women adept at decorative

needlework. As described in her manuscript, Springett treated other eye illnesses including ocular smallpox, conjunctivitis, puncture wounds, severe
bruises, and potentially blinding maladies called "pin and web," which referred to corneal opacities or overgrowths of conjunctival tissue. Springett
recorded over one hundred complex recipes for eye ailments, which sup-
ports her reputation as a skilled specialist.[24]

Springett's eye remedies refer to ingredients that were commonplace in
women healers' manuscripts and in physicians' writings, including animal
products, homegrown herbs, and chemicals purchased at apothecary (pharmacy) shops. "For pains in ye Eyes," Springett advised a sufferer to "prick a
white shell snayl [snail] & drop it [the mucus] into your eyes 3 times a day." To
modern readers, crushed snails and their slime might seem to invoke the magical potions of "old wife" healers. However, snails were standard ingredients in
physicians' medical prescriptions from the first century into the nineteenth
century. The London College of Physicians' authoritative guide for doctors and
apothecaries, the *Pharmacopoeia Londinensis* (1618), included a recipe for snail
slime to treat wasting pulmonary illnesses and other diseases.[25]

Additional ingredients in the Penn manuscript that might seem unusual
were commonplace. Both the manuscript and the *Pharmacopoeia* recommended a medicinal water made from eyebright flowers to "clear and
strengthen the sight," based on the ancient "doctrine of signatures." According
to this theory, practitioners prescribed a plant that resembled a part of the
human body to treat illnesses of that aspect of a person's anatomy. Eyebright
flowers look like eyes and thus could cure ophthalmological diseases. Although
the "Dragon's blood" in Springett's recipe for "a defensative for ye Eyes" may
seem like a mystical ingredient, it was the commonly used red sap of the
Middle Eastern *Dracaena cinnabari*, or dragon's blood tree. Springett provided
preparation instructions that demonstrated her familiarity with the precise
drams, grains, and ounces used by apothecaries, as well as culinary spoonfuls
and handfuls. Her recipe for "a Water to recover ye Sight" required "3 drames
[drams] of Tutia [copper sulfate] made in a very small powder, 11 drames of fine
sugar, [and] six ounces of Rose-water" mixed in white wine then steeped in the
sun for a month. Springett attested to the efficacy and veracity of the remedy on
the basis of her own experiments: "This I know is proved for an excellent water."
She added, "I know one yt [that] could not thread a needle without spectacles"
who, after using the eye drops, could "thread a needle without spectacles."
Springett assessed the cure by her patient's ability to return to domestic needlework or to her occupation as a seamstress without the need for eyeglasses. As

Springett's reputation as a skilled oculist and healer grew, her practice's geographical scope also expanded.[26]

However, Springett's specialization in eye problems was not unique. Another seventeenth-century English healer named E. Ashby also recorded remedies for eye diseases in her 370-page medical manuscript. One of Ashby's sources was a well-known ocular specialist named Mrs. Crick, who "makes a famous Eye Wash & yt [that] cures Red Rheumatic Eyes." Even in the mid-eighteenth century, an Englishwoman named Hannah Walker wrote to the prominent natural philosopher Benjamin Franklin regarding her son's consultation with a female eye specialist, "a very famais [famous] gentlewoman at Banbury [England]," to whom "people go for her Advice." These anecdotes suggest that women such as Catherine Springett developed medical specialty practices that were recognized beyond their immediate communities.[27]

Although elite women such as Springett and Penn received acclaim for their successful work, their reputations depended on the almost invisible labors of servants and impoverished local women healers. According to Penington, Springett "kept several poor women constantly employed simpling [gathering medicinal herbs] for her in the summer" and preparing pharmaceuticals in the winter. One can imagine Springett or Penn instructing her servants in the preparation of "A Medison [Medicine] for a Wound." They must "first gather those buds on Hartshorne and bramble, the younger the better then gather the herbs following: wormwood burgott mugwort woodbettony agrimony poppy . . . [and] violet leaves." Elite women often participated in the distillation of herbs and other ingredients to create a medicinal "Liquor." Springett and her servants produced "oils, salves, balsams," syrups, conserves, therapeutic waters, medicinal spirits, and "pills and lozenges." The Penn manuscript includes recipes for "oyle of St. John's Wort" to treat wounds, joint pain, and bruises, "The Black Salve" for wounds and cancers, and "An Oyntment for the [intestinal] Worms." Gulielma Penn also recorded recipes for distilled medical drinks such as "The Lady Oxendons Cowslip and Marigold Wine" and "Sir Walter Rawley's [Raleigh's] Cordiall given by him first to the Countess of Rutland." These preparations were produced using specialized utensils in the household kitchen or in a separate space called a stillroom. The equipment listed in the Penn family's book is similar to that found in seventeenth-century English household inventories and includes scales, sieves, mortars, pestles, alembics for distilling, and medicinal containers called gallipots. These tools were also integral to early modern pharmaceutical manufactories and chemical laboratories.[28]

In this period before the professionalization of science, Springett, Penn, and their servants, like innumerable other Englishwomen, experimented with healing remedies and participated in the production of medical knowledge. As they prepared tinctures and distillations and measured ingredients using apothecaries' notations, women healers developed the skills of the chemical laboratory as well as the distilling room. Using her research on recipe manuscripts, the historian Elaine Leong challenges scholars to look beyond the male enclaves of universities and philosophical societies to consider the household as a key site of investigations into the bodily inner workings of medicine and science.[29]

Producing Knowledge: Women's Engagement
with Early Modern Science and Medicine

Gulielma Penn, like her grandmother before her, participated in a culture of avid medical recipe sharing and bodily experimentation that reflected the empirical principles of seventeenth-century science and medicine. As Leong explains, "early modern English gentlemen and gentlewomen were gripped by recipe fever," and their extensive remedy exchanges generated new healing practices and information. The mid-seventeenth century antiestablishment religious ferment that swept the Penns into the Quaker movement intertwined with a shift in natural philosophical thought. While historians argue against the "Scientific Revolution" as a precipitous break from tradition, most agree that during the long seventeenth century, numerous scholars began to challenge the wisdom of the Bible and ancient experts such as Aristotle. Natural philosophers argued that it was possible to discover the laws of nature by reasoned empirical observation, hands-on experimentation, precise measurements, and mathematical calculations.[30]

Empirical science facilitated new sites of knowledge production outside universities and new ways of constructing knowledge that differed from traditional scholasticism, which had prevailed in Europe since the medieval period. Elite males and men in religious orders held a monopoly on this type of knowledge. At the heart of the scholastic method was the "disputation," in which professors and students interrogated theological or philosophical questions through dialectical arguments based on the writings of ancient authorities. By contrast, the "New Science," pioneered by scholars like Francis Bacon, challenged ancient philosophers' authority and focused instead on observing, mapping, and mastering the natural world. Both educated people and those with artisanal skills could generate experiments that manipulated chemical or biological processes. These anti-hierarchical sentiments increased the public's mistrust of elite medical cliques, leading to a concomitant decline in the authority and regulatory power of university-trained physicians. Englishwomen such as Springett and Penn took advantage of these new experimental methods that authorized their explorations into medicine and natural philosophy outside the male sphere of universities.[31]

Literate women familiarized themselves with the New Science by reading books about natural philosophy and by interacting with male kin and friends who shared their interests. Within household settings, women and "gentlemen of science" made notes in recipe books documenting their pragmatic experiments in medically related fields such as botany, pharmacy, and alchemy. Gulielma Penn was acquainted with her contemporary Anne, Viscountess Conway, who exemplifies how elite women claimed medical expertise and became part of natural philosophical networks. Conway's circles included family members, physicians, men of science, and members of the premier English scientific organization, the London Royal Society. In her letters and in her published book, *Principles of the Most Ancient and Modern Philosophy*, Conway engaged contemporary debates on science, religion, alchemy, and medicine. She converted to Quakerism, befriended the Penns, and opened her home to the Quaker movement. Conway may have been influenced by the Friends' interest in the sciences as well as their emphasis on women's literacy and spiritual equality. Many long-standing Quakers also embraced empirical science because they were denied access to universities for failing to acknowledge the primacy of the Church of England. As documented in his letter to Gulielma, William Penn considered medicine and science humanitarian pursuits that were important aspects of the "useful" education of girls as well as boys. The Quakers' promotion of equality and their interest in female education supported women's participation in the potentially benevolent studies of medicine and the sciences.[32]

The intellectual and humanitarian foundations of natural science masked its close connections with European imperial designs to exploit the natural resources of colonized territories. Although women such as Penn and Conway were denied formal membership in the Royal Society, they interacted with "gentlemen of science" who traveled globally on behalf of their countries in search of flora, fauna, and minerals with commercial value. During the seventeenth century, European imports of pharmaceuticals from the

Americas and Asia expanded dramatically, rising twenty-five-fold. Internationally traded medicines such as cochineal from Mexico, cinchona bark (quinine) from South America, and gum guaiacum from the West Indies appear in women's medical recipe books. Although they rarely received credit in papers presented at the Royal Society, Indigenous peoples were critical sources of information about the medical significance of these local plants and animals. Englishwomen healers participated in these wide-ranging networks of science and commerce when they purchased imported pharmaceuticals, used them in their practices, and recorded them in their recipe books.[33]

It is not surprising that literate women practitioners such as Springett and Penn shared the same medical worldview as educated physicians and surgeons. Their manuscripts demonstrate these healers' up-to-date knowledge of botanical remedies, animal-based drugs, and chemical medicines. Female healers' therapeutics were also like those of trained male practitioners, and they included purging, scarifying, cupping, and bleeding. Springett's and Penn's recipes reflect humoral medical theories established by the second-century Roman physician Galen, which undergirded standard medical practice into the nineteenth century. According to Galenic principles, the four humors—phlegm, black bile, yellow bile, and blood—were linked to the corresponding elements of water, earth, fire, and air as well as qualities of warmth, wetness, coolness, and dryness. To treat a patient appropriately, a doctor or practitioner had to "read" the patient's dominant humoral bodily constitution and provide treatments that rebalanced the humors.[34]

A recipe in the Penn manuscript "for pain of ye Eares" illustrates women healers' use of Galenic therapies as well as their participation in the commerce in transatlantic pharmaceuticals. The ear pain remedy removed maladaptive humors through purges, poultices, scarification, cupping, and therapeutic bloodletting. As the entry explains, "A young woman having for ye space of a fortnight suffered extreme pain in the left ear, together with ye pain of her teeth on yt [that] side so yt she could not sleep nor Eat by reason of yt intolerable pain." The patient "at last sent for me, first I purged her with pills of cochine [cochineal] . . . then I applied coping [cupping] glasses to her shoulders with scarification, & venoses [venesection] . . . and lastly I applyed this pultis [poultice] to her Ear wherewith she was miraculously freed from all pain." The remedy used several Galenic methods to evacuate unbalanced humors via the bowels and the skin. It called for cochineal, an imported powder made from the dried remains of insects that live on cacti in Mexico and Central America. Cochineal induced diarrhea and sweating which, in Galenic practice, expelled offending humors. The Aztecs had cultivated and hybridized the cochineal insect for centuries to create a brilliant red dye as well as an effective medicine. Aztec women harvested and processed the insects. Europeans recognized cochineal's commercial value, and its trade burgeoned in the seventeenth century. The chemist Robert Boyle and the microscopist Antonie van Leeuwenhoek studied cochineal insects and reported their findings to the Royal Society. However, cochineal's Aztec origins were obscured as it became part of the English materia medica and was recorded as an ingredient in women's medical recipe books.[35]

Although women healers are often associated only with mild homespun herbal potions, Penn's recipe reveals that their remedies also included invasive medical practices such as therapeutic bloodletting that rebalanced the humors. Some healers placed leeches (bloodsucking worms) on patients' skin to draw out blood. However, Penn's recipe advocated venesection performed by incising a large vein in the arm or neck and draining blood into a cup. In scarification, the practitioner made small incisions in the skin often followed by cupping: the application of a warmed glass cup over the cuts. As the glass cooled, it formed a vacuum against the skin, which drew small amounts of stagnant maladaptive blood from the body. The final therapy described in the recipe was a warm mixture of onions, chamomile, dill, saffron, and butter spread on a cloth and applied to the ear as a poultice, which eased inflammation and pain.[36]

In addition to prescribing medical therapies, simple herbs, and compounded pharmaceuticals in an effort to balance the humors, patients and practitioners could manipulate Galen's "six things non-natural": food and drink, motion and rest, sleep and wakefulness, retention and evacuation, air, and passions of the mind. For example, a choleric person with fever symptoms (doubly hot and dry) might be prescribed oppositional therapies like cool baths and rest. A practitioner could also advise cooling food, drinks, and medicines that might include artichokes, melons, raisins, or strawberries. The Penn manuscript provides humoral instructions to cure "a Rheume [discharge] in ye Eyes." Houseleek and white copperas were mixed with honey or snow water "if you perceive ye humour very hot," but "if ye humor be cold," mix the ingredients in "half-stilled water." The manuscript also describes a remedy for an old man who "was taken with a grievous pain" in his ear when traveling in a freezing and snowy wind. From a humoral perspective, the cold air exacerbated the elderly man's cold constitution, creating a painful imbalance. He was prescribed warm eardrops made from rue and bitter almond

oil and advised to wear a quilted hat to prevent ear pain. According to humoral theories, optimal health required changes to personal habits and a well-
balanced diet.[37]

Because diet was so central to Galenic practice, medicinal cookery was an
important aspect of women's domestic healing work. The word *diet* derives
from the Greek word *diaita*, meaning "regular way of life," and it follows that
humoral precepts promoted healthful living, including appropriate food and
beverage consumption. Skilled healers determined the appropriate holistic
therapies to maintain a delicate balance in vulnerable sufferers' bodies. It is
not surprising that the playwright Farquhar portrays his fictional Lady Bountiful prescribing a "diet drink" to treat a man's infected leg, an imbalance that
left untreated might send him careening into a death spiral. Indeed, recipes
for diet or "dyett" drinks are ubiquitous in women's recipe books.[38]

Diet drinks were complicated concoctions prescribed for a variety of illnesses, including scurvy, inflammations, kidney stones, menstrual disorders,
and tumors. The Penn manuscript contains two similar diet drink recipes,
while Lady Frescheville's Receipt Book includes "A Diet drinke to open the
Liver & for the Scurvie." The Chantrell recipe collection includes two recipes:
"An Excellent dyett drinke for the Scurvey" and "A Clensing Dyett Drink."
Both recipes are followed by the Latin phrase *probatum est*, meaning "it has
been proven or tested." In addition to signifying the authors' familiarity with
Latin as the language of science, this phrase suggests that women healers understood that the science-based skills of observation, record keeping, and
analysis of experimental outcomes were essential to assessing a recipe's authenticity as well as efficacy. All these recipes include the common ingredients scurvy grass, watercress, and brooklime. The Chantrell recipes add
oranges and lemon juice, signaling citrus fruits' increasing use to treat scurvy
in the late seventeenth century. A twenty-first-century reader might recognize that scurvy grass, watercress, and citrus fruits are rich in vitamin C and
would thus treat the vitamin deficiency that causes scurvy's symptoms of inflamed limbs, bleeding gums, tooth loss, anemia, and hemorrhages. However, vitamins were not discovered until the early twentieth century. Gulielma
Penn and her fellow healers would have understood the success of these remedies from a Galenic perspective: diet drinks cleansed the body of maladaptive humors. Through chains of information sharing, women healers
internalized authoritative medical knowledge and developed their own stan-
dardized and empirically "proven" cures.[39]

The Penn manuscript also reveals the compilers' familiarity with the opposing medical theories of the Renaissance physician Paracelsus and his seventeenth-century acolyte Jan Baptiste van Helmont. In contrast to Galenic theories, these physicians linked bodily disease to chemical imbalances, which could be cured by mineral-based remedies targeting specific symptoms and diseases. The success of Paracelsus's chemically mediated paradigm is reflected in the way recipe books were increasingly organized to record remedies for a specific illness that could cure any person of that particular disease. This universalized perception of the human body contrasted with the individualized Galenic analysis of a patient's bodily constitution. These competing medical theories and perceptions of the human body caused intense debates in medical communities in Europe and England in the seventeenth and early eighteenth centuries.[40] As one chemical physician explained, "The Practice of Physick being various, (and in the Judgment of most very uncertain) because the Galenists have one Theory, and Chymists another."[41]

Mary Trye, the daughter of a chemical doctor, waded into these debates in her book *Medicatrix, or the Woman-Physician* (1675). In addition to defending her father against the "calumnies" of an Oxford-educated humoral doctor named Henry Stubbe, Trye promoted her own skills as a chemical physician. She argued for the superiority of chemical cures in ailments such as gout, kidney stones, dropsy, smallpox, and consumption. In her chapter "The Defense of the Female Sex," Trye claimed that women were capable physicians and could engage effectively in medical debates. She advised Stubbe, "I am satisfied that there is enough ability in my sex, both to discourse his envy, and equal the arguments of his pen." Despite rancorous debates, both Galenic humoral and Paracelsian chemical theories and therapies became intermixed as part of the standard healing practices of trained physicians and women healers.[42]

Remedies in the Penn manuscript illustrate this syncretism. Springett recorded a recipe using both eggs (a Galenic remedy) and copperas or iron sulfate (a Paracelsian therapy) to treat "pin and web." Similar hybrid remedies appear in women's manuscripts of the period. Penn also signaled her familiarity with chemical medicine by using saltpeter, alum, brimstone, and "Oyl [oil] of Sulphur" in her remedies. Her recipes for "Helmont's Elixir Proprietatis" and "Helmont's Scorbutick Tincture" reveal how Jan van Helmont's moniker added the authority of an alchemical expert to her medications. Penn's complex, page-long recipe for Helmont's Elixir Proprietatis includes creating a tincture by combining oil of vitriol (her "Oyl of Sulfur"), myrrh, aloes, saffron, and Canary (Island) wine in a flask and boiling them over a flame to distill the contents. A popular treatise describes Helmont's Elixir as a panacea for countless illnesses and a recipe for a "long and sound life." Rather than relinquishing her medical authority to Helmont, Penn made his remedy her own by transcribing it into her recipe book, modifying the ingredients, and deploying it in her practice. In her extensive analysis of women's transcriptions from male-authored medical handbooks, Rebecca Laroche concludes, "In the circulation of knowledge through the printed text, women became owners of the textual truth that was then modified and recontextualized in their own experience."[43]

The boundaries between mystical alchemy and what we would recognize as pragmatic chemistry were blurry, and Penn would not have viewed them separately. In her home library, Penn had access to numerous alchemical reference books, including *Secrets in Chymestry, Basil Valentine's Last Testament*, and *Mercury's Caducean Rod: or, the Great and Wonderful Office of the Universal Mercury, or . . . the Mysterious Medicine of the Ancient Philosopher.* The latter was purportedly written by a fifteenth-century alchemist intent on discovering the philosopher's stone that could transmute base metals into precious gold and confer immortality and healing. Penn and her fellow healers combined long-standing medical lore with Galenic practices and newer Paracelsian theories as they produced medical knowledge and experimented with innovations in botany, pharmacy, and alchemy. As their recipe books demonstrate, Englishwomen healers participated in intertextual conversations with printed medical books as well as with manuscripts.[44]

The Circulation of Medical Knowledge in Print and Manuscript

An increasing market demand for printed medical works facilitated the emergence of an early popular medicine and science movement, which expanded the scope of medical information exchanges. Sixteenth- and seventeenth-century improvements in printing technologies made books and pamphlets more affordable for increasingly literate audiences. The printed word imparted a new sense of authenticity to published medical and scientific works, which bolstered literate Englishwomen's assertions of healing authority. Anti-hierarchical and anti-professional sentiments fueled an increased production of books in English rather than Latin. The mysterious secrets of alchemical and medical knowledge that were previously accessible only to educated men fluent in Latin were now exposed to the discerning minds of literate women and less educated men.[45] Household manuals became a best-selling genre, as exemplified by John Partridge's *The Widdowes Treasure: Plentifully Furnished with Sundry Precious and Approved Secrets in Phisicke and Chirurgery*. It was published in 1593 and remained popular into the seventeenth century. As Wendy Wall points out, the book's affordable price of four pence was comparable to the cost of a pint of beer. Although male recipe-book authors attempted to consolidate their own medical authority by invoking the works of other "men of great knowledge," they also had to market their works to a new audience of women readers.[46]

Male writers such as Partridge understood that they could lay claim to women's recognized healing authority by featuring the recipes of an elite female healer. Partridge explained that he wrote the *Widdowes Treasure* "at the erneste requeste" of a "Gentlewoman in the Cuntrye [country]" with a renowned medical practice. He included medical "secrets" and "profitable experiments" that he knew "by the Widdowes owne practise, to be most singuler [exceptional] and approued [approved]." Although scholars have attempted to link Catherine Partridge Springett to this author, she was too young to be the "Widdowe," despite sharing a comparable healing reputation.[47] Women's long-standing roles as authoritative healers were difficult for male authors to displace. In his *English Hus-wife* (1615), Gervase Markham encouraged women to practice their healing arts under the guidance of physicians. However, he admitted that sections of his book were based on the manuscript of an "Honourable Contesse [Countess]" who was a skilled medical practitioner. In his accessible English translation of the Latin *Pharmacopeia Londinensis*, titled *The London Dispensatory* (1649), Nicholas Culpeper recognized his female readership by extolling those "kind Gentlewomen . . . (who freely bestow your pains [,] brains [,] and cost, to your poor wounded and diseased neighbors)" and who "must not be forgotten." These authors encouraged female readers to imagine themselves as refined arbiters of healing acumen, natural philosophical expertise, and humanitarian benevolence.[48]

Several works attributed to medically proficient noblewomen gained a wide readership and were reprinted into the eighteenth century. Elizabeth Talbot Grey's *Choice Manual of Rare and Select Secrets in Physick and Chyrurgery: Collected and Practised by the . . . Countess of Kent* (1653) and a book by her sister, Lady Alethea Talbot, *Natura Exenterata: Nature Unbowelled by the Most Exquisite Anatomizers of Her* (1655), were directed at a female audience. According to a contemporary, Elizabeth Grey was an educated

Lady Bountiful who spent the extravagant sums of "twenty thousand pounds yearly in physick, receipts, and experiments and in charity towards the poor." She visited sufferers and "dress[ed] their soars [sores] with her own hands." Like her sister, Alethea Talbot encouraged readers to follow the precepts of the New Science, which emphasized the importance of exact measurement of ingredients, hands-on experimentation, and the authority of anatomical knowledge. The sisters' elite status imbued their recipe books with an aura of aristocratic legitimacy.[49]

As Springett, Penn, and their fellow healers transcribed medical recipes from printed works, they incorporated the authority of print into their own manuscripts. However, as Sara Pennell and Michelle DiMeo argue, recipe books were also "a means of self-formation and self-presentation" as women compilers read, interpreted, and annotated information from other texts and modified it on the basis of their own healing experiences.[50] The movement of various iterations of the popular recipe for Gascon's Powder between women's manuscripts and printed texts demonstrates this dynamic intertextuality. Gascon's Powder (also spelled Gaskon's or Gascoigne's) was featured in Elizabeth Talbot Grey's *Choice Manual* as a treatment "for all malignant and Pestilent diseases, French pox [syphilis], Small Pox, Measles, Plague, Pestilence, malignant or Scarlet Fevers." This "sovereign remedy" was known as "the Countess of Kent's Special Powder," and her manual provided four versions. Only the wealthy could afford the recipe's expensive, internationally sourced ingredients, and its inclusion in remedy books was a marker of elite status. Although Gulielma Penn did not cite a source, her "Gaskon Powder" recipe is similar to the first recipe listed in the *Choice Manual*. Grey's recipe instructs the reader to "take of the pouder of Pearl, of red Corral, of Crabs eye, of Harts-horn, and white Amber of each one ounce." Penn uses the same ingredients, but she lists them in a different order and her preparation instructions are not as detailed.[51]

Recipes for Gascon's Powder appear in numerous medical manuscripts of the period. In her 1680 recipe book, Johanna St. John used a recipe that followed the countess's third iteration of Gascon's Powder, which was taken from the *London Dispensatory*. The print versions advised readers to blend the ingredients in a "jelly made with the skins or castings of our vipers," while St. John says simply, "a Jelly of Snakeskins." Although the Countess of Kent's recipe suggests that the "crabs-eyes" should be obtained "in May or September," the St. John manuscript offers specific astrological instructions: "The crabs are to be taken when the Sun & Moon are both in Cancer, wch [which] happens but two days in a year."[52] In "Her Booke of Receipts or Medicines," Penn's contemporary Mrs. Anne Brumwich copied the Countess of Kent's second recipe for "Mr. Gascon's Powder" almost verbatim. Unlike Penn, the Brumwich compiler added practical information on the powder's uses, which included "ye ague [paroxysmal chills and fever,] burning feavour [fever,] Consumption [,] ye smallpoxes & will preserve age, health and strength." The version in *Natura Exenterata*, written by the countess's sister, provided additional educational information on the differences between the fevers of the "quotidian, tertian and double tertian Ague." A compiler of the Brumwich manuscript explicitly framed her recipe book as an intellectual pursuit. She explained poetically, "Lerning [learning] I would desire and knowledge crave, If I were halfe sepulcered [buried] in my grave." Both the Brumwich and St. John manuscripts include the proprietary phrase "Her Booke" on the fly-leaves. St. John bequeathed her recipe book to her daughter, along with curated medical knowledge. As they exchanged remedies from printed texts and manuscripts, literate healers appropriated the authority of others' collective experiments to create their own recipes derived from personal experience.[53]

Increased female literacy and a market for medical print and proprietary medicines allowed aspiring Englishwomen of the middling and lower orders to support themselves through authorship and pharmaceutical sales, and to situate themselves as Ladies Bountiful as they attempted to move upward in the social hierarchy. Although women writers were a minority, Hannah Woolley exemplifies a successful female household manual author. Woolley was orphaned as a child, but she gained literacy and domestic skills in service to a gentry family. The historian Wendy Wall calls Woolley "a domestic female celebrity" who published five best-selling manuals directed at women readers with instructions in cookery, deportment, and medical practice.[54] Woolley also generated income by selling her home-produced medicines. The authorship of one of Woolley's latter works, *The Gentlewoman's Companion; or, A Guide to the Female Sex*, has been contested, but its popularity demonstrates the market demand for self-help manuals for upwardly mobile women. *The Gentlewoman's Companion* asserted that visiting the sick was a "commendable quality in Gentlewomen," and thus women needed "knowledge in Physick [medicine]." The "grounds" for the author's knowledge in "the Sciences" was "practice and experience." Woolley appropriated the authority of print, noting, "When I was to write of Physick and Chyrurgery [surgery], I have consulted all Books I could meet with in that kind, to compleat my own Experiences." According to Woolley, "competent skill in Physick and Chyrurgery" furthered the refined humanitarian pursuit of "Usefulness," which allowed women to accrue social capital. Woolley's manuals, and those attributed to her, provided women of the middling and lower orders with information on how to present themselves as medically proficient "gentlewomen" and, when needed, to support themselves as authors or as pharmaceutical vendors.[55]

The Diffusion of Englishwomen's Healing Authority

The Penn manuscript and those of her contemporaries demonstrate women's recognized skills in diagnosis, medical therapeutics, nursing, and pharmacy. Literate women healers consulted medical manuals written by women and men that gave them access to new theories in medicine and science. Intertextual comparisons between published works and recipe books reveal how women transcribed printed information, customized it, and applied it to their practices using the precepts of empirical science. Recipes for patent medicines such as Gascon's Powder, Helmont's Elixir, and Stoughton's Waters also evince women's participation in the intertwined markets for self-help pharmaceuticals and popular printed medical works that would flourish in the American colonies. The themes of women's engagement with medical print, the New Science, transatlantic pharmaceutical commerce, and health care consumerism will be reprised throughout this book, but it is important to locate their roots in the mid to late seventeenth century. Catherine Partridge Springett, Gulielma Springett Penn, and their fellow healers created foundational legacies on which immigrants to the Delaware Valley built their healing practices.[56]

When Quaker women colonists set sail for Pennsylvania in 1682 as passengers in William Penn's fleet, they conveyed their authoritative healing cultures and their roles as spiritual leaders in their communities. While few aristocrats or upper gentry settled in Pennsylvania, women of the merchant and artisanal orders could model themselves after their founding mother, Gulielma Penn, and take on the mantle of Lady Bountiful while providing medical care in their communities. Like their foremothers, women healers in the early waves of immigration trained their female kin in the healing arts.

CHAPTER 2

Medical Networks

In her medical recipe manuscript, Elizabeth Coates Paschall asserted her ingenuity and authority with the bold strokes of her pen. Paschall was a widowed Philadelphia Quaker merchant who ran a dry goods business on the main floor of her house on High Street. She was also well known in the community as a skilled healer. Friends, kin, neighbors, and strangers sought her health care advice. Paschall's manuscript is a uniquely discursive document in which she described her interactions with her patients and her networks of medical information exchanges. In the mid-1750s, Paschall recorded a remedy for "an Asthma or Phthisick" in her medical manuscript. This entry was prompted by an encounter with "an Elderly woman one Mary Toms," who consulted Paschall for a cure for a serious respiratory ailment. According to Paschall, Toms was so short of breath that "she could scarce bare to lye Down." Paschall did not specify whether Toms had a severe case of asthma or a wasting disease called phthisic, which could have been consumption (tuberculosis) or another degenerative pulmonary condition. Mary Toms was certainly quite ill. As Paschall understood, people in respiratory distress have difficulty lying flat and must sit up in their effort to catch a breath. Paschall prescribed a remedy made of ground raisins and mustard pounded into a conserve, and she advised Toms to "take a tea Spoonfull or two Every morning." Toms's grateful granddaughter informed Paschall that the remedy was a success, as evidenced by Toms's ability to "ly down very well after she had taken it a little while." Paschall mitigated human suffering and proved her medical expertise. She recorded with satisfaction that Toms "her selfe wrote me word that it quickly relieved her."[1]

Documented interactions like this one between a woman practitioner and her appreciative patient are rare in eighteenth-century records in the British North American colonies. In her medical manuscript, Paschall cites remedies

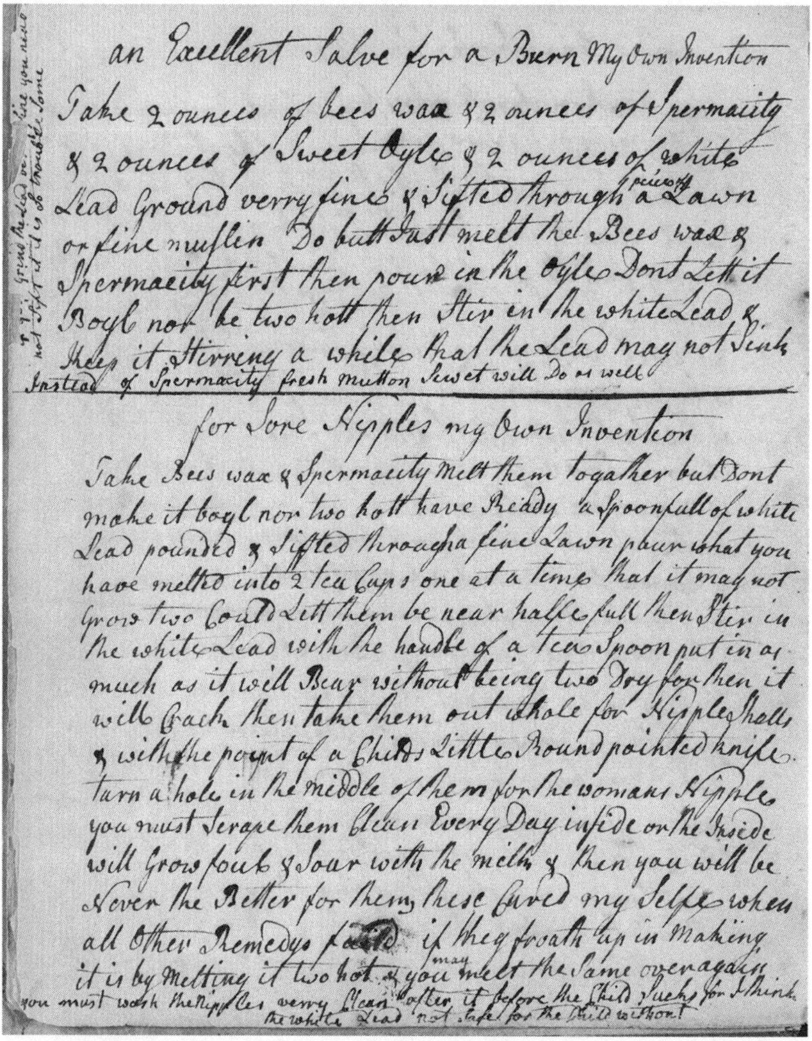
an Excellent Salve for a Bern My Own Invention
Take 2 ounces of bees wax & 2 ounces of Spermacity
& 2 ounces of Sweet Oyle & 2 ounces of white
Lead Ground verry fine & Sifted through a finest Lawn
or fine muslin Do butt Just melt the Bees wax &
Spermacity first then pour in the Oyle Dont Lett it
Boyl nor be two hott then Stir in the white Lead &
Keep it Stirring a while that the Lead may not Sink
Instead of Spermacity fresh mutton Suet will Do as well

N.B. grind the Lead or fine you need not Sift it it is So trouble Some

for Sore Nipples my Own Invention
Take Bees wax & Spermacity Melt them togather but Dont
make it boyl nor two hott have Ready a Spoonfull of white
Lead pounded & Sifted through a fine Lawn pour what you
have melted into 2 tea Cups one at a time that it may not
Grow two Could Lett them be near halfe full then Stir in
the white Lead with the handle of a tea Spoon put in as
much as it will Bear without being two Dry for then it
will Crack then take them out whole for Nipple Shells
& with the point of a Childs Little Round pointed knife
turn a hole in the middle of them for the womans Nipple
you must Scrape them Clean Every Day inside or the Inside
will Grow foul & Sour with the milk & then you will be
Never the Better for them these Cured my Selfe when
all Other Remedys failed if they froath up in Making
it is by Melting it two hot & you may melt the Same over again
you must wash the Nipples verry Clean after it before the Child Sucks for I think
the white Lead not safe for the Child without

Figure 4. Excerpts from Elizabeth Coates Paschall's mid-eighteenth-century medical manuscript. Paschall signaled her innovative practice by describing remedies as "My Own Invention." Courtesy College of Physicians, Philadelphia.

from her mother, Beulah Jaques Coates, a healer who joined the waves of Quaker immigrants to Pennsylvania after Penn's founding fleet arrived in 1682. However, neither Coates's recipe book nor her letters have survived. In the early days of settlement, few women would have had the time or resources to record their healing practices. As we saw in the previous chapter, Gulielma Springett Penn's medical manuscript helps to fill in the gaps for this first generation of colonial Pennsylvania healers. However, extant medical remedy manuscripts from second-generation women practitioners are also scarce. These manuscripts usually include only the recipes rather than details of the sufferer's symptoms or the outcome of medical therapies.[2]

By contrast, Paschall included symptoms and outcomes, as well as the webs of medical information exchanges that imbued her remedies with multiple layers of authority. In her recipe for "Asthma or Phthisick," Paschall not only described her consultation with Mary Toms, she also cited her brother-in-law John Reynell, Reynell's sister Mary Reynell Groth, and an English physician. John Reynell was a Philadelphia merchant whose commercial reputation stretched from Philadelphia to London and throughout the Atlantic world. Mary Groth gave Paschall's recipe "an Extraordinary Carracter [reference] as a Medicine Being the advice of some Eminent Physician in England." Groth, who lived in England, provided a personal testimonial from across the Atlantic. The "eminent" physician's endorsement further augmented the remedy's legitimacy. Indeed, all the ingredients listed by Paschall were included in Dr. Benjamin Marten's medical treatise on phthisic published in London in 1720. In a postscript, Paschall added yet another layer of medical validity based on her personal experimentation. She noted that the addition of honey, syrup of cloves, or molasses made the phthisick remedy "more pleasant & slides down easier." Like many practitioners, Paschall tested her medicines on own body. Paschall explained that she also enhanced the recipe with dried figs, lard, and licorice, which "helped me Grately when almost choaked up with tough phlegm." Medical recipes were not static. They were part of collaborative and innovative healing exchanges that extended across time and geographic spaces. Euro-American women built on their foremothers' health care traditions and claimed medical authority as they participated in complex, mutually affirming healing networks.[3]

Elizabeth Coates Paschall's recipe book is a point of entry into the hidden sphere of women's healing practices and their health care networks in the mid-eighteenth-century Philadelphia region. Although women of various ethnicities and social classes provided the bulk of medical care during this period, they left minimal traces in the documentary record. Paschall's recipe book and two business ledgers are the only extant documents in her own hand. None of her letters or diaries have been found. In-depth analyses of recipe books such as Paschall's provide important clues to women's diverse healing work that crossed the colonial divides of gender, race, and social status. Paschall exchanged medical information with midwives, female lay healers, male physicians and surgeons, female and male apothecaries, and Indigenous and African American practitioners. In the absence of a colonial system of medical licensure or regulation, Paschall and other lay practitioners were free to work as healers in their communities. Their successful practices and grateful patients reinforced women healers' identities as experienced and legitimate health care providers.

Medicine and Mercantile

As a member of one of the first Quaker families who settled in Pennsylvania, the young Elizabeth Coates would have felt comfortable taking on the role of a benevolent "Lady Bountiful" healer. Her father, Thomas Coates, came to Pennsylvania from Leicester, England, in 1684. By 1696, he had developed a successful shipping and merchant business and had prospered enough to marry an English Huguenot immigrant named Beulah Jacques. Early settlers were likely aware of Gulielma Penn's legacy as a Quaker founder and skilled healer, and Elizabeth had an additional female role model in her mother. Family historians praised Beulah Jacques Coates for her "upright life" and her "promotion of the cause of Truth." Coates converted to Quakerism and was remembered for her leadership in the Darby and Philadelphia Monthly Quaker Meetings. In January 1702, the Coates welcomed their third child and first daughter, Elizabeth, into their home at the corner of Philadelphia's High (later Market) and Second Streets. The Coates' dry goods shop was on the first floor of their house, which followed the pattern of most of the city's merchants and artisans. Elizabeth was raised with her brothers and sisters in a merchant's household, where she acquired business acumen from both parents.[4]

Beulah Coates was remembered as "a woman of considerable business ability" who participated in the family's mercantile enterprises. She was known to family descendants as a "bluestocking," a late eighteenth-century term for a learned woman with literary interests, and she likely educated Elizabeth at home. Beulah Coates demonstrated her financial aplomb by serving as the first treasurer of the Women's Yearly Meeting. She was later commissioned as an elder in the Society of Friends. That every generation of her family line has included a daughter named Beulah is a measure of her powerful personality and her family's esteem. As the historian Laurel Thatcher Ulrich explains, women in the patriarchal and patrilineal society of colonial America used naming patterns and moveable objects to establish strong female lineages and to create a sense of women's autonomous identities. Beulah Jacques Coates passed down her intricate, Boston-made silver chocolate pot to Elizabeth, who transmitted it through six generations of her female line. In addition to decorative domestic treasures, Beulah conveyed to Elizabeth her healing skills and her commitment to education.[5]

Elizabeth grew up in the family shop, which sold a wide variety of goods including fabrics, hardware, hats, watches, flour, and groceries. Like many Philadelphia general merchandizers, the Coates family also sold medicines. Family wills, ledgers, and surviving furniture from the period indicate that the Coates were comfortable financially and purchased tasteful consumer goods. Near the end of his life, Thomas Coates's handwriting in his business account book tapers off and appears to change to Elizabeth's hand. If Elizabeth kept her father's books as he became enfeebled, it helps to explain why she was cited, along with her elder brother, as an executor of her father's 1719 will. Daughters were rarely named as executors because they were legally under the guardianship of male kin and were considered less rational than sons. Quakers' beliefs in equality allowed Philadelphia women to circumvent the constraints of English common law.[6]

Two years after her father's death, nineteen-year-old Elizabeth married Joseph Paschall, the scion of another prominent Quaker family. In 1682, Joseph's grandfather Thomas Paschall Sr. and his wife, Joanna Sloper Paschall, had joined Penn's Fleet and sailed to Philadelphia from Bristol, England. Thomas Paschall Sr. was a pewterer, alchemist, and apothecary, and he passed down these skills to his descendants. Joseph's father, also named Thomas Paschall, operated a mill west of Philadelphia in Chester County and, like Thomas Senior, served in the Pennsylvania Assembly. Joseph Paschall was raised in a Quaker household in the fold of the Darby Monthly Meeting, where he married Elizabeth in 1721. The couple started their life together in the Coates' house on High Street, which Elizabeth had inherited from her father. Joseph's brothers shared their alchemical and medical remedies with Elizabeth.[7]

Like his sires, Joseph Paschall was civic minded, which placed the family in circles of prominent Philadelphians. Joseph was elected to positions on the

Philadelphia City Council in the 1730s. In 1736, he established Philadelphia's Union Fire Company along with Benjamin Franklin. In addition to her work in the business, Elizabeth would have been responsible for entertaining assemblymen, city councilmen, and upwardly mobile Philadelphians like Franklin. Influential men in the Paschall's civic, political, and natural philosophical circles are cited as medical recipe sources in Elizabeth's manuscript. Paschall and her mother also practiced civic benevolence. They joined "charitable widows and other good women of the city" to contribute funds for the Pennsylvania Hospital founded by Franklin and Dr. Thomas Bond. Paschall also checked out medical books from Franklin's Library Company of Philadelphia. It is not surprising that an elderly Franklin remembered Elizabeth Paschall as "my dear old friend." Of course, these networks included wives and female kin, whom Paschall also cited in her medical recipe manuscript.[8]

In 1742, after her husband Joseph's untimely death, the "Widow Paschall" was left with a merchant business to run and three children to rear: fourteen-year-old Isaac, ten-year-old Beulah, and two-year-old Joseph. As an elite, widowed woman of property, Paschall had the option to remarry. However, she chose to remain single and to take advantage of her legal status as feme sole, which, unlike that of married women, allowed her to conduct legal, business, and real estate transactions without the oversight of male kin. Paschall embraced the role of merchant and prospered, despite the political turbulence of the 1740s. British North American colonists participated in the War of Austrian Succession, also called King George's War. However, the New England colonies did the bulk of the fighting. Philadelphia merchants such as Paschall celebrated the British forces' 1745 capture of Fort Louisburg in French Canada, while continuing their successful trade with the West Indies and Britain. A 1746 announcement in the *Pennsylvania Gazette* that began "Elizabeth Paschall, Shopkeeper, in Market Street" proclaimed a key aspect of Paschall's identity, which informed her healing work. An entry in her medical recipe book counters romanticized notions of shopkeeping and suggests the physical hardships of Paschall's long workdays. She recorded a remedy for "a Most Racking Torture in Every Joynt [joint] from head to foot & in the Bowells," especially "every Single Joynt of my Back." She believed that the tormenting pain was caused by a chill from "standing too Long in the Shop without having my meals in Due time." According to Paschall, a warm glister (enema) made from oatmeal, chamomile, sweet oil, molasses, and salt counteracted the cold humor, "warmed my Bowells," "drawed the pain from Every Joynt," and "revived [me] to perfect ease in less than an hour's time." Paschall was fortunate that she could treat herself for work-related illnesses, and she applied this knowledge in her healing work.[9]

Despite the physical demands of her shop, Paschall's business ledger reveals that she participated in supportive networks of female merchants and shopkeepers that included her sister-in-law Mary Coates Reynell as well as Mary Jacobs, Rebecca Steel, Magdalena Devine, and Elizabeth Whartnaby. Both Reynell and Steel appear in Paschall's business ledger book as partners at public auctions or "vendues." They also contributed remedies to Paschall's medical manuscript. Perhaps it was during a conversation in one of their shops that the merchant Mary Jacobs shared with Paschall an "approved" remedy for the flux (diarrheal disease).[10] Elizabeth Duckworth Whartnaby, a Quaker minister, healer, and medicine vendor, also exchanged remedies with Paschall. Two decades earlier, Whartnaby had published one of the first pharmaceutical advertisements in Pennsylvania newspapers. In the *American Weekly Mercury*, Whartnaby had touted her "Spirit of Scurvey-grass" and her "right and genuine Spirit of Venice Treacle, truly and only prepared by her in Philadelphia." She asserted that she was "the original and first promoter of it in this city." Venice Treacle or Venetian Theriac was a pastiche of over fifty ingredients used to treat plague, which was prevalent in Atlantic maritime ports in the early 1720s. Whartnaby was an experienced pharmaceutical entrepreneur as well as a healer. She was not unusual. According to the historian Karin Wulf, women were heads of 20 percent of households in late colonial Philadelphia, and Patricia Cleary counted more than 160 women retailers in the city between 1740 and 1755. Shopkeeping women offered each other health information along with commercial networking opportunities.[11]

In addition to her business responsibilities and healing work, Paschall supervised the remodeling of her Philadelphia house as well as the construction of a country home in the suburb of Frankford. In a 1746 newspaper advertisement, Paschall notified her customers that she would "continue to sell all Sorts of Merchant's Goods as usual" in her temporary lodgings in Strawberry Alley during the demolition and reconstruction of her Market Street house.[12] Although reform-minded Quakers, such as Paschall's friend Anthony Benezet, exhorted Friends to live simply, Paschall shared Philadelphians' mid-century mania for real estate improvement and conspicuous consumption. Even an Anglican minister complained that the city was "one eternal scene of pulling down and putting up" characterized by endless "additions, alterations, [and] decorations." The Philadelphia Contributorship Insurance Company assessed Paschall's remodeled townhouse at £150, including

its newly added marble chimneypiece, decorative ironwork, and newel stair-
case. Extant mahogany furniture testifies to Paschall's preference for simple
designs made from the best materials. Her relationships with other elite merchant families are evident in the names recorded in her recipe book, which
included the Reynells, Logans, Pembertons, Shoemakers, and Wistars. Paschall's purchase of a carriage confirmed her status as one of Philadelphia's
"merchant grandees." In 1748, she personally supervised the construction of
a country house in Frankford, adjacent to her sister Mary's family's property.
Country homes were a mark of refinement and they offered a healthful escape from the pestilential summers in Philadelphia. Although it was far less
grand than estates such as the Penn's Pennsbury Manor, Paschall christened
her second home Cedar Grove. Contributors to Paschall's recipe book reflect
new circles of medical information sharing in Frankford. Paschall's business
activities, construction projects, and healing practice reflect her energy, self-
confidence, and competencies in a variety of endeavors.[13]

"She Cures All Her Neighbors of All Distempers"

When the Murray and Keane theatrical company brought George Farquhar's
play *The Beaux-Stratagem* to Philadelphia in 1749, skilled women healers were
a familiar presence in the city. Playgoers would have known actual women
represented by Farquhar's character Lady Bountiful, an "old, civil, country
gentlewoman" who "cures all her neighbors of all distempers [diseases]." As
a practicing Quaker, Paschall was unlikely to have attended a production of
The Beaux-Stratagem. Even wealthy Friends opposed the theater and considered it a decadent pastime. However, in Philadelphia's face-to-face community, it is likely that Paschall heard gossip about the bawdy comedy from shop
customers and non-Quaker friends. Her neighbors may have noted the parallels between Lady Bountiful's healing benevolence and the free medical care
that Paschall provided to neighbors, friends, and impoverished people. Although there were few aristocratic "ladies" in Philadelphia, women of the rising merchant elite and flourishing artisanal orders could accrue social
capital by providing health care in their communities.[14]

   In her mid-forties Paschall began to document her healing work in a clear
but unpolished script in her manuscript book. Paschall's inelegant handwriting may be evidence of her basic schooling, or it could suggest that she recorded her remedies in haste as she carved out spare moments in her

exceptionally busy life. Apart from several cooking and household recipes, all the entries in Paschall's 167-page manuscript document medical remedies and patient encounters. Her manuscript does not contain subheadings, and she appears to have recorded a remedy when she developed a new therapy or when she received recipes from a medical informant. One can imagine Paschall copying several remedies endorsed by her neighbor Mary Deshler while the women took tea in the parlor or chatted in the dry goods shop. Paschall's leather-bound book with its stains and signs of wear was certainly a workaday document. It is possible that it sat on her shop's countertop alongside her business ledger book, because some recipe exchanges took place as part of her commercial interactions. Paschall's dry goods shop on the first floor of her strategically located Market Street townhouse bridged the spheres of private domesticity, communal neighborliness, healing, and commerce.

Paschall's recipe book attests to her wide-ranging health care networks. Her sources for medical remedies included women healers, midwives, women shopkeepers, and female neighbors and kin. However, Paschall's book shatters any notion of separate gendered spheres of domestic healing. In her manuscript, she charted the ways that medical cures passed from father to son as easily as they flowed from mother to daughter. Men shared remedies with their male friends as well as female kin and neighbors. In her manuscript, Paschall maps the urban geography of the north side of Market Street by documenting her healing interactions with her neighbors, the Vernons, Wistars, Jacobs, Harmons, and Deshlers. Over 70 of the 162 names mentioned in Paschall's recipe book belonged to Quakers. However, along with documenting the close ties within the Quaker community, Paschall also delineates the connections between Philadelphians of different religions, ethnicities, and social orders. Paschall's healing networks extended beyond the city of Philadelphia to the greater Delaware Valley and across the Atlantic. Her manuscript demonstrates that she collaborated with university-educated physicians as well as lay healers, even as she asserted her own medical expertise. A close reading of Paschall's recipe book allows us to listen in on these medical conversations and to understand how healing networks reinforced practitioners' credibility and authority.[15]

Although Paschall did not appear to practice midwifery, her recipe book reveals the persistence of women's traditional networks of healing and social support in the face of frequent obstetrical and gynecological problems. For many eighteenth-century colonial women, childbearing was the focus of their lives from puberty to menopause. Pregnancy, childbirth, and the postpartum

period were fraught with the potential for ill health or death, and healers in-
tervened during these moments of physical, emotional, and spiritual crisis.
For example, Paschall was called in to treat her niece Beulah Coates, who was
"violent ill of a Chollick" during her "lying in" one week after her baby's delivery. It is unclear what caused Beulah's "colic" with its symptoms of severe abdominal pain. However, Paschall recorded that a "glister" or enema made
from oatmeal, chamomile, sweet oil, and brown sugar effected the cure. The
recipe is similar to one that Paschall used on herself to cure the "Racking Torture in Every Joynt" and in her abdomen. Like Gulielma Springett Penn, Paschall based her remedies on the theories of humoral medicine that called for
evacuating the maladaptive humors from the body. Although this unpleasant
therapy called for injecting the medicinal liquid into the rectum, the resulting
"evacuation" would have assured Paschall's niece of its effectiveness. Following the enema, Paschall prescribed a piece of toast dipped in pennyroyal tea
with a spoonful of rum, noting that the tea and toast would warm the stomach, thus balancing the humors without generating the excesses of fever. Healers such as Paschall provided supportive hands-on remedies that included
intimate bodily contact. Paschall's confidence in her expertise and her therapeutic touch could help to soothe her patients' fears of death or disability.[16]

Paschall herself endured obstetrical problems, including frequent miscarriages. She gave birth to nine children, with six dying in infancy. Fortunately
for Paschall, at a moment of crisis in the late stages of a pregnancy in 1727, her
mother, Beulah Jacques Coates, was on hand. Paschall recalled being so struck
with heat exhaustion and shortness of breath that she felt that she would "drop
down dead." Her mother "compelled" her to drink a ginger tea remedy, which
gave relief "in an instant." Other women healers provided medical advice for
Paschall's childbearing difficulties. In her "Excellent Remedy against Abortion or Miscarriages," Paschall reveals, "It was the advice of my friend Eliza
Wartnaby [Elizabeth Whartnaby]" that "helped me after so Long a habit of
miscarriage and So much weakness that I never expected health again." As
the historian Susan Klepp notes, in the mid-eighteenth century childbearing
was viewed positively and pregnant bodies were perceived as productive,
abundant, and fruitful. This image contrasted sharply with a popular rhetoric
describing the desolate "barrenness" of childlessness or the miscarriages that
Paschall experienced. While it is difficult to assess Paschall's feelings about
her childbearing problems, her recipe notations reflect the physical and emotional exhaustion of women's reproductive years. As a Quaker minister and a
healer, Elizabeth Whartnaby provided both medical care and religious coun-

seling, which might have included the spiritual work of accepting what Friends would perceive as God's will for their lives. Healers who provided authoritative emotional, spiritual, and physical interventions at critical life moments gained their patients' respect and appreciation.[17]

Women family members figure prominently in Paschall's manuscript book as both sources and patients, including her mother, sisters, sisters-in-law, female cousins, and nieces. In one entry, Paschall explained, "My Cousin Parnell Sutton tould me that her mother ordered raw onions chopd fine" to be placed in Mr. Sutton's chamber pot, which cured his kidney stones. In another instance, Paschall's servant Polly Webb shared her grandmother's topical application of sweet oil, brimstone, and pitch "that has cured many" suffering from oozing sores. Paschall readily credited this secondhand advice on the basis of her assessment of the reliability, expertise, and authority of the sources. On a more personal note, Paschall described her mother's effective poultice for infections, and her recipe "for Children's Sore heads" that used beer, butter, and cabbage leaves to draw "the humour from their Eyes & Face." By embedding themselves in intergenerational family networks, healers like Paschall enhanced their medical skills and competence. In the process, they also developed circles of women who cared for each other in times of illness, thus creating medical safety nets for themselves and for their families.[18]

Health care for children was considered women's domain, and Paschall's manuscript includes additional recipes for childhood ailments, shared between female kin, friends, and neighbors. These entries include remedies for smallpox, scarlet fever, pleurisy, and a "Most Malignant Sort of Measles." Paschall advised her "Neighbor Vernon" to give "her Eldest Son" a recipe to "cool and abate" an "Inward Fever" when the boy was "so reduced that he could scarce Creep 200 foot with a stick to support him." With a tone of satisfaction, Paschall added that she cured the lad, "tho' the Doctor Could not help him." She also documented the instances when she treated her own children successfully when physicians' remedies failed. Paschall recorded a recipe for an "Eye Water" made from "egg white and alum" that cured her son Isaac's red, inflamed eyes and the ocular infections of "diverse others when the Doctors could not." Like Gulielma Penn, Paschall mixed ingredients based on ancient humoral theories with newer chemical medicines such as alum. She noted that this hybrid remedy was effective because it "repells the humours." Paschall included information on appropriate medication doses for children. Infant's and children's death rates were high in early Philadelphia, and parents looked to skilled women healers to treat young loved ones during potentially life-threatening childhood illnesses. Paschall recommended the patent medicine "Daffy's Elixir" for the "Bloody Flux," but she cautioned that the adult dose of two tablespoons was "too strong for a child." Instead, Paschall prescribed a smaller dose of "one pap spoonful" for children two to three years old.[19]

Paschall's recipe book demonstrates that merchant class and artisanal healers were not the only trusted female practitioners. Her manuscript entries shed light on the practices of women of the lower orders known as "old wives" or "wise women," whose work has left few traces in the historical record. As previously noted, in Anglo-American popular culture, "old wives" were dismissed as mere charlatans who charged for their services and allegedly peddled regressive superstitious remedies. Nonetheless, Paschall placed her confidence in actual elder women's expertise, which she often found more valuable than physicians' advice. In one instance, Paschall described a sufferer who "was cured of a Cancer in her face" with a recipe using celandine and May butter. The remedy had been prescribed by "an Old Woman after she [the patient] had Spent Some Scores of pounds on the Docter." Paschall recorded another successful tar-based remedy suggested "by a poor old woman," which cured a cancer that had "eaten Grate [great] parts away" of a man's lips. In another case, a man was "so costive" (constipated) that "he was in such torture that could not help Continually Crying out," which "was Dreadful to hear." However, the man "could find no Relief from the Docters." "At last," explained Paschall, "he was advised by antient [old] woman" to take a preparation of hog's lard and molasses. The man's "stool flew from him . . . and he found immediate Relief." Celandine, tar, lard, and molasses were effective therapies used by experienced women healers and also are listed as ingredients in physicians' handbooks.[20]

In a recollection of one of her miscarriages, Paschall maintained that an expert elderly healer saved her life. Paschall was three months pregnant and experiencing "violent pain in her "Back & Bowells" that was "so extreem Bad that I Sweat to the very fingers ends." She was in premature labor, but she "could not be delivered" by the midwife. Paschall called in a doctor to induce an abortion. By the mid-eighteenth century, obstetricians called "male midwives" were entering women's birthing chambers, particularly in difficult cases. According to Paschall, both the doctor and midwife determined "that if I was not speedily delivered I should Dye." They understood that if a fetus dies in utero and is not expelled, it must be aborted to prevent hemorrhage, infection, and maternal death. In this dire moment, "an Elderly woman

proposed giving me a Glister [enema] which was prepared immediately." Paschall then delivered the fetus successfully "with very little pain." When the
midwife and the physician failed to provide a cure, Paschall turned to a healer
with a lifetime of experience who was assisting with the birth. The elderly
healer's remedy contained the abortifacient chamomile. This "wise woman"
may have been a "lying-in" (childbirth) nurse or an expert in reproductive
health whom women consulted for contraceptives, emmenagogues, and obstetrical advice. Both the doctor and midwife witnessed the "Elderly woman's"
expertise. In addition to providing a venue for medical information exchanges
between people of different social orders, local healing networks provided patients with an array of skilled advice when they faced health crises.[21]

Weaving Webs of Healing Authority

Sufferers often ventured beyond their neighbors and kin in search of laywomen practitioners. Paschall's Quaker neighbor Catherine Wistar, who was
of German descent, consulted a Pennsylvania Deutsch (German) healer to
treat a swelling on her newborn son's head after several doctors were unable
to effect a cure. The woman healer advised Wistar to rub the swelling with
"fasting spittle" and to "cover it with a piece of thin Lead."[22] This remedy
contains elements of magical and alchemical cures, and it demonstrates a
chain of information sharing that extended beyond the Quaker fold into the
Pennsylvania German community. The healing authority of the unnamed
German woman, whom Paschall never met, as told to Paschall by her trusted
neighbor and friend Catherine Wistar, was greater than that of physicians
because it produced a successful cure. Folk remedies were common among
Anglo-American healers, but they were also part of *braucherei*, a Pennsylvania German vernacular healing culture. *Braucherei* practitioners combined
alchemical theories, religious practices, and vernacular charms. William
Penn had promoted immigration from the German states and as many as
one-third of Pennsylvanians were of German descent in the early eighteenth
century. While a few university-trained physicians immigrated from German
provinces, numerous nonphysician healers from these areas brought their
unique medical ideologies and folk healing customs, which Paschall blended
with English healing traditions.[23]

The German-born merchant David Deshler and his French Huguenot
wife, Mary, both Quaker converts, were skilled healers who shared their

western European medical cures with their friend and neighbor, Elizabeth Paschall. Mary Lefevre Deshler gave Paschall the details of a cure for a felon [infected fingertip] using ground earthworms, which cured a boy "whose hand was much swell'd & in Such and agony that he could scarce get any sleep." In a period before antibiotics, a felon could quickly become a serious generalized infection. Mary Deshler was renowned for her Deshler's Salve, which was made of beeswax, turpentine, resin, linseed oil, and sheep or deer's tallow. The medication was used to treat burns, wounds, and abscesses. Deshler's legacy was long-lived. References to Deshler's Salve appear in women's recipe books, letters, published pharmaceutical dispensatories, and advertisements into the mid-twentieth century. Elizabeth Paschall passed down this remedy, along with her healing skills, to her daughter Beulah, who was named for her grandmother. Beulah recorded the Deshler's Salve recipe in her own extensive household manuscript. Mary's husband, David, was also an adept healer. Perhaps when Paschall purchased "six penny nails" from him in November 1749, David shared with her his balsam apple remedy to cure an open wound. Although female networks were clearly important sites of health information transmission, Paschall included remedies from male lay healers and other men who were part of her business dealings, community interactions, and Quaker networks.[24]

Male nonphysician healing experts like David Deshler provided medical care for Philadelphia area residents alongside women healers. Paschall recorded remedies from other male healers, including Joseph Linington, and her brothers-in-law John and Stephen Paschall, who were "alchymical doctors." Men handed down recipes in their families and shared remedies with their male kin and friends. Paschall related that her uncle John Holme got a "Receipt from a Small Manuscript book of his father's" that "cured Severall verry Bad Scald Heads (tinea capitis or ringworm)." The term "scald" referred not to burns but to the scaly and scabby inflamed patches of scalp that we now understand to be caused by a fungal infection. Although the intense itch, circular peeling skin, and subsequent hair loss of ringworm was common in children, it carried the social stigma of poverty. Paschall considered her uncle an authoritative source for a scald head ointment recipe using verdigris (a green chemical pigment), butter, and deer's suet. Through her own experiments, Paschall found that an ointment made with cream promoted healing when the inflammation was resolving, and she "imparted the secret" to her cousin Elizabeth Adams.[25]

Men's and women's medical information networks overlapped and extended across religious denominations. John Holme was a leader in Philadelphia's First Baptist Church congregation, and he connected Paschall with healers from this religious group. A respected lay healer named Joseph Watkins, who owned a lumber business, was another male medical source from the First Baptist Church. Watkins told Paschall about a cure for whitlow (infected fingertip) using elder leaves or roots, which an American Indian woman had imparted to Henry Clifton's wife. The Cliftons shared the recipe with Watkins, who, according to Paschall, "has cured many with it since." Watkins also shared a nosebleed remedy he had received from a "man who had Treasured up many valuable Receipts." Paschall did not let her preoccupation with her building projects stop the flow of medical information. According to a notation in Paschall's business receipt book, Watkins delivered beams for Paschall's country house, Cedar Grove, in October 1748. Perhaps it was in this transaction that Watkins shared with Paschall a recipe that cured a "violent swelling in his leg" after a "Pile of Boards" fell on him. Watkins feared that his leg would putrefy and require amputation. He remembered that his father taught him to use an application of the leaves of black snakeweed. However, "it Being then winter season he could not get Leaves But took the Roots." Watkins prepared a decoction, bathed his foot, and gained relief. Paschall advised her readers how to locate and identify black snakeweed. Other names in Paschall's business ledger book coincide with those in her recipe book, demonstrating the connections between her business, personal, and health care networks.[26]

Without apparent reticence, Paschall documented her open discussions with men regarding intimate bodily topics. Paschall's brother-in-law John Reynell gave her the details of a remedy that had given Richard Blackham "admirable relief" from a case of piles (hemorrhoids), "which he himself experienced." George Wood of the Darby Quaker Meeting was equally open about sharing with Paschall a recipe for an ointment-soaked rag to be "putt up the fundament" that cured his bleeding hemorrhoids "when Severall Docters failed." Her daughter Beulah copied the recipe into her own manuscript. Paschall's descriptions of conversations between women and men about deeply personal health issues are similar to those found in newspapers and almanacs of the period.[27]

Health information sharing reached across the boundaries of race and class as well as gender, but the exchange did not alter social hierarchies.

Although Paschall was a friend of the abolitionist Anthony Benezet, her recipe book demonstrates the racialized distinctions that even reformers maintained. Benezet reaffirmed Quakers' assertion that all peoples, including Native Americans and African Americans, possessed God's inner light and were thus the spiritual equals of Euro-Americans. However, the Society of Friends had few successes in converting these groups, and they rarely joined Quaker congregations. The historian David Brion Davis notes with irony that Philadelphia Quakers practiced a "fraternal relationship of unequals." Abolitionists like Benezet challenged Quaker slaveholders to manumit their enslaved people, but some, like Elizabeth's brother-in-law John Paschall, never did. Quaker practices that preserved racialized hierarchies amid egalitarian ideology are echoed in the ways that Paschall fails to identify Indigenous and African American practitioners or patients by name in her manuscript.[28]

Although Paschall cited Euro-American servants by name, and even noted the name of a stranger she met in a tavern, African Americans and Native Americans, including servants in neighboring households, remain tellingly nameless. After an extensive healing encounter, Paschall called a Native American patient "a Jersey Indian Man," and a neighbor's servant suffering from smallpox "an Indian girl at Isaac Lane's." In another instance, Paschall described an "Old Negro Man" who was either enslaved or a servant to one of her neighbors, whose "limb was so mortified that the Surgeon ordered it to be Cutt off." The man refused surgery, and instead sent for another "Old Negro Man" who was a healer from Merion, about eight miles outside Philadelphia. Although she maintained a social distance by failing to cite his name, Paschall recognized the elderly Black healer's expertise and recorded his remedy in her manuscript. The Black healer cured the "Old Negro Man" without subjecting him to the risks of amputation. He washed the man's ulcerated joint with herbal tea by "spirting the warm tea out of his mouth" and applied a copper penny to the area. The idea that spittle contains a healing force was common in both African and European folk healing traditions, and the use of copper dates to the ancient Mediterranean. In addition, the healer cleaned out "dead flesh," and applied a poultice of verdigris and deer suet to the wound. Indeed, Paschall noted that these were the chief ingredients of her own scald head remedy. Although she relegated the elderly African American healer to anonymity, Paschall clearly valued his healing expertise and recorded his successful therapy, which shared elements with her own medical practices.[29]

Paschall's recipe book also suggests that female servants' healing work was often subsumed under that of their employers. Although Paschall employed several servants, who likely helped to prepare remedies and to assist in gathering medicinal herbs, their adjunct work is not mentioned in the manuscript. However, Paschall did provide several examples of household servants' successful remedies. For example, she noted, "our [servant] Nancy Donaldson" had "verry sore nipples in her Lyeing Inn [postpartum period]." Donaldson informed Paschall about a recipe for balsam apple steeped in rum, which "speedily cured" the problem. Paschall acknowledged Donaldson's healing expertise and she recorded the proven recipe. However, Paschall always described her servants with the patronizing prefix "our," such as "our Martha Owen" or "our Phebe." She also failed to name several older healers of the lower orders, identifying them only as "elderly women." Although Paschall likely enacted her healing role with benevolent Quaker intentions, her practice also provided her with social capital and served as a marker of her status.[30]

Medical Collaboration and Competition

Paschall's status as a Quaker merchant and a member of a prominent Philadelphia family allowed her to collaborate with physicians while simultaneously asserting her own role as an elite healer. She described a trusting relationship with the university-trained Dr. John Kearsley Sr., whom she likely met in her husband's political circles. Kearsley appears to have been the Paschall's family physician, and the families' social positions would have been relatively equal. Paschall records several instances in which she sought Kearsley's guidance, and others in which she collaborated with Kearsley to treat a patient. She also noted that Dr. Benjamin Morris tried her larkspur flower tea for "a violent vomiting," and "he said it was an excellent medicine." Like Kearsley, Morris received a formal medical education in Europe, and he was respected in the community. Although she collaborated with doctors, Paschall was quick to assert the many times that her remedies succeeded when those of physicians were ineffective. Phrases such as "cured when the doctors failed" or "cured when all the Doctor's medicines proved ineffectual" run like a refrain in her manuscript.[31]

Paschall could practice healing alongside physicians such as Kearsley and Morris because the medical marketplace in early Philadelphia was unregulated. Colonial governments did not enforce medical educational or licensure requirements, and the first professional medical association would not be established until 1787. Female as well as male practitioners had the freedom to declare themselves doctors, doctresses, apothecaries, surgeons, bonesetters, therapeutic bleeders, or cancer specialists. As we saw in Chapter 1, physicians and nonphysicians practiced within the same medical worldview, often using similar therapies and medications. Sufferers recognized that doctors did not have a monopoly on medical knowledge or practice. Indeed, patients shared the sneaking suspicion that no practitioner had a consistently proven panacea for a specific illness. It was up to the individual physician or practitioner to win a patient's trust.

This lack of medical hegemony diffused doctors' health care authority. Plays, books, and political cartoons that ridiculed doctors reflected the public's mistrust of the medical profession. Recall that although George Farquhar mocked Lady Bountiful in his play *The Beaux-Stratagem*, he also derided physicians. As a character in the play opined, Lady Bountiful "has cured more people in and about Litchfield within ten years than the doctors have killed in twenty."[32] Tobias Smollett, an English physician and popular satiric author, jeered at doctors who affected the wigs, clothing, carriages, and silver-headed canes of elites in a pathetic attempt to escape their roots as mere tradesmen and win a place among the gentry class. Smollett understood that upwardly mobile young physicians depended on the approval of upper-class women healers and their social circles to gain important elite patient referrals. In one novel, Smollett described how his protagonist Dr. Ferdinand Fathom had "to exert himself in winning the favour of those sage sibyls, who keep . . . the temple of medicine, and admit the young priest to the service of the altar." Smollett humorously referenced classical Greek female oracles, who were often skilled healers, to underline physicians' need to win over women practitioners. Like the fictional Dr. Fathom, Kearsley likely needed patient referrals from the "sage sybil" Elizabeth Paschall, and he would have sought to retain Paschall's family in his practice. The need for physicians to garner the approval of elite women healers opened the way for collaboration as well as competition between these groups.[33]

Claiming Healing Authority

It is tempting to imagine that patients sought cures by moving upward on a health care chain of command by first seeking healing experts within the household, then less expensive nonphysician healers, and finally trained physicians. However, in practice, this process was inconsistent. In analyzing a health care marketplace, medical anthropologists attempt to determine patients' "hierarchy of resort," or the sequence and criteria that patients use in seeking a particular practitioner or therapy to cure their illness. The cases in Paschall's manuscript demonstrate that sufferers might try self-care, seek the advice of a physician, consult a woman healer, obtain a remedy from an apothecary or woman herb seller, seek treatment from a cancer specialist, find an Indigenous or African American practitioner, or see a midwife—in no particular sequence. Their choices might be influenced by their social status, the cost or accessibility of a provider, their previous health care experiences, or any number of personal preferences. Although some patients sought a laywoman practitioner before seeking a doctor's care, some sufferers consulted lay healers such as Paschall when doctors were unsuccessful. The most important element was a patient's trust in a practitioner.[34]

Paschall narrated several cases of severe poison ivy that demonstrated complex hierarchies of resort. According to Paschall, "My Friend Eliza Brooks said she had one of her Sons was so Poison'd with it" that his "private parts became so Swollen that he could not make water [urinate]." The son had apparently put his knife smeared with the oil from the poison ivy vine into "his britches pocket." Brooks went to a nearby inn to consult with a female healer, but instead found "a studious man that heard her Complaints" and advised her to bathe the area with warm honey and apply a cabbage leaf, "which quickly relieved him [her son]." Innkeepers and tavern keepers were frequent sources of health care referrals, and practitioners could often be found in these public places. Brooks's husband subsequently had such a severe case of poison ivy, his face "swelld till he was blind." A doctor prescribed an ointment of "house Leek & Cream which Did no Good." Brooks applied the honey and warm cabbage leaves suggested by the "studious man," which "quickly cured" her husband. Brooks used the same remedy to cure a man "from Salem [New Jersey]" with a similarly severe facial swelling from poison ivy. In these cases, there was little to differentiate physicians and lay healers' remedies: all used herbal cures. A practitioner's personal credibility and healing successes convinced patients to implement a remedy, rather than his or her formal credentials.[35]

The very language of women's recipe books asserted the truth-value and authority of their healing expertise. The common opening phrase of a recipe usually began in the second person imperative, which compelled a reader to "take!" Paschall's manuscript exhibits exclamatory and imperative linguistic patterns such as "Cured when the Doctors failed!" and "*Take* Sweet Marjoram Dryed and Distilled." The authoritative admonition "take" reflected the Latin word *recipere,* the root of the word *recipe.* The apothecaries' abbreviation *Rx* denoting a set of instructions for a medical remedy derives from this root, and it can still be found on prescriptions. This etymology helps to explain the sense of authority that a recipe author could generate, whether the prescriber was a female healer or a male practitioner. Healers' use of the active tense allowed recipe book readers to become dynamic participants in the process of recreating the recipe and then prescribing it for a patient. A healer's affirmation of the remedy's efficacy or "virtue" was generally stated in the present tense, which increased the emphasis on the validity of the statement. The Latin term *probatum est,* "it is proved," appeared in eighteenth-century recipe books as well as in the seventeenth-century manuscripts of Gulielma Penn's contemporaries. Although Paschall did not use this term, she often included similar confident assertions at the end of a recipe, such as "infallibly cures" or "perfected the cure." Paschall took her proof statements to the next level by testifying to actual patient successes. In other recipes, she identified the names of the people she had healed, so that a recipe book reader could verify the cure with an individual sufferer.[36]

It is not surprising that Paschall and her fellow women healers legitimized their remedies by assessing and asserting the personal honor, credibility, or "credit" of their recipe book contributors. Samuel Johnson's influential *Dictionary of the English Language* (1755) and other popular dictionaries reflected contemporary definitions of authority. In addition to defining *authority* as formal legal control, Johnson invoked the notion of informal power by including the synonyms *influence, credibility,* and *testimony. Credibility, reputation,* and *honor* were interchangeable terms. Paschall frequently gave a character reference for her informants, along with a testimonial to the efficacy of their empirical cures. Paschall advocated a cure for a "Fellon" on the basis of her informant Susannah Fowler's "Good Reputation" and her history as "an Acquaintance of mine from her Childhood." A cure for consumption was of value because it came from "a young woman that was well dressed and Seemed like a person of credit." A cancer remedy from a "Country man" was worth recording because Paschall deemed him "Sober & Sollid." Paschall described Mrs. Thomas Penrose, a prominent Philadelphia merchant's wife, as "an acquaintance of mine & a person of undoubted credit." Thus, without reservation, Paschall recorded that Penrose "cured a young man that mostly Pised [pissed or wet] the Bed Every Night" and included the remedy in her manuscript. Paschall also accepted the legitimacy of one reliable informant who she averred "has known ten or twelve peoples cured." As a creative woman in her own right who touted remedies of "my own invention," Paschall valued a recipe to treat poison ivy from "Rebecca McVaugh who is an ingenious woman of good credit." For Paschall, a "woman of credit" with an honorable practice was as legitimate a healer as the university-educated Dr. John Kearsley. A healer's personal credibility was a critical form of currency in mid-eighteenth-century Philadelphia that informed perceptions of healing authority.[37]

In addition to garnering patients' faith in her cures, Paschall deployed her dynamic personality, social capital, and close interpersonal relationships to become an authoritative "node" in a web of health care information exchanges. Sociologists are intensely interested in analyzing how influence is created within social networks, particularly in the current context of online communities. However, their theories are applicable to the face-to-face society of Paschall's Philadelphia. Like other esteemed Delaware Valley healers, Paschall successfully won the hearts and minds of her patients and the regard of her fellow practitioners. According to the social network theorist Mark Granovetter, once a person is identified as an influential node within a social network, new network participants also look to that person for information and advice, and the process becomes self-reinforcing. Network participants continue to cluster around a person imbued with authority, and the clustering tends to snowball. Paschall's health care networks demonstrate the power of strong social ties exemplified by the medical legitimacy generated by the reputable testimonials of patients, kin, fellow Quakers, and other merchants.[38]

Paschall increased the scope of her influence by reaching beyond her immediate networks to participate in wider communities. Her actions are consistent with Granovetter's argument that a trusted person's contacts with people outside of close-knit networks facilitate an ingress of new information and creativity that strengthens that person's claims as an authoritative node. Paschall imported new health information into her practice from areas outside Philadelphia. She gleaned a new medicine for deafness from Jane Davis of Goshen, Pennsylvania, a brimstone-based remedy for the measles that she learned from "People from New England," and a cure for ringworm from a "Gentleman Traveller" named Paul Tooks. She described a complex rheumatism cure that was "a True Coppey [copy] from Jno. [John] Pyle of North Carolina, Doctor: Given to me by his Aunt Sarah Way." As she cultivated her extensive networks of medical knowledge in the greater Philadelphia area and beyond, Paschall developed a captivating aura of healing authority.[39]

Paschall's medical book reveals the complex inner workings of Philadelphia's mid-eighteenth-century health care marketplace, in which free Euro-American women healers played a vital role. Her manuscript details the ways that medical knowledge traveled intricate pathways before finding its way into her collection. Paschall assessed medical knowledge on the basis of the credibility and credit of the informant and the evidence of successful cures. She then dispensed her medical prescriptions to her many patients, including the deeply grateful Mary Toms. Although women healers were often the first line of medical therapy for their families, some developed extensive practices outside their households that included health care for women, children, and men. Nonphysician practitioners such as Paschall participated in an unregulated medical marketplace in which university-trained doctors had not achieved hegemony. Patients often sought out female healers for primary medical care, as well as for consultations, when the remedies of physicians or other healers failed. Paschall developed close-knit and extended networks of healers who helped her to develop and sustain her reputation as a skilled healer. Indeed, Paschall's healing networks extended beyond the Quaker, Anglo-American, and Pennsylvania German communities to include valuable health care information from Lenape women healers, who established their own healing authority. As Paschall understood, medical knowledge was powerful. Her recipe book was a definitive repository of her lifetime of healing experiences that she handed down to her daughter Beulah and her other descendants. Free Euro-American women in the mid-eighteenth-century Delaware Valley built on their foremothers' legitimate healing practices and carved out places for themselves as authoritative healers.

CHAPTER 3

Healing Borderlands

Local histories of Chester County, Pennsylvania, recount the story of an eighteenth-century Lenape woman called Hannah Freeman or "Indian Hannah," who sold medicinal herbs and handmade baskets to Quaker families. When Hannah was born in 1730, there were still Lenapes (Delawares) living on the Wawassan or Brandywine River, which ran through the western part of the county, about twenty-five miles southwest of Philadelphia. In her youth, Hannah planted corn, wove baskets, and culled medicinal herbs along with her grandmother Jane, her mother, Sarah, and the female kin of her matrilineal turtle clan. Freeman's Brandywine River Lenapes used the Unami language, and they were affiliated with other groups that spoke related Lenape languages who lived along a broad swath of the mid-Atlantic piedmont and coastal plain. Lenape leaders had signed land treaties with William Penn and other colonial officials that resulted in decades of relative peace. However, increasing waves of Euro-American settlers forced Lenapes from their lands, and epidemics of Old World diseases caused the depopulation of Lenape groups. By mid-century, only a small Lenape community remained in the Brandywine River Valley.[1]

Despite settler encroachment, Hannah Freeman chose to live, work, and practice healing among Quaker farmers in Chester County and New Castle County (later Delaware). In a newspaper account, the Quaker minister John Parker identified Freeman as a "doctress as well as a basket maker." Parker remembered visiting her "wigwam" and paying five shillings for a remedy for his sick children. Freeman furnished Parker with "herbs and pounded roots" and "directions for their use." Although there are few traces of her medical practice, available sources suggest that Chester County Quakers valued Freeman's healing acumen and paid for her medical services. Her acknowledged skills helped Freeman make the transition to an emerging market economy. By selling medicinal herbs, healing advice, and baskets,

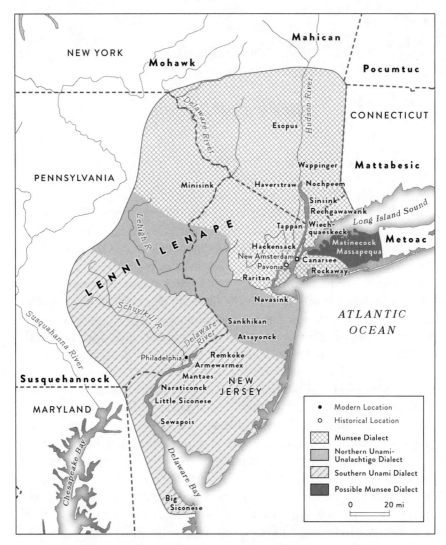

Figure 5. The lands inhabited by the Lenapes (Delawares) at the time of European contact. Lenapes are sometimes called Lenni-Lenapes (Original People).

along with paid domestic and day labor work, Freeman earned the income that allowed her to remain near her homeplaces. Healing facilitated Hannah Freeman's cultural and geographic persistence amid the dislocations and violence of European colonization.[2]

Native American women healers' medical authority had long been recognized within their communities. Their knowledge of locally grown herbs and remedies also exerted an exotic power that was sought after and appropriated by Euro-American colonists. On the cultural borderlands of health care exchanges, healing power relations between Native Americans and Euro-Americans could be relatively equalized by urgent needs for lifesaving cures. Shared medical information and remedies resulted in hybrid healing cultures, which altered practices and conferred medical legitimacy for women in both communities. While healing exchanges could result in mutual understandings, these interactions could also erupt in intercultural misunderstandings and conflicts. Whether they involved empathy or aggression, healing interactions provide a rich space to consider cross-cultural relations of authority, power, and gender.[3]

However, Indigenous female healers in the greater Delaware Valley are particularly invisible in the historical record. Like Euro-American women healers, their medical activities were part of daily gendered duties that included plant cultivation, cloth dyeing, and cooking. The herbs and flora grown and processed for each of these tasks were often the same, further blurring the boundaries between healing and other responsibilities. Childbirth and women's health were embedded in a female-centered sphere. Thus, eighteenth-century Euro-American male traders, missionaries, and natural philosophers often overlooked Native American women's healing work. Instead, these observers preferred to document the activities of male sachems and "medicine men" who exerted obvious political influence and spiritual power. Nonetheless, Lenape women in the Delaware Valley were also recognized as medical authorities, as evidenced in the healing encounters between Native Americans and Euro-American colonists that appear sporadically in the historical record.[4]

A Lenape Healer's Persistence

Hannah Freeman's story comes to us filtered through an interview by an overseer of the poor, romanticized local histories, newspaper accounts, Lenape oral traditions, and archaeological evidence. In the early nineteenth century, some residents remembered Freeman as "the Last of the Lenni-Lenape Indians in Chester County." She was later commemorated in poetry and prose as a symbol of a lost and purportedly "primitive" Lenape culture. As one newspaper story explained derisively, "Indian Hannah's" death marked the moment when "the red man was no longer seen tilling small plots of land with crude and primitive plows and harrows."[5] In the mid-twentieth century, the historian C. A. Weslager noted the pathos of Hannah's solitary death in 1802 at age seventy-two in the Chester County Poorhouse. According to Weslager, "There was loneliness in the two hands withering still and useless on the white muslin sheet . . . she belonged to no country, she was of the wind, the rains, and the sun." Depictions of "Indian Hannah" have been used to perpetuate offensive stereotypes of Native Americans as wandering peoples with no fixed homeland. Euro-Americans used this pretext to justify their appropriation of Lenape lands. They mourned Lenapes' passing only after they believed that these original inhabitants had supposedly "vanished" from the landscape. Nonetheless, Hannah Freeman was more than a useful fiction in the narrative of European colonization. She was an actual Lenape woman who, along with her people, adapted lifeways and deployed skills so that their culture could survive the economic changes, land expropriation, and warfare wrought by settler colonialism in the eighteenth-century Delaware Valley.[6]

Freeman's medical exchanges and economic relationships with Euro-American settlers reflected Lenapes' creative subsistence strategies in the face of the increasing dispossession of their lands and their social marginalization. According to Freeman's 1797 interview with Moses Marshall, a Chester County justice of the peace, she was born in a cabin in Newlin Township, Pennsylvania, "on William Webb's place." Marshall was attempting to determine Freeman's status as a pauper, so his transcription must be read carefully. It is likely that the land that Freeman described near the Brandywine River had belonged to Lenapes long before the Quaker Webb family arrived. Hannah, her parents, her grandmother Jane, and her aunts Betty and Nanny "lived in Kennett [Pennsylvania] in the winter and in the summer moved to Newlin to Plant Corn." Gender defined the political and economic pursuits of Lenape women and men. Elder female clan members held political advisory positions in council meetings. Women like Freeman had charge over agricultural lands and the production of corn, beans, squash, and other products vital for their communities' survival.[7]

Freeman and her family negotiated with Quaker colonists so that they could continue the Lenape pattern of seasonal migrations to lands that had previously belonged to their people. Lenapes were matrilineal, with clan descent proceeding down female lines, and matrilocal, meaning that a husband usually moved from his mother's household to that of his wife. Hannah may have had a common-law marriage with a man named Andrew Freeman, but there is no evidence that the couple had any surviving children. Freeman was a common surname taken by Lenapes and emancipated African Americans, but Andrew's identity is unclear. Nonetheless, Hannah Freeman's narrative retains elements of Lenape cultural forms, particularly in her choice to stay in the Brandywine River Valley with her mother, grandmother, and aunts, even when her father moved north to the village of Shamokin sometime in the 1750s. Around this time, as Freeman's narrative states, "the rest of the family moved to Centre in Christiana Hundred, New Castle County and lived in a Cabin on Swithin Chandler's place." Lenapes had inhabited this area prior to Quaker settlement. Freeman and her family "continued living in their Cabins sometimes in Kennett and sometimes at Centre." They may have traded work, baskets, medications, or healing skills for permission to live on the Chandlers' land.[8]

However, Freeman and her family faced a crisis when "the Indians were killed at Lancaster soon after which, they being afraid, moved over the Delaware [River] to N[ew] Jersey and lived with the Jersey Indians for about Seven Years." Freeman was referring to the December 1763 massacre of unarmed Conestoga women, men, and children in their village near Lancaster, Pennsylvania, at the hands of Scots-Irish men who were called the "Paxton Boys." One hundred of these vigilantes marched on Philadelphia to attack Christian Indians who had fled there for safety. An anti-Paxton delegation led by Benjamin Franklin and Governor John Penn diffused further violence. Earlier that year, the Ottawa leader, Pontiac, had formed a Pan-Indian alliance with Great Lakes and other Native American groups, and began a war against the British to oust them from Indigenous lands. As warfare erupted in western Pennsylvania between British troops and Pontiac's forces, it was clear that William Penn's vision of a peaceable commonwealth was on the wane. Amid increasing anti-Indigenous violence by colonists, Freeman and her female family members found refuge with their distant kin, the "Jersey Indians," possibly in the reservation communities at Bethel Indian Town or Brotherton.[9]

In about 1770, Freeman, her "Granny Jane," mother, and aunts returned to their "cabin" at Kennett, and then moved seasonally to lodgings at Centre. In addition to John Parker's recollections, the Chalfourt family remembered Freeman successfully treating their daughter for the whooping cough with herbal medicines. A romanticized local history described how Freeman "spent the summers collecting herbs and roots, then sold her nostrums, brooms and beautifully woven baskets of oak and ash splints . . . at farm and village kitchen doors." The local historian invoked the trope of "old wives'" familiarity with the supernatural, adding, "At friendly hearthsides she told fortunes and shared ancient wisdoms." At some point, all her kin died, and Freeman lived alone, selling baskets, brooms, herbal medicines, and healing advice to local Quaker families.[10]

Freeman's brief narrative makes it difficult to gain a clear picture of her healing practice. However, her story shares similarities with an Abenaki healer and midwife named Molly Ockett, whose account provides corroborating evidence of intercultural healing practices in early colonial settler spaces. Ockett (or Ocutt) practiced healing in the Androscoggin River Valley in Maine and is remembered in local histories as the "last Pigwacket [Ozogwakiak or Sokokis] Indian," which was an Abenaki subgroup. Her lifespan, from the 1730s through 1816, parallels that of Freeman. Ockett retained a seasonally migratory lifestyle typical of Abenakis, who, like the Lenapes, were an Algonquian-speaking group. The Abenakis in Maine were increasingly dispossessed, but, like Freeman, Ockett chose to stay on Abenaki lands and live in proximity to the increasingly numerous English settlements. In addition to selling baskets and needlework goods, Ockett had an extensive practice as a midwife and healer, treating both Euro-Americans and Abenakis. Local accounts record the irony of Ockett curing the wife of a soldier who had fought in wars against Native Americans. Healers such as Ockett provided lifesaving care in the intimate spaces of Euro-American and Native American households, and they acted as mediators between these communities.[11]

Ockett was known as a skilled healer throughout New England. In his autobiography, the adventurer Henry Tufts described Ockett as "the great Indian doctress." He sought her advice to treat a severe knife wound on his thigh and to "superintend the recovery of [his] health." As Tufts explained, "Having much faith in the skill of my physician, I continued to swallow . . . every potion she prescribed." Within two months the "kind doctress" had cured his injury. From 1772 to 1775, Tufts lived in Ockett's village in order to learn her "secret" cures and to devote himself "to the study of Indian botany and physic [medicine]." Tufts described "attending my patroness when she visited her patients" and thus gaining "better insights into the Indian methods of cure." Tufts' tone is generally patronizing toward Native Americans. However, his choice to seek medical care from Ockett, his profession of a cure, and his decision to serve as her apprentice demonstrate Tufts' respect for Ockett's acumen. Both Ockett and Freeman used their healing skills to earn income and to develop social capital so that they could live in relative independence near their homeplaces that had become Euro-American communities.[12]

Guardians of Culture and Mediators of Change

For Lenape women such as Hannah Freeman, healing conferred cultural authority within their communities. Lenapes valued two types of healers: *nentpikes*, who provided herbal cures for wounds and diseases, and *medew* (or *meteinu*), who were also adept at diagnosing and treating illnesses of spiritual origins. Although female herbalists and midwives tended to be *nentpikes*, these roles overlapped, and both demonstrated spiritual power. For Lenapes, healing authority flowed from specialized health care knowledge and skills that allowed female healers to wield medical and spiritual influence, which contributed to the wellness of their communities. Women practitioners taught their female kin the healing and harming properties of plants and the correct ways to collect, process, store, and dispense them. Herbal remedies might be accompanied by songs, prayers, dreams, dances, and the rhythmic sound of turtle shell rattles to counter disease-causing malevolent spiritual entities. Lenape women's roles as child bearers, midwives, and cultivators of food for their villages also conferred life-giving power. Although it is important not to overemphasize Lenape women's leadership roles, the diffusion of political and healing power, even among male leaders, provided spaces for women's healing authority.[13]

Healing was part of a general culture of reciprocity that bound kin, communities, and clans together. Personal, community, and cosmological health depended on the balance between the deeply interconnected natural and spiritual realms inhabited by humans and other powerful beings called *manitou*. Lenapes' ceremonial use of sweat lodges reflects these connections. In a January 1684 account of his journey up the Schuylkill River, William Penn described his encounter with Tenoughan, a Lenape sachem (leader) ill with a fever, who entered a sweat lodge adjacent to the river. As Penn reported, sweat lodges were like ovens constructed with branches covered by clay. He explained that Tenoughan's wife poured water on hot stones inside the hut to create a steamy environment. Tenoughan sang songs as part of the ceremony attended by others in the village. "In less than half an hour" the sachem

emerged from the hut in "so great a sweat" and immersed himself in the freezing river. According to Penn, Tenoughan was soon "easie, and well in Health."
Lenapes used sweat lodges for individual healing and as part of rituals to
cleanse their communities and restore spiritual balance.[14]

Although their medical theories and spiritual belief systems differed, European and Lenape women healers shared some ideas and practices. Both groups
believed that bodily wellness required physical and spiritual equilibrium, and
they valued therapeutic bleeding, purging, and diaphoresis (sweating) to rid
bodies of unhealthy substances. Euro-Americans sought information on Indigenous therapeutics, which included sweat lodges, wound cauterization,
smoke therapy, and immersion in hot springs. Sweat baths and sulfur springs
evoked Western medical practices dating back to classical Greece and Rome
that were well-known in Europe. One mid-eighteenth-century Moravian missionary was so convinced by Indigenous therapies that he tried "sweating in a
hot hut," which successfully cured his rheumatism. What Europeans called
hospitality and Lenapes considered reciprocity were fundamental cultural values that also promoted communal balance. Rituals of hospitality facilitated
reciprocal health care exchanges between women in household and communal
spaces. While Indigenous groups' power structures differed from those in European societies, the notion of healing authority based on interpersonal influence rather than intimidation would have been mutually understandable.[15]

However, some European missionaries and travel writers attempted to
create false dichotomies between science-based European medical practices
and what they considered Native Americans' healing superstitions. Nonetheless, Euro-American physicians, as well as women healers, continued to incorporate astrology, alchemy, and magic into their practices. Most people of
European descent also operated within a religious worldview and recognized
the power of prayer. Like their Native American counterparts, European
women healers taught their acolytes rituals for gathering herbs that might
coincide with the seasons, time of day, or phases of the moon.[16] Similar healing customs generated medical interactions between culture groups.

Exchanges of compatible healing practices between Lenapes and early
Swedish and Dutch settlers set a precedent for subsequent relationships when
English Quakers settled in the Delaware Valley. The early eighteenth-century
missionary journals of Andreas Hesselius, a Swedish Reformed minister to
Christiana (southeast of present-day Wilmington, Delaware), suggest that
healing encounters were commonplace. In one instance, Hesselius sought

medical advice from the Lenape female healer, Chicalicka Nanni Kettelev, to treat his son who was desperately ill from intestinal worms. The minister copied down Kettelev's herbal remedy that cured the boy, but she admonished Hesselius to keep the remedy secret.[17] English Quakers also valued Lenapes' "secret" healing practices. Elizabeth Haddon Estaugh, a leader of the Newton, West Jersey Quaker Meeting, learned remedies and herbal cures from Lenape women, which enhanced her lifelong practice as a healer. Like ceremonial gift exchanges, shared medicinal herbs and remedies facilitated mutually beneficial political and economic alliances between Lenapes and colonists.[18] Hannah Freeman's grandmother would have passed down stories from this period of European incursions along with Lenapes' attempts at coexistence.

In the new disease environment created by colonial settlement, vulnerable sufferers from various culture groups were especially motivated to share healing information. Europeans transmitted numerous devastating diseases such as smallpox, measles, influenza, and dysentery, which were particularly virulent for Native Americans, whose immune systems had never encountered Old World organisms. Historians estimate that in some Indigenous communities, death rates may have been as high as 80 percent. These new maladies often eluded the curative powers of male and female Native American healers, and they sought medical information from colonists. Meanwhile, early European settlers faced morbidity and mortality from diseases they called pleurisies, throat distempers, the flux [dysentery] and "fever and ague." Although Europeans brought their own healing remedies along with their infectious diseases, they eagerly sought cures from Native peoples, who were acknowledged experts in treating festering wounds, burns, and broken bones. As William Penn noted, Native Americans knew of "diverse Plants" to treat "Swellings, Burnings, Cuts, etc. that are of great virtue in suddenly curing the patient."[19]

Western European medical theories asserted that diseases arose from specific environments and that God had mercifully provided cures for diseases in the areas in which illnesses were endemic. Indigenous healers were critical sources for herbal remedies to cure medical problems that were new to settlers, such as using rattlesnake root to treat bites of venomous snakes unknown in Europe. Native Americans understood the healing properties of numerous North American plants, including sassafras, dogwood, tobacco, staghorn sumac, bloodroot, and American ginseng. Euro-Americans learned that the Lenapes used sassafras root as a treatment for wounds, dropsy, eye ailments, and venereal diseases. As the Finnish naturalist Pehr (Peter) Kalm recorded, "An old Swede remembered that his mother cured numerous people of dropsy by a decoction of the root of sassafras in water, drank every morning." Dropsy was identified by severe swelling in the extremities, which we now understand is caused by heart, liver, or kidney failure. The woman augmented the dropsy remedy by adding the European practice of cupping, which involved placing heated glass cups on skin to draw out maladaptive humors. The Swedish healer combined an Indigenous botanical with a European humoral therapy, creating an intercultural remedy.[20]

Kalm and other European and colonial natural philosophers or "Gentlemen of Science" recognized the medical and commercial value of North American flora such as sassafras and ginseng, which became major export commodities to England. American sassafras appeared in Britain's popular *Pharmacopoeia Londinensis* in the mid-seventeenth century. In the 1730s, Pennsylvania colonists marketed North American ginseng as an economical substitute for expensive Chinese ginseng. Natural philosophers traveled throughout North America prospecting for botanicals and recording their medical encounters. Although these naturalists often reported their source merely as "an Indian" with uncertain affiliations or gender, in some cases the healer was identified as a woman. During his plant-collecting travels in the mid-Atlantic region in the 1740s, Kalm recorded some encounters between Native American women healers and Europeans. Kalm noted in his journal that the "wife of Colonel Lydius" suffered from severe leg pain, which caused her to limp with the aid of a crutch. "Finally," Kalm continued, "a native woman came to the house, who cured her [Mrs. Lydius]." Kalm described the Indigenous healer's remedy: "She went into the forest, took twigs and cuttings of the dogwood, removed the bark, boiled them in water and rubbed the legs with this water." He added, "The pain disappeared within two or three days." The missionary David Zeisberger also observed colonists' use of dogwood root, noting that Pennsylvania apothecaries sold it to treat fevers in place of expensive imported cinchona bark (quinine). Colonel and Mrs. Lydius provided Kalm with additional Indigenous recipes, including an iris root–based remedy for leg sores and a sassafras decoction used to cure ocular diseases.[21]

Kalm sought Native Americans women's recipes for the common problem of abscessed teeth, which he ascribed to Native peoples' adoption of tea drinking. Indeed, the usual addition of sugar to tea likely exacerbated dental problems. During his travels in New York, Kalm reported, "I saw a young Indian woman, who, by frequent drinking of tea, had got a violent tooth-ache." To "cure it, she boiled the *Myrica aspleniifolia* [sweet fern], and tied it as hot as she could bear it, on the whole cheek." Other Indigenous healers applied the boiled inner bark of the "*Sambucus canadensis*, or Canada Elder" to the site of the abscessed tooth. An Anglo-American woman, the wife of a Captain Lindsey, shared an additional Native American toothache remedy with Kalm. According to Mrs. Lindsey, "They take the seed capsules of the Virginian Anemone, as soon as the seed is ripe," and grind them until they are "a cotton-like substance," which they dip into brandy and "put into the hollow tooth." Kalm published these healing exchanges between Euro-American and Indigenous women in his travel journals. His works were translated into French, Dutch, and English and reached a wide international audience of female as well as male readers. Subscribers to the London version included prominent physicians and natural philosophers as well as a number of women interested in science.[22]

In addition to his international connections, Kalm was part of a circle of Philadelphia's natural philosophers that included Benjamin Franklin and the self-taught Quaker botanist John Bartram. Women healers, such as Bartram's wife, Ann, and his cousin Elizabeth Coates Paschall, were also part of these networks. Kalm recorded in his journal that John Bartram told him of a Virginia woman who used sassafras to cure herself of severe foot pain of three years duration, which "almost hindered her from walking." In her Indigenous-derived recipe, the Virginia woman described boiling sassafras berries to extract essential oils, which she rubbed into her feet daily. According to Bartram, the woman was "entirely freed from the pain and recovered completely." Although these natural philosophers appropriated Native American's botanical information for their own scientific and commercial use, they clearly recognized Indigenous women and men as producers of authoritative medical knowledge.[23]

To borrow a phrase from the historian Kathryn Holland Braund, during the devastating cultural, political, and economic dislocations caused by European colonization, Lenape women such as Hannah Freeman were "guardians of tradition" as well as mediators of change. Their healing expertise allowed them to maintain their cultural practices, forge intercultural alliances, and earn needed wages while adapting to rapid social transformations. Some Lenape communities persisted in New Jersey and Pennsylvania, while other Lenapes joined displaced groups in towns on the borderlands of European settlement.[24]

Intercultural Healing: Collaboration and Conflict

Despite the presence of intercultural medical exchanges, conflict percolated beneath the surface of the precarious peace negotiated by the Penns and Lenape leaders. New waves of European settlement challenged Native peoples' lifeways and health through the expropriation of lands, rapid environmental changes, and epidemic diseases. Hannah Freeman's Brandywine group increasingly faced land-hungry settlers and squatters. A Chester County historian recorded the Lenapes' legal battles with the Pennsylvania Assembly over land rights "on this spot" where "Indian Hannah, the last of her race dwelt for many years."[25] When Freeman was a child in the 1730s, the Lenapes faced Euro-Americans' continued land grabs, exemplified by the so-called Walking Purchase of 1737. William Penn's sons and the provincial secretary, James Logan, reprised a flimsy 1680s deed purporting that Lenapes had previously promised to sell prime lands at the confluence of the Delaware and Lehigh Rivers. Rather than stake out the territory with a leisurely walk along the line, the Penns hired fast runners on cleared paths, thus falsely appropriating more than one million acres of Lenape lands. Lenapes' simmering anger over this land swindle would erupt two decades later during the Seven Years' War.[26]

Many Lenapes who were evicted from their lands migrated northwest to Pennsylvania's Susquehanna and Wyoming River valleys. In villages such as Shamokin, some Lenape women and men stayed and recreated their lives among Shawnees, Susquehannocks, Tutleos, Senecas, and other transplanted residents. In her transcribed narrative Freeman recalled, "The Country becoming more settled the Indians were not allowed to Plant Corn any longer" so her "Father went to Shamokin and never returned." During the 1750s, Freeman's father would have found diverse groups of Native American peoples who were adapting to new cultural, religious, diplomatic, and physical environments. Although Shamokin was periodically wracked with conflict during the Seven Years' War, its strategic location at the forks of the Susquehanna River and at intersections of overland trade routes also made it a commercial hub with linkages to the important village of Onondaga to the north and the Philadelphia area to the southeast. An influential Oneida leader named Shikellamy presided over the town, except when he traveled to diplomatic meetings to negotiate treaties between colonial governments and Native American groups. Shamokin attracted displaced Indigenous people, trappers, traders, missionaries, and soldiers. Along with its commerce in furs, guns, cloth, and export pharmaceuticals such as ginseng, Shamokin was a place where people sought cross-cultural medical information.[27]

In one healing encounter at Shamokin, the German-born trader and colonial negotiator Conrad Weiser requested medical care from the Métis trader, diplomat, and interpreter Isabelle Montour, often called "Madame Montour." To treat Weiser's chronic stomach problem, which he described as a "fever," Montour prescribed fever powders that were her own secret recipe. The languages through which they chose to communicate are unknown since they were both multilingual, but sometime in the mid-1740s Weiser copied Montour's instructions in German at the back of his account book. Translated into English, he wrote, "Memorandum of Madame Montour: Take a good thimbleful [of her fever powder] tied in a rag and dissolve it in a half pint of water." He noted, "When the fever comes the patient must be given this half pint of water, to be drunk, and if the fever returns, it is repeated; for a child, according to proportion." Had Montour shared the actual recipe for her fever powders, the ingredients might have provided insights into the networks of medicinal exchanges in which she participated throughout her lifetime.[28]

Madame Montour exemplifies skilled healers who navigated intercultural borderlands successfully. Born to a French trader father and a Ozogwakiak (Sokokis) mother, Montour was captured and adopted by Oneidas and raised by an Oneida family. In his youth, Conrad Weiser had lived with a Mohawk family, so he and Montour had both experienced intercultural adaptations. Along with her Oneida husband, Montour served as a valued interpreter and diplomat for the governor of New York and the Pennsylvania Provincial Council. She also had worked as a negotiator between Haudenosaunee (Iroquois) and Great Lakes Indigenous groups. After her husband's death in 1729, Montour moved with her three children to Pennsylvania, just north of her colleague Shikellamy's home at Shamokin. She visited Philadelphia and learned English from "the gentlewomen of that city." In Pennsylvania, Montour continued her role as an interpreter and cultural mediator. She played a key role, along with Conrad Weiser, at the 1744 Treaty of Lancaster, where she may have shared her fever powders with him.[29] In her travels to treaty conferences, Montour likely met another female mediator named Molly Brant (Degonwadonti), a Mohawk woman, who was the common-law wife of William Johnson, the British superintendent of Indian affairs in the Northern Colonies.

There is evidence that Brant also practiced healing as part of her diplomatic interactions, and she was well known for her hospitality to Native American and Euro-American guests at Johnson Hall in New York. As Johnson knew from his personal experiences, "There are many simples [herbal medicines] in this country which are, I believe, unknown to the learned, notwithstanding the surprizing [sic] success with which they are administered by the Indians." Effective herbal remedies administered by skilled healers such as Montour and Brant were interwoven with their diplomatic encounters.[30]

In her later years, Madame Montour would have had ample occasions to practice her healing skills in her homes at Otstuagy and at Shamokin, both plagued with recurring epidemics. As Weiser noted in a 1747 letter to Provincial Secretary Richard Peters, "The Indians about Shamokin have been sick with the fever and ague very much." Shikellamy, his wife, and his children were desperately ill, and Weiser administered a cinchona bark (quinine) remedy, "which had a very good effect." He noted that "Indian doctors" treated other sufferers. Reports of Native American and Euro-Americans' frequent illnesses and deaths from epidemics run like a refrain through Weiser's writings. Sickness, along with healing remedies, crossed ethnic, geographic, and religious boundaries with impunity, and sufferers sought successful cures from those outside their culture groups. Amid the anxieties of an epidemic, Weiser, Shikellamy, and the unnamed Indigenous healers shared medical prescriptions and offered healing care, which strengthened their interpersonal and diplomatic ties.[31]

Although healing encounters could forge intercultural understandings, for some missionaries such as the Presbyterian minister David Brainerd, healing was a site of religious antipathy rather than cross-cultural bonding. Brainerd viewed the rowdy, diverse town of Shamokin as a city of sin in need of the Christian gospel. In his journal, he noted the political, spiritual, and healing power of male leaders like Shikellamy, whom he scornfully called "powwows, conjurers, and jugglers." These adepts challenged the authority of the Christian message and its missionaries. In one instance at Shamokin, Brainerd attempted to preach to a group of Native Americans, but "they gathered together all their powwows (or conjurers) and set about half a dozen of them to playing their juggling tricks, and acting their frantic distracted postures, in order to find out why they were then so sickly . . . with a fever, and bloody flux [diarrhea]." Brainerd was exasperated by what he described as "heathenish dance and revel" because he believed that a sick Indigenous man's "disorder was much aggravated by the noise." He failed to understand that the ceremonies, songs, and dances were rituals aimed at healing the ill man and restoring wellness to the community by quelling malevolent spirits. Brainerd's journal with his outlandish descriptions of Native Americans' healing rituals was published in Philadelphia in 1746. The popular journal likely fed Delaware Valley readers' negative stereotypes of Indigenous peoples, making it difficult to find commonalities.[32]

While Moravian missionaries also viewed Shamokin as a fertile mission field, unlike Brainerd, they learned Native Americans' languages and attempted to understand their cultures. Moravians were a German Pietist, evangelical sect that sent immigrants to Native American villages in Pennsylvania from their enclave in Saxony. The sect sent single as well as married women as missionaries. Some of these female evangelists were trained in the healing arts and in Lenape and Iroquoian languages. Before beginning their resident mission at Shamokin in 1745, Moravian missionaries Martin and Jeanette Rau Mack lived with the elderly Madame Montour at her home north of Shamokin, apparently seeking Montour's intercultural expertise. Montour also entertained the Moravian founder Count Nickolas van Zinzendorf, missionary David Zeisberger, and Moravian bishop August Gottlieb Spangenberg. Her son Andrew Montour was also a well-respected diplomatic negotiator and guide, and he had worked closely with Zinzendorf, Weiser, and Shikellamy. Moravian missionaries clearly recognized the Montours as an important diplomatic family. Their writings also suggest that some Moravians understood the social, spiritual, and diplomatic significance of Native American rituals of gift exchanges.[33]

Shared healing remedies and personal care in household spaces could forge alliances. In 1745, Madame Montour consulted with Bishop Spangenberg regarding her daughter Margaret's skin abscesses. The bishop, who had studied medicine as well as the ministry, recorded that he lanced and dressed Margaret's boils. Spangenberg's European treatment was consonant with a Native American therapy for infected skin lesions. In his missionary journal, David Zeisberger noted, "Indians applied a warm poultice of Indian cornmeal to boils, which were lanced when ripe." Montour may have preferred that another skilled practitioner implement this painful procedure on her daughter.[34]

On other occasions, Spangenberg deployed his healing skills as part of diplomatic gift exchanges and spiritual ceremonies. From Montour's house at Shamokin, Spangenberg traveled with Conrad Weiser to Onondaga, the Iroquois League's geographic, political, and spiritual center. According to Spangenberg, upon his arrival "there came many sick people and demanded some medicine" and "the Lord blessed it." When the Onondaga leader Canassatego saw Spangenberg's boat arriving for a second visit, he "built a fire and prepared food" for a ritual feast. A Moravian companion noted, "When Bro. [Brother] Spangenberg landed, he [Canassatego] requested him to bleed him" as part of the welcoming ritual. For Lenapes, Haudenosaunees, and Moravians, diplomatic, spiritual, and healing power were closely intertwined. Exchanges like those between Spangenberg, Montour, Weiser, and Canassatego cemented intercultural ties on multiple levels.[35]

Female Moravian missionaries such as Jeanette Rau Mack also found that healing bridged cultural differences. During their mission at Shamokin in the mid-1740s, Mack and her husband provided health care services and therapeutic bleeding. According to one account, the Macks were "especially held in high esteem" because they were "always ready to assist in case of sickness." Mack, who was fluent in Mohawk and Lenape dialects, noted that she and other Moravian women cared for sick Indigenous women and assisted at childbirths. Moravian healers' therapeutic bleedings were accompanied by prayers and religious songs, a practice that would have been comprehensible to their Native American patients. Bloodletting was a remedy valued by both Indigenous peoples and Euro-Americans for numerous illnesses, including fevers and smallpox. In his journal of his travels in "the Indian Territories" during the 1760s, Alexander Henry recorded Indigenous healers' practices that were shared by Euro-Americans, including "emetics, cathartics, and the lancet [therapeutic bleeding]; but especially the last." Bloodletting and purging corresponded with Native American practices that focused on removing disease-causing poisons. Moreover, blood held ritual power for Euro-American Christians, Lenapes, and Haudenosaunees, and it appears to have had particular salience for Algonquian-speaking women. Henry added, "Bleeding is so favorite an operation among the women that they never lose an occasion for enjoying it, whether sick or well." For Lenapes and other Algonquian-speakers, menstruating women were considered spiritually powerful, and therapeutic bleeding may have invoked a similar authority.[36]

Native American women accepted healing therapies from Euro-Americans, but they also demonstrated their medical acumen by treating settlers' wounds and other diseases. Alexander Henry noted that a wounded priest was cured after he was left in the care of "some praying [Christianized Native American] women." The Moravian missionary David Zeisberger confirmed Henry's observations, asserting, "Wounds and external injuries they [Indigenous peoples] treat very successfully." As John Heckewelder, another Moravian, explained, "There are [Lenape] physicians of both sexes, who take considerable pains to acquire a correct knowledge of the properties and medical virtues of plants, roots and barks, for the benefit of their fellow-men." Heckewelder perceived similarities with Europeans' empirical approach to medicine. He noted approvingly, "Their science is entirely founded on observation, experience, and the well tried efficacy of remedies." In a personal testimonial, Heckewelder recalled, "I have myself been benefited and cured by taking their [Lenape] emetics and their medicines in fevers" and "have known many, both whites and Indians," who experienced similar successes." He also lauded Lenape women healers' expertise with gynecological problems. According to Heckewelder, "The wives of Missionaries, in every instance in which they had to apply to the female [Lenape] physicians, for the cure of complaints peculiar to their sex, experienced good results from their abilities." Heckewelder's use of the European term "female physicians" may have been a mark of his respect for Lenape women's healing skills. There are also several recorded instances of Moravian women seeking care from female Native American midwives. At vulnerable moments of childbirth or illness, a healer's ministrations and care had the potential to create connections between people from different communities.[37]

Multicultural healing information could be handed down to the next generation. Conrad and Anna Feck Weiser's daughter Anna Maria would have learned skills of intercultural mediation and healing acumen from her parents and from frequent visitors to the family's home at Tulpehocken. Young Anna Maria met Moravian women missionaries, Native American women, and other travelers of various ethnicities. She later married the Lutheran minister Heinrich Melchior Muhlenberg, and they imported and sold medications from a Pietist pharmaceutical manufactory in the German state of Saxony. Anna Maria Muhlenberg's diverse childhood experiences were of inestimable value as she and her minister husband established a church and a medicinal business in a rural town north of Philadelphia. For the Muhlenbergs, Montours, Weisers, Macks, and those in their networks, healing was deeply interwoven with webs of diplomacy and intercultural alliances.[38]

Medical Diplomacy and Secret Indigenous Cures

These relatively peaceful interactions became more difficult to maintain over the course of the Seven Years' War. Colonists on the Pennsylvania frontier under British rule who faced both encroaching French combatants and raids by their American Indigenous allies increasingly viewed mediators like Conrad Weiser, as well as pacifist Moravians and Quakers, as potential conspirators with hostile enemies. After French and Native American troops defeated the British general Edward Braddock and the Virginian colonel George Washington at Fort Duquesne in 1755, Indigenous peoples dispossessed from their homes in Pennsylvania began attacking settlements as part of a strategy to regain their lands. Scots-Irish, German, and English settlers in western Pennsylvania retaliated, beginning a long cycle of violence that resulted in the deaths of Native American and Euro-American men, women, and children. To protest Euro-Americans' dispossession of their lands, Lenapes on the western frontiers tended to side with the French after 1756. This led some colonists to question the loyalties of New Jersey's remaining Lenapes, including those in Christianized Indian communities. In 1756, the governors of Pennsylvania and New Jersey declared war on France and offered bounties on French-allied Native Americans' scalps. Newspaper editors found that salacious accounts of Indigenous reprisals sold copy, which further inflated colonists' anxieties. In a 1760 diary entry, the Quaker healer Ann Cooper Whitall opined, "O the dismal nuse [news] of the Endians cilling [Indians killing] of the white people," underscoring the rumors' racialized undertones. Yet, despite her qualms about Lenapes, Whitall used their remedies like sumac, snakeroot, and chestnut bark. However, Whitall remembered dreaming of "Endians cilling of me" as a child, and she now feared for her own children. Even Lenapes like Hannah Freeman who shared medical knowledge and who lived near Euro-American settlements understood that they could be targeted as enemies.[39]

Pacifist Quakers were also at risk because they were accused of aiding and abetting the Lenape's attacks on frontier settlements. The Philadelphia merchant and healer Elizabeth Coates Paschall stayed in contact with the Webb and Pyle families in the Chester County Quaker community that interacted with Freeman, so she had likely heard of the Lenape healer.[40] Paschall was well aware of the virulent anti-Quaker backlash that targeted her family. Prominent Quakers such as Paschall's brother-in-law John Reynell and her friend Israel Pemberton sought extrapolitical measures to stem the escalating backcountry violence. In 1756, they formed a nongovernmental organization called the "Friendly Association for Regaining and Preserving Peace with the Indians by Pacific Measures" to mediate for Lenapes in colonial affairs. Leaders of the Friendly Association attended treaty meetings at Easton and Lancaster where they supported the Lenapes' long-standing land claims. Tunda (Moses) Tatamy, a Lenape leader from the Bethel Christian Indian Town in New Jersey, worked alongside the Friendly Association as a treaty negotiator. The association also provided material goods to facilitate ceremonies of exchange at treaty conferences, which included needed supplies and medicine for Lenapes and other groups.[41]

During this period, Elizabeth Paschall recorded treating several Lenapes, despite the potential to arouse colonial settler suspicions of collusion. In one instance, "a Jersey Indian man of about 50 years who was in consumption" sought Paschall's diagnosis and treatment at her Philadelphia dry goods shop. The man, who was accompanied by his son, may have been from the Bethel Lenape community, since they were called "Jersey Indians." His "consumption" was likely tuberculosis or another debilitating respiratory ailment. Paschall prescribed a decoction of "Blackberry Bryer Roots" and "Sassafras Roots & White Beach [Beech] Bark," which were "brewed up" with yeast. Ironically, she used a recipe compiled from standard Lenape botanicals to treat the Lenape man. "While I was dosing him to it," Paschall explained, "a woman that was well Dressed & Seemed like a person of credit commended this highly." This reputable woman added that "a lady" in her neighborhood was "cured of a consumption by this same Drink when She had been Given Over as past Recovery." Paschall also noted that her friend, the skilled healer Nathaniel Thomas, "perfectly cured a man who was brought so Low as to keep to his bed." The Native American father and son were sent on their way with these encouraging words and with additional medications. Paschall wrote with satisfaction that in a few months, the son "came looking for me at my house & gave me thanks for what I had done for his father," who was cured in a month. Despite the potential for a negative backlash, some Quakers like Paschall chose to assist Lenapes in need. However, Paschall maintained some social distance by declining to either discover or note the "Jersey Indian" man's name. Although healing encounters created moments of empathy, they did not alter racialized hierarchies. In more subtle ways than the minister David Brainerd's patronizing journal, Paschall's recipe book traces the personal as well as the cultural barriers created by the choice not to learn or remember the name of a Lenape man.[42]

Paschall's manuscript also charts how wartime movements of troops and refugees exacerbated epidemics that threatened Lenape communities. She listed a remedy from 1759 for the "untolorable itching of the worst sort of Small Pox." That winter, there was a smallpox outbreak in the Philadelphia area and in the Quaker community of Mount Holly, New Jersey, likely affecting the nearby Bethel Indian community. In her diary, the Quaker Ann Whitall confirmed that it was "a sickly time" in the greater Philadelphia area, with "20 or 15 or 16 to be put in the ground every day." Paschall recorded that a castile soap bath cured "an Indian girl at Isaac Lane's" whose "Corroding,

Eating" smallpox sores were so ulcerated "that People Could Scarce Come near her." The nameless "Indian girl," who might have been enslaved or a paid or indentured servant, suffered from smallpox in a Euro-American home away from the care of her family and community. Her putrid and foul-smelling smallpox sores only increased her isolation. Nonetheless, either Paschall or one of the female family members or servants in the Lane household personally bathed the girl's lesions with the curative castile soap.[43]

Paschall also recorded a Native American woman's successful remedy that used parts from the North American elder tree (*Sambucus canadensis*) to cure a "Whittloe" (whitlow), an infected fingertip. To a twenty-first-century reader with access to antibiotics, this may sound like a minor first aid injury. However, in this period, even a local infection left untreated could quickly become serious. The internal pressure caused by an infection in the closed compartment of the fingertip could lead to cell death, tissue sloughing, bone infection, a septic joint, and the need for amputation. In her recipe book, Paschall directed, "Take Elder leaves or if you Cannot Get Leaves the Winter Roots or Bark will do." She advised pounding "them fine with Cream to Moisten it" and applying the mixture to the finger as a poultice. Then Paschall shared her sources: "An Indian woman cured Henry Clifton's wife of one & he Imparted the Secret to Joseph Watkins, who has cured many with it since." Recall that Watkins was a lay healer and a frequent informant in Paschall's recipe book whose male kin also passed down "secret cures." As we saw in the exchange between Andreas Hesselius and Chicalicka Nanni Kettelev, Europeans and Native Americans shared the notion that effective remedies should be divulged only to trusted recipients, and these recipes were often unrecorded. As the Moravian minister John Heckewelder noted, "The Materia Medica of the Indians consist of various roots and plants known to themselves, the properties of which they are not fond of disclosing to strangers." They kept their compounding techniques "a profound secret." Paschall's recipe book provides insights into the ways in which a secret cure was transmitted between an Indigenous woman healer and an Anglo-American woman.[44]

Paschall's recipe "for a Sore Legg" from the late 1750s also suggests cooperation between settlers and Native Americans. However, it also underscores the wartime conflicts between Native American groups who sided with the English or the French in their own geopolitical struggles. Paschall wrote, "Susannah Mason said that William Logan Informed her that there was a Boy in the Country that had a verry Bad Sore Legg." William, like his late father James Logan, was interested in botany. According to Paschall, the Quaker boy's knee was so infected that the family feared his leg would have to be amputated. However, "an Indian whome his Enemies of a Different Nation Persued [pursued] had taken Shelter in their house and was Concealed." Despite the atmosphere of fear and violence, a settler family chose to hide the fleeing Indigenous man despite the risk that they might be attacked by his enemies. In return for saving his life, Paschall noted that the man "revealed this Secret of an Indian Cure to them." Paschall explained, "Take the dried powder of yellow poplar bark and blow it into the Deep Sores & Bathe it with a Strong Decoction of the Same, which quickly Cured" the boy. Her dispassionate recording of the recipe contrasts with the intensely emotional scenario that she portrayed. In the context of two potentially life-and-death situations, and in the intimate space of the household, the settler family's offer of a safe haven resulted in the Native American man's choice to divulge an effective medical recipe that saved their boy's leg. Amid the violence of warfare and the encroachment of the colonial settler presence, healing could be an act of compassion that created bonds of appreciation and obligation. The episode generated a narrative of intercultural cooperation that moved through networks of healers along with the appropriated "secret Indian cure."[45]

In the tense war years, healing exchanges might create interpersonal bonds, but medical issues could also rise to the level of a formal diplomatic crisis. The July 1757 shooting of the Lenape interpreter William Tatamy by a Euro-American youth threatened to derail the preliminary diplomatic discussions that would lead to the 1758 Treaty of Easton. Moravian women's domestic healing skills were a subtext in the episode. The goal of the 1757 diplomatic council between Native American and Pennsylvanian leaders was to reconcile Indigenous land disputes and to persuade the Lenape leader Teedyescung to side with the British against the French. The skilled mediators Tunda Tatamy and his son William traveled in Teedyescung's delegation to the town of Easton, north of Philadelphia. Tunda Tatamy, a Christian convert christened Moses, was well-respected among Euro-American Pennsylvanians, including Conrad Weiser and the Quaker Friendly Association.[46]

When the diplomatic delegation stopped overnight at the Moravian town of Bethlehem, William Tatamy went by himself into the town. In an anxious letter to the Pennsylvania governor at Easton, Army Captain Jacob Orndt explained subsequent events: "A foolish wite [white] boy aboud[t] 15 years of eage [age], followed him [William Tatamy], and Shot him in the Right Thigh of the outside bone, but not morterly [mortally]." Orndt understood the potential for racialized violence, and he expressed a need to station troops "to

Protackt [protect] the Indians and to hinder a Scrabel [scuffle] . . . which might fall out between Wite Peoble [white people] and the Indians." William Tatamy was taken to a nearby Moravian farm, where he received nursing care. In this diplomatically sensitive situation, Drs. John Otto and Charles Moore were called in to examine and treat Tatamy. Initially, Otto had good news for Governor Denny and the delegation, noting on July 27 that the "wound looks well, is without inflammation." He did not name the Moravian women caring for Tatamy, but Otto reported, "I believe, with good nursing & attendance, if nothing unforeseen happens, he may, by God's Help recover."[47]

The conference at Easton was meeting that same day. As the doctors and the Moravian women labored to save William Tatamy's life, the implications of the shooting were dire enough to be included in the treaty records. Pennsylvania officials offered William's father a ceremonial strand of wampum and assured him that "strict Justice shall be done" to the jailed shooter. They prayed "that the Almighty would bless the Medicines that are administered for this Cure." The doctors and the Moravian women kept William Tatamy alive long enough for the Easton peace treaty to be completed. Their nursing care had a profound effect on wartime diplomacy. In the wake of the treaty, Hannah Freeman felt safe enough to move back to her home in Chester County. However, despite prayers and the "good nursing" by the Moravian family, William Tatamy died in August. There was no balm to heal Moses Tatamy's grief and disillusionment with colonial diplomacy after his son's murder, particularly when treaties increasingly dispossessed the Lenapes.[48]

Narratives of Euro-Americans who were taken captive and adopted by Native Americans during the Seven Years' War also reflect wartime violence as well as healing exchanges in household and village settings. In the war's aftermath, diplomats and negotiators worked to release thousands of settlers abducted from western Pennsylvania and Virginia. Captivity narratives suggest that some detained Euro-Americans learned Indigenous women's healing remedies. Taking captives was part of a mourning war culture practiced by Haudenosaunee and some Algonquian groups when they faced population losses caused by warfare and diseases. In a ritual of adoption, the captives, usually women and children, took the place of lost clan members. Although captivity could be a coercive space, some younger captives, like the Pennsylvanian Mary Jemison, adapted to their Native American families and chose to remain in their adoptive villages.[49]

Other captives, such as Margaret Frantz, returned to their Pennsylvania towns with new cultural knowledge and healing skills. In 1760, a Lenape raiding party kidnapped fifteen-year-old Frantz and her friend "Soltz" while they washed flax in the creek near their homes. According to her narrative, Frantz lived with a Lenape group near the Delaware Water Gap "for seven years during which time she learned the Indians' use of herbs and roots for medicinal purposes." Frantz chose to return to her community in Lehigh County as part of the Pennsylvania government's negotiations in 1767. A local historian records, "She was known far and wide for her knowledge of herbs which she had acquired of the Indians," and "her services for relieving the sick were in great demand." Frantz's friend Soltz "lived with an Indian as his wife and had two children," and "she was allowed to keep the girl when she was returned to the whites." These abbreviated accounts downplay a myriad of intercultural experiences of grief, change, and personal adaptations. Frantz married Nicholas Wotring in 1769 and used her experiences in Lenape communities to create an authoritative healing practice near Allentown, Pennsylvania.[50]

In the aftermath of the Seven Years' War and Pontiac's Rebellion, Euro-American antipathy toward Indigenous peoples was rife, and there were fewer possibilities for positive intercultural encounters in the colony that William Penn had envisioned as a place of peace between settlers and Lenapes. According to her narrative, Hannah Freeman left Chester County for New Jersey in the wake of the Paxton Boys' massacre of Conestoga Indians in 1763. Although she returned to Pennsylvania around 1770, it would have been difficult for her to feel safe in an environment of increasing anti-Indigenous violence. Nonetheless, the narratives of Moravian women's cooperation with Native American women and the relationships recorded by Elizabeth Coates Paschall suggest the possibilities for collaborative healing exchanges. The cultural borderlands of healing could be spaces where the hierarchies of race and gender might be temporarily suspended when sufferers sought pain-relieving remedies or life-giving cures from people outside their ethnic group. These moments of understanding are a reminder that despite the increasing pressures of colonization, intercultural conflict was not inevitable.[51]

Remembering and Forgetting Native American Women Healers

Although Euro-Americans recognized Indigenous women's healing skills, Lenape practitioners such as Hannah Freeman became increasingly marginalized during the latter half of the eighteenth century. In her sixties, Freeman returned to her homeplace near Kennett. As the women in her kin networks died, she had to rely on her Quaker neighbors. According to the Chester County Poorhouse record, she worked as a live-in laborer, and "she got no money except for baskets, besoms (handmade brooms) &c." The "et cetera" included Freeman's healing practice and sales of herbs. As she aged, the healer was "afflicted with rheumatism" and required health care. Freeman requested medical services from a Jacob Peirce, and he recorded bleeding her in 1795, 1799, and 1800, perhaps reflecting her own confidence in Lenape women's partiality to therapeutic bloodletting. The Webbs and several other Quaker families took up a subscription to defray the costs for board and for Freeman's medical care. It must have been a poignant moment for Freeman as she was admitted to the newly built Chester County Poorhouse so close to the traditional lands of the Brandywine Lenapes.[52]

Over the course of seventy years, Freeman had witnessed the dispossession of the majority of Lenapes in Pennsylvania and the marginalization of those who remained. Freeman died in the Chester County home in 1802. She was buried with other paupers on the poorhouse grounds rather than in the sacred burial ground of Brandywine Lenapes. Nonetheless, during her life, Freeman chose to remain near her homeplaces, adapting to dramatic cultural change while mobilizing the healing, agricultural, and basket-making skills that she had learned from her female kin. Hannah's grandmother, mother, and aunts had provided mutual support as they shared the lifelong challenges of their roles as custodians of tradition and mediators of change. Despite the narratives of their disappearance, small communities of Lenapes persisted in the greater Delaware Valley, living quietly alongside Euro-American villages. Lenape women treasured their healing traditions and passed down their medical knowledge to subsequent generations in New Jersey and Delaware, and in tribal groups in Oklahoma, Wisconsin, and Ontario, Canada. Minnie Fouts (Wèmeehëlèxkwe, 1871–1949) exemplifies later women who were recognized as skilled healers and leaders in their Lenape communities. Oral histories and fragments of written documents attest to this rich repository of healing knowledge and acumen, which are the legacies of Lenape women like Hannah Freeman.[53]

Eighteenth-century Euro-American naturalists also remembered "secret Indian cures" because they continued to exploit and appropriate Native Americans' remedies. In 1751, Benjamin Franklin and David Hall published the botanist John Bartram's edited version of Thomas Short's *Medicina Britannica*. The book included Bartram's appendix titled "Descriptions, Virtues and Uses of Sundry Plants of these Northern Parts of America; and Particularly of the Newly Discovered Indian cure for the Venereal Disease." Bartram detailed the path of medical knowledge transmission: "The learned Peter Kalm who gained the Knowledge of it from [Indian Agent] Colonel [William] Johnson, who learned it from the Indians." He noted, "After great Rewards were bestowed," the Native American healers revealed their "lobelia remedy for syphilis more effective than mercury." As natural philosophers learned new "secret" Indigenous botanicals, American merchants exported them to Europe and editors added them to English and American pharmaceutical manuals. However, over time, naturalists, physicians, and apothecaries obscured the origins of Native American botanicals by hiding them under the façade of Enlightenment science. Late eighteenth-century English and American pharmacopeias cited numerous Indigenous remedies but failed to note their sources, thus appropriating them as standard Euro-American pharmaceuticals. Just as depictions of Hannah Freeman as the "last Lenape in Chester County" served to marginalize remaining Lenape communities, male natural philosophers and university-trained physicians sidelined Native American women healers' medical expertise and remedies.[54]

Nonetheless, in their medical recipe books, the women in Elizabeth Coates Paschall's networks continued to cite and value Native American medicines. Paschall passed down her recipe for "An Indian Cure" for burns to her daughter Beulah, who recorded the remedy that featured linden tree bark. Paschall's acquaintance James Logan also transmitted Native American remedies to female healers in his family. Logan recorded "An Indian Cure for a Felon or Whitlow" using violet roots provided by John Heckewelder, and he transmitted the recipe to women in his family. It appeared in the medical recipe book of Logan's granddaughter Sarah. And yet, even as Euro-American women healers continued to record "secret Indian cures," they also learned that the emerging authority of European Enlightenment science and the prestige of the printed word could be used to denigrate the healing expertise of both Native American and Euro-American women.[55]

CHAPTER 4

The Authority of Science

In her mid-eighteenth-century medical recipe book, Elizabeth Coates Paschall recorded an outbreak of an illness in her Philadelphia neighborhood characterized by "a Violent Swelling in the Throat." Paschall herself was "allmost Choaked [almost choked] with the Swelling" and she was "Scarce able to Swallow a Drop of Drink." She described the illness as quinsy, a pustular swelling around the tonsils, which might have been related to diphtheria or another infection. In severe cases, quinsy could lead to suffocation. Paschall's daughter was also afflicted, which doubtless caused additional anxiety. Amid her family health crisis, Paschall's neighbors sought her skilled healing advice. Fortunately, she knew a Native American herb that would perform the cure. As Paschall explained, she made "a Strong tea of Rattlesnake weed & putt a vial funnel, bottom upwards over the top of the tea pot." She advised the sufferers to "suck the steam strongly Down your throat through the funnel" and then gargle with rattlesnake weed tea. Paschall and her daughter "were relieved in an hour" and her neighbors could "Eat & Swallow anything in a few hours."

In the face of this severe illness, Paschall knew that she needed to describe rattlesnake weed with botanical precision so that it would not be confused with the similar sounding herbs, Seneca snakeroot and rattlesnake root. According to Paschall, rattlesnake weed "grows wilde on poor barren land, the stalks are about two foot high, straight and woody . . . of a deep red the color of Birch." Her half-page depiction classified the plant with specific characteristics, including leaves "the size and shape of tea leaves Indented Round the edges" with "small yellow flowers" that bloom in September. The plant is easily recognizable in botanical atlases as *Hieracium venosum* or rattlesnake weed. Paschall's entry invokes Native American and Euro-American women healers' long-standing skills in herb lore. However, her detailed observations also speak to her familiarity with natural philosophers' discourses and their project to reframe the vernacular knowledge of medicinal plants within the new science of botany.[1]

Paschall's final recipe notations on rattlesnake weed make this connection clear. She cited her cousin John Bartram, a reputed botanist who participated in transatlantic circuits of natural philosophers, also known as "gentlemen of science" or "virtuosi." She added, "John Bartram says its good apply'd as a pultice [poultice] to dispel swelling on the Limbs or Body." As we saw in Chapter 2, Paschall's extensive healing networks bolstered her medical credibility. Over the course of her recipe book, Paschall increasingly incorporated sources that demonstrate her recognition of the new authority of experimental science. She collected medical information from local experts such as Bartram, as well as medical recipes from her brothers-in-law John and Stephen Paschall, both chemical experts and respected "alchymical doctors." In addition, Paschall compiled information from authoritative medical texts that she checked out from the Library Company of Philadelphia. For example, after reading a section in Dr. Robert James's *Medicinal Dictionary* describing a public anatomical dissection at London's Royal Society, Paschall transcribed a passage that lauded not the university-educated physicians but rather an Englishwoman healer who cured patients' tumors without exposing them to risky surgery. In her recipe manuscript, Paschall details her extensive natural philosophical networks and invites her recipe book readers, as well as twenty-first-century scholars, to read the same medical texts that she consulted at the Library Company. Through her self-directed studies, documented observations, and medical experiments, Paschall embraced the emerging authority of botany, chemistry, and anatomy. As Paschall shared medical trials and remedies that she described as her "own invention," she became an influential link in wide-ranging networks of natural philosophers. Paschall positioned herself alongside learned male experts as a legitimate producer of medical knowledge.[2]

Nonetheless, male physicians and natural philosophers created structural barriers to prevent women's participation in medicine and the sciences. The seventeenth-century culture of experimental science influenced the eighteenth-century intellectual movement called the Enlightenment, which celebrated logical thinking and mathematical reasoning deployed to solve medical, social, and political problems. According to the German philosopher Immanuel Kant, the motto of the Enlightenment was "Dare to know!" or, as he explained, "Have the courage to use your *own* understanding."[3] However, most eighteenth-century Enlightenment natural philosophers, including Kant and Jean-Jacques Rousseau, maintained that reason and logic were male attributes. They argued that women were innately illogical and passionately emotional, and thus unfit for the "rational" and orderly enterprises of medicine and science. In continental western Europe, regulations governing health care practice, early attempts at medical professionalization, and the emergence of male natural philosophical societies combined to curb women healers' unlicensed practices. By contrast, government officials in Britain and its North American colonies were far less successful than their European counterparts in regulating medical practice.

Even so, British medical and philosophical societies were exclusively elite, male organizations. According to its secretary, the prestigious Royal Society of London for Improving Natural Knowledge was founded to advance "Masculine Philosophy." In London and other imperial centers, formally trained male physicians and natural philosophers claimed authority over the medically related fields of botany, chemistry, and anatomy. Their gendered language and exclusively male institutions marginalized women. Until recently, the historiography has mirrored this discourse by sidelining women in the histories of science and medicine. As the scholar Patricia Fara contends, romanticized histories of science have celebrated solitary male geniuses in heroic battles against the forces of ignorance and superstition. According to Fara, "Women have not been written out of the history of science: they have never been written in."[4]

However, if we flip the traditional narrative and examine the history of science from the "bottom up," the lines between science and folk healing are blurrier, and the story includes numerous women and men of various ethnicities and social orders. Fara encourages us to look beyond the limits of an "intellectual class system that rates the achievements of gentlemen far higher than artisans and women." Indeed, the settler colonial context facilitated wider participation in natural philosophical enterprises. European imperial governments and universities sent natural philosophers to the Americas to discover commercially valuable medicinal plants and minerals. "Gentlemen of science" recognized Native Americans, people of African descent, and ordinary colonists as critical sources of information about the natural world in conquered territories. By necessity, natural philosophy became a collective enterprise that developed among diverse networks of people who acquired information and nature's specimens within the context of imperial expansion.[5]

Elizabeth Coates Paschall and her colleagues demonstrate that households, gardens, woods, and shops were important sites of medical and scientific knowledge production. Paschall's extensive networks reveal that the flow of natural knowledge was multidirectional, moving among intercolonial circles as well as between the colonies and the philosophical societies in European metropoles. An emerging culture of popular science in Philadelphia made this new natural philosophical information accessible to the public. The city's unregulated medical milieu was also favorable. Numerous non-physician healers practiced in Philadelphia, which prevented doctors from dominating the health care market or cornering the intellectual landscape. Quakers promoted gender equality, female education, and the pursuit of "useful knowledge" with humanitarian applications, which facilitated women's engagement in medical and science-related pursuits. Paschall and her networks provide evidence that helps to re-center women practitioners in the historiography of mid-eighteenth-century Enlightenment science. Her recipe book demonstrates the pathways that women healers forged to resist marginalization and to assert their expertise and authority in medicine and the sciences.[6]

Useful Knowledge and the Gendered Uses of Knowledge

For Paschall and her fellow Quakers, medicine, science, education, and benevolent religious ministry intertwined seamlessly. Philadelphia Friends' proclivity for accessible and useful experimental science was the product of a unique confluence of anti-hierarchical philosophical and religious movements in mid-seventeenth-century England. As we saw in Chapter 1, radical religious denominations like the Society of Friends, as well as the gradual paradigm shift historians have called the Scientific Revolution, emerged out of the social ferment of this period. Natural philosophers challenged ancient wisdom and created new sites of knowledge production outside the elite male sphere of universities. They sought to discover the laws of nature by reasoned empirical observation, hands-on experimentation, precise measurements, and mathematical calculations. The phrase *natural philosophy* encompassed the systematic study of the natural and physical sciences, including medicine. By the mid-eighteenth century, the word *science* also began to refer more specifically to what we consider the sciences rather than merely diffuse knowledge. Medicine was interwoven into natural philosophy, and women as well as men experimented with novel medical practices that emerged from the "New Science."[7]

In this period before the professionalization of science, the household was an important site of experimentation and scientific knowledge production. Seventeenth-century "gentlemen of science" such as the English chemist Robert Boyle, whose works were read and admired by Elizabeth Paschall, often did not have formal positions in universities. Some of Boyle's most productive years were those in which he shared a London household, along with medical recipes, with his sister Katherine Boyle Jones, Lady Ranelagh. As the historian Michelle DiMeo has shown, Jones participated as a "gentlewoman of science" in her brother's philosophical networks and his medical and chemical experiments, which were shared with members of the Royal Society. However, because she could not present findings at the Royal Society or publish in its *Philosophical Transactions*, her own contributions have been overshadowed by those of her brother.

Despite women's exclusion from male organizations, scholars have described numerous elite Englishwomen who experimented, published, and served as important conduits of natural philosophical information. As noted in Chapter 1, Anne Finch Conway, a Quaker convert and friend of William and Gulielma Penn, was an important node in circles of medical and scientific exchange. She published *The Principles of the Most Ancient and Modern Philosophy*, and her writings influenced the mathematician and philosopher Gottfried Leibniz.[8] Her contemporary Lady Damaris Cudworth Masham was a correspondent of Leibniz who also influenced his philosophy. Masham contended, "I see no Reason why it should not be thought that all Science lyes as open to a Lady as to a Man." Elizabeth Paschall and other colonial women healers stood on the shoulders of these outspoken and intellectually curious Englishwomen. When English Quakers immigrated to Philadelphia in the late seventeenth and early eighteenth centuries, they transmitted a culture of empirical science and household knowledge production inscribed in their recipe manuscripts.[9]

Paschall became a healer, businesswoman, and "gentlewoman of science" in a cosmopolitan port city and within a family network engaged in benevolent medical and natural philosophical pursuits. By the mid-eighteenth century, Philadelphia was a flourishing metropolis with a population of over twelve thousand people. It was the premier British colonial city in science and medicine and was home to the colonies' first hospital, medical school, lending library, and philosophical society. Although the Quaker population had dwindled from a majority to only about one-sixth of Philadelphia's population by 1750, their culture that valued equality and humanitarian benevolence still exerted influence.[10] Benjamin Franklin represented himself as the city's quintessential "gentleman of science" or philosophical "virtuoso." The Quaker Paschall and Coates families participated in his numerous medical, literary, and natural philosophical enterprises. Franklin's philosophical society and his charity hospital dovetailed with Quakers' pragmatic philanthropic goals. In the philosophical society's 1743 founding statement, Franklin and Paschall's cousin John Bartram articulated an enlightened vision for "promoting Useful Knowledge" for the "benefit of mankind." This organization, which would become the American Philosophical Society, encouraged medical, botanical, and chemical innovations. Men in the Paschall and Coates family were early members. Paschall and Coates men also served on the board of the Pennsylvania Hospital, a charitable institution for the sick poor founded by Franklin and Dr. Thomas Bond in 1751. Elizabeth Paschall and her mother, Beulah Coates, joined "charitable widows and other good women of the city" to contribute funds for the hospital's pharmacy in 1754. Quaker women like Paschall participated informally but significantly in the city's medical and science-related organizations.[11]

Elizabeth Paschall also valued literacy and learning. Her brothers-in-law John and Stephen Paschall were charter members of Franklin's Library Company of Philadelphia, founded in 1731. Although women were initially denied library membership, Paschall circumvented this barrier by borrowing books under the auspices of male family members. The library directors also allowed Elizabeth's sister-in-law Margaret Paschall to check out books. Elizabeth North and "a Widow Coates" (likely Elizabeth Paschall's sister) inherited male family members' shares in the company. Women's de facto library participation opened the way for their later official membership in the 1770s. The library's extensive collection of works in medicine and the sciences gave literate women access to new information that could be digested and discussed in the reading room or in their households. When Franklin and Bartram's Society for Promoting Useful Knowledge was disbanded from 1746 through 1767, the Library Company took its place as a natural philosophical society.[12]

Despite its imposing location in the Pennsylvania State House, women participated in the Library Company's science-related activities even as they continued to borrow books. As early as the 1730s, the Library Company had received donations of scientific instruments, including a vacuum pump, an

Figure 6. *An Experiment on a Bird in the Air Pump*, by Joseph Wright of Derby, 1768, National Gallery, London. Although natural philosophers presented themselves as masterful impresarios of science, elite women also participated in popular public demonstrations that opened the secrets of science to the masses.

electrical apparatus, a telescope, and a microscope from the Penn family. Over time, fossils, shells, botanical specimens, and other "curiosities of nature" found their places on the library's shelves. These collections embodied naturalists' drive to gather, organize, and classify nature's objects in an attempt to master and control the natural world. The foundation of natural knowledge was constructed with this bricolage of flora, fauna, minerals, and observations from the Americas. Literate colonial women participated in this enterprise by collecting specimens, creating botanical drawings, and recording new information about the natural world in their letters and manuscripts. Philadelphia's naturalists sought to convince the patronizing natural philosophers in London that colonists were refined virtuosi whose North American knowledge and specimens were crucial to imperial science. While Elizabeth Paschall was likely influenced by the exalted visions of transatlantic natural philosophers, her recipe book also demonstrates that for medical practitioners, the knowledge of the natural world had pragmatic applications in their work of healing and alleviating suffering. In addition, an emerging popular science movement served to bring highbrow natural philosophy down to earth by making it accessible to ordinary women and men.[13]

The Library Company's scientific instruments and natural curiosities were displayed and deployed to feed a fashionable appetite for popular science. The library sponsored lectures and demonstrations that attracted spellbound spectators, including women. A 1750 advertisement in the *Pennsylvania Gazette* publicized the Library Company's courses in "Experimental Philosophy," which included "*Physics, Pneumaticks, Hydrostatics*, Opticks, *Geography*, and *Astronomy* . . . illustrated by a large and curious Orery [orrery, model of the solar system]." "Each subscriber" received "a Gratis Ticket for one Lady to attend the whole Course." Spectators could observe natural philosophical virtuosi experimenting with air pumps to discover the role of atmospheric components in respiration. Audiences watched anxiously as these impresarios of science placed birds in glass beakers evacuated by a vacuum pump, until the animals gasped for breath or died. Onlookers served as fact witnesses to an experiment's apparent scientific truth. Franklin and his colleague Ebenezer Kinnersley awed audiences with the sparks and jolts produced by electrical machines while lecturing on the "Newly Discovered Electrical Fire."[14]

Franklin and Kinnersley experimented with electricity's medical applications by delivering mild electrical shocks to patients in attempts to treat paralysis, gout, headaches, deafness, and tetanus. As a minister and member of Philadelphia's First Baptist Church, Kinnersley also lectured on electricity from the pulpit. His parishioner Elizabeth Byles, whose recipe book demonstrates her medical acumen, may have learned about electricity at church or at a public demonstration. She appropriated Kinnersley's language of science in a letter to a friend, anticipating the "pleasure of a nearer Acquaintance in a happy Electricity." Considering Paschall's friendship with Franklin and Bartram, as well as her record of borrowing medical books from the library, she may well have attended popular scientific demonstrations.[15]

Paschall's recipe manuscript certainly reflects her self-education in the "New Science." Her source documentation, innovative experiments, observations of patients' symptoms, and records of medical outcomes are consistent with the methods of empirical natural philosophy. One detects a note of pride in Paschall's description of "an Excellent Salve for a Burn" that was her "own Invention," as well as her unique "Invention" of a cup-shaped plaster made of beeswax, lead, and spermaceti to cure nursing mothers' inflamed breasts. In their recipe books, women demonstrated how they validated their new empirical knowledge by sharing experiments, comparing results, and disseminating new knowledge by word of mouth and in manuscripts. Paschall created networks of male and female experts in the medically related fields of botany, chemistry, and anatomy to augment her natural philosophical knowledge.[16]

"An Useful Study and Labour to Mankind": Claiming Botanical Authority

Compared to the disciplines of chemistry and anatomy, women's participation in botanical studies was considered an acceptable "feminine" pursuit in the mid-eighteenth century. Women healers' long-standing expertise in herbalism was difficult for male natural philosophers to displace. Nonetheless, preeminent European men of science such as the English botanist and physician Sir Hans Sloane and the Swedish botanist Carl Linnaeus sought to relegate the interpretation and classification of botanical knowledge to elite male natural philosophers, particularly those in European cities. It was fortunate for Paschall that the Philadelphia area was home to John Bartram and other virtuosi who corresponded with these international experts. Bartram's networks included over fifty prominent male naturalists and a few women with whom he exchanged letters and botanical specimens. However, Paschall's recipe manuscript demonstrates that the oral circuits of botanical sharing encompassed even more people than Bartram's correspondence network suggests. Many elite women such as Paschall did not leave behind an archive of letters. Nonetheless, her discursive manuscript reveals that numerous colonial women participated in botanical knowledge gathering, medical experimentation, and interpretation of evidence.[17]

Along with the rattlesnake weed cure for quinsy, Paschall recorded other recipes from her cousin John Bartram, a farmer and self-taught botanist, and his botanically proficient wife, Ann. Although he had no formal secondary education, John Bartram read extensively, observed plant anatomy with a microscope, experimented with hybridization in the family's botanical garden, and sold seeds and plants to naturalists in Britain. Paschall must have known John Bartram all her life. Like Paschall's parents, Bartram was a member of the Darby Quaker Monthly Meeting. The Bartram's house and botanical garden were located three miles south of Philadelphia and adjacent to a tract of land belonging to the Paschalls. Paschall had access to the Bartram family's home library, which contained classic herbal texts including those authored by John Parkinson and Nicholas Culpeper. Although Bartram was disowned by his Quaker meeting in 1758 for deism, his heterodoxy did not preclude Paschall's continued friendship and her participation in his extensive botanical networks.[18]

Bartram recognized that the desire for commercially and medically useful flora had long fueled European powers' bioprospecting expeditions in search of American plants. In his *Pennsylvania Gazette*, Benjamin Franklin posted an advertisement encouraging Philadelphians to volunteer monetary subscriptions to support Bartram's travels throughout the mid-Atlantic colonies "in Search of curious Vegetables, Fossils, &c." In the 1742 advertisement, Bartram explained that "Botany, or the Science of Herbs and Plants, has always been accounted" as "an useful Study and Labour to Mankind, as it has furnished them with Cures for many Diseases." Making a case for the exceptionalism of the colonial environment, he added, "The Wildernesses, Mountains and Swamps in America, abound with Variety of Simples [medical herbs] and Trees, whose Virtues [medicinal value] and proper Uses are yet unknown to Physicians." In 1751, Bartram documented his findings in his appendix to Thomas Short's *Medicina Britannica*, titled *Descriptions, Virtues and Uses of Sundry Plants of These Northern Parts of America; and Particularly of the Newly Discovered Indian cure for the Venereal Disease.*[19]

To discover new botanical pharmaceuticals, Bartram interrogated "the Country People" for information on plants like "Chelidonium" to cure jaundice. Paschall used the comparable terms "countryman" or "countrywoman" to describe her recipe book informants who lived outside of cities and had valuable vernacular healing knowledge. As we saw in Chapter 3, Bartram also sought botanical remedies from Native American healers, such as dogbane for the "Bloody Flux" (dysentery) and a lobelia decoction to cure syphilis. Like Paschall, he recognized Indigenous peoples' expert knowledge of North American "medicinal roots, herbs, and barks, used with success amongst the common people." The botanical knowledge of Euro-American women healers, "country people," and Indigenous women and men circulated in transatlantic natural philosophical networks.[20]

Like many naturalists, John Bartram's scientific and benevolent pursuits in botany were intertwined with his commercial interests. To help finance his botanical expeditions from New York to Florida, Bartram sold medicinal and ornamental plants and seeds to Peter Collinson, a London Quaker botanist, Royal Society member, and merchant, who marketed these products in Britain. Collinson was an important philosophical as well as commercial contact. He connected Bartram to the correspondence networks of the foremost European "gentlemen of science," including Carl Linnaeus, the founder of systematic botany. Some of Bartram's letters to Collinson were read to the London Royal Society, which gave the colonial farmer's findings and specimens its imprimatur. Although metropolitan natural philosophers sought to assert their own expertise, they also recognized the authority of colonial inhabitants' firsthand observations, grassroots natural knowledge, and commercially valuable botanical specimens. Bartram and Paschall participated in vast networks composed of people of various classes and ethnicities who participated less visibly in the practice of natural history.[21]

The popular penchant for collecting medical recipes that is evident in Paschall's manuscript was an aspect of this widespread culture of scientific prospecting. Information on medical plants moved within oral circuits among local botanical experts in their shops, gardens, and households. Following a consumption remedy deploying beech bark, Paschall noted, "[John] Bartram says there is but one beech in the country besides the water beech or Buttonwood and you cannot mistake that." John Bartram was a recognized healer and Paschall trusted his medical as well as botanical expertise. Paschall also consulted the Bartrams' sons Moses and Isaac, both botanists and practicing apothecaries, whose shop was on Second Street in Philadelphia near Paschall's business. Next to her recipe book entry on rattlesnake weed, Paschall scribbled a sideways note in the margin explaining that she asked Moses Bartram whether the weed could be taken orally. In her medical trials on herself, family, and neighbors to treat quinsy, Paschall had only used it as an inhalant or gargle. Moses assured her that rattlesnake weed could be taken "inwardly," but only in small quantities.[22]

The Bartrams' advice regarding medicinal plant identification was invaluable. Paschall transcribed a recipe for rheumatism that was "a True Copy" given to her by her Quaker friend Sarah Way of Chester County, who got it from her nephew Dr. John Pyle, who had migrated to North Carolina. Despite an additional authoritative testimonial from Way's granddaughter, Paschall voiced concern about the toxicity of the nightshade plant used in the remedy. Paschall noted, "There is a Deadly Nightshade" and "I never heard of Nightshade given Inwardly, & I know but one Sort which is Excellent in Salves."

Before experimenting with this recipe on her family or patients, Paschall wrote herself a reminder to "inquire of John Bartram or Sons if that be wholesome taken inward." Paschall was right to question the recipe because there were two types of plants called nightshade. "Deadly Nightshade" or belladonna (*Atropa belladonna*) is extremely poisonous and hallucinogenic if not dosed correctly. Although it originated in Europe and Asia, it had become naturalized in mid-Atlantic forests. Paschall describes one of several subspecies of American nightshade whose green berries are toxic but whose ripe black berries are edible. Eastern black nightshade (*Solanum ptycanthum*) fits her description: "It has a little berry the sparrows grab & leaves full of holes [from beetles] and reddish lavender underneath." Cooking decreases this plant's toxicity, and Pyle's rheumatism recipe calls for nightshade and other herbs to be pounded and boiled down in water. Paschal documented complex oral circuits of women healers' information gathering and medical experimentation that are often not apparent in written correspondence networks.[23]

Despite her relative invisibility in the historical record, John Bartram's second wife, Ann Mendenhall Bartram, also participated in local, intercolonial, and international webs of botanical information sharing and knowledge production. Ann worked in the family's botanical garden and plant export business. She had access to her family's medical books as well as those at the Library Company, since John was an early member. Evidence in Paschall's recipe book suggests that Ann Bartram, like her husband and sons, practiced healing outside her family circle. Paschall gave Ann's botanical and medical information equal weight with that of the Bartram men. After citing a remedy for "the Dropsy," Paschall noted, "Coz [cousin] Ann Bartram says this cured [a tavern keeper] Thomas Worth when his Leggs were very much swelled." Dropsy was a life-threatening ailment characterized by swelling of the lower extremities which, as we now understand, can be caused by heart or kidney failure. Ann's testimonial augmented the cure's authority.[24]

Unfortunately, none of Ann Bartram's correspondence is extant. However, a letter survives that was written to Ann in 1761 from the widowed botanical expert Martha Daniell Logan of Charleston, South Carolina, who sent plants and seeds to the Bartrams. Logan thanked Ann for her letter, and she sent along a tub of "roots of the Indian or Worm Pink [*Spigelia marilandica*], as the seeds were all fallen before I had yours [your letter] about them." Logan also conveyed "some Slips of Mrs. Bees Littel flower" and she signed the letter "your well-wisher and friend."[25] Logan listed almost thirty plants that she sent to the Bartrams, including pinkroot and a purple flower that John

had admired during his visit to the garden of a Charleston botanical specialist aptly named Mrs. Bee. This letter underscores the importance of reciprocal material exchanges of seeds and plants along with botanical information.
Although Indian pinkroot provides showy blooms for gardens, Ann Bartram
would have known that it was also an effective treatment for colonists' per-
vasive and debilitating infestations of tapeworms or roundworms. Logan's acquaintance the Charleston botanist and physician Dr. Alexander Garden
had introduced her to this medicine. In his essays on pinkroot presented to
the Philosophical Society of Edinburgh in 1764, Garden explained that the
plant's medical properties were "discovered by the Indians" about "40 years
ago," and Native Americans shared the information with South Carolina's
white settlers. Garden was an important node in the Bartrams' intercolonial
and transatlantic networks, and it is not surprising that Indian pinkroot's
medical uses spread to other colonial "gentlemen of science" such as Dr. Cadwallader Colden in New York and Dr. Benjamin Rush in Philadelphia, as
well as botanists, apothecaries, and physicians in England. Although historical memory has privileged John Bartram and his Euro-American male
correspondents, Ann Bartram, Martha Logan, Mrs. Bee, and unnamed Indigenous healers were important links in chains of botanical and medical
information sharing.[26]

The Bartrams connected Paschall to other literate white colonial women
interested in botany. In a plant-collecting trip in the southern colonies, John
Bartram visited the stately home and garden of the Tidewater Virginia planter
and botanist William Byrd II. His wife, Maria Taylor Byrd, shared Bartram's
natural philosophical interests and encouraged him to document his discoveries in botanical illustrations, which were important to his success. Jane
Colden, the daughter of New York "gentleman of science" Cadwallader
Colden, also corresponded with Bartram regarding her botanical interests.
In 1755, her father wrote to Peter Collinson in London that he was encouraging his daughter to pursue botanical studies "as it is not unusual for woemen
to take pleasure in Botany as a Science." Collinson described Jane Colden as
an "accomplished lady" who "is scientifically skillful in the Linnaean [bo-
tanical classification] system." Jane Colden became a natural philosophical
authority in her own right and was recognized for her "Botanic Manuscript,"
her discoveries of medically useful plants, and her chemical experiments to
create an improved type of cheese. Elite women capitalized on the notion that
botany and horticultural experimentation were appropriate pursuits for "accomplished ladies."[27]

The popularization of botanical gardens provided additional venues that were accessible to women. Informants in Paschall's medical recipe manuscript who developed experimental horticultural gardens included the Bartrams, Dr. Christopher Witt, James Logan, and James Alexander, the head gardener for the Pennsylvania proprietor Thomas Penn. Paschall would have examined specimens in the Bartrams' garden, which gained additional recognition after John was named King's Botanist for North America in 1765. Christopher Witt of Germantown created one of the first horticultural gardens in the Philadelphia area, and Paschall trusted the elderly doctor's herbal and medical expertise. James Logan, a prominent government official and botanical expert, hybridized plants in his garden and published his experiments in philosophical society tracts. From Logan, Paschall gleaned a wound cure that used the "Root of Cat Tails," which Logan had likely learned from Native Americans.[28]

When Paschall visited James Alexander at the Penn family's garden at Pennsbury Manor, he shared an Indigenous remedy using the "inner bark of the Linden Tree" that cured a child whose head was so severely burned in a fire "that there could be no expectation of life." Paschall confirmed the efficacy of Alexander's remedy by citing a female healer who successfully cured "a boy who fell upon his backside into a large pot of scalding hot mush." She noted that linden could be found in both the Penn family's botanical garden as well as in "the widdow Jekyl's Garden on Second Street." Alexander was a self-taught botanist who developed a seed export business that competed with Collinson and Bartram. Collinson attributed Alexander's success to his "discourses with all the people he can get any intelligence of" outside elite gentlemen's circles. Paschall's sources for medicinal botanicals spanned women's kitchen gardens and formal horticultural gardens. She developed her sense of botanical authority within a network that included female herbalists, Native American healers, and "country people," as well as gentlemen virtuosi.[29]

Although botanical experts such as Paschall, Ann Bartram, Martha Logan, and Jane Colden did not receive the international recognition accorded to "gentlemen of science," evidence suggests that they were valued within their wide-ranging horticultural and healing circles. These women exemplify numerous others who contributed to botanical knowledge through their medical or horticultural experiments but left behind few documentary traces. Women healers, including those from Native American communities, acquired the grassroots knowledge of medicinal plants that male naturalists needed to construct the edifices of botanical and medical science. Paschall's manuscript provides glimpses into the local accolades that she received for her botanical cures. As we saw in Chapter 3, the son of a Lenape man from New Jersey returned to Paschall's shop to thank her for prescribing an herbal remedy that healed his father's severe consumption. In another dramatic instance, Paschall's botanical medicine cured a woman who had suffered with a long-standing case of weeping ulcers on her hands that prevented her from working. The woman came to Paschall's house "spreading Both her hands held up with these Acclamations, the Lord in Heaven bless you, for what you advised me to do has Cured me!" Paschall's unflagging confidence in her botanical knowledge and healing authority contrasted sharply with eighteenth-century natural philosophers' notions of women as dependent and irrational.[30]

"Philosophers by Fire": Authoritative Alchemical Networks

In addition to botanical information, Elizabeth Paschall sought out medical knowledge from alchemical specialists. Unlike botany, which was a culturally approved science for women, chemistry was considered a male pursuit. However, Paschall had no qualms about obtaining information on chemical medicine from her brothers-in-law John and Stephen Paschall. In their commonplace books, the Paschall brothers recorded alchemical experiments, innovative diagrams of chemical apparatuses, and medical information handed down from their grandfather, who was a pewterer, apothecary, and alchemist. The Paschalls also sought the alchemical philosopher's stone that allegedly transmuted base metals into gold, cured all illnesses, and conferred eternal life. "Dr." John Paschall was a well-respected, self-taught "alchymical doctor" who was known for his proprietary chemical medicine, "Paschall's Golden Elixir."[31] Elizabeth Paschall's and her brothers' alchemical cures might appear to be artifacts of a regressive vernacular culture of mystical healing at odds with the putative march of eighteenth-century science. Instead, their manuscripts underscore continued debates between humoral medicine and alchemically based medical theories introduced by Paracelsus, a Swiss-born Renaissance physician. As we saw in Chapter 1, the chemical theories of Paracelsus's followers, such as Jan Baptiste van Helmont, became part of lay medical practice, further blurring the lines between learned medicine, vernacular healing, alchemy, magic, and mysticism.[32]

Elizabeth recorded her brother John's recipe for severe nosebleeds derived from Helmont's theories. Helmont's concept of "vitalism" argued for a vital primal force within humans and its invisible "sympathetic" connections between living beings and material objects. Although Isaac Newton opposed vitalism, his theories of unseen gravitational forces lent weight to the proponents of sympathetic bonds. As Elizabeth noted in her medical recipe book, "Brother John" healed nosebleeds by carrying "a handkerchief that has catched the warm blood" under his arm for "6 or 8 miles, then anointing it [the handkerchief] with Cato's Roman Vitriol." Elizabeth explained, "Brother John Says it Cures it by Sympathy." The English philosopher Sir Kenelm Digby, a follower of Helmont, elaborated on the theory of vitalism with his "weapon salve" or "powder of sympathy," a preparation made with the same Roman vitriol used in John Paschall's nosebleed cure. According to Digby, the "powder of sympathy" applied to a blood-soaked weapon or cloth cured wounds from afar by the power of sympathetic bonds. Digby's seventeenth-century treatise, *The Powder of Sympathy*, went through twenty-nine editions, keeping the debate alive into the eighteenth century. Although physicians argued over the validity of chemically mediated medical practices versus long-standing humoral theories, most North American colonial doctors and healers melded aspects of each into their practices. Elizabeth Paschall's eclectic medical recipes underline this syncretism. She recorded distillations and decoctions that used classic alchemical ingredients such as Armenian bole, white lead, oil of amber, and "Pilgrim's Salve."[33]

In addition to her brothers-in-law, Paschall sought chemical healing information from local experts with roots in western Europe. Healers from the Netherlands and the German states were more likely than British immigrants to transmit the legacy of Paracelsian chemical medicine, vitalism, and transmutational alchemy to the colonies. They represented religious groups like German Pietists, Lutherans, Moravians, Schwenkfelders, Kelpian mystics, and Dutch Reformed believers. In her manuscript, Paschall related the account of a "Dutch Dr. Diemer" who saved the life of her sister Mary Reynell's washerwoman when she "had Bled at the Nose almost to Death, an Immeasurable quantity" so that "they could scarce keep life in her." Although Paschall calls him Dutch, Dr. Johann Jacob Diemer was Deutsch or German, from the Palatine area of Rhenish Bavaria. His medical training is uncertain, but he called himself a "practitioner in physick and surgery." According to Paschall, to stop the persistent nosebleed, Diemer prescribed a mixture of the washerwoman's blood, salt, ashes, and hog's dung applied as a cloth poultice on the wrists and neck. Paschall relates, "Imediately [sic] after it was laid on the Back of her Neck the Bleeding Stop'd." Diemer's remedy confirmed the efficacy of the Helmontian sympathetic theory behind her brother John's nosebleed regimen. Paschall may have also known Dr. Diemer's wife, Catherine Fischer Diemer, a healer who practiced with her husband in the Philadelphia suburb of Germantown. Catherine Diemer publicized her practice in the *Pennsylvania Gazette*, where she marketed her proprietary salve to cure "that most raging distemper called The Scald Head" in her shop "at the sign of the Comb." Paschall had her own "Certain Cure for a Scald Head [severe fungal infection]," whose main ingredient was the chemical pigment verdigris, which was commonly used among Pennsylvania German practitioners.[34]

Sufferers often ventured beyond their ethnic communities in search of women practitioners, particularly those whose chemical remedies might help them to avoid surgery recommended by a doctor. Paschall noted that her Quaker friend Martha Pettit, who suffered from a "hard white swelling on her Neck," sought the advice of "Lodowich Christian Sprogell's wife." Mrs. Sprogell was likely Catherina Sprogell, the widow of a Dutch-born Mennonite Philadelphia merchant and assemblyman. Pettit's physician diagnosed the swelling as the "King's Evil [scrofula]," and he recommended surgery. However, Pettit demurred, fearing the pain and the potentially fatal consequences of an excision. In the absence of anesthesia, sterilization techniques, or antibiotics, postoperative complications and deadly infections were frequent. Patients' fears of surgery were well-founded. Catherina Sprogell prescribed a classic alchemical recipe, a plaster of "Pilgrim's Salve," made from "Human Dung and Hogs Lard." According to Paschall, Sprogell had seen this remedy perform an "Extraordinary Cure" in "Holland or Germany" on a woman's gangrenous hand. This "surprised the Surgeons" who had recommended amputation. Pilgrim's Salve successfully cured Pettit's tumor without surgery "& compleated the Cure to the Docter's [sic] admiration." Paschall's informants underscore the religious and cultural diversity that informed the mix of alchemical and vernacular remedies in Philadelphia's mid-century medical marketplace.[35]

Paschall's friend Dr. Christopher Witt of Germantown demonstrates the connections between chemical and botanical medicine, as well as the presence of medical mysticism amid the dissemination of enlightenment science. Witt was a polymath "gentleman of science" who practiced as a physician, alchemist, astronomer, astrologer, botanist, and clockmaker. Paschall recorded Witt's recipe for rheumatism that included the alchemical "Oyle of Amber" and "unguinieum nervenium." Witt was likely acquainted with John and Stephen Paschall because he shared their interest in alchemy and chemical medicine. However, like Paschall, Witt interwove herbal cures with his chemical remedies. Witt participated in botanical networks that included the Bartrams, Peter Collinson, and the German printer and herbalist Christopher Sauer. Along with his pursuit of science, Witt was a *braucher*, a practitioner of German folk medicine, and a member of the mystical alchemical and religious Rosicrucian order. Local histories recall that some of Witt's neighbors called him "hexenmeister" or sorcerer, and they crossed themselves when he passed. Witt's close friend Christopher Sauer included sympathetic cures in his German-language home remedy handbook *Kurzgefasstes Kräuter-Buch* (The compendious herbal), which was one of the first herbals published in the North American colonies. Sauer's remedy called for laying a smartweed poultice upon a painful body part and then burying it in a manure pile to transfer the pain away from the patient. Witt and Sauer represent the ongoing interconnections between sympathetic magic, folk beliefs, humoral medicine, and alchemical theories.[36]

Paschall's recipe book underlines this lack of consensus regarding what constituted authoritative medical practice and scientific expertise. Although Philadelphia physicians who studied at Edinburgh University at mid-century were exposed to professors' attempts to separate applied chemistry from mystical transmutational alchemy, a variety of chemical theories persisted. Newtonian mechanistic matter theories could not completely displace Helmontian vitalism. The tenacity of chemical cures is exemplified by the popularity of "Dr. John Paschall's Golden Elixir," "Dr. Witt's celebrated medicines," and "Catherine Diemer's Ointment," which were marketed and sold by female and male druggists for decades. Rather than solidifying the boundaries of the "New Science," the increasing commercialization of pharmaceuticals and the profusion of popular medical literature provided practitioners with additional spaces to assert the efficacy of their own healing style in a medical landscape replete with diverse theories and practitioners.[37]

The Malleable Authority of Print: Reading Alongside Elizabeth Paschall

Paschall and the women healers in her networks augmented their botanical and chemical knowledge by reading both popular and scholarly medical and scientific print. The fashion for popular science legitimized popular printed works and provided an impetus to move science out of male-centered spaces and into heterosocial places where women could participate. As the London editors of the prominent and urbane journal *Spectator* explained, their goal was to bring "philosophy out of Closets and Libraries, Schools and Colleges, to dwell in Clubs and Assemblies, at Tea-Tables and in Coffee-Houses." The democratization of scientific print provided women with natural philosophical knowledge that they could share and discuss in letters, manuscripts, domestic spaces, and in mixed public places like dance assemblies. Following this trend, Paschall began to include medical information from printed sources midway through her recipe book. She cited Benjamin Franklin's *Pennsylvania Gazette* and *Poor Richard's Almanac*, as well as the *Gentleman's Magazine* published in London. Health-related topics, self-help medicines, and discoveries in the popular fields of electricity and pneumatics featured prominently in these publications, as well as in those marketed toward women, such as the *Ladies Library* and the *Female Spectator*. In chatty columns and letters to the editor, readers frequently shared intimate details of their self-help remedies and medical experiments.[38]

The English healer Joanna Stephens's successful cure for kidney stones exemplifies a woman's celebrated medicine that circulated widely throughout the British Atlantic. In 1739, the *Gentlemen's Magazine* reported that Stephens's discovery earned her a prodigious five-thousand-pound award from Parliament. The *London Gazette* revealed Stephens's secret recipe, which included "Egg shells and Snails both calcinated." Physicians wrote pamphlets describing their experiments to discover the chemical essence of Stephens's medicine. Her success inspired other women healers. Variations of Stephens's cure appeared in women's recipe manuscripts in Britain and its mid-Atlantic colonies. In a letter to his parents, Paschall's friend Benjamin Franklin shared Stephens's recipe and name-dropped the famed chemist Herman Boerhaave, who had experimented with the acidity and alkalinity of kidney stones. Franklin confidently practiced self-help medicine and published health care information. As he humorously explained in his letter, "I am too busy in prescribing and meddling in the doctor's sphere." Medical and scientific information circulated in print and was dispersed in personal letters and manuscripts, creating a transatlantic virtual community of scientifically minded and health-conscious readers.[39]

Paschall shared Franklin's continued interest in remedies for the common problem of kidney stones. She directed her recipe book readers to "look in *The Gentleman's Magazine* in June 1761 for a man cured of the stone." After her transcription of another kidney stone recipe from the magazine using chicken broth and onions, Paschal advised her readers, "I Believe onions are an excellent remedy for the stone." She then recorded another successful kidney stone cure using an onion poultice on the navel given to her by a male customer in her shop. The customer received the recipe from a woman healer in his village. Paschall's in-person consultations overlap on her manuscript pages with local experts' advice and magazine writers' printed endorsements, generating expansive but intimate virtual healing networks. Healing adepts such as Franklin and Paschall copied published sources into their personal letters and manuscript recipe books, which were shared in their medical circles, further widening their spheres of health care influence.[40]

One of Paschall's contemporaries, the Quaker healer Susanna Wright, also consulted the *Gentleman's Magazine* as well as scientific books sent to her by correspondents such as Benjamin Franklin. According to the historian Frederick Tolles, Wright functioned as a "physician and apothecary, distilling simples [single herb medicines] and compounding medicinal herbs, which she prescribed and dispensed gratis to her neighbors." At her home in Wright's Ferry, west of Philadelphia, Wright was active in politics, participated in a circle of women poets, and experimented with botany. Her article on silkworm cultivation was published in the *Philadelphia Medical and Physical Journal*. Although Wright's medical manuscript is not extant, the healer Elizabeth Coultas transcribed Wright's "proven" recipe for the popular patent medicine "Turlington's Balsam of Life" into her remedy book. Recipes were transcribed, altered, and enhanced as they circulated between printed sources, oral networks, letters, and manuscripts, gaining credibility as they moved through healing circuits. As women shared natural philosophical information, they fashioned identities as learned individuals within a community of writers.[41]

Although the "New Science" created fresh challenges to women's healing legitimacy, Paschall and her colleagues buttressed their medical authority within networks of philosophically minded women. However, Paschall complicated her assertions of authority when she began citing male-authored printed sources one-third of the way through her recipe book. As Paschall's recipes of her "own invention" change to remedies recorded "in his own words taken from the book," it might seem that she relinquished her own authority to that of published, learned male experts. Nevertheless, on closer examination it is clear that Paschall appropriated and revised male medical and natural philosophical knowledge to affirm her own healing expertise. Paschall's detailed and annotated transcriptions from medical and scientific books allow us to follow in her footsteps and to examine how she claimed ownership of male-authored texts.[42]

Because the Library Company of Philadelphia has been in continuous operation from the time of its founding, a twenty-first-century reader can obtain, read, and analyze the exact volumes listed in Paschall's manuscript. Paschall assumed that her family members and recipe book readers could also access the Library Company of Philadelphia. She advised readers to "look in James' Grate Folio Dictionary," providing the volume and page number for easy reference. Dr. Robert James's *Medicinal Dictionary* is an imposing three-volume folio set that offers histories of medicine, biographies, scientific theories, and anatomical diagrams. The book's full title evokes its encyclopedic scope: *A Medicinal Dictionary, Including Physic, Surgery, Anatomy, Chymistry, and Botany . . . Together with a History of Drugs, an Account of Their Various Preparations, Combinations, and Uses; and an Introductory Preface, Tracing the Progress of Physic and Explaining the Theories Which Have Principally Prevail'd in All Ages of the World.* James was an Oxford-educated London physician whose weighty dictionary purveyed his medical authority. One can imagine Paschall hefting one of these fifteen-pound volumes onto the reading room desk and discussing James's theories with other library patrons.[43]

In her transcriptions, Paschall applied James's expert knowledge to her practice. She noted the similarities between James's remedies and her own for the "Bloody Flux," fevers, and smallpox. Paschall transcribed James's recipe "for the Convulsive Colic" in which he advocated "carefully anointing the Navel with oil of Turpentine," cautioning readers not to try the remedy without the "advice of a Skillfull Physician." According to James, an anatomical understanding of how the "umbilical arteries adhere to the sides of the bladder" was crucial for the remedy's success. Paschall was apparently undaunted by James's warning, as she had already recorded a similar navel-applied remedy that she used without a doctor's consultation. If she required a better understanding of urinary tract anatomy, she could simply study James's extensive anatomical drawings at the end of each volume. Although she transcribed a fever recipe from James's *Medicinal Dictionary* describing how the "viscid Juices Coagulated by the febrile Heat are Resolved" by medicinal tar water's "Diaphoretic" qualities, Paschall was not daunted by this exclusive jargon. She explained in accessible terms, "It was tarr water that cured our neighbor Matthias Bush of a long lingering wasting Flux when all other medicine failed." Paschall's entries exhibit her confidence in her healing acumen. She resisted male authors' demands to defer to their expertise. Like Gulielma Penn, Paschall did not relinquish her medical legitimacy when she read, interpreted, and transcribed the printed text of a physician's remedy. Instead, Paschall synthesized, recontextualized, and internalized new medical information to authorize her own health care work.[44]

The paragraph that Paschall copied from James's lengthy article on the famed physician Herman Boerhaave exemplifies how she appropriated and reinterpreted male-authored texts. Boerhaave was a recognized authority who chaired the departments of medicine, chemistry, botany, and anatomy at the Netherlands' prestigious University of Leyden. Rather than focusing on his later accomplishments that underscore women's lack of access to higher education, Paschall transcribed Boerhaave's personal experiences that led him to choose healing as a profession. At age twelve, Boerhaave developed an excruciating ulcer on his thigh lasting five years that "defeated all the art of the Surgeons & Physicians." Their treatments were "so tormenting" that the "Disease & Remedies were Equally Insufferable." As Paschall recorded, Boerhaave's "own anguish taught him to [be] compassionate [to] that of others," perhaps thinking of her own painful illnesses that she self-treated. Like Paschall, Boerhaave experimented on himself, finding a cure for his ulcer similar to one of Paschall's. Out of James's five-page hagiographical tribute to the great man, Paschall focused on the narrative that made Boerhaave a kindred spirit as a compassionate empirical healer who began his practice by self-experimentation.[45]

Paschall demonstrated her continued interest in chemical theories by reading Dr. Peter Shaw's translation and abridgement of Boerhaave's *New Method of Chemistry.* Shaw was a fellow of London's Royal College of Physicians who wrote and marketed his medical books to "the unlearned and the novice" as well as "the philosopher and scholar," leaving readers like Paschall to categorize themselves as they desired. Boerhaave's chemical experiments supported Paschall's use of simple remedies like vinegar. She transcribed his assertion, "I have often endeavored in vain by Elaborate Chemical productions to Relieve persons" suffering from "Lethargic Dropsy and Vomiting Disorders," when vinegar "effected the cure." *New Method of Chemistry* supported knowledge production through observation and experimentation—skills available to Paschall and her chemist brothers-in-law. Boerhaave argued, "Chemistry is no science form'd *a priori* . . . it took its rise from a number of experiments casually made" and by "collecting and comparing the effects of such unpremeditated experiments." Paschall's recipe book follows this pattern of observing, collecting, and comparing information with an eye to discovering and confirming remedies.[46]

Boerhaave's text provided Paschall with additional information on the chemical bases of diseases, an interest shared by a fellow Philadelphia Quaker, Mary Pemberton. Both women were intrigued by seawater's potential as a chemical remedy for stomach complaints. While visiting the New Jersey shore in 1759, Pemberton "consulted a treatise" on the subject and experimented on her female companion. Mary Pemberton was one of the Library Company's first official women members, and the library's copy of Richard Russell's *Dissertation on the Use of Sea-Water* would have been available to her. Her interest in seawater reflected her engagement in the Pennsylvania Hospital's healing networks, as her husband, the prominent merchant Israel Pemberton, was on the hospital's board. Paschall's brother-in-law John Reynell informed Paschall that "they keep a barrel of fresh sea water" at the hospital to cure "Billious Chollick," which caused paroxysmal abdominal pain. Reynell was a merchant and a hospital founder, and he shared Paschall's medical interests. Paschall wrote in her recipe book that, according to "Brother Reynell," draughts of seawater cured their friend John Armitt of a severe case of colic. Like the Library Company's reading room, the Pennsylvania Hospital created a context in which to share information and medical experiments.[47]

The recipes that Paschall copied from Peter Shaw's abridgement of *The Philosophical Works of the Honourable Robert Boyle* also enhanced her knowledge of chemical theories and medicines. In a three-volume set comprising 2,215 pages, Shaw compiled works by the famed chemist Boyle, renowned for his fundamental gas law and his presidency of London's Royal Society. Although he was not a physician, Boyle's chemical and healing acumen were well known in the mid-Atlantic colonies. In his *Almanak*, Benjamin Franklin touted "The great Mr. Boyle's remedy for the Dysentery or bloody flux" and "A remedy for the Stone and Gravel strongly recommended by Mr. Boyle." Like Boerhaave, Boyle asserted the superiority of "simple" or single herb remedies, rather than compound medicines, because complex preparations made it difficult to discern which component was effective. Editor Shaw anticipated readers' potential objections: "The remedies, cries one, are simple, such as the good women prescribe, and some . . . appear ridiculous [but] Mr. Boyle cou'd have prescribed as elegant compounds as any physician." In other words, although Boyle's recipes were easily recognized as the "simples" prescribed by women healers, they were still as authoritative as those prescribed by doctors.[48]

Boyle's recipes are so similar to the "simples" in women's recipe books that some scholars believe that Boyle obtained them from his medically and alchemically adept sister. Katherine Boyle Jones wrote her own book of medical recipes called *Kitchin-Physic*, and she shared her medical recipes with her brother. Paschall may have recognized a common remedy used by women healers when she transcribed a passage in which Boyle averred that "the chin cough [whooping cough] in children . . . often frustrates the endeavors of Physicians," and "I have not known any Magisterial composition so effectual as the simple juice of Pennyroyal." Paschall used this herb in her practice, and, like Boyle, she noted remedies that "cured when the doctors failed." Popular works by "gentlemen of science" provided the basis for Paschall and other women healers to assert their own empirical medical expertise.[49]

Printed works also expanded Paschall's botanical knowledge as she digested the Latin language of Carl Linnaeus's new hierarchical plant classification system while reading *A History of the Materia Medica* by the English botanist John Hill. This source reinforced information that Paschall gleaned from local experts like John and Ann Bartram. Hill's tome likely sparked lively conversations, particularly since Hill had written an imperious letter to John demanding plant specimens, including the syphilis remedy *Lobelia syphilitca*, for his patron, the Prime Minister Lord Bute. When Paschall consulted Hill for information on hyssop's usefulness to cure bruises or contusions, she digested the authoritative Linnaean name, *Didynamia gymnospermia*, on a page liberally sprinkled with Latin monikers. The *Materia Medica* provides pages of details on plants' characteristics, habitats, and anatomical structures, as well as quotes from Linnaeus. Hill opined, "A Man is hardly qualified to write on any Subject, who has not read everything that has been well written on it." Like Paschall, after reading scientific works, Hill brought "them to the Test of Nature" by his "own Experiments." Both recognized the authority of print as well as experiment.[50]

As she read these texts, Paschall entered the halls of science inhabited by authoritative male natural philosophers speaking in recondite Latin and Greek jargon. However, her transcriptions from London apothecary John Quincy's *Pharmacopoeia Officinalis Extemporanea* demonstrate that she recognized the exclusionary potential of this gentleman's club. She included translated Latin diagnoses and apothecaries' terminology for her readers, who may have included family members and those in her health care network. Although the *Pharmacopoeia* was geared for a professional audience, Paschall was not deterred. For example, she interpreted Quincy's listing

"Emplastrum Mamillare" into the more comprehensible "For Sore Breasts." Paschall clarified that "Emplastrum" means a "plaister" or plaster—a topical medication. She translated apothecary symbols for pounds and ounces and explained that the term "S.A." signifies "according to art." Paschall advised readers to add "a Dram of Venice Turpentine" to Quincy's recipe, improving on the expert's advice on the basis of her own experience. As she mastered new material, Paschall appropriated the role of an educator by explaining and augmenting expert medical information for her readers. Clearly, Paschall did not simply defer to male medical authors' authority. As a synthesizing reader, she compiled new information, tested it against her own healing experiences, improved on it, and translated it into plain language for her readers.[51]

The Embodied Authority of Anatomy

Printed medical works also reinforced Paschall's interest in the authoritative discipline of anatomy, which was becoming the most important marker of a learned physician. Paschall's references to anatomy date from the mid-1760s, when Dr. William Shippen returned to Philadelphia from his medical and anatomical education in Edinburgh and London. Shippen had trained as a man-midwife or obstetrician, and he was part of a movement to supplant female midwives with university-trained male physicians. Man-midwives and natural philosophers were beginning to deploy anatomy to argue for women's innate bodily and intellectual inferiority. Along with advertising his practice as a man-midwife, Shippen opened a medical museum at the Pennsylvania Hospital that featured anatomical drawings and plaster casts of the decapitated torsos of pregnant women. In his lectures to physicians, midwives, and curious Philadelphians, Shippen used these anatomical representations to assert his knowledge of hidden gynecological and fetal anatomical structures that were previously confined to the sphere of women-centered childbearing. Revealing nature's secrets to the masses was central to popular science. Shippen charged the hefty sum of one dollar for "such Persons who from Curiosity may apply to view the said Paintings &c [the casts]." In England, both women and men visited anatomical museums, and Philadelphians like Paschall may have followed suit. In 1765, Shippen also invited the public to view human dissections at his new "Anatomical Theatre," which provoked shocking rumors that he had desecrated and robbed graves to procure corpses.

Paschall would have certainly been aware of these religiously charged anatomical controversies.[52]

At the same time that Paschall discovered the new authority of anatomical studies, a number of eighteenth-century European women learned the
art of creating wax anatomical models, which required extensive knowledge
of anatomy. The Parisian Marie Biheron's anatomical sculptures were recognized throughout western Europe, and natural philosophers such as Benjamin Franklin acknowledged her skill. Waxwork sculptures displayed in
museums or traveling shows were also popular in the Philadelphia region.
Considering the closeness of the Quaker community, Paschall was likely familiar with the Quaker artists Rachel Lovell Wells and her sister Patience
Lovell Wright, who lived in New Jersey, just across the Delaware River from
Philadelphia. Both women excelled in the art of wax sculpture. In 1767,
Dr. Shippen sent Benjamin Franklin, who was in London, a wax preparation
for the Royal Society that scholars believe was created by Wells. The model
represented "a very extraordinary Lusus Naturae [freak of nature], two female children joined firmly together from the breast bone as low as the navel" and Shippen hoped it would be of "use & amusement of the curious &
learned." He advised Franklin that the "preparation of wax was made by a
gentlewoman who is a great tho unimproved genius in this way, tis the exact
semblance of the original wch [which] I have in spirits." It is telling that Shippen did not divulge the woman's name and that he denigrated her "great"
genius by describing it as unlearned. Wells and Wright would later receive
acclaim for their waxworks exhibits in Philadelphia, New York, and London.
Despite being dismissed by men such as Shippen, women artists continued
their work in anatomical sculpture, just as female midwives continued their
practices.[53]

Paschall demonstrates that she was able to successfully navigate the cultural quagmires of anatomical study. When one follows her reading pathway,
it leads from a recipe in her manuscript to the section that Paschall transcribed from Dr. Robert James's *Medicinal Dictionary* on the subject of a
bronchocele tumor. It is clear from the placement of the passage and the lack
of a reference in the index that she could have found the source for her transcription only while reading fifteen densely written folio pages in an entry
titled "Anatomy." To discover the passage about a bronchocele cured by a
respected woman healer, Paschall plowed through James's transcription
of "an Account . . . presented by the ingenious Dr. *Douglass* to the *Royal
Society*." According to the prominent anatomist Douglass, "I had lately the

Opportunity of opening a Woman about fifty Years old, who had a very large Tumor . . . in the fore Part of the Neck." He proceeded with a detailed description of the dissection, peppered liberally with anatomical terminology: "The fleshy Fibres of the *Latissimus Colli* were scarcely visible, the *Mastoidoeus* and *Coracohyoidoeus* were extremely thin . . . it was connected to the *Levator Scapulae* and the *Cucullaris*." Through the medium of print, Paschall could virtually "sit in" on Douglass's dissection of the woman presented before the London Royal Society. If she had questions about the terminology, she could refer to the anatomical diagrams in the *Medicinal Dictionary*.[54]

As she pored through Douglass's esoteric anatomical language, Paschall discovered and documented more earthy similes that matched her own tactile diagnostic experiences. She found resonance with Douglass's description of the tumor as having the "Consistence of a Cow's Udder when boiled," and she included this passage in her transcription. Significantly, Paschall also copied a section in which Douglass explained, "I was formerly acquainted with a Woman who was in great Reputation for resolving these Tumors. Her Secret consisted in anointing the Part frequently with the Oil of Chamomile made by Infusion." Paschall sifted through the words of Drs. James and Douglass to discover a passage that lauded a woman healer's medicinal expertise that prevented risky surgery. As she copied down Douglass's accolades for the woman healer's successful remedy, Paschall extended her medical networks to include a female practitioner who inhabited the virtual world of print. By recording the account of a woman of "great Reputation," Paschall identified and foregrounded the contributions of a woman healer like herself who might otherwise be effaced in scholarly writings. In her recipe book, Paschall constructed a more inclusive narrative of women in science and wrote herself into the story.[55]

It is easy to dismiss women's participation in medicine and the sciences in the mid-eighteenth century because they were barred from universities, scientific organizations, and medical societies, and they rarely received formal recognition. Fortunately, Elizabeth Coates Paschall's recipe book helps us to view the history of science from a grassroots rather than a top-down perspective. Paschall allows us to catch glimpses of women healers' extensive botanical, chemical, and anatomical networks, which are almost invisible in the elite correspondence of European and colonial "gentlemen of science." Women's specimen exchanges and information sharing demonstrate that they were active participants in the construction of scientific knowledge at local, intercolonial, and transatlantic levels. Paschall and her colleagues recognized the emerging authority of empirical science, and they deployed its new rhetoric and methods of observation, experimentation, and documentation to authorize their healing practices.

Empowered by her Quaker beliefs in equality and humanitarian benevolence, Paschall ignored prescriptive literature that denigrated women as too irrational to pursue medicine and science. Her recipe book is replete with her own innovative recipes and treatments, followed with the confident accolades "cured to admiration" and "cured when the doctors failed." Paschall embodied the philosopher Immanuel Kant's Enlightenment appeal to "have the courage to use your *own* understanding." Philadelphia's public scientific demonstrations provided additional venues for women such as Paschall to learn novel ideas about the respiratory, nervous, and cardiovascular systems as they viewed pneumatic, electrical, and anatomical experiments. A lack of consensus regarding new theories in medicine and science provided literate women opportunities to enter debates regarding the validity of older humoral and chemical ideologies in the face of new discoveries in the fields of anatomy and electricity. As they imbibed new medical findings in newspapers, journals, and medical texts, Paschall and her fellow healers appropriated remedies and theories from recognized male experts without relinquishing their own authority. As synthesizing readers, they digested new information, tested it against their own healing expertise, recorded their findings in their recipe books, and incorporated it into their practices. These women took "his words found in a book" and blended them with information from their female and male expert networks, as well as their own life experiences, to narrate themselves as authoritative women healers and "gentlewomen of science."[56]

In her later years, as tensions increased between Britain and the American colonies in response to parliamentary taxation measures, Paschall demonstrated her assertive personality in the political as well as the medical sphere. In 1765, along with four hundred fellow merchants and health care practitioners, she signed a nonimportation agreement to protest the Stamp Act. After reading a July 1766 edition of the *Pennsylvania Gazette* that heralded the repeal of the despised Stamp Act, Paschall copied a recipe for "Daucus Ale" to treat kidney stones, along with the testimonial of a Thomas Butler, Esquire. Like many Philadelphians, Butler consulted a variety of sources, including "Physicians, Apothecaries, Quacks, Old Women," and "Mrs. [Joanna] Stephens' Medicine," until he found a successful kidney stone cure in a "Daucus or Wild Carrot" remedy that was "recommended by the chemist Robert Boyle." However, two years after penning this recipe, Paschall's vibrant healing practice was cut short. In 1768, Elizabeth Coates Paschall, merchant, healer, and gentlewoman of science, died at age sixty-six of unknown causes. One of the final entries in her recipe book is "To Roast a Pig My Way." Paschall lived life "her way" until the end. She did not survive to see her healing, scientific, and economic networks strain and break under the stresses of impending war.[57]

CHAPTER 5

Medical Entrepreneurship

The American Revolution challenged Margaret Hill Morris's economic independence. Morris was known as a medically skilled Quaker woman who provided health care gratis for her kin and community. However, by 1778, wartime inflation and currency depreciation had left the widowed Morris in financial distress. She wrote to her sister Hannah that she hated to "spunge" off their wealthy brother because she desired fiscal self-sufficiency. Having prayerfully considered a plan for "getting into a little business," Morris opened a medical and apothecary practice in Burlington, New Jersey. She diagnosed, prescribed, compounded drugs, dispensed medicines, and provided nursing care. With her usual dry wit, Morris quipped, "When a patient comes by for advice, if I am at a loss, I open the bookcase, w[hi]ch. is my Apothecary shop, & fumble about the bottles & turn over [William] Buchan's [*Domestic Medicine*], till I meet with something like the case, & then with a grave face prescribe." While she was proud of her new business venture, Morris also lampooned her makeshift medical office, Buchan's popular self-help manual, and physicians' alleged gravitas. She deployed eighteenth-century satirists' classic puns that transformed "grave and learned" doctors, along with their patronizing claims of professional authority, into quacks whose "grave business" put patients into early graves. Morris seems to paraphrase the author Robert Campbell's sardonic portrait of physicians: "To acquire this Art of Physic [medicine]" one needed only to be "acquainted with a few books . . . put on a grave face, and Sword, and a wig," then "the pert Coxcomb is dubbed a Doctor and has a License to kill as many as trust him with their Health." However, Morris's characteristic humor may have masked her anxiety. Although her benevolent free healing practice was well respected in Burlington and Philadelphia, would patients value Morris's medical authority enough to actually pay for her services?[1]

Figure 7. *Margaret Hill Morris* (1737–1816), artist unknown, oil on canvas, ca. 1750s, private collection.

Morris was fortunate that her move from a benevolent Quaker healer to a paid doctress and apothecary occurred during the late eighteenth-century transition to market capitalism and a concomitant rise of a consumer culture that encompassed medical practice and the pharmaceutical trade. As we saw in Chapter 1, during the seventeenth century, healers' legitimacy was based on their ability to assess a patient's physical constitution within the context of environmental conditions. An effective practitioner offered advice on changes of habits and prescribed medications that would resolve an imbalance in the patient's bodily humors. As the historian Harold Cook explains, the adage was that physicians and healers offered "good advice and a little medicine." However, by the late eighteenth century, the success of the patent medicine trade caused patients to expect just the opposite, or a little advice and lots of medicines. Pharmaceuticals circulated as consumer goods offering sufferers the promise that health was something that money could buy. A healer's credibility became more closely tied to the efficacy of their medications. Patients were willing to pay for pharmaceuticals because their monetary value seemed easier to judge than the worth of a healer's advice. By opening an apothecary and medical practice, Morris was able to assert the value of her effective medicines along with her good advice. Indeed, Morris's practice was an immediate success. She noted proudly in a letter to her sister, "I have more custom [business] than I expected!" That patients readily purchased medical products and services from practitioners such as Morris provides evidence of women's ongoing healing authority amid the health care sector's transition to market capitalism.[2]

Although economic historians argue persuasively that women were embedded in the development of market capitalism in late eighteenth-century British North America, the scarcity of sources on women healers has made it difficult to incorporate their practices into this narrative. The historian Ellen Hartigan-O'Connor demonstrates that women were "quintessential market participants," and she places them at the center of urban economic networks.[3] Women were also central to medical commerce because they provided the bulk of health care in their communities. However, their economic contributions remain understudied. In addition, some older medical histories imply that women healers were static traditional practitioners destined to fall victim to the onward march of scientific medicine and capitalism. By contrast, Morris exemplifies free Euro-American women healers who mobilized their expert health care knowledge and healing skills as economic assets in an unregulated consumer marketplace. Women healers such as Morris were not frozen relics

of an idealized precapitalist world. Instead, these women adapted their entrepreneurial practices to weather the perils of emerging market capitalism, which
introduced new regimes of credit, cash exchange, and wage labor. Female
medical entrepreneurs' reimbursement strategies blended nonmonetized barter economies and cash/credit transactions, which suggests their participation
in the uneven economic transformations of the late eighteenth century. Morris
and her networks offer insights into the business strategies that women deployed to maintain their medical credibility while transitioning from unpaid
to remunerative health care work.[4]

Women Healers and the Business of Medicine

Although local historians remember Morris as the first woman physician and
apothecary in Burlington, that is only because they neglected to record the
practices of numerous other women healers. Morris's friend Grace Buchannan trained as an apothecary in London before moving to Burlington in the
mid-eighteenth century. Buchannan located her apothecary shop on Burlington's prestigious High Street, where she marketed pharmaceuticals and
medical advice until the end of the Revolutionary War. Morris and Buchannan
had counterparts in nearby Philadelphia who had practiced as apothecaries
for decades. Elizabeth Paschall's friend Elizabeth Duckworth Whartnaby
served as a healer and itinerant Quaker minister. To supplement her ministerial stipends, she opened an apothecary shop on Philadelphia's Market
Street. Whartnaby ran one of the first pharmaceutical advertisements in
Pennsylvania newspapers, which appeared in several editions of the *American Weekly Mercury* in the early 1720s. Whartnaby touted her "Spirit of
Scurvey-grass" and her "right and genuine Spirit of Venice Treacle, truly and
only prepared by her in Philadelphia, who was the original and first promoter
of it in this city." Venice Treacle or Venetian Theriac was a popular medicine
made of over fifty ingredients used to treat plague.[5]

However, Whartnaby faced competition. On the same page as her ad in
the *Mercury*, another woman announced that her mother's preparation of
Venice Treacle, called "Mary Banister's Drops," was the only authentic and
effective brand. Hannah Harkum Hodge and other Philadelphia shopkeepers advertised and sold this medication for decades. In the 1730s, Philadelphia printer Benjamin Franklin announced in his *Pennsylvania Gazette* that
his mother-in-law, "The Widow READ," had moved her business into his

print shop and continued "to make and sell her well-known ointment for the ITCH [scabies] . . . always effectual for that purpose and never fails to perform the cure speedily." Her daughter Deborah continued to sell salves and medicines in the Franklins' print shop, along with popular medical books and a novel titled *The Amiable Doctress*. By the 1760s, medical consumerism flourished, and Delaware Valley newspapers' columns were filled with pharmaceutical ads. Ann Tucker advertised in the *Pennsylvania Gazette*, touting her "CHOICE Ointment for curing the Piles, Rheumatisms, strains, all kinds of Pains, Ringworm," sore breasts, "Scurvy from Gums," and intractable sores. The "widow of Augustus Schubart" advertised her chemically based "Gold tincture" in a Philadelphia German-language newspaper. By the time of the American Revolution, women doctresses, apothecaries, and drug vendors were visible medical entrepreneurs in Philadelphia and Burlington.[6]

Women's healing roles were fluid, often changing over the course of a lifetime. They deployed their expertise across an economic continuum—from the provision of free medical care to the creation of flexible health care businesses that required cash, credit, or bartered goods in exchange for pharmaceuticals and services. Morris began at one end of the continuum by providing free healing services. Her benevolent medical work reflected her social status within the community and invoked what economic historians call the preindustrial "moral economy" of mutually beneficial exchanges between the "lower sorts" and their "betters."

The historians Elaine Leong and Sara Pennell argue that, even in the absence of cash exchanges, healing recipes and health care knowledge functioned as forms of "currency," which they define as "a commodity which flowed between people and the authority and reliability which was inflected by the circumstances of that movement." Women who did not charge for their services used their health care "currency" to create economic safety nets: chains of nonmonetary indebtedness and dependency that could be called on in the future to reinforce their social capital or to acquire needed goods and services. As the historian Craig Muldrew explains, economic encounters were enmeshed in webs "of tangled interpersonal obligation."[7]

Recipe exchanges embodied relationships of trust and credit between the givers and receivers of valuable healing information. In this period, the terms *authority, reputation, honor, trustworthiness*, and *credit* were closely linked. Entries in women's recipe books describing a medical information source as "a person of credit" or "a woman of reputation," reflect the importance of assessing a healer's trustworthiness along with the value of their medical advice and pharmaceuticals. Women entrepreneurs understood that credit represented informal relations of influence and power. They guarded their reputations and personal credibility carefully because once lost, these attributes were difficult to regain. However, credit also became a formal commercial term connoting that a business owner allowed a customer to obtain money, goods, or services without immediate payment, trusting that the customer would pay in the future. Women's accrued medical credibility and interpersonal "credit" were valuable resources when they transitioned to fee-for-service practices.[8]

Women healers in the late eighteenth-century British North American colonies were able to excel in a variety of venues because health care practice continued to lack regulation by the state or by nascent physicians' organizations. However, even during wartime, Morris had to compete with a profusion of healers for patients' business. To borrow a phrase from the historian Colin Jones, well-informed customers sought health care à la carte in a cafeteria line of practitioners that included laywomen healers, midwives, nurses, physicians, surgeons, apothecaries, cancer specialists, Native American doctors, oculists, bonesetters, African conjure doctors, ministers, and patent medicine vendors. Consumers also faced a market awash with a bewildering array of "all the most useful kinds of patent medicines for sale." Newspapers hawked popular panaceas such as Dr. James's Fever Powder, Lockyer's Pills, Turlington's Balsam of Life, Bateman's Drops, Hooper's Pills, Stoughton's Bitters, Anderson's Pills, Godfrey's Cordial, and Daffy's Elixir. Women healers vended these proprietary medicines from apothecary shops, dry goods stores, print shops, bookstores, market stalls, their homes, and door-to-door. In this laissez-faire milieu, a woman like Morris could call herself an apothecary or a doctress and set up practice without outside interference. On the downside, it was a "let the buyer beware" marketplace in which medical consumers faced uncertainties regarding practitioners' education and credentials, as well as anxieties concerning the safety and efficacy of pharmaceuticals. Medical legitimacy was based on a healer's ability to convince consumers that her skilled medical advice and remedies were effective, safe, and economical.[9]

When women healers developed medical businesses, their operating expenses could vary. Their practice options ranged from the sale of health care services and home-processed herbs and pharmaceuticals that required low up-front costs and overhead, to more structured businesses like apothecary shops, which necessitated start-up funds, capital investment, operating budgets, and credit lines with European drug manufacturers. Free and unfree women with modest financial assets, including African Americans and Native Americans, participated mainly in less capital-intensive enterprises. They produced pharmaceuticals using homegrown herbs and readily available equipment such as mortars, pestles, gallipots, and alembics, which were also employed in food processing and cookery. Middling and elite Euro-American women who possessed start-up funds or who had inherited a business from male kin were more likely to be proprietors of formal shops. Morris's practice was at a midpoint on this business continuum. Whatever their practice styles, women healers had to gain patients' confidence in their prescriptive advice.

Patients took advantage of a flourishing market in self-help medical publications and they educated themselves about their bodies and their health. Self-taught sufferers often tried self-diagnosis and their own prescriptions before seeking care from a practitioner. Increasingly literate health care consumers read medical manuals such as John Tennent's *Every Man His Own Doctor*, John Ball's *The Female Physician: or, Every Woman Her Own Doctress*, and Dr. William Buchan's *Domestic Medicine*.[10] Circulating subscription libraries also provided access to pharmaceutical, medical, scientific, and popular self-help information. Women as well as men consumed popular medical print. By the 1770s, women had borrowing privileges as members of subscription libraries and participated in the public discourse on health and illness. Morris and the women in her literary circle were active members of the Library Company of Burlington and the Library Company of Philadelphia. As we have seen, medical print exerted its own authority, allowing literate patients to affirm their medical knowledge. Patients' claims of medical proficiency challenged physicians' credibility and leveled the playing field for women healers, particularly if women practitioners validated patients' knowledge while carefully asserting their own expertise.[11]

Medical works authored by women appealed to a literate female audience and confirmed women practitioners' healing and pharmaceutical skills, as exemplified by Eliza Smith's *Compleat Housewife*. This popular household manual is remembered for its cooking recipes, but it also contains over three hundred complex medical remedies, including "secret" recipes for proprietary medicines. The book's remedies appear to be drawn from a woman's medical recipe manuscript. According to Smith, a woman's healing knowledge could generate needed income as well as increase her social capital. Smith explained that her medical recipes were for families and "publick-spirited Gentlewomen as would be beneficent to their poor neighbors," who in turn gain the poor's "Good will and wishes" and a reward in the life to come. However, Smith emphasized that her book could also be used as a how-to manual for the aspiring doctress and apothecary. She noted, "I communicated [the recipes] to a Friend [who] procured a very handsome Livelihood." *The Compleat Housewife* was readily available at booksellers and at the Library Companies of Burlington and Philadelphia. Smith provided information that facilitated women's transition from benevolent healers to medical entrepreneurs.[12]

Women who sold pharmaceuticals had to develop innovative marketing strategies to remain competitive. As the historian Patrick Wallis argues, apothecaries were among the first retail businesses to understand the importance of catchy advertising and packaging that reinforced brand names. Women who sold drugs in their shops or homes learned to use bombastic language to make exaggerated claims in their advertisements to differentiate their products from a raft of other patent medicines. Proprietors of formal apothecary shops installed bowfront leaded glass shop windows displaying richly decorated majolica and delftware apothecary jars to entice customers inside. Uniquely colored, shaped, and stamped glassware served as product advertisements and attested to medicines' authenticity. The smells of herbs and chemicals, the sights of beautiful glassware, and the visions of exotic animal specimens made pharmaceutical shopping a rich sensory experience.[13]

Morris reflected this trend by purchasing a glass-front apothecary cabinet for her practice. By locating the business in her home and situating her apothecary shop in her bookcase, Morris minimized her initial costs and reinvested some of the proceeds to build her practice incrementally. Yet, Morris also purchased pharmaceuticals from the Philadelphia Quaker apothecary Townsend Speakman, who in turn imported from the London Quaker drug manufacturer Thomas Corbyn. Women healers like Morris formed critical ligaments that connected individual health care consumers to the broader structures of a transatlantic market for pharmaceuticals and healing services. Morris developed her medical acumen over the course of her long lifetime, from 1737 to 1816. Her career as a healer provides a detailed case study of how a woman could translate her healing skills into an entrepreneurial medical practice in the greater Philadelphia area.[14]

Formative Health Care Networks

To understand Morris's transition from the provision of free health care to a paid medical practice, we must look back to the economic circumstances and medical influences of her younger years. Unlike Gulielma Penn, Hannah Freeman, and Elizabeth Paschall, Morris left behind numerous written documents. Although her medical recipe book is short and succinct, Morris's American Revolutionary diary and her extensive letter collection provide a rich context for her healing work. From early childhood, Margaret Hill experienced on a deeply personal level the devastating risks of capitalism. She was born near Annapolis, Maryland, in 1737 into a medical and commercial Quaker family that subsequently moved to Philadelphia. Her father, Richard Hill, a physician and merchant, provides an early example of colonial traders whose companies, credit, and masculine honor were shipwrecked on the shoals of merchant capitalism. In 1739 Hill's commercial partnership failed, and he and his wife Deborah fled their creditors to the island of Madeira to start a wine business. The Hills left baby Margaret and three other siblings in Philadelphia in the care of their fifteen-year-old daughter, Hannah, who had recently married the Quaker merchant-physician, Samuel Preston Moore. The Moores served as surrogate parents, and their respectability helped the Hill children overcome the personal humiliation of their father's economic embarrassments, as well as the anger of unpaid creditors.[15]

Despite this early setback, Margaret grew up in comfortable circumstances in a family of merchants, physicians, and women healers who served as role models and educators. Her mother, Deborah Hill, and her eldest sister, Hannah, were both respected healers whose expertise was passed down through generations in the Hill family. Hill family letters document extensive transatlantic networks that included Funchal (Madeira) and London as well as Philadelphia and other colonial ports. Along with personal and business news, family members shared healing advice and medical materials. For example, Deborah Hill asked a daughter in Philadelphia to send the medicinal herb tansy in addition to snakeroot and elecampane, noting that "Cousin Lloyd hath both in his garden." From Madeira, Deborah sent dragon's blood tree extract, a botanical that was used in remedies and dyes. Even at an early age, Margaret learned to meld Old and New World remedies into her pharmaceutical repertoire.[16]

By the mid-eighteenth century, Margaret Hill's hometown, Philadelphia, was the most populous city in British North America and a vital commercial port with close connections to West Jersey's capital, Burlington. As we have seen, the "Quaker City" was also the premier British North American metropolis of medicine and science. Like her distant cousin Elizabeth Coates Paschall, Margaret and her family participated in the city's culture of popular and scholarly science as well as its medical benevolent organizations. Although Philadelphia's population became increasingly diverse over the course of the eighteenth century, the Quakers' relatively egalitarian beliefs continued to influence the way gender operated in the city. Young Margaret imbibed the foundational and potentially subversive Quaker testimonies of peace, integrity, simplicity, and equality.[17]

Margaret grew up surrounded by assertive Quaker women who assumed authoritative public positions within a culture that accepted unconventional gender roles. Quaker women ministers, such as Margaret's cousin Rebecca Jones, embodied the equality testimony by speaking to both men and women on preaching tours throughout the Atlantic world, and by publishing their sermons and diaries. This contrasted sharply with Protestantism's usual admonitions that women should remain silent in church, avoid public roles, and tend only to domestic duties. Margaret's friends Martha Routh and Mary Swett combined skilled healing with their public itinerant religious ministries. Susanna Wright, a prominent healer, tavernkeeper, poet, and politician in Margaret's circle of friends, argued that women could avoid the "chains of matrimony," remain single, and still have fulfilling lives and ministries. These women's successful public work destabilized traditional gender hierarchies and supported women's claims to healing knowledge and authority.[18]

Not surprisingly, Quaker women were well represented in Philadelphia and Burlington's business communities. The number of female-run local businesses in Philadelphia grew from a few dozen in the 1740s to approximately 160 by 1775. Quaker girls like young Margaret Hill learned business and healing and skills through formal schooling and informal studies in natural philosophy, which included medicine as well as the sciences. In an environment open to female entrepreneurship, some schools taught girls skills that enabled them to excel in a variety of trades. Rebecca Jones ran a Quaker school to help finance her ministerial travels. Jones educated girls about compounding interest, brokerage, metallurgy measurements, and apothecaries' terminology and conversions. Since Jones was single, she knew from personal experience that women needed business and mathematical abilities to be financially secure. Margaret Morris shared her cousin Rebecca's understanding of the importance of these skills. When Morris opened her medical practice during the American Revolution, she voiced frustration when her sister Sarah refused to assist with compounding pharmaceuticals. Sarah reminded her elder sister that she was not trained in apothecaries' nomenclature and she feared making medical errors. Morris, on the other hand, had acquired these skills, either from a Quaker school or from knowledgeable family members.[19]

Education facilitated women's sense of confidence as they pursued public endeavors. As a young woman, Margaret enhanced her knowledge by participating in literary and medical networks that fostered her self-assurance in her healing acumen. Her circle included her cousin Hannah Griffitts, Susanna Wright, the Philadelphia salonnière Elizabeth Graeme Ferguson, and her siblings Dr. Samuel and Hannah Hill Moore, Dr. Charles and Milcah Martha Hill Moore, and George and Sarah Hill Dillwyn. The scholars Karin Wulf and Catherine Blecki demonstrate that women in this web of literati empowered themselves through literacy, writing, and exchanges of self-authored poetry and manuscripts. In addition, medical recipes, medicinal herbs, and health care information flowed through these oral and written networks, confirming healing authority along with female authorship. Margaret's sisters and brothers-in-law supplemented her schooling by teaching her the medical and pharmaceutical knowledge and expertise necessary for a successful healing practice. Her equal interactions with her physician brothers-in-law and their colleagues were reflected in the confidence that Margaret exhibited in her collaborations with other doctors in Philadelphia and Burlington.[20]

Margaret also exchanged letters and poetry with the dry goods merchant William Morris, a scion of a prominent Quaker family. They married in 1758. William shared Margaret's medical interests, and they both supported the new charitable Pennsylvania Hospital. Because William was a merchant who marketed imported goods to shops in the Pennsylvania backcountry, the couple was also concerned about a series of new taxes imposed by the British Parliament under the guidance of Prime Minister George Grenville, culminating in the Stamp Act.[21]

Healers at the Crossroads of Revolution

The 1765 Stamp Act crisis and the associated nonimportation movement politicized the home production of medicines in Morris's circles and motivated these women to hone their pharmaceutical skills. The act, which required that stamps purchased with hard currency be affixed to innumerable colonial documents, had far-reaching implications. In October 1765, William Morris joined the healer and merchant Elizabeth Coates Paschall and four hundred business owners, including eight female shopkeepers, seven physicians, and fourteen apothecaries, in signing a nonimportation petition to protest the Stamp Act, declaring it "unconstitutional" as well as detrimental to trade. As these men and women in health care–related occupations understood, the Stamp Act interfered with the business of medicine as well as other trades. A typical *Pennsylvania Gazette* article announced, "Just imported . . . from London . . . by Isaac and Moses Bartram . . . a Fresh and Large assortment of drugs and medicines," underlining the importance that apothecaries and other medical experts attached to open and affordable trade. The petition signers maintained that the act increased the cost of imports, enlarged the colony's debt to Great Britain, and decreased the availability of specie, thus curtailing the merchants' "ability to pay the duties imposed on us, much less to serve as a medium of our trade." Elizabeth Paschall, William Morris, and their fellow merchants agreed that until the Stamp Act was repealed, they would not import or export British goods. The petition encouraged colonists to buy home-produced American products and to boycott British imports such as tea and textiles. Female merchants like Elizabeth Paschall who signed the petition supported boycotts in which women throughout the colonies were key participants. Although women in Margaret Morris's circle had exchanged healing recipes and parcels of herbs within their social networks for decades, nonimportation added a politicized urgency and authority to these productions. The movement also provided opportunities for these women to enhance their healing and pharmaceutical skills, which they could redeploy to earn income during the war.[22]

Within a year of the Stamp Act's repeal in 1766, Margaret Morris's husband died suddenly, leaving her widowed after only eight years of marriage. The grieving widow and her four children left Philadelphia to live in Burlington, New Jersey, with her sister Sarah and brother-in-law George Dillwyn, a prominent Quaker minister. Morris leaned on her Quaker faith to cope with her loss. As she wrote to a sister, "My heart still bleeds and the wound remains unclosed." Like the Dillwyns and their colleague Anthony Benezet, Morris took part in a Quaker reform movement that challenged Friends to avow pacifism along with the testimonies of equality, integrity, and simplicity. For Morris, the American Revolution was neither a glorious cause nor a rebellion against imperial Britain: it was pointless social confusion, and she longed for the day when the battling parties would be reunited. She prayed that Heaven "would interpose & spare the effusion of more blood." In addition, the Quaker community was painfully fractured, dividing along a political continuum that included reformist Quakers like Morris who avowed pacifist neutrality, Free Quakers who rejected pacifism and fought in the Revolution, and Quaker loyalists to Great Britain. As Morris advised her sister in Philadelphia, "Things are low in a religious sense" for "we are a living People scattered" and seeking a "resting place from the Stormy Day." Morris's devout Quaker beliefs and her pacifism informed her healing practice.[23]

The Delaware Valley's location in a military theater of war from 1776 through 1779, and again in the war's last phases, had disastrous economic, personal, and health consequences for residents in the path of the conflict. Despite the expansion of colonial trade during the third quarter of the eighteenth century, monetary and taxation policies created inequalities in wealth distribution in the greater Philadelphia area. The onset of the Revolutionary War exacerbated crippling scarcities of specie, collapsing chains of credit, and property foreclosures that had dogged Delaware Valley families and businesses since the aftermath of the Seven Years' War. Women left in charge of homes and businesses struggled to provide for themselves and their families when their male kin joined the military or were killed in combat. Epidemics of smallpox, dysentery, and "camp fever" (typhus) followed troop movements and ravaged families on the home front as well as combatants on battlefronts. In 1777, Morris noted, "I never knew such a sickly time since I came to Burlington." Continental Army physicians and surgeons had difficulty procuring medicines for the troops in the face of increased disease prevalence and scarcities of imported pharmaceuticals caused by wartime disruptions in shipping. British soldiers also seized private-practice physicians' medicines and equipment as they marched through the countryside, creating shortages for civilians as well as combatants. Doctors and surgeons sought women healers' advice on how to obtain local herbs such as American senna and white walnut bark to replace depleted stores of imported pharmaceuticals. The increase of diseases, shortages of physicians, difficulties in accessing available doctors' expensive services, and the dearth of medical supplies made women healers' skills and herbal knowledge particularly marketable during wartime.[24]

Adding to the dislocations of disease and warfare, the presence of numerous loyalists and politically neutral residents in West Jersey and Philadelphia created an atmosphere of civil strife. In Burlington, Morris faced shelling by patriot gunboats as well as the confiscation of food and household goods by both Continental and British soldiers. American officials suspected pacifist Quakers of treason, and rioters vandalized the homes of Morris's relatives. In April 1776, the Philadelphia Committee of Safety declared Morris's friend, the apothecary Townsend Speakman, "an enemy to his country and precluded from all trade" for "refusing to receive Bills of Credit emitted by the authority of Congress." Speakman and other reformist Quakers argued that the bills were linked to violent warfare, and thus their use was contrary to Quakers' pacifist beliefs. According to the committee, the apothecary was "lost to all virtue."[25] Although Speakman avoided imprisonment, in 1777 seventeen of Morris's prominent Quaker friends were charged with treason and sent to prison in Winchester, Virginia. Writing to his sister from Winchester, the merchant John Pemberton noted, "Besides the sword, & sickness which hath carried off multitudes, the want of Bread is like to prevail." As Revolutionary warfare escalated in western New Jersey, Morris treated soldiers and civilians on both sides of the conflict without charge in accordance with her Quaker pacifism and political neutrality.[26]

In her journal, Morris detailed the personal and economic results of her healing work. On June 14, 1777, American gunboats cruising the Delaware shot at Morris's home, thinking it was a British loyalist stronghold, particularly when they saw Morris's son observing them though a spyglass. Fortunately, no one was injured. Later in the day Morris noted in her journal, "Some sailors and their wives being sick, and no doctor in town . . . were told Mrs. Morris was a skillful woman, and kept medicines to give to the poor." She added wryly, "And notwithstanding their late attempts to shoot my [son], they . . . begged me to come" and help them. As "they were very ill with a fever," Morris "treated them according to art" and they recovered. In appreciation, one of the American sailors contacted Morris's sister Hannah in Philadelphia and described the supply shortages in Burlington. Hannah sent the sailor back to Burlington with "a bushel of salt, a jug of molasses, a bag of rice, some tea, coffee, and sugar" for Morris and her family. In this chain of favors and gifts, Morris's healing skills produced an unexpected windfall of necessities. Morris tearfully thanked the soldier and her "Heavenly Father" for the "seasonable supplies" and in turn "divided the bushel and gave a pint to every poor person who came for it—having abundance left for our own use." Morris viewed her experiences from a providential perspective, likening the episode to the biblical miracle story of Jesus feeding the hungry multitude with a few fish. However, Morris's account also demonstrates how her healing skills provided her family with an economic safety net.[27]

Women's healing labor could serve political allegiances as well as religious convictions, from the battlefields to the households that were commandeered as hospitals. Like Morris, Ann Cooper Whitall embodied Quaker pacifism while treating hundreds of British-affiliated Hessian solders as well as American troops when her home became a military hospital after the 1777 Battle of Red Bank, New Jersey. Abigail Marshall received accolades for her work as a "faithful nurse" for soldiers billeted in her home. Her husband, the apothecary Christopher Marshall, was the chairman of the Committee in Philadelphia for Sick Soldiers, and Abigail's health care work supported her family's position as leading members of the "fighting Quaker" patriot opposition to Great Britain.[28] Other Philadelphia women reached out to needy soldiers after the disastrous Battle of Germantown in October 1777. As the elite Quaker Deborah Norris Logan recounted, "wagons full of the wounded arrived in the city, who's Groans and sufferings would be enough to move the most inhuman to pity." American troops sustained significant casualties, and hundreds of injured Americans waited in agony at the statehouse while British physicians first treated their own soldiers. According to Logan, "The street was filled with women of the city" bringing food and bandages to care for the wounded. The Quaker midwife Lydia Darragh used her health care networks to gather intelligence from the British and to warn General George Washington of a surprise attack at White Marsh, Pennsylvania, in December 1777. The American Revolution offered new medical challenges for women healers as well as visibility in politicized public roles.[29]

The war also supplied formal opportunities for women to earn wages as nurses in military hospitals and to gain medical and organizational skills that they could later use to create health care businesses. If they survived the dangers and rigors of an army hospital, nurses received a hands-on education in sanitation, wound care, fever therapies, dietary interventions, and the procedures surrounding smallpox inoculation. Nurses also found time to develop medical networks that bolstered their healing reputations and authority. At the Yellow Springs Hospital west of Philadelphia, the army chaplain Rev. James Sproat praised Nurse Adams for her effective administrative skills, noting that the hospital was "very neat, and the sick comfortably provided for." Sproat explained that he "drank tea with the doctors and matron [supervising nurse]" and was "genteelly treated" by "the matron, Mrs. Adams." By performing rituals of sociability, Adams fashioned herself as a refined healer, which deflected negative stereotypes that depicted hired nurses as inebriates and prostitutes.[30] The army nurse Mary Watters, a widowed Irish immigrant, also created collegial relationships with Benjamin Rush and other military doctors that established her healing credentials and boosted her social status. As we will see in the next chapter, Watters marketed her extensive wartime healing experiences and her relationships with physicians to launch a successful medical business as a nurse, doctress, and apothecary in postwar Philadelphia. The American Revolution provided Margaret Morris and other healers with examples of women who received payment and public visibility for their medical work. Unlike the nurses Mrs. Adams and Mary Watters, Morris was a member of a prominent Quaker family, and she did not have to struggle to assert her refined social status. However, Morris had to reconfigure her role as a benevolent healer into that of a paid proprietor of a medical practice.[31]

"Then with a Grave Face Prescribe"

Like other healers who sought paid employment during the war, the widowed Morris needed to translate her medical knowledge into income to support her family. Persistent wartime economic instability and inflation continued to create financial problems for Morris. Although she held several properties in the Philadelphia area, she had difficulty collecting rents from lessees who experienced financial reversals that were exacerbated by the British occupation. However, Morris hated to "spunge" off her wealthy merchant brother, Henry Hill, who ran the Philadelphia office of the family wine-importing partnership. Henry Hill's choice to reject pacifist Quaker principles and enlist in the military may have also influenced Morris's desire not to be indebted to him. In her quest for financial self-sufficiency, Morris had to tread carefully to remain true to the Quaker testimonies. As the popular minister Samuel Fothergill admonished another Quaker physician, "an *anxious* pursuit of business in the medical way is very unsuitable to our situation on the borders of eternity." With a sense of God's peace, Morris opened a modest medical practice in her home in March 1779.[32]

   If Morris kept ledgers for her business, they are not extant. One can only discern the outlines of her practice through her letters, diaries, and medical recipe book. With a touch of humor, Morris told her sister Hannah that, as she had "long supplied many gratuitously," she might as well charge for her services now. She was pleased at the "custom" she attracted in this "first attempt at business," and it appears that her previously nonpaying patients accepted the change. In 1779 Morris noted, "There is not a dose of physic [medicine] to be got in this town without coming to me for it. . . . I feel quite alert at the thoughts of doing something that may set me a little step above absolute dependence." Although Morris was supported by family and community networks, she clearly sought to maintain a personal sense of economic autonomy.[33]

Morris's paid healing work encompassed a spectrum of roles that, in the early twenty-first century, we typically divide into rigid categories regulated by the state licensure of physicians, nurses, physicians' assistants, nurse practitioners, and pharmacists. However, in the unregulated environment of late eighteenth-century Pennsylvania and New Jersey, Morris's practice would have included all these health care roles. Morris's extensive letter collection provides detailed information on her medical work that is not recorded in Elizabeth Paschall's manuscript or in other women's medical recipe books. To appreciate the scope of Morris's practice, we will examine separately her roles as a doctor, a nurse, and an apothecary, and compare them with the practices of other women healers in West Jersey and Philadelphia.

In her medical role, Morris diagnosed health conditions and prescribed therapeutic bloodletting, pharmaceuticals, or Galenic humoral alterations in the patient's activities, including changes in diet, exercise, and access to fresh air. Patients visited Morris in a consulting room in her home, but her practice spaces were also flexible. On one occasion, in the midst of a Quaker meeting (religious service), Morris bled an acutely ill woman "on the spot." The patient's symptoms were relieved "considerably." At another time, she was "called in after meeting" to examine a young woman who had a film growing over her eye. Morris explained to a sister, "I directed Molasses to be dropt in at Night, & and to take a dose of Rhubarb." She added facetiously, "It was rec'd. [received] as Gospel, & the sale of the Rhubarb may pay for heeltaps." Morris referred to the pieces of leather used to repair the heels of shoes. Considering her wry sense of humor, Morris may have used the term to joke about her shabby "down-at-heel" impoverishment during the war. Like her physician counterparts, Morris also visited clients in their homes. Morris's grandson remembers her making house calls in a borrowed carriage, appropriating this symbol of physicians' status and authority along with the lancet for therapeutic bleeding. Other women healers also deployed bloodletting to treat patients. In 1778, the Methodist minister Freeborn Garrettson was "in an insensible state" after receiving a beating for preaching without a license in Delaware. He was "taken to a house near-by and [was] bled by a doctress, who was just then passing by" who "restored him to his senses." Like Morris, the doctress always "carried her lancet when called out." Although women healers are often associated with milder, herbal remedies, most followed the standard humoral medical practices of bleeding and purging.[34]

Sometimes Morris stayed overnight to monitor an acutely ill patient. In one instance, she stayed with a patient to titrate and administer the dose of the cinchona bark (quinine) that she prescribed to treat the woman's remitting fever. Apparently, Morris did not like the family, and she hesitated to make the house call because of previous negative encounters. As she told her sister, "I am not fond of works of Supererogation [showy good works] and did not offer to set up with JB's wife." However, he "intreated me to come . . . to watch the going off of the fever to give her the bark . . . [and] I went without expecting any reward." She concluded with surprise, "But behold he . . . [paid me with] a Chest of fresh imported medicines!" In the face of wartime shipping disruptions, the chest was a scarce and valuable commodity. In letters to her sisters, Morris cites other barter payments, including a tea set and baskets of potatoes, turnips, and eggs.[35]

In the absence of a business receipt book, it is difficult to assess Morris's income from bartered goods or cash. This is not surprising, since there are few extant Delaware Valley physicians' ledgers from the mid to late eighteenth century. However, Morris's friends Drs. Thomas and Phineas Bond did leave behind a rare copartnership ledger. In the 1760s, the Bonds charged an average of one to two English pounds sterling for an overnight house call and approximately one pound for an obstetrical delivery. They provided services on credit that at times were not settled "by cash in full" for years. Like Morris, they compounded and sold pharmaceuticals. Women healers may also have kept either written or remembered credit-and-debit accounts that might be settled for cash, barter, or exchange of services. In her analysis of Maine frontier midwife Martha Ballard's post-Revolutionary diary, the historian Laurel Thatcher Ulrich discovered that Ballard accepted both cash and bartered goods, and she suggests that Ballard charged less than local physicians. Ballard's average fee for a delivery was six shillings, whereas a standard physician's fee in her town was one pound or even one guinea. Morris was not a midwife, but she attended and assisted with deliveries. She did not leave behind financial accounts like Ballard's, but it is clear from her letters that she was satisfied with a practice that set her "above absolute dependence."[36]

Morris's doctress role overlapped with the provision of personal nursing services. Women healers may have been more likely than physicians to nurse patients, as it was typical for women to take turns watching over their kin and neighbors during illnesses. For example, Morris treated a patient for a serious disease, and he credited her with saving his life. During his convalescence, he called on Morris for nursing care as well. As Morris commented to a sister, "When others try to get him out of bed he cries out I'm too weak, then they send for me, & I warm the gown & tell him it is time for him to set in the Chair & he never refuses—and all the while I stay he is wishing . . . [me] Blessings & Comforts." Morris also cared for patients in her home while they convalesced after smallpox inoculation, which was becoming a profitable business as more advanced methods increased the safety of the practice.[37]

In addition, Morris provided supportive care for patients facing death. The Carey family had engaged Morris to treat their father for a serious case of dropsy, a disease characterized by abdominal swelling and swollen, fluid-filled limbs that we now understand to be caused by heart or kidney failure. When Morris concluded that the case was terminal, some family members became alarmed and called in John Jones, a prominent Philadelphia consulting physician. Although Morris enjoyed excellent relationships with numerous doctors in the Philadelphia area, she apparently had little patience with the pompous Dr. Jones. As she wrote to a sister, "Dr. Jones is come—& there is to be a grand Consultation this afternoon about poor Neighbr. Carey—but I doubt if it's in the power of Med[icine] to save him." She added, "The Dropsical symptoms advance fast upon him—he feels it in his belly & his face begins to bloat." When Jones returned to Philadelphia without explaining the gravity of the man's illness, Morris was left with the difficult task of informing the patient that his case was incurable. She offered Carey spiritual support by describing the "comforts that await a weary traveler when the journey is at an end." Jones validated Morris's assessment of her patient's condition and she remained Carey's physician until the end.[38]

Good Advice and a Profusion of Pharmaceuticals

Whether they provided nursing care, medical diagnoses, or minor surgical procedures, female healers like Morris often met their patients' expectations by prescribing, compounding, and administering pharmaceuticals. Although some women advertised drugs in newspapers and broadsides, others used their health care and community networks to market their medicines and healing knowledge. Burlington and Philadelphia women of the lower and middling social orders who sold pharmaceuticals are difficult to recover in the historical record, but these healing experts were well known to their communities. Burlington residents Mary Harris, Widow Barker, Mrs. Shaw, and Mrs. Elton sold healing herbs, medicinal waters, patent medicines, and salves out of their homes and door-to-door. By producing pharmaceuticals in their households, women could attest that they had made their products with authentic and safe ingredients, which contrasted with the uncertain provenance of imported drugs.[39]

However, because medical botanicals were also used as cooking spices and ornamental plants, their pharmaceutical applications can be obscured in women's documents. For example, the elite Burlingtonian Mary Burd Campbell recorded that she purchased a half pound of Carolina pinkroot from Mary Harris for five shillings. The plant's striking red blossoms were decorative, but it was also known as worm grass. Pinkroot was a standard remedy for the persistent and debilitating problem of intestinal worms in children and adults. It was also commonly used an emmenagogue to regulate menstruation or as an abortifacient. Margaret Morris vended her own medicines in her shop, but she also worked in cooperation with Burlington women like Harris who had less formal businesses. In one instance, she encouraged a fellow healer to charge more for her proprietary salve, arguing that the healer "undervalued" her remedy "by setting so low a price as 2 shillings." Morris quipped, "I'd chearfully pay 15!" Although Burlington County's large community of free and enslaved African Americans and its population of resident Lenape Indians must have included female healing adepts such as Hannah Freeman, they left scant documentary traces. The sale of homegrown and home-processed medicines entailed low up-front costs, thus allowing women of various classes and ethnicities to earn income by starting home businesses.[40]

Morris home-produced numerous medicines, harvesting herbs from her garden and distilling medicines in her alembic. Her garden and kitchen were pharmaceutical and culinary spaces, making the medical aspect of her work less visible to historians. As we have seen, compounding medicines required skills in chemistry and botany, and it allowed women to create novel scientific knowledge and products. Patients and family members often requested Morris's proprietary fever powders. However, sometimes kitchen chemistry spilled over into other household activities. For example, Morris apologized for sending her sister Hannah a foul-smelling letter. According to Morris, "Son John [and I] had been making musk julep for [Mr.] Carey on the Counter, where my paper laid and scented it." The musk used in the recipe was indeed a malodorous substance extracted from the gland of the Asian musk deer. Morris may have gotten the recipe from her copy of Buchan's *Domestic Medicine*, since he recommended it for a variety of "nervous fevers" and "spasmodic affections." Morris had apprenticed her son John to his uncle Dr. Charles

Moore, who lived northwest of Philadelphia, in part to hide this able-bodied youth from military recruiting officers. Still, Morris relished John's stealthy visits home, where "the business of an Apothecary be still carried on by a diligent apprentice, & watchful Mother." Morris's kitchen was a site of medical education as well as medicinal production.[41]

Morris's medical recipe book and letters demonstrate that she purchased imported pharmaceuticals to supplement the local herbs that she used to make her medicines. Her Musk Julep recipe required store-bought musk and sugar as well as homemade rose water. Morris recorded her efforts to find scarce cash to pay off her apothecary bills, often relying on family members. She noted, "I think upon the whole I had best buy this list of Meds. with hard money—as the sum in Dr. Br[other] M[oore]'s hand will clear my last year's score for wood." Morris traded with the Philadelphia Quaker apothecary Townsend Speakman, whose avowed pacifism likely made his business more popular with reformist Quakers than that of "fighting Quaker" apothecaries Christopher Marshall and his sons. Moreover, according to Morris, Speakman's products were less expensive than Marshall's, and he granted credit. In a letter to her sister, Morris wrote that she planned to send a list to Speakman to "add to my shop by a little at a time." Speakman had managed to avoid imprisonment for his treasonous refusal to accept Continental currency, which his Quaker beliefs linked to war. His religious principles requiring payment in specie also made good business sense, as Continental currency rapidly depreciated.[42] Morris hoped to have a similar credit arrangement with the apothecary Isaac Bartram: credit granted up front with a promise to pay cash later. However, he insisted on cash payments. In response to a package of medicine that her sister sent from Philadelphia, Morris grumbled, "I'm sorry thee paid for the medicines . . . as I've dealt so much with Bartram, he might have let them come without the money." Bartram and Speakman linked Morris to transatlantic networks of pharmaceutical credit, but they also kept her tied to the uncertainties of wartime currency in Philadelphia.[43]

Morris participated as a retailer in the transatlantic economic channels connected to Thomas Corbyn's London pharmaceutical manufactory and wholesale distribution center. Corbyn was particularly influential among Quaker merchant networks. Along with Speakman, Corbyn supplied other Philadelphia apothecaries, including the Marshalls, Esther White, and Isaac and Moses Bartram.[44] However, he faced competition from an established drug manufactory in Halle, Brandenburg-Prussia. The prominent Pennsylvania German Lutheran minister Heinrich Melchior Muhlenberg and his wife, Anna Maria, imported medications from Halle, which they sold to parishioners and generated needed income. Anna Maria processed the raw ingredients, created medicinal compounds, and vended pharmaceuticals out of her home in Trappe and later in Philadelphia. She likely paid for the wholesale shipments out of her own substantial inheritance, until both the Halle and the Corbyn manufactories faced shipping disruptions during the Revolutionary war. However, despite these supply chain problems, the war did not preclude an ongoing business in pharmaceutical sales.[45]

The Philadelphia apothecary Elizabeth Weed exemplifies women who took over family pharmaceutical businesses after the death of male kin during the war years. Like the widowed Morris, Weed needed to support her family during difficult economic times. Before the Revolution, Weed and her husband, George, ran an apothecary shop out of their home on Front and Arch Streets. In 1770, the self-styled "Dr. George Weed" advertised in both the *Pennsylvania Gazette* and the *Pennsylvania Chronicle* a "neat assortment of medicines," including the proprietary "Weed's Syrup" for the bloody flux (a severe gastrointestinal illness). George Weed's first career as a counterfeiter of Continental currency and his subsequent job as the apothecary for the Pennsylvania Hospital gave him the skills to produce medicines and to concoct the extravagant claims that were typical for pharmaceutical advertisements. The Weeds compounded drugs to treat a variety of illnesses, including "venereal disease in all its stages," consumption, "colds, coughs, shortness of breath, spitting of blood," rheumatism (arthritis), and gout. They also marketed pediatric medicines, including the opiate paregoric for curing children's intestinal complaints and ensuring that an infant is "easy and quiet, more healthy, and requires less tending." Their Syrup of Balsam cured "whooping coughs in children," and the Essence of Tar healed "the greensickness in virgins." Because women traditionally provided the bulk of children's and women's health care, Elizabeth would have been comfortable advising mothers, dispensing pediatric medications, and discreetly treating female clients' gynecological issues and sexually transmitted diseases. To undercut their competition and to reach a wider audience, the Weeds advertised reasonably priced products so that "the poor may be able to purchase them," and provided "printed directions" with their medications "gratis." According to the ads, "Persons in both town and country" testified that the Weeds' remedies had been "under God, the means of saving their lives."[46]

Like Margaret Morris, the Weeds diversified their practice in the early 1770s by offering smallpox inoculation. The Weeds advertised that they had

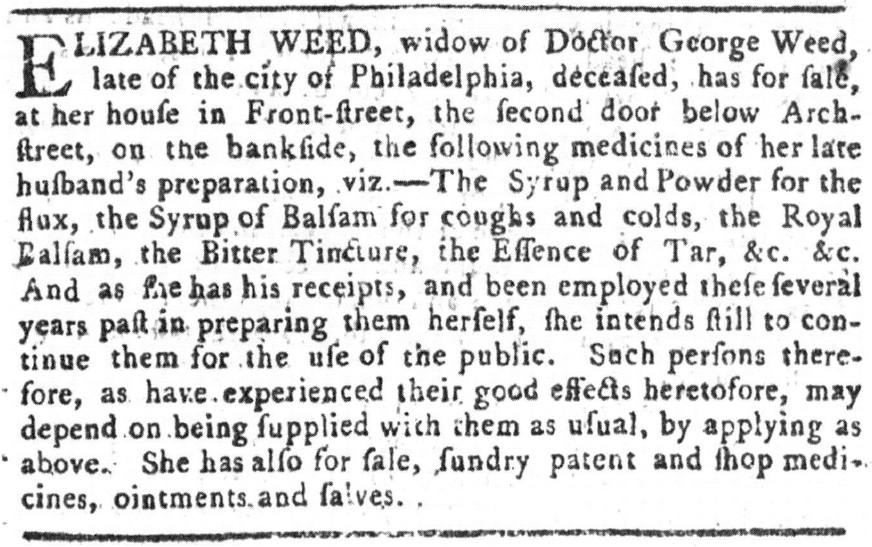

ELIZABETH WEED, widow of Doctor George Weed, late of the city of Philadelphia, deceased, has for sale, at her houfe in Front-ftreet, the fecond door below Arch-ftreet, on the bankfide, the following medicines of her late hufband's preparation, viz.—The Syrup and Powder for the flux, the Syrup of Balfam for coughs and colds, the Royal Balfam, the Bitter Tincture, the Effence of Tar, &c. &c. And as fhe has his receipts, and been employed thefe feveral years paft in preparing them herfelf, fhe intends ftill to continue them for the ufe of the public. Such perfons therefore, as have experienced their good effects heretofore, may depend on being fupplied with them as ufual, by applying as above. She has alfo for fale, fundry patent and fhop medicines, ointments and falves.

Figure 8. Apothecary Elizabeth Weed, advertisement in the *Pennsylvania Evening Post*, Philadelphia, October 11, 1777. Weed was an active participant in the family apothecary practice. Courtesy American Antiquarian Society.

developed a new inoculation method such "as the great Dr. Boerhaave hinted at," which made the ordeal "light and easy for the patient to undergo." By citing the renowned Leiden physician and chemist Herman Boerhaave, admired by scientifically minded Philadelphians like Elizabeth Paschall, the Weeds appealed to literate patients abreast of innovations in Enlightenment science. New techniques had indeed made smallpox inoculation a safer and more popular procedure. The Weeds' advertisement touted their successful inoculation of eighty patients, noting, "What greater proof can there be of the utility of medicines than the great success that attends them?" Elizabeth may well have prepped patients with the pre-inoculation diet and medications and cared for them following the procedure in the rooms above the shop. Her apothecary work required an understanding of botany, chemistry, and apothecaries' weights and measures, as well as methods to produce tinctures, decoctions, distillations, plasters, and ointments. Although Elizabeth was not named in these early advertisements, her later ads clarified that she had been an active partner in the business. She gained valuable medical, pharmaceutical, and marketing experience in her early years in the apothecary shop.[47]

After the devastating defeat of General George Washington's Continentals at Germantown, followed by the British occupation of Philadelphia in September 1777, Elizabeth Weed announced her husband's death in the *Pennsylvania Evening Post*. She advised customers that she would carry on his apothecary practice "as she has his receipts, and been employed these several years past in preparing them herself." She assured readers that they could "depend on being supplied" as usual with "patent and shop medicines, ointments, and salves" including the "Syrup and Powder for the flux, the Syrup of Balsam four coughs and colds, the Royal Balsam, the Bitter Tincture, the Essence of Tar &c &c." She advised her patrons that those who experienced the "good effects" of her products "may depend on being supplied with them as usual." After years of work in the apothecary shop, Elizabeth Weed confirmed that she had the acumen to compound pharmaceuticals and offer medical advice. Despite the economic dislocations of occupation, Weed had to sustain her apothecary business to support herself and her sickly toddler, George Junior. Unfortunately, like many female artisanal entrepreneurs of this period, Elizabeth Weed left few documentary traces. Aspects of her life and her apothecary practice must be reconstructed from newspapers, wills, city directories, local histories, her third husband's commonplace book, and public records.[48]

Along with other women healers, the widowed Weed faced the economic vicissitudes of the British occupation of Philadelphia, which disrupted businesses, markets, and monetary systems. Prices for staples such as salt, sugar, coffee, and flour, which had increased sixfold earlier in the year, more than doubled again by the fall of 1777. Newspaper notices publicized business closures and partnership dissolutions. Instead of dampening pharmaceutical sales, the occupation provided new opportunities for apothecaries and druggists. Inflated prices, combined with decreased availability of physicians, increased the value of affordable self-help pharmaceuticals. Weed advertised to a new, transient pool of customers, including British soldiers and speculators.[49]

With shortages of supplies and stiff competition, Weed had to rely on her marketing expertise to differentiate her pharmaceuticals from those of other Philadelphia drug retailers. Apothecary William Smith's advertisement in the *Pennsylvania Evening Post* in March 1777 assured customers that despite the British occupation, "they may still be supplied with all kinds of DRUGS AND MEDICINES as usual at his shop . . . on reasonable terms." Dry goods merchant Nicholas Brooks advised clients that he continued to sell "DR. RYAN'S incomparable WORM DESTROYING SUGAR PLUMBS," which "cured a great many children of whooping or chin coughs, and agues." Below this advertisement, the itinerant patent medicine purveyor Dr. Anthony Yeldall, "well known for his travels through most of the United States," offered consultations at his "medicinal warehouse" in Philadelphia, in patients' homes, or by post. Yeldall also followed the example of British patent medicine vendors by selling his products in medicine shows performed on stages in public spaces accompanied by his "Merry Andrew," a common moniker for a clown. Salesmen such as Yeldall had long been called mountebanks because they mounted benches in town squares to flamboyantly hawk their wares. Medicine shows capitalized on consumers' demand for public scientific spectacles, their desire for entertainments, and their hopes that a patent panacea would cure all ills. Despite this competitive marketplace, Weed successfully marketed her products and gained brand-name recognition for her "genuine" proprietary "Weed's Syrup."[50]

Margaret Morris's patients also continued to patronize her medical practice in the later years of the Revolution. Like the nurse Mary Watters, Morris won the esteem of Benjamin Rush and other prominent physicians, including the imperious John Jones. In a 1781 letter, Dr. Jones wrote to a patient, confirming that the man's medical condition had been "very sensibly penned by Mrs. Morris." Morris had written to this university-trained physician, whose patients included George Washington and Benjamin Franklin. Despite his credentials, Morris confidently questioned Jones's diagnosis. In response, Jones admitted to his patient grudgingly, "It is very possible that I may have mistaken the nature of your disease for it is not an uncommon thing for Doctors to be mistaken." Physicians as well as nonphysician patients also consulted Morris's friend and itinerant Quaker minister and healer Martha Routh. Routh had visited Morris's brother-in-law Dr. Charles Moore and had prescribed her proprietary anodyne (pain-relieving medicine) for his chronic pain. When Routh returned to Burlington, she delivered the medicine to Morris, who sent her "dear Brother a phial of M. Routh's Anodyne" to be "taken about half an hour before bed." Although women healers were theoretically doctors' competitors, women of the diverse social orders represented by Routh, Morris, and Watters created collaborative relationships within physician networks.[51]

In the Revolution's wake, Morris moved back to Philadelphia and continued her busy healing practice. Despite her pacifism during the war, Morris was able to maintain her status as a creditable healer within her like-minded Quaker community. In a letter to her daughter, Morris noted that once again her home had become like a "little hospital," but she admitted that she relished her healing role. Morris added, "Dr. G[riffitts] being obliged to be out of Town for some days requested me to prepare medicines & visit several of his patients in his absence, saying he could depend on me to do it." For Samuel Powel Griffitts to ask Morris to cover his practice was a clear mark of his trust in her medical authority. Although Griffitts, a Quaker, was elected professor of materia medica and pharmacy at the University of Pennsylvania, he depended on the well-connected Morris for patient referrals and trusted her to care for his patients in his absence.[52]

Women's authoritative healing work deserves more consideration in economic history and in the historiography of the American Revolution. Shortages of medicines and difficulties accessing physicians' care made women healers' expertise even more important during wartime than in peacetime. As Morris and her practitioner colleagues demonstrate, healing knowledge was particularly suited for translation into a variety of paying occupations that accommodated a range of start-up and operating costs. Women of diverse social standings could enter the medical market and deploy their formidable skills by vending pharmaceuticals and providing health care advice. Morris was not an exception. Elizabeth Weed, Martha Routh, and Anna Maria Muhlenberg exemplify women who inventively marketed their wares to meet the demands of an informed, self-help-oriented clientele. These women were members of a frontline sales force linked to transatlantic supply chains of pharmaceutical manufacturers and distributors. Their practices straddled older, nonmonetized healing exchanges and newer emphases on credit and cash transactions. Margaret Hill Morris and her fellow healing practitioners connected and actuated the economic structures of the increasingly commercialized business of medicine. In a competitive health care marketplace, these healers established reputations as paid providers of beneficial healing advice and pharmaceuticals, which demonstrated their economic legitimacy and reinforced their healing authority. Women healers' wartime experiences continued to inform their medical work in the early Republic.

CHAPTER 6

Marketing Health

Mary Watters, a widowed Irish immigrant, learned valuable healing skills as a nurse in Continental Army hospitals during the American Revolution. After the war, she deployed her medical acumen and wartime contacts with Philadelphia doctors to create physician and patient referrals for her practice as a nurse, doctress, and apothecary. Watters strategically publicized her medicines and her practice in an advertisement on the wrapper cover of the *Weekly Magazine* in 1798. The magazine entered hundreds of Philadelphians' homes and was available at lending libraries, which introduced her pharmaceuticals to a wide audience. On the back cover of the *Weekly Magazine*, Watters advertised her signature "Worm Cakes" along with *"Huxham's Tincture of Bark, Lavender Compound, and a Variety of other Medicines, particularly Eye-Water, Pills, and Tooth-Powder."* Watters promoted the safety and efficacy of her medicine, which expelled intestinal worms. She marketed her Worm Cakes as lacking "any of those pernicious or dangerous Properties so evidently prevalent in other Remedies for the Worms." Watters claimed that the medicine "effectually clears the Body" of worms and other stomach complaints. Although Watters's ads were quite visible to subscribers, advertisements on magazine wrappers are often lost to historians. Wrappers were blue-tinted magazine covers that featured ads on the reverse face of the front and on the last wrapper pages. Most eighteenth-century magazine wrappers were discarded by libraries when magazine editions were bound together into single volumes. Fortunately, the Library Company of Philadelphia kept some of the original wrappers from the *Weekly Magazine* so that reference librarians and a historian could discover Watters's advertisement while digging in the library's secure collections.[1]

The ephemeral nature of an eighteenth-century magazine wrapper is an apt metaphor for the relative lack of documentary evidence for the healing

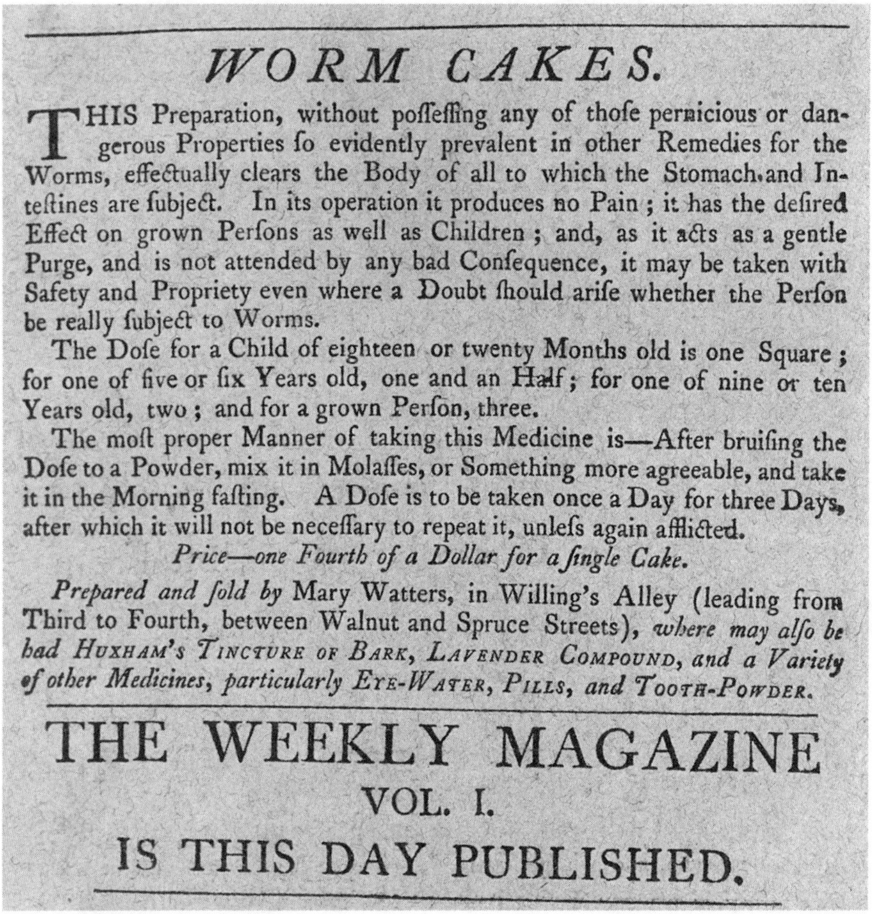

WORM CAKES.

THIS Preparation, without poſſeſſing any of thoſe pernicious or dangerous Properties ſo evidently prevalent in other Remedies for the Worms, effectually clears the Body of all to which the Stomach and Inteſtines are ſubject. In its operation it produces no Pain; it has the deſired Effect on grown Perſons as well as Children; and, as it acts as a gentle Purge, and is not attended by any bad Conſequence, it may be taken with Safety and Propriety even where a Doubt ſhould ariſe whether the Perſon be really ſubject to Worms.

The Doſe for a Child of eighteen or twenty Months old is one Square; for one of five or ſix Years old, one and an Half; for one of nine or ten Years old, two; and for a grown Perſon, three.

The moſt proper Manner of taking this Medicine is—After bruiſing the Doſe to a Powder, mix it in Molaſſes, or Something more agreeable, and take it in the Morning faſting. A Doſe is to be taken once a Day for three Days, after which it will not be neceſſary to repeat it, unleſs again afflicted.

Price—one Fourth of a Dollar for a ſingle Cake.

Prepared and ſold by Mary Watters, *in Willing's Alley (leading from Third to Fourth, between Walnut and Spruce Streets), where may alſo be had* Huxham's Tincture of Bark, Lavender Compound, *and a Variety of other Medicines, particularly* Eye-Water, Pills, *and* Tooth-Powder.

THE WEEKLY MAGAZINE
VOL. I.
IS THIS DAY PUBLISHED.

Figure 9. The healer Mary Watters's pharmaceutical advertisement in the *Weekly Magazine* (February 3–April 28, 1798), bound edition, back cover. Courtesy Library Company of Philadelphia.

practices of women of the artisanal or lower social orders in the early Republic. Unlike Elizabeth Coates Paschall and Margaret Hill Morris, Watters left no personal letters, diaries, recipe books, or business records. To reconstruct Watters's healing work, one must place her practice in its historical context, examine public records, and analyze the few documents that refer to her. Fortunately, Watters's healing acumen caught the attention of Dr. Benjamin Rush, a prominent Edinburgh-educated member of Philadelphia's medical community, and his writings provide glimpses into Watters's background and practice.

Watters encountered Rush during his stint as surgeon general of the Continental Army's Middle Department. Rush was so impressed with Watters that he penned a biographical sketch in his commonplace book and contemplated writing a full biography of her achievements. According to Rush, Watters "served during the whole war in the military hospitals where she was esteemed and beloved by all who knew her." Rush wondered why there were not more narratives of accomplished women. In his manuscript, Rush asked the striking question, "Why not?" As he explained, Watters's "occupation was a noble one—and her example may be interesting to thousands. Only [a] few men can be Kings—& yet biography for a while had few other subjects." However, Rush recognized that the life story of a female nurse would likely meet with objections because standard historical narratives featured famous men rather than women. Rush preempted the British novelist Jane Austen's well-known critique of history as a tiresome retelling of "the quarrels of popes and kings, with wars and pestilences in every page . . . and hardly any women at all." By contrast, Rush viewed women's healing work as a pursuit that warranted biographical studies. Although Rush never published his short chronicle of Watters's life, his query regarding the lack of biographies on women healers is still germane. By foregrounding the narratives of middling and lower-class women such as Watters, this chapter constructs a more complete picture of the diverse health care practitioners that populated Philadelphia's late eighteenth-century medical marketplace.[2]

The healing practices of Watters and her fellow healers demonstrate that a culture of medical consumerism continued to flourish in the early Republic, offering a profusion of patent medicine cure-alls, novel medical appliances, and health care services. The commodification of bodily health that accompanied an increasingly impersonal capitalist market raised questions for medical consumers regarding practitioners' credibility and the authenticity of the pharmaceuticals they sold. How could consumers know if a healer or a patent medicine was authentic or counterfeit? A patient's perception of a practitioner's healing authority was critical in determining whether medical goods or services were genuine and effective or fraudulent and harmful. Medical authority itself became a marketable commodity. In a democratizing political culture, Philadelphians were suspicious of elite physician cabals and continued to depend on medical care provided by female and male nonphysician healers. A postwar economic downturn made affordable health care even more important. Far from being sidelined by the rise of medical consumerism, female healing entrepreneurs took advantage of increasing demand for accessible and effective patent medicines, and they marketed themselves as authentic and reputable practitioners. Mary Watters's work as a nurse, doctress, and apothecary exemplifies the variety of innovative business strategies that practitioners of the artisanal and laboring classes deployed to cultivate and market their healing authority during the early national period.

Conflicting Representations of Nurses: A Noble Occupation?

Rush's depiction of Nurse Watters's calling as "a noble one" was at odds with standard representations of nurses. In order to market her healing acumen and practice successfully, Watters had to first overturn anti-Irish prejudices and negative images of working-class nurses who were paid for their services. As an Irish Catholic immigrant in a predominantly Protestant city, Watters lacked Margaret Morris's extensive family and Quaker support systems. Instead, she relied on the smaller Catholic community in Philadelphia as she forged a livelihood for herself and her young son, James. According to Rush's biography, Watters was born in Dublin and immigrated to Philadelphia in 1766 after the end of Britain's Seven Years' War with Catholic France. Although a few Dubliners from the artisanal class emigrated, most came to the Delaware Valley as laboring class redemptioners who negotiated indentured labor contracts upon arrival. Anti-Irish and anti-Catholic bigotry were rife in Philadelphia, making it difficult for Dubliners to find jobs. Many Irish American women found work as indentured domestics. However, some fled their undesirable posts, as evidenced by numerous newspaper advertisements for runaway female Irish servants. The expendable character of indentured servants' labor is exemplified in a *Pennsylvania Gazette* advertisement seeking someone to buy out a woman's contract: "The Time of an Irish Servant Woman . . . to be disposed of . . . she is sold for want of employment." Women of Irish descent often had to resort to entering the Philadelphia almshouse when they lost their jobs, were unable to find work, or fell ill. Widows with children had particular difficulties gaining employment and frequently became impoverished. Irishwomen's bodies and labor were considered commodities that could be discarded when they were no longer productive.[3]

Watters's social and marital status upon her arrival in the city are un-known, but at some point during the Revolutionary period she was widowed. Despite the unfavorable employment environment for Irish immigrants, she was able to deploy her healing skills as an army nurse to make a living for herself and her son. Catholic women such as Watters had positive role mod-els in nuns who had provided nursing care as a benevolent religious calling in European hospitals for centuries. However, in Protestant countries and colonies, hired nursing in the army, in public hospitals, or in nonfamilial homes was considered a servile job of last resort, even below domestic ser-vice. As we have seen, eighteenth-century discourses lauded Ladies Bounti-ful who provided free health care and derided allegedly degraded lower-class "old wife" healers and nurses who worked for pay in the public sphere. Paid nurses of the lower orders had a long-standing association with criminality, drunkenness, theft, and prostitution. The historian Kathleen Brown notes that some early modern Englishwomen mixed the roles of nurse, laundress, and sex worker in order to earn income for their families, especially in households without a male head. Nonetheless, their work fostered stereo-types that linked nurses with the epithets *whore* or *bawd*. Records from late eighteenth-century hospitals in England suggest that some nurses were in-deed discharged for drunkenness, sexual relationships with staff, and neglect of patients. Female nurses working in army hospitals among male soldiers were particularly suspect. Despite potential censure, women such as Watters chose to work as paid army nurses during the American Revolution. It is possible that Watters joined the Continental Army because she needed the work, and, unlike domestic service, it was a job that allowed her son to ac-company her.[4]

Rush's biography suggests that after the Revolution, Watters touted her wartime experience as a measure of her healing experience and acumen. In-deed, the conditions in army hospitals challenged even the most capable healers. Although General George Washington initially balked at hiring fe-male nurses, he ultimately recognized that they relieved soldiers from the task of caring for the wounded, which allowed male medical attendants to be re-deployed to the battlefield. Medical officers placed advertisements in news-papers to recruit experienced women healers from local communities. They also enlisted nurses from the pool of soldiers' wives and other women who followed the army, working as cooks, seamstresses, and washerwomen for rations or minimal pay. Nurses received two dollars per month and one ration a day. Their pay was later increased to four dollars and then to eight dollars per month by 1777, in order to recruit and retain quality caregivers in the face of nursing shortages. Supervising nurses, called "matrons," received fifteen dollars per month along with a daily ration. However, nurses did not receive formal commissions and they were paid on average less than a third of soldiers' promised wages.[5]

Dr. John Morgan, the army's chief medical officer, detailed nurses' tasks in his 1776 "Plan for Conducting the Hospital Department." Morgan's orders demonstrate physicians' new emphasis on cleanliness as a vital element in preventing and treating soldiers' illnesses. Watters's jobs included maintaining patients' personal hygiene and hospital sanitation. According to Morgan, nurses should "empty chamber pots as soon as possible after use, wash new patients, wash the hands and faces of old patients, comb patients' hair daily, change linen, sweep out the hospital, [and] sprinkle the wards with vinegar three to four times a day." Rush, who served as the surgeon general of the army's Middle Department, seconded his colleague Morgan's precepts, arguing, "Too much cannot be said in favour of CLEANLINESS." Nonetheless, Morgan's injunction that the nurses "must stay clean and sober" speaks to assumptions that they were filthy inebriates. To counter these long-standing stereotypes, army nurses had to present themselves as physically and morally pure, while simultaneously providing intimate personal health care and labor-intensive hospital cleaning services.[6]

In addition to battling misogynistic rhetoric, Watters and her nurse colleagues faced the challenges of squalid, disorganized, and poorly supplied military hospitals that threatened their health and thwarted their attempts to implement sanitary protocols. Dr. Lewis Beebe, a physician for the Continental Army's Northern Department, described his "Compassionate feelings for poor Distressed Soldiers" who were "thrown into this dirty, stinking place [the hospital] and left to care for themselves," some with "large maggots, an inch long, Crawl[ing] out of their ears." After documenting persistent epidemics of smallpox and "camp fever" (typhus), he added morosely, "Death is now become a daily visitor." Beebe described his own frequent illnesses and the deaths of hospital staff. When physicians and surgeons fell ill, nurses were left to perform medical as well as hygienic duties, unless they also contracted debilitating diseases. Although later histories romanticize women's army hospital work as "errands of mercy," close bodily contact with soldiers suffering from smallpox, typhus, and other communicable diseases exacted a deadly cost. Even at the well-run Yellow Springs Hospital west of Philadelphia, the nurses Abigail Hartman Rice and a Mrs. Christian Hench contracted typhus, a disease associated with crowded unsanitary living conditions, which we now understand is spread by body lice, fleas, and ticks. Hench died from her hospital-acquired illness. Rush's accolades to Watters's wartime heroism were well earned.[7]

Rush would also later cite Watters's skills in nursing patients with smallpox, and it is likely that Watters gave soldiers smallpox inoculations as part of a broader effort to prevent the epidemics that were decimating Continental Army troops. Doctors inoculated soldiers by placing smallpox-infected pus into an incision on the men's arms. Nurses provided supportive care while, in theory, the men developed a mild case of smallpox that conferred lifetime immunity. However, the feverish soldiers' oozing pustules were contagious, and inoculated men could infect others during the process. Some inoculations failed, and soldiers and their caregivers died from smallpox. Wartime nursing involved physically taxing work, harsh living conditions, and exposure to communicable diseases. Nurse Watters survived this difficult hospital environment and gained valuable health care experience as well as income during the American Revolution.[8]

Nonetheless, as Watters developed her postwar practice in Philadelphia, negative images of nurses would have followed her as she sought work. Even civilian institutions, such as Philadelphia's Pennsylvania Hospital, were considered dangerous to the reputation and health of their inmates because they were charity institutions intended only for impoverished patients and those with mental illness. The perceived depravity of their nurses added to hospitals' disreputable character. A newspaper article reported that two attendants at the Pennsylvania Hospital were imprisoned for theft, noting darkly, "Apprehensions had been, for some time, entertained . . . that illicit practices were carried on at that place." By contrast, people of the middling and upper orders eschewed hospitals and instead nursed sick family members in the privacy of their homes. Another article promoting the Philadelphia Dispensary argued that outpatient services, along with domestic nursing care by family members, prevented the genteel poor from "exposing [dishonoring] themselves as patients in a public hospital." However, sometimes people of the middle classes sought care in public hospitals. In a letter to a newspaper editor, a traveler to Philadelphia from New York described the crisis of his sudden illness and his inability to obtain health care in a household because he lacked acquaintances. He admitted

MISERIES OF HUMAN LIFE

While confined to your bed by sickness — the humours of a hired Nurse, who among other attractions like
a drop of comfort — leaves your door wide open — stamps about the chamber like a horse, in a boat — slop
you, dost you tie, with scalding posset — attacks the fire, instead of courting it — falls into a dead sleep the mom
when you want her, and then snores you down when you call to her — wakes you at the wrong hours, to to
your physic, and then gives you a dose of aqua fortis for a composing draught &c.° &c.°

Figure 10. *Humours of a Hired Nurse*, satiric print. Hand-colored aquatint engraving by Thomas Rowlandson from *Miseries of Human Life: Designed and Etched by T. Rowlandson* (London: R. Ackermann, 1808). Women who practiced nursing for pay faced negative stereotypes as depicted in this image.

himself reluctantly to the Pennsylvania Hospital. However, he noted with pleasant surprise that he had received excellent care from "sober attentive nurses," as if he had expected negligent treatment from frivolous or inebriated caregivers. The man's backhanded compliment suggests that excellent nursing care in public hospitals was considered the exception rather than the rule.[9]

Nurses such as Watters also faced denigrating stereotypes when they sought work as paid home care nurses and healers. Satirical prints like Thomas Rowlandson's *Humours of a Hired Nurse*, from his collection *Miseries of Human Life*, intertwined middle-class derision for the allegedly depraved lower classes with the older representations of disreputable "old wives." Rowlandson depicts a slovenly dressed, obese, and inebriated nurse slumbering in a chair in a female patient's room. The caption explains that the hired nurse, "among other attractions, likes a drop of comfort [liquor]" and "stamps about the chamber like a horse." After she "slops you as you lie with scalding possets," the negligent nurse "falls into a dead sleep the moment before you want her, and then snores you down when you call to her." In a final delinquent act, the nurse knocks over a candle and ignites a house fire, while the helpless bedridden patient looks on in horror. This disparaging representation of a callous and drunken hired nurse persisted into the nineteenth century, notably in Charles Dickens's character Sairey Gamp. Rowlandson's caricature clashed with Rush's representation of Watters's paid work as "noble" Christian benevolence.[10]

Within her Catholic community, Watters could attempt to deflect defamatory portrayals of nurses by appropriating the image of a chaste, compassionate, and religiously motived nun to frame her practice. Nuns in nursing orders evoked religious as well as healing authority. Along with Rush's advocacy, Watters found a proponent in Father Ferdinand Farmer at Philadelphia's St. Joseph's Catholic Church. According to Rush, Watters "once left off nursing, but was induced to undertake it again by the advice of her minister the late Revd. Mr. Farmer." Farmer was a Jesuit priest who served St. Joseph's predominantly Irish 150-person congregation. Rush was acquainted with Farmer through their membership in the American Philosophical Society and their connections to the College of Philadelphia. Farmer told Watters that "her skill in nursing was a commission sent to her from heaven, w[h]ich she was bound never to resign, and that she might merit heaven by it." The priest used the military term "commission" to represent Watters's nursing practice as an irrevocable, God-given mandate. However, in Philadelphia's anti-Irish

and anti-Catholic Protestant circles, women in religious orders elicited suspicion rather than trustworthiness or pious commitment.[11]

The Culture of Sensibility: Reframing Nurses
as Benevolent Healers

Nonetheless, in the late eighteenth century, nursing became associated with
an emerging culture of sensibility, which provided a Protestant antidote to
negative portrayals of nurses as drunken bawds. The culture of sensibility encompassed an emphasis on markers of refinement and civility as well as a
rhetoric of feeling benevolence that promoted social reform. Books, pamphlets, and newspaper articles modeled reforming sensibility by evoking
feelings of sympathy that would inspire compassionate actions to comfort pathetic sufferers. This sentimental language was readily adopted by middle-
class white women to elevate the mundane task of domestic nursing into an
admirable benevolent act. In a letter "fill'd with tender sentiments" the
nineteen-year-old Quaker Philadelphian Deborah Norris lauded a friend who
was caring for her sick mother. Norris gushed, "How I admire and reverence
thee in the character of a nurse!" Her sentimental style paralleled the language of popular literature.[12]

Moreover, some early women's rights advocates further expanded on the
rhetoric of sensibility to promote female education and women's access to traditionally male professions such as medicine. In *The Gleaner*, Judith Sargent
Murray introduces a successful New England village healer who exemplifies
"female capability" and who "feelingly sympathizes with every invalid." The
widowed healer's "extensive acquaintance with herbs, contributes to render
her a skillful and truly valuable nurse" and makes her "the idol and standing theme of the village." Murray also lauded the woman's habit of extensive
reading to hone her skills as "a botanist." Her description of an accomplished
and "feelingly" compassionate healer contrasts with portrayals of nurses as
negligent "bawds." Mary Wollstonecraft also employed the rhetoric of sensibility in her writings, even as she recognized its potential to emphasize
women's irrational passions rather than their virtuous humanitarian reason.
In her *Vindication of the Rights of Woman*, Wollstonecraft stated her case
more directly than Murray, arguing, "Women might certainly study the art
of healing, and be physicians as well as nurses." Both Wollstonecraft and
Murray sought to identify respectable occupations outside the household that

would provide economic independence for single women and for those whose profligate husbands, like Murray's, did not provide financial support.[13]

In his biography of Watters, Benjamin Rush also reimagined nursing outside the domestic sphere as a "noble" endeavor characterized by sympathetic altruism as well as skill. As a physician, temperance advocate, and antislavery activist, Rush fashioned himself as the quintessential "man of feeling" and an arbiter of moral instruction. Although Watters was a paid nurse, Rush explained that "she was truly charitable," as exemplified by her compassionate care for her patients and her propensity to lend money to needy sufferers and their families. Rush combined examples of Watters's humanitarianism with details of her upbeat bedside manner and healing acumen. As he explained in the biography, "I never saw her out of humor—she is chatty—and tells a merry story very agreeably." He added, "She possesses a good deal of skill—and an uncommon regard to cleanliness." Apparently, Watters shared Rush's interest in new theories regarding the importance of sanitation in disease prevention. Her insistence on cleanliness evinced her refined sensibility and set her above the stereotypes of slovenly lower-class nurses captured in Rowlandson's *Humours of a Hired Nurse.*[14]

Rush further described Watters's desire for medical challenges beyond routine home health care. As he explained, "She dislikes <u>nursing lying in women</u> [childbirth caregiving]—as well as all such persons as <u>are not very ill</u>. Nothing but very great danger rouses her into great activity and humanity." Rush portrayed Watters's skilled nursing as courageous medical benevolence. The historian Marjorie Levine-Clark argues that working women "constructed an ideal of womanhood based upon able-bodied-ness" that was "associated with health, strength, and work," as opposed to the biblically prescribed notion of women as the "weaker vessels." According to Rush, Watters managed to find a middle ground between charitable nunlike nurse and audacious healer with the strength to battle disease.[15]

Health Care Authority in a Fractious Medical Community

Mary Watters's efforts to create business networks required careful navigation in Philadelphia's contentious medical community. In the wake of the Revolution, medical authority and older hierarchies of social deference were contested. Rush's endorsement of Watters's work was high praise from a physician who freely criticized his medical colleagues' therapeutics and politics.

Physicians in the City of Brotherly Love had been fractured since the founding of Pennsylvania's first medical school in 1765, and this prevented doctors
from creating a hegemonic presence. Erstwhile friends and colleagues Drs.
John Morgan and William Shippen Jr. had battled over the prestige of being
considered the medical school's founding physician, with Morgan winning
the title.

Their simmering conflict erupted again in 1777 amid the American Revolution. As an army nurse, Watters would have been aware of the public professional battles and the associated hum of gossip. Dr. William Shippen had
mobilized his family and political ties with General George Washington to
have Morgan fired from the position of director general of the Army Medical
Department. In his 1777 pamphlet *A Vindication of his Public Character*, Morgan attributed his dismissal to Shippen's "dark purposes" designed to "injure
my character with the public." Morgan anguished, "How truly Machiavellian
has been his conduct!" In response, Shippen merely scoffed: "Ha! ha! ha! He
[Morgan] is truly ridiculous and contemptible!" Watters's medical officer Benjamin Rush sided with Morgan and called Shippen a "monster of public iniq-
uity." Shippen smugly took over Morgan's position, but his ascendancy did
not last long. In 1780, Morgan had Shippen court-martialed on the basis of
substantive evidence of his profiteering on medical supplies. The military tri-
bunal acquitted Shippen by only one vote, leaving him under a cloud of suspicion. Both physicians recognized that the defamation of their reputations
could adversely affect their medical credibility and their practices.[16]

The public responded negatively to this ongoing acrimonious brawl
enacted in the press. After the war, Philadelphia physicians chose sides with
either Morgan or Shippen, which frustrated attempts to align doctors into one
medical society. Physicians also divided along political lines, signaling their
allegiance to the emerging Federalist or Anti-Federalist factions. Many of the
physicians in Watters's consulting network were in the Morgan/Rush camp,
but she also created ties with the Shippen partisans. Although they formed
two medical societies to control nonphysician health care practices and to
promote the sciences in the new United States, these associations had no
power to enforce practice standards or licensure. Philadelphia's medical marketplace remained unregulated. As medical consumers became frustrated with
their battling physicians, they continued to appeal to skilled healers and
apothecaries such as Watters for diagnosis, treatment, and pharmaceuticals.[17]

University-educated physicians did succeed in radiating an aura of learned
authority that attracted some patients, particularly those of the higher social

orders. Eight of the approximately thirty Philadelphia physicians had received their medical education at European universities, which conferred prestige. Some doctors also used their wartime medical experiences to launch political careers and to situate themselves as arbiters of public health. Nonetheless, as part of a movement toward democratization, working people expressed anxieties over the monopoly power of professional associations. For example, in his *Key of Libberty, Shewing the Causes Why a Free Government Has Always Failed*, the populist writer William Manning decried the attempts of physician societies to control access to health care and the diffusion of medical knowledge. According to Manning, "The Doctors have established their Medical Societyes . . . by which they have so nearly enielated Quarcary [annihilated Quackery] of all kinds." However, the results were negative, because "a poor man cant git so grate [get so great] cures of them now for a ginna [guinea], as he could 50 year ago of an old Squaw for halfe a pint of Rhum [rum]." As Manning argued, "The business of a Midwife could be purformed [performed] 50 years ago for halfe a doller & now it costs a poor man 5 hole [whole] ones." The subtext of Manning's folksy wit was that physicians' organizations had decreased accessibility to nonphysician practitioners and increased the cost of medical care. His term "squaw" was derogatory, but it also represented the reality of people who sought affordable care from Native American women healers and other lay practitioners. Although Manning was from New England, he succinctly expressed Philadelphia-area residents' suspicions of exclusive professional cabals. This mindset was part of the "every man his own doctor" self-help movement, which advocated publicizing the secrets of medical practices and pharmaceutical ingredients.[18]

Watters had to cultivate savvy business skills to succeed in this socially and politically complex environment. Available documents suggest that she advertised her practice, fashioned social ties with her patients, and developed collegial relationships with physicians such as Rush. Watters described herself as a "doctress" and "apothecary" in Philadelphia City Directories using terms that inferred an independent practice and professional status. In addition to bedside nursing care, Watters diagnosed illnesses and prescribed, compounded, and dispensed medicines. However, Watters was skilled at reshaping her professional image to cater to the desires of her patients and referral networks. In their writings, Rush and the elite Quaker Elizabeth Drinker refer to her with the more subservient term "nurse." Drinker was the wife of a prominent Philadelphia merchant, who left an extensive diary chronicling almost half a century of her life experiences. She was adept at providing medical care and healing remedies for her kin and she carefully supervised the physicians who treated the Drinker family. In the late 1780s and early 1790s, Drinker noted several times in her diary that "Nurse Waters [*sic*]" visited a sick family member in the Drinker household accompanied by the elderly Dr. John Redman. After the house calls, Redman and Watters took tea or dined with the Drinker family. Redman, a distinguished physician who served as the president of the Philadelphia College of Physicians, had trained numerous younger doctors, including Rush. Watters also drank tea and dined at the Drinkers with Dr. Adam Kuhn, a professor in the Medical Department at the College of Philadelphia (later the University of Pennsylvania). Drinker included Watters in rituals of middle-class sociability, which placed her above the usual hired wage worker. By demonstrating her gentility alongside prominent physicians, Watters deflected the negative associations with hired nurses. Both Rush and Drinker commented on Watters's affable loquacity. While their assessments may reflect stereotypes of garrulous Irish people, Watters did appear to successfully deploy her social skills in her practice.[19]

However, even as she embedded herself in physician networks, Watters was discreetly in competition with them. Watters's professional shape-shifting can obscure the fragments of evidence that document her actual practice as she alternated between the roles of skilled but deferential nurse and authoritative doctress/apothecary. As Rush recounted, Watters was "once sent for to prescribe for a lady in consumption, for her skill was known to many people." Consumption encompassed a variety of serious wasting illnesses and was often associated with lung diseases that we would identify as tuberculosis or lung cancer. According to Rush, before Watters made the house call, "she found out whose patient this lady was." After ascertaining the name of the woman's attending physician, Watters complemented the absent doctor. She then exclaimed to the patient, "Indeed Madam I know nothing but what I learned from Dr.____ (mentioning the name of the physician who attended her) in the military hospitals." Rush infers that Watters would fill in the blank for the attending doctor's name on the basis of her reconnaissance before the house call. From Rush's perspective, Watters renewed the lady's "confidence in her physician" and "showed a disposition to support their [the doctors'] influence in medicine." But Rush's assessment must be read critically. As a shrewd entrepreneur, Watters was able to simultaneously garner Philadelphia physicians' approval while reminding patients of her own authoritative wartime healing experiences. We must consider the subtext of this encounter:

before consulting a physician, the patient had called in Watters to diagnose and to *prescribe* for the woman's pulmonary condition. "Nurse" Watters assumed these customary diagnostic and prescriptive roles of physicians and apothecaries. Contrary to Rush's notions of Watters's deference to physicians, his account provides insights into Watters's independent practice.[20]

Although women healers such as Watters might work collaboratively with physicians, they often trusted their own medical judgment. Margaret Hill Morris's extensive letters provide examples of these practice details that are not available for Watters. As we have seen, Morris questioned the therapies of the Philadelphia consultant Dr. John Jones in his attempt to treat a patient who was in the terminal stages of dropsy. In another instance, when Morris's youngest daughter, Deborah, experienced severe dropsical swelling in her extremities, Morris's brother stepped in and called in a team of prominent physicians, Dr. John Cadwallader and Drs. Thomas and Phineas Bond. The physicians examined Deborah and bled her "to little effect." Morris wryly quipped to a sister, "From the appearances I believe [the doctors] were doubtful what name to give her disorder." In the face of the consultants' uncertainty, Morris took charge of Deborah's care. After her prescriptions of a decoction of vinegar whey and sulfur poultices, Morris noted the Deborah was "much better indeed." When her sister Rachel Hill Wells was confined to bed with severe rheumatic [arthritic or joint] pains, Morris prescribed therapeutic bleeding. However, Rachel's pulse "was so low" that Morris suggested she consult a physician. Morris noted with some pride that Rachel and her husband were "not willing to consult any other doctor!" Instead of calling in a male physician, Morris watched anxiously over her sister after administering a blister, tincture of guaiacum, and laudanum to evoke the appropriate humoral response of "plentiful perspiration." By morning, Rachel was "vastly better." Like Watters, Morris relied frequently on her own diagnostic and therapeutic skills.[21]

Morris's friend and fellow Quaker healer Lowry Jones Wister also had cause to question physicians' authority and the efficacy of their therapies to treat her three-year-old son, William. Wister penned a poignant retrospective account of her son's death from smallpox. She wrote mournfully, "The recollection of my sweet infant's suffering rends my very soul." Wister berated herself for leaving "Little Willy's" bedside in the early stages of his illness to attend a pregnant woman who was in labor. Upon returning home to find Willy's health deteriorating, she called in Dr. John Jones, who prescribed emetics and therapeutic bleeding. However, as she cared for her son, Wister observed that the vomiting caused by the emetics and the depletion from the bloodletting only made Willy worse. Despite Wister's assessment of her son's decline, Dr. Jones assured her that Willy's case was not dangerous. Wister's memories of her son's death were "most painfully encrease'd [increased]" by her "doubts respecting the propriety of medicine that was given to him, and by my hand administered." She feared that she had killed Willy by following the doctor's orders, even as she recognized that emetics and bloodletting made him worse. Wister wondered if her own less interventionist therapies might have saved her son.[22]

Watters, Morris, and Wister were comfortable collaborating with physicians, but sometimes they doubted doctors' judgments and instead made their own independent medical diagnoses. Nonphysician practitioners and patients recognized that many illnesses had no definitive cures and that physicians did not necessarily have superior therapies or medical wisdom. Thus, patients continued to seek care from a variety of health care providers. Despite physicians' attempts to organize and to control medical practice during the early years of the new republic, women healers created their own less visible but persistent networks of female health care practitioners and loyal patients.

Authentic or Counterfeit: The Intellectual Property of Women

In addition to her practice as a doctress and a nurse, Mary Watters compounded and sold medicines, which placed her in competition with other female drug vendors and male apothecaries, as well as physicians. However, there are few details of her pharmaceutical practice. The apothecary Elizabeth Weed, introduced in the previous chapter, provides additional insights into Watters's work as a pharmaceutical vendor, even though Weed's sources are also scanty. Judging by her advertisements, city directories, wills, tax records, and court documents, Weed assumed the family apothecary shop after her husband's death during the American Revolution. Near the end of the war, Elizabeth Weed married master carpenter Thomas Nevell, whose artisanal reputation, military service, and solid patriot credentials would quell any rumors of loyalism related to Elizabeth's residence in Philadelphia during the British occupation. However, Elizabeth did not marry Thomas for his fortune: he struggled with debt and served time in debtor's prison. Elizabeth might have considered that he was well-connected and he would have provided her with valuable business contacts. The Nevells lived in Elizabeth's house and shop, which was in her name. Her son George, rather than Thomas, was slated to inherit the property. Elizabeth used the legal system to maintain her own property and to secure a competence for her son.[23]

The first floor of the Nevell's Front Street house served as their workplace. According to city directories, Elizabeth practiced as an "apothecary who prepares medicines against the ague &c." while Thomas contracted work as a carpenter and a coffin maker. Apparently, this grave trade was not off-putting to Elizabeth's sick clients. One would hope that her therapeutics were effective and did not contribute to her husband's coffin business. Moreover, Elizabeth continued to face competition from other female healers like a Mrs. Kayser, who advertised in the *Pennsylvania Packet* that she "had a safe and peculiar method for the cure of fever and ague . . . and she has great pleasure in the general way of Physic and Surgery." Elizabeth Weed Nevell had to deploy her substantial marketing skills to remain competitive and to attract customers to her pharmaceutical business.[24]

In July 1787, while Philadelphians debated the tenets proposed by the Constitutional Convention, including a clause on intellectual property rights, Weed Nevell was more concerned about the state of her business. She was so successful in marketing her proprietary "Weed's Syrup" that it gained brand-name recognition. However, Weed Nevell was shocked to discover that the crafty James Craft, "a barber and a shoemaker," was guilty of counterfeiting her medicine. Weed Nevell announced in the *Pennsylvania Gazette* that she was suing the "base, vile forger." She used the press and the courts to assert her intellectual property rights in Weed's Syrup. Her newspaper ad began with moderate language and an ostensible civic service announcement "TO THE PUBLIC," affirming that "HEALTH" was the "greatest temporal blessing." She advised customers that she possessed the skills to maintain bodily vigor, including "a knowledge of the 'virtues' (medicinal values) of 'the vegetable and mineral kingdoms'" and "the art of restoring health when lost." Weed Nevell reminded readers that she alone possessed "the Doctor's genuine recipe." By peddling his counterfeit cures, Craft "imposed on the public, and may possibly have injured many" with his potentially harmful and fraudulent drugs.[25]

As an artisanal woman, Weed Nevell defied prescriptive norms of restrained and private elite female behavior by naming herself in print and promoting her products in public. Her use of the courts to battle for her intellectual property rights challenged the stereotypes propounded by Enlightenment philosophers, who argued for women's innate intellectual inferiority compared to men. Weed Nevell marketed herself as a civic-minded and authoritative healer in opposition to the alleged forger, James Craft. She claimed that her customers could place their trust in her reliable diagnoses and her authentic, effective, and safe medicines. Although Craft worked as a barber/shoemaker, he is described as a Burlington wholesaler and retailer in a later advertisement for "Hopkins Celebrated Razor Strops," which prevented "Human Blood From Being Spilled" by "blunt razors . . . A Fact Clearly Proved!!!" Craft likely perceived himself as a legitimate health care provider, since barbers and barber-surgeons practiced tooth-drawing, minor surgery, and therapeutic bloodletting. He confidently countersued Thomas and Elizabeth Nevell for slander, declaring in the press that he was merely reselling Weed's Syrup, which he had purchased from Elizabeth. Unfortunately, the Philadelphia County Court of Common Pleas records are not complete for this period, and the outcomes of the lawsuits are unknown. Nonetheless, in addition to developing skills in sales and marketing, Weed Nevell learned to defend her products in the courts and in print, and to compete in a cutthroat commercial environment.[26]

Despite the distractions of litigation, Weed Nevell continued her work and educated her son George to take over her practice. After twenty-two years in the apothecary business, Elizabeth Weed Nevell died in 1790. Her successful practice enabled her to secure a legacy for George. Weed's legal maneuvers suggest she was intent on facilitating George's social mobility. The 1790 census listed sixteen-year-old "Doctor" George Weed as head of the household, with the sixty-nine-year-old Thomas Nevell, "house carpenter," listed second. George Weed held the title to the Front Street house, finding success, first as an apothecary marketing "the only authentic Weed's Syrup" and then as a self-styled physician, adding the title "M.D." to his name in city directories. In the late 1790s, he purchased and managed Grays Ferry Inn, a venue with its own pleasure garden, "a veritable fairy scene, with bowers, grottoes, [and] waterfalls." The "eminently successful" George Weed was quartermaster for the Second Troop Philadelphia City Cavalry, whose members he entertained in style at his inn. Through her apothecary business acumen and shrewd financial planning, Elizabeth Weed Nevell's healing practice secured for her son a successful livelihood and a place in Philadelphia society.[27]

However, Weed Nevell's medicinal legacy did not remain with her menfolk. In the back of carpenter Thomas Nevell's commonplace book, there is an affidavit written by Rebecca Reed Nicholson dated September 21, 1795, which states, "I certify that the foregoing recipes are in Doctor Weeds own handwriting and that his widow after the Death of her Husband the Doctr. continued to make the preparations agreeable to the foregoing Recipes." Detailed instructions for "Weed's Essence of the Essentials" and "Syrup for the Flux" are crossed out but visible. Nicholson continued, "That for & in consideration of a sum of mony to me in hand paid I now deliver them to Samuel Wetherill & Sons to be prepared & sold by them as they may think proper, & I hereby engage that I will not give or cause to be given the recipes to any other person or persons." Rebecca Nicholson had provided nursing care for the ailing septuagenarian Thomas Nevell. It is possible that Elizabeth gave the secret remedies to Thomas or George, and they bartered the recipes to pay for Thomas's health care. Or perhaps Elizabeth Nevell bequeathed them directly to Nicholson. In either case, Nicholson sold them to the prominent Philadelphia druggists Samuel Wetherill and Sons. Another woman, then another business kept the Weeds' authentic remedies and pharmaceutical legacy alive. In 1796, Elizabeth Drinker noted that Samuel Wetherill gave her son a bottle of Weed's Syrup to treat his cough. Weed's Syrup also appeared among popular patent medicines in an early nineteenth-century druggist's manual. Its secret ingredients included opium, peppermint, aniseed, and fennel, which were typical for flux (diarrhea) remedies and likely effective. Medicinal knowledge served as a transferrable commodity that networks of women could appropriate to maintain their financial independence.[28]

Therapeutic Multitasking in a Competitive Marketplace

Like Elizabeth Weed, Mary Watters recognized the lucrative potential of selling pharmaceuticals, and she added an apothecary business to her work as a nurse and doctress. Watters was also intent on generating enough income to support and educate her son, James, and to set him up in business. She continued to rely on the support of physicians, patrons, and the St. Joseph's Catholic Church community. Watters is listed in the important role of godparent in St. Joseph's baptismal rolls in 1784, 1785, 1794, and 1797. Mary's extensive social networks gave James access to prominent Philadelphians who facilitated his entry into the field of magazine publishing. This was quite an accomplishment for a widowed Irish immigrant. Her many achievements may have inspired Rush to sketch her biography as a woman with a "noble" calling. Beginning in 1789, James Watters learned his trade under the prominent printer Thomas Dobson, who specialized in medically related printed works.

As he advanced to chief editor, James became part of a group of ambitious young literati that included Charles Brockden Brown, one of America's first recognized novelists. After completing the first edition of Dobson's *Encyclopaedia* in the 1790s, James had gained enough experience to launch his own enterprise, the *Weekly Magazine*. The magazine's subscriber list featured Mary Watters's social, business, and religious contacts, including the Drinker family, Saint Joseph's Catholic Church parishioners, and most of the physicians in Philadelphia from both the Morgan and Shippen factions.[29]

While James established his publishing credentials, Mary continued her healing work as a nurse, doctress, and apothecary. In 1793, Rush published an article in the *Transactions of the College of Physicians of Philadelphia* describing his successful treatment of a man with smallpox, which highlighted Mary Watters's healing acumen. The College of Physicians and its publications were part of a medical public sphere that excluded women, and it is significant that Rush chose to commend Watters's practice in the medical society's journal. The *Transactions* were published by James Watters's mentor, Thomas Dobson, and Mary's inclusion in the article may have been discussed in the family's literary circles. In his article, Rush commended Watters for her "fidelity, judgment, and humanity, which contributed greatly to the recovery" of the patient described in his case study. According to Rush, Watters "cut off the heads of the pocks with a pair of scissors," bathed the wounds with rum and vinegar, administered medications, provided a strengthening diet, and maintained the sanitation of the patient's room. These were all skills that she would have learned during her wartime nursing service. Understanding the informal rules regarding the inclusion of a "lady's" name in print, Rush wrote that he hoped that the "College will permit me to mention her name in this commemoration." Perhaps thinking of his unfinished biography of Watters, he opined, "Whole pages of history have been filled with the exploits of persons less worthy of being known to the public." Apparently, Watters did not share Benjamin Rush's compunctions about displaying her name in print because she publicly promoted herself and her business.[30]

In her advertisement for Worm Cakes and other medicines on the back cover of the *Weekly Magazine*, Watters demonstrated her fluency in competitive advertising rhetoric. She marketed her Worm Cakes as both safe and effective in contrast to the "pernicious or dangerous Properties so evidently prevalent" in her competitors' products. Intestinal worms were a persistent and debilitating problem for children and adults in the late eighteenth century. Hookworms cause blood loss and anemia, tapeworms invade human tissues and organs, and roundworms migrate throughout the body and can infest the lungs. Standard medicines for worms included mercury, alcoholic distillations of wormwood (absinthe), and spirit of vitriol (sulfuric acid), which could be unpleasant or potentially toxic in high doses. By contrast, a customer could purchase Watters's secret preparation that, according to her ad, "effectively cleared the body" of intestinal worms and could be "taken with Safety and Propriety." Watters reassured customers that the purging operation of Worm Cakes was painless and effective in "grown persons as well as Children," and was "not attended by any bad Consequence." Her proprietary remedy could be had for the rather steep price of "*one Fourth of a Dollar for a single Cake.*" Watters noted that her preparation could be taken safely "even where a Doubt should arise whether the Person be really subject to Worms." Worm preparations were also used as an emmenagogues to regulate menstruation or as abortifacients, and Watters may have been signaling patients that she also treated women's health issues.[31]

In addition to Worm Cakes, Watters sold the popular patent medicine Huxham's Tincture of Bark, as well as remedies that appear frequently in women's medical recipe books, such as a compound tincture of lavender and remedies for eye ailments. She may have imported Huxham's Tincture or compounded it herself. The tincture was composed of Peruvian bark (cinchona bark or quinine), orange peel, cinnamon, and Virginia snakeroot, which were bruised and infused in brandy. Watters would have prescribed it for gastrointestinal ailments and for fevers, particularly during recurring summer and fall epidemics. Recipes for Huxham's Tincture were readily available in printed self-help medical manuals, such as Buchan's *Domestic Medicine*. Watters likely had access to a revised Philadelphia edition of *Domestic Medicine* printed by James's mentor, Thomas Dobson. Just as Elizabeth Weed provided medical advice along with her pharmaceuticals, it is likely that Watters provided consultations in the family shop as well as on house calls.[32]

As an Irish immigrant whose health care work had supported her son and connected him to prominent Philadelphians, Mary Watters must have felt personal satisfaction in James's accomplishments. In addition to the author Charles Brockden Brown, James's literary circle of upwardly mobile young men included the printer James Maxwell and the physician and poet Elihu Hubbard Smith, a founding editor of the *Medical Repository*, the first medical journal in the United States. Brown chose James Watters's *Weekly Magazine* to introduce his first serial novel, *The Man at Home*, followed by *Arthur Mervyn*. James Watters shared Brown's progressive views on women's rights and abolition, and his magazine articles deployed the rhetoric of sensibility to win his readers' hearts to these causes. Brown was a member of the Philadelphia Belles Lettres Club, and he helped to establish the Society for the Attainment of Useful Knowledge. Topics highlighted in the *Weekly Magazine* included the plight of enslaved people, self-help medical remedies, the culture of sensibility, women's rights, and women's access to the professions.[33]

Brown's article titled "The Rights of Women," which appeared in March 1798 editions of the *Weekly Magazine*, exemplifies the radical topics that James published. The article presents the contemporary debates over women's rights as a dialogue between Alcuin, a young schoolmaster, and Mrs. Carter, a wealthy, educated salonnière. Carter decried women's exclusion from "the liberal professions," including "the class of physicians." She argued that her grandmother practiced as a physician and "was in much request among her neighbours."[34] Brown's article reflected his literary circles' positive response to the publication of Mary Wollstonecraft's *Vindication of the Rights of Women* in 1792. After reading *Vindication*, Dr. Elihu Smith wrote to his sister, "Women are formed for something nobler than merely to be wives and mothers. Think for yourself." Mary Watters moved in circles that were proximate to these reformist ideas and conversations.[35]

Tragically, James Watters's promising career was cut short in the fall of 1798. He died of yellow fever even as he was publishing the serialized version of Charles Brockden Brown's novel *Arthur Mervyn*, which chronicled the disastrous 1793 epidemic. Mary Watters briefly took over the *Weekly Magazine* and then sold it to another editor. In the February 1799 edition, the new editor eulogized James Watters as an "excellent young man" who was "gifted with a clear and steady mind, strong intellect, and judicious taste, combined with a benevolent and virtuous heart." He "bid fair to rise into public notice—a pattern of worth to his associates . . . and the support of a declining parent's age." In her diary, Elizabeth Drinker noted James's death, calling him "an industrious young man." Drinker recognized that "his poor mother, Nurse Waters [*sic*], will be almost heartbroken." However, Drinker noted wryly that Watters's grief had not deprived her of "her faculty of talking." Elizabeth Drinker's husband, Henry, administered James's will. Mary Watters must have felt the genuine pain of the *Weekly Magazine*'s florid tribute to James: "But alas! the gay and flattering prospects are forever flown; and he, on whom these budding hopes were founded, now rests in the cold and dreary tomb!" Unlike George Weed Junior, James did not survive to rise in Philadelphia society. Nonetheless, by effectively publicizing their healing practices, Mary Watters and Elizabeth Weed Nevell ensured that their sons had the educational and financial foundations to excel in the early Republic's emerging market economy.[36]

Mary Waters and Elizabeth Weed Nevell exemplify female medical entrepreneurs who successfully navigated the rise of medical consumerism in the early Republic. They leveraged increasing consumer demand for affordable health care and accessible pharmaceuticals to sustain their businesses in a competitive marketplace. When needed, women practitioners used the press and the courts to promote their products and protect their intellectual property. In an expanding and commercializing nation, Delaware Valley residents wondered how to tell the difference between authentic and counterfeit medical providers and medicines. The public, printed battles among Philadelphia's fractious physicians increased medical consumers' anxieties over the trustworthiness of practitioners' claims to authority. Women healers such as Watters and Weed Nevell learned the business and advertising skills that bolstered their reputations as authoritative and authentic healers. In the process, they shaped customers' expectations that health was a commodity that money could buy.

One of Mary and James Watters' legacies is the serial publication of Charles Brockden Brown's novel *Arthur Mervyn*, which chronicles the 1793 Philadelphia yellow fever epidemic. In the book's preface, Brown opined, "The evils of pestilence by which this city has lately been afflicted will probably form an aera in its history." *Arthur Mervyn* is awash with the rhetoric of sensibility and with characters that embody self-sacrificing benevolence in the face of a health care crisis. The novel's physician-narrator and his wife demonstrate sensibility by risking their lives to nurse fever-stricken patients. Brown hoped that the epidemic would promote "schemes of reformation and improvement" in the City of Brotherly Love. He explained, "Men only require to be made acquainted with distress for their compassion and their charity to be awakened," because "the evils of disease and poverty" call "forth benevolence." The deadly 1793 yellow fever epidemic provided opportunities for women of the lower social orders to demonstrate their compassionate medical acumen. However, when the city's African American women stepped forward to provide nursing care for white Philadelphians, debates over issues of race as well as class framed anxiety-filled discourses.[37]

CHAPTER 7

The Fevered Racial Politics of Healing

The mysterious illness appeared first on the Delaware River waterfront in early August 1793. Initially, Philadelphians were not alarmed by a few fever-induced deaths on Water Street because the city could be a sickly place in the sweltering heat of late summer. However, by August 19, as cases spread toward the market district, Dr. Benjamin Rush announced the advent of a devastating epidemic. As church bells tolled the mounting fever deaths, Philadelphia elites fled the city, leaving local, state, and federal governments in disarray. Those left behind hid in their homes, ignoring the plight of dying neighbors. Skilled healers were in demand, but they were scarce amid a yellow fever epidemic that ultimately killed approximately 10 percent of the city's population. The enormity of the disaster reprised American Revolutionary discourses of martial masculinity and self-sacrificing republican virtues, as few people of benevolent sensibility defended the city from the epidemical invader. Some African American women seized this opportunity to display their humanitarian civic service by delivering desperately needed nursing care.[1]

On September 7, a public notice appeared in the Philadelphia *Independent Gazetteer* next to a dramatic rendition of France's radical Declaration of the Rights of Man and Citizen. Mayor Matthew Clarkson announced that Absalom Jones and Richard Allen, the leaders of "the [Free] *African Society*," touched by the distresses" of the prevailing epidemic, offered to mobilize women and men in their community to provide nurses to attend the sick. Volunteers Sarah Bass, Mary Scott, and other members of this Black benevolent organization risked their lives to provide twenty-four-hour nursing care for white Philadelphians whom sources describe as raging "with all the fury [of] madness," "vomiting blood, and screaming enough to chill" their caregivers "with horror." Bass and her fellow Free African Society (FAS) nurses

Figure 11. *Sarah Bass Allen* (1764–1849). Free African Society nurse and founding mother of Bethel AME Church. Courtesy Mother Bethel AME Church,
Philadelphia.

asserted their healing authority as humanitarian activist healers to validate
African Americans' worthiness for civil equality.[2]

The yellow fever epidemic conveyed FAS nurses out of historiographical
obscurity and onto center stage in a documented public debate over African
American citizenship. However, instead of offering accolades for their public service, the Philadelphia publisher Mathew Carey accused "the vilest" of
the African American nurses of theft and profiteering in his best-selling "real-
time" October 1793 pamphlet titled *A Short Account of the Malignant Fever.*
His vehement response suggests that he recognized the power of the nurses'

performance of healing humanitarianism. Carey tapped into long-standing racialized discourses that denigrated people of African descent. He exploited stereotypes that portrayed hired nurses as drunkards, thieves, and prostitutes. At the FAS nurses' insistence, Jones and Allen published a pamphlet in the epidemic's aftermath titled *A Narrative of the Proceedings of the Black People, during the Late Awful Calamity . . . And a Refutation of Some Censures Thrown upon Them.* In their account the FAS leaders asserted, "In consequence of a partial representation of the conduct of the people who were employed to nurse the sick . . . we are solicited, by a number of those who feel themselves injured thereby . . . to step forward and declare the facts." Although historians emphasize Jones and Allen's authorship, Bass, Scott, and the FAS nurses provided the impetus for the pamphlet. The *Narrative* refutes Cary's slander and mobilizes the popular rhetoric of sensibility to argue that the nurses were model "Good Samaritans" and soldiers whose valiant service was forgotten in the battle's aftermath.[3]

For Sarah Bass, Mary Scott, and their colleagues, nursing was both an act of medical benevolence and an enactment of political street theater. The nurses' performance embodied complex, intertwined conceptual strands reflecting gendered notions of evangelical sensibility and virtuous republican self-sacrifice that were complicated by conflicting, evolving meanings of nursing in the public sphere. While the dramatic narrative of the 1793 Philadelphia yellow fever epidemic has long interested historians, it still raises unanswered questions. Who were the nurse volunteers? Why did they think that public volunteer nursing would convince the Philadelphia community of their civic virtue? Unfortunately, like those of many eighteenth-century Black women, the voices of the FAS nurses, their healing practices, and their early politicized activism are difficult to recover because they left few documentary traces. The historian Erica Armstrong Dunbar has built on classic works by Gary Nash, Julie Winch, and Richard Newman to emphasize African American women's central role in Philadelphia's Black community formation. However, Black women healers are particularly invisible in historiographies of nursing and medicine in the late eighteenth century.[4]

In the *Narrative*, Jones and Allen explicitly linked nursing to the culture of "feeling" sensibility while making the striking assertion that nursing is "a considerable art, derived from experience, as well as the exercise of the finer feelings of humanity." As we saw in the previous chapter, hired nurses were associated with prostitution, drunkenness, and disorderliness. By contrast, the FAS nurses reframed African American women's public health care work as an act of benevolent civic virtue, rather than as mere menial service for financial gain. This was sixty years before Florence Nightingale introduced a global audience to the notion of nursing as a humanitarian pursuit for white middle-class "ladies" through her work in military hospitals during the Crimean War. Nightingale famously argued that "nursing is an art . . . the finest of Fine Arts." Although Nightingale and her British nurses initially engendered censure, they ultimately garnered international accolades for their soldierly services. However, Bass and her colleagues preempted Nightingale with their public nursing service during a national crisis. In 1793, they advanced a unique, positive image of African American nurses who exhibited "finer feelings" and defended their city from an invading epidemic with compassionate care. Through their public healing actions, the nurses wrote themselves and their community into narratives of national belonging. For Bass and the FAS nurses, healing authority was deeply intertwined with their assertions of religious power, political legitimacy, and antislavery resistance.[5]

Of the numerous female nurses, only Sarah Bass and Mary Scott are named in the *Narrative*. Mary Scott may have been related to a William Scott, cited as a founding member of Absalom Jones's St. Thomas Church in 1794, or a "John Scott (African)" listed as a "mariner" in a 1795 Philadelphia city directory. However, no additional information has been discovered. Although the outlines of Bass's life are hazy, she left more traces than Scott because she married Richard Allen in 1801 and became the "founding mother" of the African Methodist Episcopal (AME) Church. Sarah Bass Allen's passage from slavery to freedom and then to healing activist for Black equality anticipated the path taken by many early nineteenth-century freedwomen. Bass helps to put a face on the otherwise nameless and faceless FAS nurses. A brief backward look at Sarah Bass's early years provides the context for examining Philadelphia's African American nurses' activism in 1793.[6]

Healing Authority amid the Constrictions of Slavery

Considering her importance in AME history, there are surprisingly few details of Sarah Bass's life before her marriage to Richard Allen at Philadelphia's

Saint George's Methodist Church in 1801, when she was identified as a freed-woman. Bass's death certificate, her obituary, and AME histories record that she was born enslaved in Isle of Wight County, Virginia, in 1764.[7] This coastal or Tidewater county was a tobacco-growing and mixed agricultural region on the south side of the James River. It was home to both enslaved and free African Americans. Genealogies of Nathaniel Basse (or Bass), the English founder of the county, note that his male family decedents inter-married with both Nansemond Indian and African American women and they often identified with their wives' communities. Sarah's exact relation-ship to this family is unclear, because Jones and Allen call Sarah Bass a widow in the *Narrative*. Nonetheless, Sarah grew up in a county with rich multicultural healing traditions. The county's free Black community and ethnically mixed families taught her how slavery's constrictive boundaries might be crossed.[8]

In Tidewater Virginia, young Sarah would have known free and en-slaved African American midwives, herb doctors, and nurses who devel-oped reputations as valued healers among white slaveholders and within communities of color. The historian Sara Collini has recovered evidence that free and enslaved Black women in this area were paid for their mid-wifery work. Like free white midwives, these healers also treated women's gynecological issues and provided health care for infants, children, and adults. Black midwives, nurses, and doctors grew herbs, mixed medicines, and provided the bulk of health care on slave plantations. Enslaved healers and midwives were granted unusual geographic mobility, which allowed them to create healing networks as they traveled to neighboring plantations. A midwife named Nell, enslaved on George Mason's Gunston Hall planta-tion, was paid approximately twelve shillings per delivery. Further up the Potomac River, George Washington recognized Nell's skills and hired her to care for pregnant women on his Mount Vernon estate. He paid Nell's twelve-shilling fee for delivering the enslaved woman Sall, which was comparable to what he paid white midwives. Washington later paid Nell ten dollars for attending at the childbirths of several other enslaved women at an outlying farm. Kate, another enslaved woman, petitioned Washington to pay her a regular salary to serve as Mount Vernon's midwife, arguing that "she was full as well qualified for this purpose" as those whom Washington "was pay-ing twelve or £15 a year." Although enslaved midwives garnered healing au-thority, the inhumanity of the slave system placed them in the paradoxical role of birthing children who became the property of slaveholders. Having a healthy enslaved workforce benefited slaveholders. Nonetheless, midwives were also on the front lines of slave resistance when they used their skills to protect ill patients from coercive work or to assist enslaved people in feigning sickness to thwart the plantation labor regime. As the historian Sharla Fett argues, health and healing were arenas of power struggles on slave plantations, particularly when enslaved people preferred practitioners of African descent rather than placing themselves under the control of white doctors or midwives.[9]

Despite scarce documentation, archaeologists and historians have demonstrated the cultural persistence of West African and West Central African healing practices on Virginia slave plantations. Although these extensive African geographical regions were home to numerous unique healing cultures, scholars have identified some broad similarities. Enslaved peoples transported to eastern Virginia shared a holistic perspective of health that encompassed the spiritual balance as well as the physical wellness of communities, families, and individuals. Women and men who were community elders, healing adepts, and spiritually gifted healers wielded healing authority within a natural world that was animated by powerful spirits of ancestors, animals, and flora. Enslaved West Africans brought the knowledge of plants used in healing, such as okra leaves, sorghum, and oil palm, which they blended with new information about European and North American medicinal herbs. Archaeologists have found artifacts near enslaved peoples' living quarters that reflect West African healing traditions. Examples include "cosmograms" inscribed on ritual medicine bowls and "conjurers' kits," which are collections of objects such as bones, shells, animal parts, or herbs used by diviners for healing rituals. Cosmograms were drawings that usually included a cross within a circle. However, depending on their cultural origins, cosmograms could include complex arrangements of arrows, rectangles, small circles, or stars. During healing rituals, practitioners deployed cosmograms to create a locus of power that mediated between different spiritual realms and between the living and the dead. Healers might combine herbs and spiritual conjuration to help individuals and communities experiencing physical suffering or emotional discord to regain a healthful balance.[10]

Their spiritual authority and their knowledge of African, Native American, and North American herbs imbued Black healers with the power to harm as well as heal. Euro-Americans' fears of this potentially harmful medical acumen is apparent in laws enacted in 1748 in Virginia and in the late 1740s in South Carolina, which prohibited enslaved people from compounding or administering medications. However, it is unclear how well the assemblies enforced the laws, as whites were torn between fears of African American healers' power and their desire for Black practitioners' expert medical knowledge.[11] For example, "Negroe Caesar's Cure for Poison and Rattlesnake Bite" circulated throughout the colonies and appeared in William Buchan's popular *Domestic Medicine*, women's recipe books, the *Pennsylvania Gazette*, and numerous other colonial newspapers. The remedy's ingredients, including horehound, sassafras, and plantain, reflect medicinal exchanges between peoples of European, American Indian, and African descent. The South Carolina Assembly so valued Caesar's healing knowledge that they granted him freedom and a lifetime annuity of one hundred pounds per year. Although some Euro-Americans attempted to disempower Black healers by devaluing their work as lowly, menial labor, their practices were also suffused with spiritual power and medical expertise. This tension between what Sharla Fett describes as "contradictory elements of skill and servitude" followed African Americans like Sarah Bass into freedom.[12]

As a founder of the African Methodist Episcopal Church, Sarah Bass was instrumental in weaving together religious and healing traditions to create an evangelical denomination that valued its African roots and supported Blacks' aspirations of freedom and equality. When free and enslaved African Americans in Virginia began to embrace the Methodist, Baptist, and other evangelical denominations in the mid-eighteenth century, they created new hybrid religious forms that incorporated aspects of West African spirituality and healing. Healing markers that were central to both West African religions and Christianity, such as the powers of water and blood, allowed African Americans to blend aspects of their religious practices. Even as a child, Sarah was exposed to radical forms of evangelicalism that promised spiritual freedom and supported antislavery tenets. Tidewater Virginia was an early hotbed of radical Methodism, and numerous Bass family members were adherents. In the late 1760s, the Methodist minister Robert Williams's fiery antislavery preaching to mixed Black and white audiences led the Norfolk mayor to exclaim, "If we permit such fellows as these to come here we shall have an Insurrection of the Negroes." Williams may have influenced the self-appointed Black Methodist minister Mary Perth, who recalled that she often strapped her infant to her back and walked twenty miles to preach in open-air meetings near Isle of Wight County. In a culture in which spiritual and healing authority were intertwined, Sarah imbibed the egalitarian tenets of radical evangelicalism, which offered opportunities for Black women to claim legitimacy as preachers, spiritual leaders, and healers.[13]

The Ambiguities of Liberty and Slavery in the City of Brotherly Love

In 1772, when Sarah was about eight years old, church histories record that she was "brought" to Philadelphia. Sarah's passage to Philadelphia coincided with Lord Chief Justice Mansfield's pathbreaking 1772 decision on the James Somerset case in London. Somerset was an enslaved man from Virginia, who upon arriving in England, fled his slaveholder and claimed to be free. English abolitionists sued for Somerset's freedom. Although Mansfield had not intended to make a broad ruling on slavery, his decision that English common law disallowed slavery on free English soil prompted rumors that if enslaved people could get to Britain, they would be freed. A *Virginia Gazette* runaway advertisement described an enslaved man "named BACCUS" who "will probably endeavor to pass for a Freeman . . . *and attempt to get on Board some Vessel bound for Great Britain, from the Knowledge he has of . . . Somerset's Case.*" Sarah arrived in Philadelphia during an uptick in the number of runaway slaves from Tidewater Virginia, where she and Somerset had lived.[14]

However, there is no record of whether Sarah was taken or sold as a slave, or whether she fled with family members. While men traveling alone or in groups predominate in runaway slave advertisements, occasionally families attempted to flee bondage.[15] A 1772 *Virginia Gazette* runaway advertisement offered a reward for the recovery of twenty-five-year-old Doll, "a short well-made woman," who was fleeing with her husband, Nat, their daughter Sarah "about six years old," and a male friend named Cato. Doll and Sarah each fetched only a twenty-shilling reward, while Nat and Cato merited three pounds. Women fled with children and male partners to escape potential sexual abuse by slaveowners, harsh work conditions, and the pain of family separations. Running away was an act of politicized resistance against a violent and disempowering labor regime that commodified women's productive work as well as their reproductive labor. Runaways often absconded to cities like Philadelphia, where they could blend into free Black communities and fashion themselves as freed people. An advertisement in the *Pennsylvania Gazette* described an enslaved runaway named Simon, who "can bleed and draw Teeth" and was "pretending to be a great Doctor and very religious." Although the slaveholder who placed the ad attempted to dismiss Simon's claims to healing expertise as counterfeit, it is more likely that Simon's medical acumen and spiritual authority would have helped him assume a free identity. The Pennsylvania Abolition Society assisted Philadelphia's runaways in obtaining their freedom, and AME church histories posit that Sarah Bass was later manumitted by this organization.[16]

Within a few years of Sarah Bass's arrival in Philadelphia, the Delaware Valley was engulfed in the Revolutionary War. The Revolutionaries' ideological cries for liberty from the yoke of imperial Britain resonated on a more personal level for Black residents living in slavery or in tenuous freedom. Free and enslaved African Americans had the difficult choice of escaping to a promised liberty in British-occupied areas or remaining to assert their personal freedom. Bass's future husband, Richard Allen, aligned with the patriots and worked as a carter for the Continental Army to earn the money to purchase his freedom. As she grew into young womanhood, Sarah Bass experienced the ambiguities of the Revolutionary promises of liberty alongside the realities of racism. In 1780, the Pennsylvania Assembly passed a Gradual Emancipation Act, and in 1787 the Pennsylvania Abolition Society reorganized under a mandate to abolish slavery. That same year, the Constitutional Convention in Philadelphia set a date to end the international slave trade but maintained the institution of slavery. Despite their early antislavery agitation, Black Philadelphians faced social, political, and economic marginalization. Nonetheless, by mid-1793, Philadelphia's African American population was 3,320 out of a total population of 51,200. Sarah Bass spent her young adulthood amid the largest free Black community in the United States.[17]

Philadelphia City Directories in the 1790s listed free Black people in a variety of occupations. Men were employed as laborers or artisans, while African American women worked or developed businesses as boardinghouse owners, midwives, teachers, vendors, herb sellers, healers, washerwomen, or live-in domestics. Many women provided nursing services as a part of their domestic duties. Although city directories listed Absalom Jones as a shopkeeper, and Richard Allen as a shoemaker and a master chimney sweep with apprentices, both also worked as therapeutic bleeders. Black women are underrepresented in these sources, and neither Sarah Bass nor Mary Scott were listed.[18]

The scarcity of documentation regarding African American practitioners belies their presence. In a journal from a slightly later period, the Philadelphia Quaker reformer Anne Parrish noted that an aged, free African

American woman named Anna Dalemoa Bellamy sought assistance from a relief society after Bellamy escaped from captivity by an unnamed Native American group. Parrish described Bellamy as "a woman of education—and called by some the black doctor—she professes—bone setting bleeding tooth drawing—and cureing wounds." During her captivity, Bellamy would have had opportunities to observe Indigenous healers' acknowledged expertise in bone-setting and wound care. Bellamy's educational accomplishments and her transcultural healing skills added weight to her healing authority. Laurel Thatcher Ulrich found similar evidence that the residents of Hallowell, Maine, sought the services of an itinerant "Negro woman doctor." Considering that women played prominent roles in health care, it is likely that some FAS women were experienced in providing healing and nursing care.[19]

In response to increasing numbers of Black workers, Allen and Jones founded the Free African Society in 1787 to provide needed social services. Although they were members of St. George's Methodist Church, they also began plans for a separate, autonomous African church. Sarah Bass was likely a congregant at St. George's and a participant in FAS activities. Bass may well have joined Allen, Jones, Sarah Dougherty, Jane Murray, and others who walked out of St. George's to protest segregated seating. Bass was certainly a founding member of the ultimately autonomous Bethel AME Church, because she appears in one of Bethel's original two Methodist Bible study class lists along with Richard Allen and his first wife, Flora. Bass and other women parishioners were central to church and community building by creating supportive female religious networks, leading "prayer bands," and preaching in public.[20]

Black churchwomen like Sarah Bass were also responsible for developing a perception of African American Christian respectability that contributed to the "social uplift" of their communities. Churchwomen also monitored the members of their community to ensure that they conformed to standards of female Christian sobriety, modesty, and sexual purity. Although this watchfulness was intrusive, it underlines Black women's early activist strategy of "social uplift" through the performance of respectability and industry. As Allen noted in the abolitionist tract appended to the *Narrative*, "much depends" on free Blacks' behavior, as "the enemies of freedom" could cite freed persons' who were "lazy and idle" as an excuse to "keep many in bondage." However, Black women's public roles conflicted with Black men's efforts to reject the vestiges of slavery's disempowerment and to assert their masculinity by conforming to gender roles that expected men to be the protectors and providers for submissive female kin. Free African American church-women often found themselves amid these conflicting gendered cross-currents that required them to assume the modest domesticity of elite white women while simultaneously working outside the home to support families, as well as engaging publicly in antislavery and civil rights activism. Nonetheless, by participating in organizations like the FAS and the African Church, Black women and men could work together to support their community.[21]

It is likely that twenty-nine-year-old Bass was among the two hundred people who attended the celebratory banquet commemorating the raising of the African Church on August 22, 1793. That miserably hot summer day must have been alive with possibilities. The smell of freshly sawn wood and the soaring roof beams evinced the proud words of the mutual aid organization's articles of incorporation: "We the free Africans and their descendants, of the City of Philadelphia." As FAS members celebrated the fulfillment of their dream of an independent church, Philadelphia newspapers reported that in revolutionary France, people of color appropriated the French National Assembly's radical assertions of liberty, equality, and brotherhood to claim citizenship and to agitate for abolition. According to the *Philadelphia Independent Gazetteer*, a marching band of Black Parisians paraded into the National Assembly, celebrating new abolitionist legislation that "raised them to the rank of MEN." Other writers feared that "the contagion of liberty is catching and spreading," since it appeared that the French Revolution was destabilizing race, class, and gender hierarchies. Liberty's fire had certainly ignited slave revolts in the French Caribbean colony of Saint-Domingue, and refugees flooding into Philadelphia brought news of people of color seizing freedom by force. James Forten, a prominent Black businessman, later remembered that members of Philadelphia's African American community were electrified by news from Saint-Domingue, but they also recognized that they needed to keep a low profile to avoid exacerbating Euro-Americans' anxieties over slave revolts. Sarah Bass and other Black Philadelphians at the African Church dedication shared a renewed community consciousness amid transatlantic waves of radical revolutionary fervor.[22]

At the church-raising celebration, FAS members served a banquet to express appreciation for their prominent white supporters in attendance. Dr. Benjamin Rush recorded that he offered two optimistic toasts: "'Peace on earth and good will to men,' and 'May African churches everywhere soon succeed African bondage.'" He added, "After which we rose, and the black people (men and women) took our seats. Six of the most respectable of the white company waited on them, while Mr. Nicholson, myself, and two others . . . set down with them." While the historian Gary Nash argues for the "separate but equal" aspects of this dining turnabout, Rush's inclusion of African American women is also significant. For women born into slavery like Sarah Bass, taking an equal place at the table with white men while being *served* by them represented a powerful reversal of racial, class, and gender hierarchies. Rush noted that the FAS leader William Gray was moved to tears of sensibility as he addressed the gathering. For Methodists like Bass, Gray, and Allen, the dinner suggested the biblical parable of the wedding feast in which marginalized people experienced justice and claimed an equal place at the millennial banquet table as the true inheritors of God's kingdom. As Nash points out, it was a short step from claims of spiritual equality to African Americans' demands for civil equality and justice.[23]

"Our Services Were the Production of Real Sensibility"

With this empowering millennial imagery fresh in their minds, Bass and the FAS volunteers placed themselves on the front lines of a deadly epidemic. According to Jones and Allen's *Narrative*, Sarah Bass was "a poor black widow" who "gave all the assistance that she could" to several families without remuneration. Mary Scott's nursing services were so valued by one family that they provided her with an annuity. A desperately ill white couple offered "great wages" to a "young black woman" for nursing services, but "she replied, 'I will not go for money.'" The nurse contracted yellow fever. An "elderly black woman nursed with great diligence" going from "place to place rendering every service in her power without an eye to reward." Although the pamphlet war between the FAS and the publisher Mathew Carey became embroiled in economic issues over the value of nurses' wages, Jones and Allen made the point that FAS nurses provided benevolent *volunteer* services, as appropriate for refined charitable women. By disengaging their actions from the dependency of wage labor, Bass and the nurses strengthened their performance of religious and civic service.[24]

However, since most free Black women were in fact dependent on employer referrals for their work as domestics and nurses, the issue of respectability was also woven into concerns that character defamation would negatively affect FAS nurses' future earning potential. The wage issue was complicated by the fact that some caregivers detached themselves from the FAS so that they could accept higher wages offered by employers competing for their services. Jones and Allen attempted to fix reasonable prices for nursing services, but they had no control over the actions of nurses outside FAS auspices amid a civic crisis in which all goods and services were wildly overpriced. Bass and the nurses inadvertently found themselves hemmed in between the performance of elite Ladies Bountiful, who benevolently provided health care gratis, and Mathew Carey's depiction of degraded, lower-class "old wives," who charged for their services. This was particularly problematic during the height of the epidemic, when some nurses received remuneration pressed on them by grateful patients in appreciation for their life-saving services.[25]

In addition, the FAS nurses' work underscored a tension between the nurses' public civic activism to advance Black equality and their private performance of respectability and sensibility as dignified African American "ladies." In a racialized milieu, Black women healers had difficulty finding the balance achieved by elite Euro-American healers such as Margaret Hill Morris and Dr. Benjamin Rush, who asserted that their services were based on religiously motivated benevolence, even as they received payment. In the *Narrative*, Jones and Allen attempted to keep the focus on benevolence rather than wages, arguing, "we could with certainty assure the public that we have seen more humanity, more real sensibility from the poor blacks than the poor whites." They further invoked the culture of sensibility by affirming, "Our services were the production of real sensibility." By refusing wages and claiming "feeling" self-sacrificing virtues, Bass and the nurses enacted their superiority to white citizens who fled the embattled city. Mathew Carey's slanderous account of the nurses demonstrates that he recognized the potentially powerful implications of the nurses' actions.[26]

Sensibility served as a compelling rhetoric for those active in the evangelical and abolitionist movements, including Bass and the FAS. As we have seen, the language of sensibility evoked sensations of sympathy to prompt benevolent actions to comfort pathetic sufferers. Even nonliterate women and men shared an active oral culture that allowed them to appropriate evangelicalism's potentially subversive, egalitarian theology through camp meetings, sermons, and hymns. Lyrics to hymns popular with Methodists underscored the shared belief that to be truly human was to feel and to bleed sympathetically along with sufferers:

Blest is the man whose softening heart
Feels all another's pain . . .

And bleeds in pity o'er the wound
He wants the power to heal.

Other hymns affirmed that providing medical care for the poor, sick, and imprisoned was akin to caring for Christ himself.[27] In his antislavery tract
Thoughts Upon Slavery, Methodism's founder John Wesley deployed the language of sensibility in questions he posed to an imagined slave trader: "Are
you a *man?* Do you never *feel* another's pain? Have you no Sympathy?" In a
description of a beaten enslaved man, Wesley invoked the image of Jesus's
crucifixion by asking, "When you saw the flowing eyes . . . or the bleeding
sides . . . of your fellow-creatures, was you a stone, or a brute?" According to
the scholar Brycchan Carey, abolitionist sensibility rested on the central tenets that "a sympathetic heart is common to all human beings" and that
"equality of feeling proves the equal status of all human beings."[28]

For evangelical ministers like Wesley and Richard Allen, healing was an
ideal way to minister to people's physical and well as spiritual health. Wesley
published his popular medical manual, *Primitive Physic: Or, An Easy and
Natural Method of Curing Most Diseases*, to educate itinerant Methodist min-
sters to treat their congregants' illnesses. He also appointed female "deacon-
ess" healers to visit the sick. Jones and Allen described the FAS nurses' work
during the epidemic as a "charge we took upon us," which, for Methodists,
implied a religious mission and a divine calling. Bass and the FAS nurses'
endeavors embodied Christlike service by laying down their lives to save
others. In Christian theology, this was the greatest act of love and paralleled
Christ's sacrifice on the cross. In evangelicalism's reverse spiritual economy,
the least became the greatest in God's millennial kingdom: a self-sacrificing
servant-healer could become an empowered leader. In this period, the discourses of religious sensibility wielded cultural power.[29]

Although Benjamin Rush and other antislavery activists used representations of "poor Africans" and pathetic, disempowered, enslaved people to
win public sympathy for their cause, these images also served to render Blacks
as helpless victims. However, as African-descended people served as leaders
in the abolition movement and entered the public sphere of print media, they
contested these stereotypes. Jones and Allen joined other Black abolitionist
writers such as the American poet Phillis Wheatley and the British authors
Olaudah Equiano and Ignatius Sancho, who used the rhetoric of sensibility
to persuade their readers of the hard-hearted immorality of slavery. African
Americans' entrance into the virtual "republic of print" posed a strong

argument for their intellectual equality as well as their humanity. Jones and Allen's *Narrative* invoked the authority of the printed word and introduced Bass and the Black nurses' humanitarian civic service to a transatlantic abolitionist audience.[30]

As the *Narrative*'s appended antislavery tract makes clear, Jones, Allen, Bass, and the nurses understood that progress toward free African American equality was predicated on the emancipation of those still enslaved. Deploying the rhetoric of sensibility, Jones and Allen invited their readers to "sympathize with us in the heart-rendering distress, when the husband is separated from the wife, and the parents from the children" by their cruel slaveholders. The ministers argued that enslaved families felt the acute pain of separations just as Euro-American families would, which should rouse "righteous indignation" as the "tear of sensibility trickles from your eye." Jones and Allen made the further theological assertion that all peoples, including those of African descent, are "children of one father who made of one blood all the nations of the earth." The abolitionist and evangelical movements provided a politico-religious platform for FAS leaders to assert African Americans' humanity and civil equality as evidenced by the FAS nurses' benevolent healing services, which were "the production of real sensibility."[31]

"Sensible" self-sacrificing evangelicalism dovetailed nicely with the "feeling" rhetoric of classical republicanism that was popularized during the American Revolution and reintroduced during the epidemic. Although classical republicanism or civic humanism originated in the ancient Greco-Roman world, it was reprised during the western European Renaissance and the Enlightenment. This ideology argued that virtuous, male, property-holding citizens should be active in public life and should subordinate their self-interest for the common good.[32] In the fall of 1793, Philadelphia newspaper articles echoed this rhetoric by emphasizing the bonds of masculine sensibility and calling for self-sacrificing citizens to battle the epidemic that was invading the city. Editors lauded benevolent Philadelphians, like the FAS's colleague Dr. Benjamin Rush, who remained "at their posts" in the city. Philadelphians were familiar with this rhetoric of "feeling" military manhood portrayed in literary fiction and in pathos-laden dramas such as Joseph Addison's *Cato*. This tear-drenched play, based on the life of a Stoic Roman statesman, features virtuous citizens who, by definition, sacrifice personal interests for the good of the republic and volunteer as soldiers to defend a besieged city. This genre lauding the virtues of classical republicanism was particularly popular among elite military officers who became politicians, including George Washington, Alexander Hamilton, and Benjamin Rush. The bonds of sympathy between martial "bands of brothers" coexisted with their assertions of "masculine" rationality. Bass and the nurses embodied this rational masculinized soldierly image, which contrasted sharply with stereotypes of African Americans as irrational and disempowered.[33]

Leaders of the early Republic like Dr. Benjamin Rush maintained that the "feeling" camaraderie that soldiers fashioned during the Revolutionary War could be redeployed to bind citizens together and build the new nation. Rush promoted a novel vision of the "man of enlightened sensibility and virtue— the new republican citizen." His model citizen embodied Christian morality and benevolence along with self-sacrificing classical republicanism. He asserted that sensibility must be constantly "exercised" by a "familiarity with scenes of distress from poverty and disease," which produce virtue in the citizen. By Rush's reckoning, their nursing role allowed Bass and the FAS nurses to "exercise" the "finer feelings" of their sensibility and thus demonstrate civic virtues. In a letter, Rush stated that he gave a "hint to the black people" that their nursing services in the epidemic offered a "noble opportunity" to "place them, on point of civil and religious privileges, upon a footing with" white Philadelphians. By explicitly linking healing, sensibility, and citizenship, Rush encouraged FAS members to envision their health care services during the invading epidemic as a pathway to incorporation into the body politic. Jones and Allen chose to "imitate the Doctor's benevolence." FAS leaders and nurses embodied evangelical, abolitionist, and classical republican sensibility. Healing bodies of the corruption of yellow fever symbolized curing the body politic of the sinful diseases of slavery and racial discrimination.[34]

By contrast, the publisher Mathew Carey promoted his version of the civic crisis to advance his own standing in Philadelphia society and to exclude African Americans from recognition as model citizens. As an Irish Catholic and a relative outsider, Carey mobilized the rhetoric of martial sensibility to opine that he served his "tour of duty" as a patriotic member of Mayor Clarkson's emergency civic committee. However, Jones and Allen noted that "Mr. Carey, although chosen a member of [Mayor Clarkson's] band of worthies," quickly fled the city. Clarkson's committee minutes confirm Carey's absence. Carey also lauded the civic virtues of other white male Philadelphians, particularly the merchant Stephen Girard, who organized the Bush Hill fever hospital. According to Carey, Girard worked as much as six hours a day and occasionally assisted patients by "wiping the sweat off their brows . . . and performing many offices of kindness to them at which nice feelings in any other circumstances would revolt." These "laudable and dangerous offices" merited "the unceasing gratitude of [his] fellow citizens." Although Girard's work deserved merit, Carey's encomiums to the merchant must have been particularly galling to Sarah Bass and the slandered FAS nurses, who soldiered on for days without respite in direct patient care.[35]

"Our Duty to Do All We Could to Our Suffering Fellow Mortals"

Nursing a yellow fever patient certainly required martial fortitude. As physicians fell ill, died, or left the city, Bass and the FAS nurses increasingly acted as primary health care providers for patients facing a complex disease process that in current medical terms could include liver impairment, bleeding disorders, shock, and multiple organ failure. Contemporaries described patients with "chills, fevers, headaches, nausea, retching, nosebleeds," and jaundiced eyes. After a brief remission, patients exhibited "puking, fearful straining of the stomach, the black vomit, comatose delirium, purplish discoloration of the whole body," and finally death. Observers noted the overpowering stench of the sickroom. Jones and Allen recorded that the FAS nurses worked alone and were "up night and day, without any one to relieve them." They were "worn down with fatigue and want of sleep" after working constantly for seven to ten days—despite warnings from the College of Physicians that overexertion and exhaustion increased the risk of contracting yellow fever.[36] Nurses administered doses of calomel, jalap, snakeroot, and laudanum, determining the timing and dosage on the basis of their assessment of patients' symptoms. Inducing vomiting and diarrhea, emetics and purgatives necessitated frequent laundering of linens, requiring nurses to haul water from wells that were running dry. Jones and Allen emphasized that African American nurses often left "their dearest connections sick" and "suffering for want" while they nursed in white Philadelphians' homes. In a letter, Rush recorded a playful comment made to an FAS nurse he met on his rounds: "'Hah! Mama,' said I, 'we black folks have come into demand at last.' She squeezed my hand and we parted." Although Rush's appropriation of African American dialect was patronizing, his underlined phrase "we black folks" suggests that he identified with the nurses' efforts and confirmed that the white community valued their services.[37]

Rush assured the FAS leaders that African Americans were less likely to contract yellow fever than white Philadelphians. However, it is clear from

Bush Hill hospital records that by the first week in September, Blacks were dying of the disease. Allen himself was seriously ill by October. At least 198 African Americans died from yellow fever out of a resident population of slightly over two thousand. Rush's beliefs about Blacks' immunity may relate to physicians' observations that people born in Africa or the Caribbean were less likely to contract the disease. Doctors did not know that yellow fever was a mosquito-borne disease that conferred lifelong immunity. Indeed, physicians were unsure of yellow fever's origins and they quarreled bitterly over its etiology in newspaper articles. Rush and his backers argued that yellow fever stemmed from miasmas arising from rotten coffee on the docks, while his opponents maintained that it was a foreign disease brought by French colonists fleeing Saint-Domingue. Nonetheless, Philadelphia's African American community recognized that those who had never been exposed to yellow fever were as susceptible as white Philadelphians. The nurses' potentially self-sacrificing services and their familial sacrifices caused Bass and the FAS nurses to feel that they deserved more than slander.[38]

Philadelphia's citizens recognized that careful nursing was critical for yellow fever patients' survival, whereas negligent nursing care was considered a death warrant. Mayor Matthew Clarkson placed a newspaper column that advertised "generous wages" for nurses at the Bush Hill fever hospital as "much depends on good nursing." Another article in the same newspaper lamented that "many of the sick suffer greatly" from the lack of "the attendance of nurses." The prominent Philadelphia physician Caspar Wistar credited his sister Catharine's skilled nursing for saving his life when he was stricken with yellow fever. When their aunt, Margaret Wistar Haines, contracted the disease, she implored her daughter to "get 2 black nurses & leave me." Haines explained, "I had rather thee would not run the risk of staying." It is unclear whether Haines believed that the Black nurses were more expendable than her daughter or if she thought they were less likely to contract the fever.[39] Haines's cousin Margaret Hill Morris also remained in Philadelphia during the epidemic because she was unable to move her eldest sister, who was bedridden after a series of strokes. In early September, Morris's daughter Deborah Morris Smith fell ill, and her husband called in Morris to treat her instead of a physician. However, when her son Dr. John Morris came down with the fever, Margaret Morris contacted Allen and Jones, who sent two African American nurses to help her care for John and his wife. Morris voiced appreciation for the nurses and detailed the intimate space of her son's sickroom. She told a sister, "I lay down by him [John]—the Negro woman sitting near the bed." After Deborah and John died, a male nurse contacted a fellow FAS member in charge of burials and they assisted with the family's hasty funerals. When the FAS nurse developed yellow fever and was thrown out of his lodgings, Morris demonstrated her appreciation by nursing this "valuable black man." However, in the Wistars' and Morrises' letters, African American caregivers remain nameless, underscoring the social distances that Bass and her colleagues sought to bridge.[40]

Nursing was especially suited to demonstrate the volunteer nurses' humanity if it could be linked to positive images of healers who benevolently nursed kin and neighbors in family households. Images of nurses that vacillated between caring womenfolk and degraded prostitutes mirrored the binary stereotypes of African American women, described by the historian Deborah Gray White as either loyal, asexual, motherly domestics or uncontrolled, sensuous, and scheming "Jezebels."[41] Although the Black men who served as nursing attendants could be denigrated for working in a servile and feminized role, Black women were particularly vulnerable to Carey's slander as African Americans, lower-class freedwomen, and nurses. Carey chose the phrase the "vilest of the nurses" strategically. The word *vile* was associated with the word *villainous* as well as the gendered epithet "vile strumpets and common prostitutes," which was common in fiction, newspapers, and pamphlets.[42] Uncivilized, vile nurses were antithetical to concepts of citizenship as well as to emerging notions of restrained and sexually pure white middle-class womanhood. Moreover, because nurses were often the only able-bodied persons in a household of sick and vulnerable patients, they were open to charges of theft, abuse, and neglect. In subsequent editions of his account, Carey presented terrifying images of an inebriated and "profligate abandoned set of nurses" at the Bush Hill fever hospital who "rioted on the provisions" and left patients "destitute of every assistance." He described the hospital as "a great human slaughterhouse." In response, Jones and Allen clarified that only two African American nurses were part of the original group of Bush Hill nurses, and their services were so valued that they were rehired after the hospital was reorganized under Stephen Girard. Although the FAS leaders conceded that with the disintegration of civic life during the epidemic, some people of all ethnicities were negligent or resorted to profiteering, they argued that the nurses under FAS auspices ministered to their patients rather than exploiting them.[43]

However, Jones and Allen had to address other concerns in their pamphlet. As yellow fever continued to ravage Philadelphia in the fall of 1793, ongoing slave revolts in Saint-Domingue caused critics to attack the antislavery movement. Philadelphia newspapers that remained in business published lurid, "affecting scenes" of slave rebellions, which placed Europeans in sensibility's classic role of distressed sufferers at the hands of militant Black revolutionaries. This evoked white Philadelphians' sympathy and apprehensions. At this crucial moment, the success of Philadelphia's Black churches had wide-reaching consequences for the transatlantic antislavery movement. If African churches were to "succeed African bondage" as the FAS leaders and members hoped, they needed a strategic narrative to promote their cause. Jones and Allen presented Sarah Bass and the FAS nurses' performance as virtuous republican soldiers robed in Christian benevolence and welcomed into the homes of whites to battle the invading epidemic with empathetic nursing care. They pointed to the dearth of humanitarian role models among white Philadelphians, including many who displayed "barbarity" instead of compassion, inverting the stereotypical depictions of African Americans as "savage barbarians."[44]

In his published reply to Jones and Allen's *Narrative*, titled *A Desultory Account of the Yellow Fever*, Carey grudgingly acknowledged the services of Jones, Allen, and a few others but chose not to retract his previous slander toward "the vilest of the nurses." In response, Jones and Allen cited a proverb that attributed classical republican sensibility to Bass and the courageous but unappreciated soldierly nurses who "exposed their lives in the late afflicting dispensation." They retorted, "God and a soldier, all men do adore, in time of war, and not before / When the war is over, and all things righted, God is forgotten, and the soldier slighted."[45] The nurses' actions were particularly notable compared with those of retired army officers like President George Washington and Treasury Secretary Alexander Hamilton, who fled the city early in the epidemic. The notion of African American women as nurse-soldiers blurred race and gender boundaries, particularly because Black male soldiers were controversial. However, FAS nurses evoked a heroic image that was less threatening than representations of armed men of African descent, like those fighting for their freedom in Saint-Domingue. Rather than merely assimilating the dominant culture's rhetoric of republican and evangelical sensibility, Jones and Allen appropriated its language and redeployed it to interpret Bass and other FAS nurses as courageous Christian soldiers risking their lives as they battled to save the city—by definition citizens of a republic. They challenged discourses that limited citizenship to white males, especially those who displayed heroic martial masculinity.[46]

Bass and her fellow nurses did not conform to the popular sentimental image of "poor Africans" enshrined in the transatlantic abolitionist logo, which portrayed persons of African descent as helpless, chained supplicants who required the patronage of sympathetic white elites. Instead, Bass and her fellow nurses were raised to the status of virtuous Good Samaritans, who "found a freedom to go forth, confiding in Him who can preserve in the midst of a fiery furnace, sensible that it was our duty to do all we could to our suffering fellow mortals." The credibility of the nascent Black church movement rested on public perceptions of the nurses' actions, because the nurses represented all peoples of African descent advancing "the cause of freedom." With so much at stake, it is not surprising that the nurses "solicited" their leaders to defend their actions in the public space of print. For Bass, civic nursing became a pathway to activism. She chose to identify herself publicly in one of the earliest African American protest pamphlets as a visible champion of the movement for Black liberation and equality.[47]

In retrospect, the egalitarian possibilities of the 1790s were not realized, and citizenship for African American women and men was contested for more than a century. Sarah Bass and her fellow nurses' concerns for their reputations were justified because Carey's slander continued to follow them in subsequent epidemics. A newspaper article on the 1797 yellow fever epidemic attributed "many deaths" to the "remissness of nurses" and warned against the "danger of entrusting" the lives of "endearing relations" to "hardened or impious creatures." Nonetheless, the Philadelphia African American community remembered the FAS nurses' public service, and some Euro-Americans memorialized their humanitarian work in print. A poem in the *Massachusetts Magazine* praised Jones and Allen and tangentially recognized the nurses' heroic "toil," divine sympathy, and "godlike zeal." A 1795 play staged in Philadelphia featured an emancipation scene to honor FAS work.[48] Jones and Allen's *Narrative* was published in London, introducing Bass and the nurses to a wide abolitionist audience. Richard Allen included a copy of the *Narrative* with his published 1833 autobiography. In 1838, when African Americans protested the new Pennsylvania constitution's revocation of Black suffrage, they invoked the memory of the FAS nurses to argue for civil equality. The activist Robert Purvis asserted, "When the yellow fever ravaged Philadelphia and the whites fled . . . many whites [who] were forsaken by their own relations and left to the mercy of this fell disease were nursed gratuitously by the colored people." The mid-nineteenth-century AME historian William Douglass situated the FAS nurses' work as foundational for the Black church movement.[49]

During the epidemic, Bass and the nurse volunteers gained critical leadership skills that positioned them to form Black churches and organizations to advance African American emancipation, education, and civil equality. After her marriage to the widowed Richard Allen in 1801, Sarah Bass Allen was a coworker in his "gospel labors," ministering to a five-hundred-member congregation as well as managing a growing family and apprentices in the Allens' business. According to an AME historian, "Sarah Allen takes a place of leadership" as the founding "Mother in Israel" of the "mother church" of the AME denomination.[50] Just as the eyes of the Philadelphia community were watching the behavior of the FAS nurses in 1793, they were also trained on Bass Allen's performance of respectability in the early nineteenth century. She served as an example of Christian courage, piety, and industry for her congregation and the Black community. Pieces of her floral china set and her mahogany linen chest on display at the Bethel AME Church Museum attest to Bass Allen's participation in the rituals of refined sociability as she entertained city worthies such as Benjamin Rush, presiding over a tea table set with delicate porcelain and freshly pressed table linens. Bass Allen's portrait on display at Bethel Church radiates the respectability that Black church women sought to achieve.[51]

Nonetheless, the strategy of "social uplift" emphasized the strictures of domesticity and patriarchy, and Methodist gender norms barred women from formal leadership. Although Richard Allen had challenged racial barriers to Methodist church leadership, he drew the line when his wife's friend Jarena Lee attempted to defy gender barriers by preaching in public. Bass Allen weighed in on the issue by caring for Jarena Lee's son so that Lee could preach as an itinerant "exhorter." She discreetly supported Lee's assertion, "As unseemly as it may appear now-a-days for a woman to preach . . . nothing is impossible with God." Lee noted that Bass Allen had encouraged to her to write her ministerial autobiography and was one of the first to purchase a copy of the book. Although Bass Allen never formally preached, her lengthy obituary emphasized that she "walked with God," the "power of which was felt as often as she opened her mouth to rebuke, to counsel, or encourage." The obituary evoked military imagery by asserting that Bass Allen "battled mightily for the establishing of our beloved Zion." At the risk of retaliation by slave catchers, Bass Allen harbored runaway slaves in her home, and in 1816, she created the first AME women's organization. As her eulogy noted, "The poor flying slave . . . has lost a friend," and the "Church has indeed lost a pillar from the building." Sarah Bass Allen continued to battle for equality and for the abolition of slavery until her death in 1849.[52]

During the 1793 Philadelphia yellow fever epidemic, Sarah Bass learned that public political activism took soldierly courage. Bass and the FAS nurses' unique representation of African American women as authoritative citizen-soldier healers challenged race and gender norms that reserved military displays of citizenship for white men. When censured, Bass and the nurses demanded vindication in print. In the mid-nineteenth century, the AME Church historian William Douglass described the early days of the FAS as "an age of searching enquiry into the equity of old and established customs," asserting that "a moral earthquake had awakened the slumber of ages." At the foundational moments of the Black church movement, FAS women as well as men created the seismic tremors that propelled their community toward self-determination. According to the *Narrative*, Sarah Bass and the nurses were slandered by "unprovoked enemies" who "begrudge us the liberty we enjoy." Nonetheless, Bass could assert, along with Jones and Allen, "We are confident, we shall stand justified." Bass and the FAS nurses mobilized their authority as activist healers who battled yellow fever with courage and humanitarian compassion. Although Sarah Bass Allen was born enslaved, according to her death certificate she died a "lady," having served as a founding mother of an influential Black church. However, as Bass Allen discovered, in the early nineteenth century, an emerging culture of domesticity created new challenges for women of all ethnicities who strove to maintain their leadership roles as humanitarian healers while engaging in activist reform movements, and as economic actors in the capitalist marketplace.[53]

CHAPTER 8

Navigating New Challenges

On May 30, 1805, Charles Marshall confessed formally to the Philadelphia Quaker Monthly Meeting that he had mismanaged his apothecary business. After making imprudent business investments, Marshall faced bankruptcy. As a Quaker, he understood that "to be in unity with the Body of our religious Society . . . the Members should walk orderly." The bankruptcy was a family calamity as well as evidence of personal disorder. Marshall was the scion of a prosperous pharmaceutical business established by his grandfather Christopher Marshall in the 1730s. Now the stately two-story brick apothecary shop on Chestnut Street with its signature sign of the golden ball would be sold. However, Marshall found consolation in reflecting, "I have not intentionally been the cause of . . . my present unhappy Situation." Surely, his fellow Quakers would understand that unseen market forces might conspire against a businessman in this new, uncertain century. Still, Marshall kept the faith. "Altho my prospects be thus gloomy," Marshall opined, "I am at times favored with a sustaining hope that He [God] . . . will not be altogether unmindful of your afflicted friend." Marshall's prayers were answered in his eldest daughter Elizabeth, who reopened the apothecary shop in the family's home and quickly placed the business on sound financial footing. When she sold the company in 1825, Elizabeth Marshall had trained numerous apprentices and had expanded the apothecary shop into a successful drug manufactory. In retirement, she added the role of philanthropic civic humanitarian to that of authoritative pharmaceutical business owner.[1]

Nonetheless, historians suppressed the memories of Marshall's achievements, as well as those of numerous other women who practiced as apothecaries and healers in the greater Philadelphia region. A definitive late twentieth-century pharmacy history text omitted Elizabeth's role in the Marshall family's apothecary business. An early twentieth-century historian called Elizabeth Marshall "the first woman pharmacist in America," with the qualifier, "the first of whom we have any knowledge." Margaret Morris, Mary Watters, and Elizabeth Weed would have presumed that their apothecary practices had predated Marshall's. However, over the course of the nineteenth century, their achievements would be obscured by a powerful discourse of domesticity that sought to relegate women to the private household sphere, safe from the perils of the business domain. Women were circumscribed as maternal physicians and home sanitarians even as female practitioners were written out of histories of pharmacy and medicine. The rhetoric of domesticity is evident in accounts by twentieth-century historians who reframed Marshall as a self-effacing city matron whose "active, yet unobtrusive duties of benevolence" exemplified "the chief ornaments of the Christian character." Marshall "was beneficent and kind to all and dispensed her charities with a liberal hand." By throwing the mantle of a newly domesticized Lady Bountiful over Elizabeth Marshall's memory, these historians marginalized the narrative of a savvy pharmaceutical businesswoman who dispensed medicines along with benevolence, and who marketed and manufactured pharmaceuticals.[2]

In the Quaker-influenced Delaware Valley, some women navigated alternative courses against the cultural currents of domesticity, and they continued their work in health care–related fields in the first decades of the nineteenth century. Although their percentages in the population were diminishing, Quaker women challenged the rhetoric of domesticity by modeling less restrictive gender roles and ideals. Women healers and entrepreneurs such as Elizabeth Marshall built on their foremothers' foundations as they participated as economic actors in a still unregulated consumer medical marketplace. Education reformers established female academies and educated girls in the sciences, countering notions of women's intellectual inferiority. Female health educators and practitioners used their newfound knowledge to position themselves as experts in the medically related fields of anatomy, botany, and chemistry. Women from among the ranks of Philadelphia's white and Black middle-class families could redeploy the rhetoric of benevolent sensibility to become knowledgeable reforming women who advanced the personal and public health of their communities, while simultaneously agitating for abolition and for humanitarian improvements in hospitals and asylums. In urban areas such as Philadelphia and in smaller towns, women doctresses, healers, and medical entrepreneurs belied domesticity's assertions of female bodily frailty as they continued public work in family businesses or as sole proprietors. In rural areas, the lack of access to physicians assured that women healers and self-help health care still held sway. A revitalized health reform movement combined the late eighteenth century's promotion of useful knowledge with new religious and scientific visions of societal perfectionism. Despite pressures to conform to emerging notions of domesticity, some women healers continued to demonstrate their healing authority as they embraced opportunities offered by the marketplace, an expansion of women's educational curriculum in the sciences, and new efforts to reform society.[3]

Manufacturing Medicinal Authority

Elizabeth Marshall identified and developed business opportunities in pharmaceutical and chemical manufacturing in Philadelphia. She was the favorite grandchild of Christopher Marshall, the founder of the family apothecary business, and she likely learned her pharmaceutical skills and business acumen from him. Elizabeth's achievements are particularly impressive because she had to restart the Marshall's apothecary shop from the ground up in the small front room of the family home. Although her brother Charles Junior was a partner with his father and shared responsibility for the 1805 bankruptcy, local histories are silent as to why he did not attempt to recover the business. As it was with Margaret Hill Morris's father a half century earlier, the forfeiture of a business was a blow to a man's sense of masculinity. The loss of the physical presence of the landmark apothecary building would have been a constant reminder of personal failure in a culture that increasingly equated manhood with providing economically for one's family. It may have been easier for Elizabeth than for Charles Jr. to open a modest home apothecary shop. She could follow female precedents like that of her cousin Margaret Morris, who appropriated a personal bookcase to house apothecary jars, or Mary Watters, who started a medical and pharmaceutical business in her home. However, Elizabeth also faced the challenge of rebuilding her customers' trust in the Marshall brand.[4]

Within a decade, Elizabeth Marshall reinvigorated and expanded the business. She reintroduced the industrial drug production begun by her father and supervised the manufacture of specialty pharmaceuticals and chemicals such as muriate of ammonia and the popular cathartic Glauber's Salts. The Philadelphia historian John F. Watson recalled childhood memories of the malodorous fumes that exuded from Elizabeth Marshall's drug manufactory.

Marshall contributed to the science of pharmacy by compounding uniquely American preparations. She worked with Dr. Benjamin Smith Barton to create a medicinal called mistura glycyrrhizae composita in 1814, which was later included in the United States Pharmacopeia. Barton was a botanist, practicing physician, and professor at the University of Pennsylvania Medical School, who sent his prescriptions to be filled at Marshall's drug store. Marshall's and Barton's innovations were part of a cultural nationalist movement aimed at demonstrating the ability of the United States to compete with Europe in the fields of science and medicine.[5]

In addition to running the business, Marshall employed and supervised between six and twelve apprentices who were recognized by contemporaries as "the representative, progressive pharmacists of Philadelphia." As one physician recalled, the Marshall establishment "was renowned for the extent and integrity of its transactions," and "numbers of the College [of Pharmacy] have received their pharmaceutical education within its walls." In a historical period when issues of counterfeit and authenticity in business transactions were particularly salient, Elizabeth Marshall made pharmaceutical integrity a fundamental aspect of her successful company. One of Marshall's apprentices was Isaac Paschall Morris, the healer Elizabeth Coates Paschall's great-grandson and a cousin of Margaret Hill Morris. Unlike Paschall and Morris, Elizabeth Marshall remained single and did not have daughters or sons to train to inherit her business. Despite her presence as a potential role model for women pharmacists, all of Marshall's apprentices were men. In 1825, Elizabeth Marshall sold the business to her former apprentices Isaac Paschall Morris and Charles Ellis, and it became the preeminent pharmaceutical firm in Philadelphia. A Philadelphia pharmacist remembered Marshall's business abilities and her "decided character" that was "well calculated to command respect." In her own time, the Philadelphia community recognized Marshall's pharmaceutical authority and her business accomplishments.[6]

Other women who were less visible than Marshall also leveraged an unregulated medical marketplace and deployed their healing skills to develop respected practices as apothecaries and drug vendors. Despite several economic downturns during the first decades of the nineteenth century, demand for patent medicines made pharmaceuticals consumer necessities, which provided opportunities for women to sell home-produced or manufactured drugs either in shops or through direct marketing. In Delaware County, Pennsylvania, Ann Pearson and several other women sold Paschall's Golden Drops, a panacea alleged to cure most ills. Elizabeth Coates Paschall's brother

John, the self-styled "alchymical doctor," created this medicine and handed it down to his son Dr. Henry Paschall. Henry manufactured Golden Drops and distributed the product among authorized women and men druggists. In the Philadelphia suburb of Kensington, Hannah West practiced as an apothecary with her husband. When he died in 1817, West followed Elizabeth Weed's pattern and continued the family apothecary business. She was listed in the 1825 *Philadelphia Directory* along with male practitioners as the apothecary to "the Out-Door Poor" for Kensington, under the auspices of the Philadelphia Almshouse. Her family retained her official certificate for this civic role. West practiced in Kensington into her late seventies, providing medical advice along with pharmaceuticals. She may have purchased drugs for her shop from Elizabeth Marshall, who expanded her Philadelphia retail practice to include a wholesale business. In another city directory that cited West, the Marshall family business was listed but not Elizabeth herself, which demonstrates the limits of city directories in creating a comprehensive picture of women's health care work.[7]

Marshall and West were part of mid-Atlantic pharmaceutical marketing networks that included Hannah Lee, who owned Lee's Patent and Family Medicine Store in New York City. Like Marshall, Lee excelled as a pharmaceutical entrepreneur. In her 1817 promotional pamphlet, Lee boasted that her medicines "have been in high estimation and general use throughout the United States for upwards of 16 years" and cure "most diseases to which the human body is liable." The market for patent medicines was even more competitive in the 1810s and 1820s than in Elizabeth's Weed's and Mary Watters's lifetimes. The health advice pamphlets that accompanied Lee's medicines were actually advertisements aimed at shaping her customers' pharmaceutical consumption patterns. However, Lee cautioned customers to "observe that an engraved label with the signature of Hannah Lee is pasted on the outside" of each bottle, "without which they are counterfeit." Her concerns were well founded. The pirated ingredients and recipes for home-produced versions of Lee's proprietary medicines appear in women's medical manuscripts in the Philadelphia area. As Elizabeth Weed had discovered, women apothecaries and druggists had to be shrewd in their marketing practices, product packaging, and aggressive prosecution of counterfeiters. These women who appeared in print or in local histories must stand in for others whose practices were unrecorded. Despite their successes as pharmaceutical entrepreneurs, women were excluded from professional organizations and had to develop their own health care networks.[8]

Although Elizabeth Marshall had rescued and revitalized the family pharmaceutical business, it is telling that her elderly father, Charles, rather than Elizabeth, was elected president at the founding of the Philadelphia College of Pharmacy in 1821. Early twentieth-century pharmacy historians remembered Charles Marshall Sr.'s pharmaceutical achievements but relegated Elizabeth Marshall to the domesticized role of a self-effacing philanthropist, thus obscuring her role as an apothecary, business owner, and founder of one of the first pharmaceutical manufactories in the United States. An early nineteenth-century culture of domesticity that sought to consign women to the household sphere played an important role in this historical amnesia. While it is important to recognize that powerful cultural movements can marginalize specific groups, it is also necessary to interrogate the differences between idealized prescriptive literature and women's lived experiences. Elizabeth Marshall likely viewed her own philanthropy as part of a broad-based reform movement spearheaded by Quakers. Women healers and health care entrepreneurs such as Marshall had to navigate the boundaries between outward-facing social movements intent on educating and reforming society and an inward-facing culture of domesticity.[9]

Female Education's Subversive Potential

In the late eighteenth century, an ideological construct that historians deem "Republican Motherhood" set the stage for a constricting culture of women's domesticity. Reformers such as Dr. Benjamin Rush argued that women should be educated to become intelligent, companionate wives and knowledgeable mothers who could train their sons to be loyal citizens of the young republic. Although this discourse validated women's roles as mothers, it limited middle-class women's participation in the political and economic spheres. However, some middle-class women subverted this restrictive rhetoric to argue that daughters also required an education, which initiated the establishment of female academies. The Delaware Valley was a locus of female educational reform. The Young Ladies' Academy of Philadelphia, founded in 1797, exemplifies institutions for middle-class girls that provided instruction in public oratory, geography, chemistry, mathematics, and natural philosophy, as well as in basic reading and literature. Women's education in the arts and sciences was intended to prepare them to teach their children, provide intellectual companionship for their husbands, and manage their households.

However, numerous women went on to deploy their newfound skills in pursuit of a variety of social reform and public health movements, including female education, women's rights, abolition, temperance, poor relief, public sanitation, and the betterment of prisons, asylums, and hospitals.[10]

Quakers increasingly founded female academies and penned textbooks for girls of the lower as well as the middle classes. The Quaker activist Anthony Benezet's school for Philadelphia's African American children continued to provide basic education for girls as well as boys into the early nineteenth century. Margaret Hill Morris's sister Milcah Martha Hill Moore organized a school for girls and boys of the lower orders and published a textbook based on her experiences. The Quaker reformer Anne Parrish, assisted by her cousin Elizabeth Marshall, founded the Society for the Free Instruction of African Females and the Aimwell School for the Free Instruction of Females in Philadelphia. Although women and girls of the artisanal and lower classes were not confined by Republican Motherhood's ideological constraints, they benefited from its impetus toward female education. Quakers and other denominations opened schools to serve girls of various social orders. Morris's cousin the Quaker minister Rebecca Jones established a school in Philadelphia that taught girls mathematics, apothecaries' terminology, bookkeeping, interest compounding, and business skills to prepare them to excel as shopkeepers as well as household managers.[11] The apothecary and healer Margaret Hill Morris recognized the new educational possibilities for girls. In 1807, Morris wrote to her namesake granddaughter studying at the prestigious Westtown Friends School of the "the many advantages that you of the present day enjoy." She urged her granddaughter, "Improve thyself in every branch of thy learning." Even in a small school in New Brunswick, New Jersey, young Rachel Van Dyke imagined that she and a female friend "would together climb the hill of science" and would reach the summit. Women such as Van Dyke had additional educational opportunities as women's science academies proliferated in the eastern United States in the 1810s and 1820s. Despite efforts to circumscribe female education, knowledge was empowering because it provided women with proof of their intellectual equality and their ability to excel in the sciences. In addition, as the historian Mary Kelley points out, women's proficiency in oratory—"learning to stand and speak"—gave young women the confidence to assume organizational leadership positions and to lecture audiences regarding a variety of reform-related topics.[12]

Philadelphia-area young women also followed Elizabeth Coates Paschall's earlier example by taking advantage of informal educational opportunities offered in printed materials and public lectures. Women members of the Library Company of Philadelphia and other lending libraries could check out books for women on the sciences by the New York educator Almira Hart Lincoln or by Priscilla Wakefield, a well-known English Quaker. The Library Company also held a copy of Wakefield's feminist tract, *Reflection on the Present Condition of the Female Sex*. Philadelphia women attended lectures and enjoyed exhibits at Charles Willson Peale's natural history museum. In the early 1820s, the Germantown Academy offered public scientific lectures that young women attended. According to the educator Charles J. Wister, "The conversation of the fair sex was no longer confined to the engrossing subjects of ribbons and laces, but was delightfully diversified with learned dissertations on philosophical questions, which mineralogical and chemical technicalities slipped off their tongues as glibly as mantuamaker's and milliner's terms had hitherto." Although his late mother, the skilled healer Lowry Wister, might not have appreciated her son's patronizing tone, she would have likely approved his promotion of young women's interest in natural philosophy. Evidence in women's medical recipe books reflects their ongoing pursuit of the sciences. Lowry Wister handed down her recipe book to her three daughters, whose remedies reflect the family's penchant for science. On the fly page of her medical manuscript, Sarah Richardson Waln, a friend of the Wisters, pasted a newspaper clipping detailing a "beautiful chemical experiment [that] may easily be performed by a lady." As their medical recipe books suggest, women healers deployed their knowledge in the sciences in their health care work.[13]

Informal as well as formal education in the sciences provided literate Delaware Valley women with the skills and confidence to found medically related benevolent organizations. Anne Parrish melded her passions for educational and health reform. In addition to founding schools for impoverished girls and women of color, Parrish created the Female Society of Philadelphia for the Relief and Employment of the Poor. Elizabeth Marshall supported the organization with donations and later wrote an account lauding Parrish's reforming endeavors. Catharine Wistar Morris, also a Quaker, continued Parrish's work into the early decades of the nineteenth century. Of course, Parrish and Morris had numerous role models of Quaker women with public ministries. According to Female Society minutes, a goal of the organization was to visit sufferers "in their solitary Dwellings, without distinction of Nation or Colour, sympathizing in their afflictions, and, as far as their Ability extends, relieving them." Catharine Wistar Morris took over the organization in the early nineteenth century, and it was officially incorporated in 1815.[14]

The Female Society's leaders and members included women from the next generations of the Wistar/Wister, Bartram, Morris, Jones, and Coates families who valued education in the sciences. Elizabeth Wetherill Jones remembered that in 1815, she and fellow society members attended "very interesting and instructive" lectures on botany given by Dr. John Waterhouse "in the rooms of the [American] Philosophical Society." According to Jones, "We were regarded as . . . very strong-minded young women." She noted, "Growing out of these lectures, a committee was appointed to collect herbs, indigenous ones, for the poor." Jones's botanical and pharmaceutical education enhanced her philanthropic health care activities.[15]

The Female Society's records also capture the poverty experienced by women in the Early Republic, often precipitated by illnesses and disability of parents, partners, and family members. Impoverished people were particularly susceptible to recurring epidemics of yellow fever and other diseases. Widowhood and personal illness could also initiate a downward spiral toward poverty. Their documents suggest that unlike other benevolent organizations of the period, the Female Society recognized that poor women were not to blame for their situations. While making a house call for the Female Society, Parrish found "the widow Agnew's children in the measles—her sister Bradshaw very poorly herself." Elizabeth Mull was found to be "much indisposed." During their home visits, the society members provided medicines, food, clothing, blankets, and money for fuel. In her journal, Catharine Morris described "Braw, a young black woman," who had "carried her infant forty miles to Philadelphia in hopes of finding employment in domestic service," but was "disappointed in her expectation." Even the skilled African American healer Anna Dalemoa Bellamy could not practice and earn income when afflicted with the dropsy. Parrish had described Bellamy as "a woman of education" and "the black doctor," who excelled at bone setting, tooth drawing, and wound healing. However, when Parrish visited Bellamy, she was "sick and destitute." Like the Lenape healer Hannah Freeman, Bellamy's condition deteriorated, and she was admitted to the "poor house." At the Philadelphia Almshouse, older women made "a little money" cultivating medicinal roots and herbs in the institution's garden. Even in grim conditions, healing skills could be part of subsistence strategies for women in economic distress.[16]

Despite their provision of necessary health care and social services, Catharine Morris and her "strong minded" Female Society women were criticized, even within Quaker circles, for visiting impoverished people in their homes. It was considered inappropriate for them, as middle-class white women, to mix in the homes of sick and destitute people of the lower orders. The Female Society continued providing relief within homes, but they also established a Female House of Industry, which offered women education and assistance in the textile trades in a less personal institutional setting. Middle-class women interested in medicine could promote health in institutions and hospitals while distancing themselves from actual patients. In 1824, Catharine Wistar Morris expanded her reforming activities to become a founding member of the Pennsylvania Hospital's "Board of Female Assistants for the Internal Management of the Hospital." The board was responsible for visiting the hospital, interviewing patients, overseeing nursing administration, and offering hospital managers suggestions for reforms. To navigate the constricting culture of domesticity, middle-class women had to find appropriate venues to bring their domestic skills to bear in public spaces.[17]

Circumscribing Maternal Physicians

Despite female education's empowering potential, authors of prescriptive and popular literature developed a countervailing culture of domesticity that sought to limit middle-class women's public roles in politics and businesses, including health care work. Building on the ideology of Republican Motherhood, this "cult of domesticity" proposed that white middle-class women's proper sphere was confined to the home, where idealized mothers created nurturing domestic spaces for children and havens for husbands to escape the stressful worlds of politics and business. Public spaces constituted a masculine sphere that was antithetical to the private household. Ironically, housework and home production of goods—including medicines—were devalued, even as middle-class women were discouraged from seeking employment outside the home. "True Women" were considered mere consumers rather than active economic producers. This gendered construct was an attempt to control the uncertainties of the emerging market economy that produced financial crises like those faced by the Marshalls. Scientific and medical "experts" bolstered the culture of domesticity by arguing that women were inherently mentally and physically inferior to men. New neurological theories that had given rise to the culture of sensibility were deployed to assert that women's nervous systems were more delicate and passionate, thus precluding women from the harsh rational world of the professions, including medicine. Women were ostensibly controlled by their childbearing bodies, which limited their occupations and public roles.[18]

For women of color, racialized stereotypes of their allegedly "inferior" bodies magnified notions of social difference. Domesticity's ideals of piety, purity, and submission purportedly differentiated middle-class white women from African American and Native American women as well as Euro-American women of the lower orders. However, in a subversive move, free African American women in Philadelphia deployed aspects of domesticity as part of a reformist strategy to "uplift" their community. Just as they did during the 1793 yellow fever epidemic, Sarah Bass Allen and other Black leaders continued to demonstrate their benevolence, respectability, and civic virtues to the white community in a bid to confirm their worthiness for full civil and social equality. Women of Philadelphia's Black elite, including Sarah Allen, Charlotte Forten, and Grace Bustill Douglass and her daughter Sarah, founded women's mutual aid societies, religious organizations, and literary societies to support their communities. They demonstrated African Americans' "respectability" and intellectual capabilities in an effort to battle the city's increasing racism. However, like their reforming white colleagues, Black middle-class women ignored the strictures of domesticity when they conveyed their domestic authority into the public sphere to agitate for abolition and equality.[19]

Discourses of respectability and physiological theories dovetailed with new medical models that emphasized the central role of sanitation and cleanliness in personal and public health. As the historian Kathleen Brown demonstrates, the emerging literary genre of "mother's manuals" posited that middle-class white women should become the guardians of the health of their children and households. In the never-ending role of home sanitarians, these women faced daily battles to keep homes and children healthy through scrupulous cleanliness. The manuals encouraged women to consult medical experts for anything more than a child's minor illness. Mary Palmer Tyler's popular book *The Maternal Physician* (1811) emphasized women's new power as arbiters of infant and childcare but simultaneously circumscribed women's authority within the domestic sphere. As they imbibed this culture reinforced by women's magazines and mothers' manuals, some women embraced new images of womanhood and motherhood to secure their middle-class status. However, prescriptive literature does not necessarily reflect their readers' medical practices. Recall how Elizabeth Coates Paschall resisted medical writers' admonitions to seek a physician's advice and instead synthesized medical information to inform her own practice. Some women sidestepped the strictures of domesticity.[20]

The culture of domesticity developed at a time when pharmacists and physicians were intent on solidifying their authoritative roles. In this context, it is not surprising that Elizabeth Marshall's elderly father was named the first president of the Philadelphia College of Pharmacy, even though it was Elizabeth who saved the company and trained young pharmacists in their profession. Cultural pressures may have also prevented middle-class women from signing on as apprentices under Elizabeth Marshall, although artisanal women continued to pursue work as apothecaries and druggists. Just as pharmacists created professional societies that marginalized women, Delaware Valley physicians built their status upon the bonds of brotherhood created by medical societies, professional journals, and medical school diplomas. The University of Pennsylvania Medical School was considered a premier institution in the United States, and its graduates increased from an average of seven men per year to sixty-five by 1810. By 1820, there were over ten medical schools affiliated with colleges and universities in the young republic. Middle-class and elite Philadelphia-area families increasingly used the proprietary term "our family physician" as a class marker, just as many women consulted with man-midwives for obstetrical care. Doctors asserted their preeminence as arbiters of physiological theories, scientific knowledge, and public health.[21]

Despite their increasing aura of authority, medical societies were unable to enforce medical school standards, and states did not regulate medical licensure. Recurring epidemics of yellow fever, scarlet fever, and other diseases augmented people's fears of bodily frailty and confirmed health care consumers' suspicions that physicians did not offer definitive cures for illnesses. Nonphysicians continued to practice as self-described doctresses, doctors, apothecaries, druggists, bonesetters, cancer specialists, therapeutic bleeders, and herbal healers.[22]

As hands-on anatomical dissections on human cadavers became the essential marker of an elite medical education, the potential for scientific advancement was tempered by the public's fears that their loved ones' bodies in sacred graveyard spaces would be violated. The Philadelphia historian John Watson remembered humorously his childhood terror of Dr. William Shippen's dissecting theater, "deemed the receptacle of the dead bodies, where their flesh was boiled and their bones were burnt down for the use of the faculty!" Watson recorded the popular ditty:

> The body-snatchers they have come
> And made a snatch at me
> They hav'nt left an atom there
> Of my anatomie![23]

Public revulsion was revived when an unmarked graveyard was discovered on the dissecting theater's grounds after Shippen's death in 1808. Philadelphia's Black community recognized that physicians' frequent use of African American cadavers for anatomical training was a form of medical racism. Debates ensued regarding medical students' appropriation of the unclaimed deceased bodies of impoverished people for dissections. The opening of new schools, such as Jefferson Medical College in 1826, reignited fear that medical students were robbing graves. As one University of Pennsylvania medical school graduate remembered, "The term 'medical student,' with many citizens, [was] intimately associated with 'roguery,' 'impudence,' 'lawlessness' and 'murderer.'" Public anxiety over the procurement of cadavers cast a cloud over physicians' medical authority.[24]

Moreover, for all but the poorest patients, health care occurred in the private spaces of the household. To physicians' chagrin, women seized their validated role as arbiters of the domestic sphere and continued to advise physicians and veto their orders. Doctors had to mind their bedside manner when entering women's domain. Elizabeth Drinker, a healing adept of the merchant class, often assumed an advisory role with physicians. In 1807, Drinker noted in her diary that after falling and injuring her chest, she sent for Dr. Adam Kuhn. According to Drinker, Kuhn "advised the parting with 10 ounces of blood, which I would not comply with . . . He then desired me to take a dose of physic, which I told him I had not done since I was ill 2 years ago." She asked if "dieting myself" would not be better, and Kuhn capitulated. Drinker also wrote in her diary that a well-known elderly African American woman named Alice Wright was so ill that several young doctors blistered her "with talk of more blisters" for "no good I fear." When Wright's health improved the next day, she "told ye Doctors that she will not take any more of their physic" and "she thinks the mercury she has taken has occasioned her to swell too much." Women gave doctors a piece of their minds when they disagreed with a treatment regimen.

In the first decades of the nineteenth century, doctors and pharmacists faced challenges to their authority from patients and nonphysician practitioners.[25]

Doctresses, Bleeders, and Midwives in an Unregulated Medical Marketplace

Despite prescriptive writers and male practitioners' attempts to restrict middle class and artisanal women's work in public places, free women in the Delaware Valley continued their medical practices in the early nineteenth century. Martha Gardiner Brand, who was known as a cancer specialist and "doctoress," exemplifies skilled Philadelphia women healers who garnered the respect of physicians and patients. From 1796 through 1799, city directories listed Brand as a "doctoress," a common term denoting a female doctor. Directories from the 1790s through the 1810s designated other women's occupation as "doctoress" or "doctress," including Mary Watters, Hannah Toy, Mary Keppler, and Hannah Myers. When *The New Trade Directory* sorted Philadelphia residents according to occupations rather than alphabetically, Brand was categorized under the heading "Physicians" along with Benjamin Rush and the city's prominent doctors, perhaps in recognition of her expertise. Rush, who had lauded Mary Watters and encouraged the Free African Society nurses, also referred patients to Brand. In one instance, Rush received a request for a consultation by mail from a colleague and fellow Edinburgh University alumnus named Dr. Peter Fayssoux. According to Rush, Fayssoux had been unable to cure his daughters' intractable and disfiguring facial skin lesions, which he diagnosed as skin cancers. Acting on Brand's reputation as cancer specialist, Rush referred Fayssoux's daughters to her. Frances and Mary Fayssoux traveled from South Carolina to Philadelphia and received treatment from Brand while boarding in her home in the early 1790s. During this same period, the apothecary Esther White sought Brand's health care expertise during her final illness.[26]

In her diary, Elizabeth Drinker also noted that she consulted Brand, a fellow Quaker, regarding a relative's cancer diagnosis. In June 1806, Drinker was dining with her relative Susannah Swett, who was suffering from an ulcerous facial lesion. Drinker sent for Martha Brand, "who is famous for cureing ill con[dition]'d sores." Brand examined Swett the next day, and she could not "pronounce the sore to be a canser." Brand prescribed an ointment, "which if it brings it to run good matter" could cure the lesion. Several days later, Drinker's sister visited Swett, who was no better. Dr. Isaac Cathrall, who was "attending at their house," examined Swett and prescribed another type of therapeutic plaster. However, Drinker felt that Swett's consultation with Cathrall was out of order. Drinker asserted, "I think she [Swett] has done wrong in applying to another [practitioner] while she was under the care of M. Brand." Drinker considered it disloyal for Swett to seek care from another physician in the middle of a treatment. Mary Fayssoux also recognized Brand's skills. In addition to citing Brand's "tenderness and unremitting care and attention," Fayssoux later bequeathed the healer eight hundred dollars in her 1804 will. Perhaps in relation to this windfall, the *Philadelphia Directory* identified Brand as a "gentlewoman" from 1804 to 1810, although other directories persisted in labeling her "doctress." Martha Brand practiced until her death in 1814 at age fifty-nine.[27]

Additional pieces of evidence help to sketch women healers' practices and their relationships with physicians. In January 1819, the twenty-two-year-old Dr. Benjamin H. Coates sought healer Ann Booth's advice for the treatment of "patients suffering from the White-swelling," a severe joint inflammation caused by tuberculosis or arthritis. Coates was on his way to becoming a prominent Philadelphia physician, but he was also the healer Elizabeth Coates Paschall's great nephew. His father, Samuel Coates, had been particularly close to his Aunt Paschall, and it is likely that Benjamin Coates had heard stories about her healing acumen. Thus, Coates had a precedent for trusting a woman healer's expertise. Booth had discussed her therapy for "white-swelling" with Coates, but she followed up with a detailed letter the next day. Booth explained, "I enjoin a strict attention to a diet of vegetables and milk—to drink freely of a tea made of Elder flowers and if convenient, some of the black Alder mixed with them," accompanied by a wine glass full of salts. She specified the dosage and prescribing directions, as well as instructions for an elder flower poultice. That Coates kept the letter among his medical papers is a mark of his respect for Booth. It is unclear from the letter whether Booth had an entrepreneurial practice, or whether she saw patients gratis.[28]

However, some Philadelphia women healers were clearly paid workers or entrepreneurs, as evidenced in city directory listings. Catherine Hailer (or Heyler), Sarah Porterfield, and a widowed Mrs. Kunitz exemplify women who had decades-long practices as therapeutic bleeders, "cuppers and bleeders," or "bleeders with leeches." Heyler had practiced as a bleeder with her husband Frederick from the mid-1790s though 1817. However, by 1819, Hailer was listed as widow, as well as a "bleeder and cupper and layer out of the dead." Practitioners of therapeutic bleeding could be called in directly by patients or by physicians, and clients would have sought their healing advice. Eleanor Culin, Elizabeth Dunlap, Hannah Simpson (widow), Hannah Albertson, Catherine Johnson, Mrs. Ring, Mrs. Curtis, and Mrs. Hutman worked as nurses and "layers out of the dead." An 1816 city directory also listed several female "nurses of the sick" and two women druggists, including the Widow Napier who sold "Napier's Pills." As we have seen, the term "nurse" can obscure women's flexible roles that might encompass a variety of health care work, including diagnosis, compounding medicines, prescribing, medical treatments, and nursing care.[29] Although nurses still had to battle images that linked them to impoverished bawds, their work became part of a consumer health care culture, particularly in urban areas. Elizabeth Drinker's diary, which she kept from 1758 to 1807, maps the change from a culture in which a woman could count on her kin and social networks to provide nursing care to a more impersonal marketplace. By the early nineteenth century, Drinker records sending out family members to search for hired nurses, and she scrutinized the nurses' abilities carefully.[30]

Although city directories and newspaper advertisements are useful sources, they rarely include women healers of color, which makes their practices less visible to historians. For many African American and American Indian practitioners, healing continued as a site of cultural persistence and as a source of income, as it was for lower-class white women. These healers were valued by people within their communities and by others who sought their expertise. Philadelphians of various ethnicities and social orders had numerous options for nonphysician practitioners, who were often more affordable than doctors.

In small towns and rural areas in the Delaware Valley with fewer physicians, women's diagnostic and prescribing skills continued to be recognized and valued. In West Chester, Pennsylvania, Elizabeth Henson practiced as a bleeder and healer, gaining the respect of the town's prominent physician, William Darlington. In Goshen Township, the Quaker farm wife and abolitionist Hannah Garrett was remembered as a healer, and her extensive recipe book outlines her therapies for acute and chronic illnesses. Elizabeth Neff Bowman, described in local histories as a "doctress," practiced in Neffsville, and she was often called to see patients in nearby Lancaster. As healers migrated west, they brought their medical skills with them. The Rappe family moved from eastern Pennsylvania to Ohio in the 1820s, and the Rappe women kept a recipe book that reflects their healing practices and ongoing interest in Native American cures. Healers who remained in the Delaware Valley also continued to compile medical recipe books through the mid-nineteenth century. The Germantown resident Letticia Billmeyer's medical manuscript from the 1810s includes recipes from women healers and physicians, along with newspaper clippings secured with sewing pins. Recipe manuscripts authored by the women in the Pennock family in Chester County and the Clymer family in Berks County also evince women's rural or suburban practices.[31]

Although women practitioners included midwives who provided family health care in addition to their obstetrical practices, the documentary evidence is thin. Newspaper advertisements and city directories provide limited information. A Philadelphian named Mrs. Beason advertised that she treated "the Yellow Jaundice, Dropsy, and other disorders peculiar to Women" in addition to her "services as a Midwife." The midwife Mrs. Spurrier's ad noted that she was trained in London and practiced across from Congress Hall. Robinson's *Philadelphia Directory* for 1806 cited twenty-two midwives, and the 1816 edition listed eighteen, with seven listings that spanned the decade.[32] Three extant early nineteenth-century Delaware Valley midwifery records provide only basic information, such as the date, the families' names, and the infant's sex. However, local histories sketch additional details. In her forty years of practice from the 1790s through 1832, the Cumberland County, New Jersey, midwife Martha Austin Reeves delivered more than one thousand babies, averaging thirty childbirths a year. Reeves also had a general medical practice and provided nursing care. In her midwifery book, she recorded recipes for fevers, the bloody flux, and other common ailments. Reeves compounded pills, ointments, and syrups, which she sold to patients during house calls. She charged two to three dollars for a delivery and twelve to thirty-six cents for medicines, which was less than physicians' charges. Reeves's need to support herself and her disabled daughter was particularly acute after her husband's death in 1811.[33]

Susannah Rohrer Müller practiced midwifery in Providence Township, Pennsylvania, from 1791 to 1815. Over those twenty-four years, she delivered 1,667 babies. Family histories attest to physicians and patients' respect for Müller's skills. According to Müller's grandson, during a difficult delivery, his grandmother sent for a doctor in nearby Lancaster in the middle of the night. However, when the physician heard that Müller was the presiding midwife, he replied, "It is all right, she knows as much about the case as I do." The midwife delivered the child safely. In addition to helping to run the family farm, Müller had a general medical practice, grew medicinal plants in her garden, and distilled pharmaceuticals to prescribe to her patients. One year, Müller distilled sixty ounces of medicinal oil of peppermint used for gastro-intestinal illnesses. Her grandson remembered that he rode seventy miles to Philadelphia and sold the peppermint oil to an apothecary for sixty dollars. Of her seven children, two daughters followed Müller in the practice of mid-wifery. Like Müller, another Pennsylvania German midwife named Mrs. Jo-seph Sarber likely combined midwifery with a more general family practice, but her casebook provides few details. Although Delaware Valley midwives faced competition from an increasing number of man-midwives, these ex-tant books reflect continuities in female healers' health care work into the first three decades of the nineteenth century.[34]

Other glimpses of rural Pennsylvania German women healers' prac-tices demonstrate their unique healing subcultures that included strains of Helmontian vitalism and religious mysticism. The German-born Anna Maria Jung, known as the "Highland Healer" of Berks County, exemplifies women called *braucherin* who deployed traditional Pennsylvania German healing practices interwoven with spiritual rituals. After her death in 1819, over one thousand grateful friends and patients attended her funeral. The persistence of German healing practices is evidenced in the popularity of John George Hohman's *The Long Lost Friend*, a self-help manual for *braucherei*, or "powwow" medicine, which was first published the year that Jung died. *The Long Lost Friend* appears to be a transcription of the Hohman's family recipe book that details herbal remedies for acute and chronic illnesses as well as miraculous cures backed up by patient testimonials. Hohman cites his wife as a skilled *braucherin*. Other recipes reprise the principles of seventeenth-century alchemy and vitalism, including the power of unseen sympathetic bonds, which were featured in Elizabeth Coates Paschall's mid-eighteenth-century medical recipe book.[35]

Although these theories became less prevalent in Anglo-American man-uscripts, they remained popular among Pennsylvania Germans, along with remedies that deployed prayers and faith healing. For example, to destroy a tape worm, the practitioner pronounced over the sufferer, "Worm, I conjure thee by the living God, that thou shalt flee this blood and this flesh." An En-glish edition of *The Long Lost Friend* appeared in 1820, which widened the book's audience. This best-selling book is a reminder that in the face of phy-sicians' attempts to consolidate their scientific medical authority, patients continued to choose trusted practitioners with whom they felt a cultural affinity. Amid social transformations, the transition to a market economy, and the uptick in westward migration in the early nineteenth century, some Delaware Valley residents longed to maintain the supposed simpler and more stable times of the past.[36]

"Modernizd" Women Reformers in the Age of Priscilla Homespun

The continued popularity of printed self-help household manuals that instructed patients how to "be their own doctors" reflected both a backward look to a golden past and a new impetus toward health reform with its potential for spiritual and physical perfectionism. In 1818, the pseudonymous author "Priscilla Homespun" published the second edition of *The Universal Receipt Book; Being a Compendious Repository of Practical Information . . . [in] All the Branches of Domestic Economy.* In addition to cooking, preserving, and household "receipts," the manual included fifty-three pages of medical recipes that suggest women's ongoing healing practices. It was printed by the Philadelphian James Maxwell, a friend of the late Mary and James Watters. As he set up the press or supervised the printing, Maxwell may well have been reminded of Mary Watters's healing and apothecary practice as he read Priscilla Homespun's homemade recipes for "The True Daffy's Elixir," "Genuine Turlington's Balsam," and "Dr. Staughton's celebrated Stomachic Elixir." In *The Age of Homespun,* the historian Laurel Thatcher Ulrich identifies a late-nineteenth-century nostalgic culture that glorified a simple, homespun world of colonial times. Apparently, the idea of "homespun" also resonated for readers in the 1810s.[37]

Judging by its organization and remedies, Priscilla Homespun's book appears to be a transcription of a woman's recipe manuscript. A recipe for "The Duchess of Rutland's Stomach Plaster for a Cough," hearkens back to the eighteenth-century pattern of citing the authority of aristocratic Englishwomen. However, *The Universal Receipt Book* incorporates contemporary newspapers, magazines, and published medical sources, including a "receipt for the cure of the Jaundice" extracted from the May 1813 *New York Medical Repository.* Like Elizabeth Paschall a half a century earlier, "Priscilla Homespun" appropriated the scientific authority of the chemist Robert Boyle by citing "The Honorable Mr. Boyle's Genuine Syrup for Coughs, Spitting of Blood, etc." These sources alluded to male medical authority, but as we saw with Paschall, a female reader could use the recipe to affirm her own healing expertise. Unlike most "mother's manuals," *The Universal Receipt Book* is an unmediated source of medical knowledge because it did not include a prescriptive preface that attempted to limit women's health care practice.[38]

If the healer Sarah Richardson Waln had picked up a copy of *The Universal Receipt Book* on her visits to Philadelphia from her Walnford estate in New Jersey, she would have found similarities with her own well-worn medical recipe manuscripts. Two of her books that date from 1800 to the mid-1820s are among the handful of extant mid-Atlantic recipe manuscripts from this period. Waln's medical networks included Philadelphia's foremost activists for abolition and health reform, which informed her practice. Skilled healers in Waln's circle included Dr. Benjamin Rush, Anthony Benezet, George and Sarah Dillwyn, their daughter Susanna Dillwyn Emlen, and their sister Margaret Hill Morris. Like others in their network, Waln and her husband, Nicholas, supported Philadelphia's Free African American community's activism for abolition, education, and economic opportunity. In 1800, the prominent Black ministers Richard Allen and Absalom Jones tapped Nicholas Waln to present their abolition petition to the United States Congress. To their chagrin, it was rejected. However, the Joneses, Allens, and Walns continued to agitate for abolition. For healers and ministers' wives such as Sarah Allen and Sarah Waln, curing social ills like slavery was integral to their religious healing ministries.[39]

Nonetheless, inspired reformist discussions could include quotidian health concerns, as evidenced by Sarah Waln's inclusion of Anthony Benezet's "Proven remedy for the Rheumatism" in her manuscript. Although Waln participated in literary, natural philosophical, and abolitionist circles, her recipe manuscripts demonstrate a mix of homespun and science-based healing that persisted into the nineteenth century. Her recipes alternated between formal prescriptions similar to printed pharmacopoeias and more folksy recipes that call for "a peck of Stallions dung" for rheumatism or a sheep's gallbladder to cure cancer. Waln also recorded an Indigenous remedy for leg ulcers that she received from her fellow Quaker friend Sarah Logan.[40] The recipe included the Indigenous herbs sassafras, nettle, and elder bark. Waln noted that Logan had received the remedy "from Wright's family at Susquehanna, & it is said to have performed great Cures, after the greatest Swellings & when the Leg had run with watry sores for some time." Women practitioners still valued remedies from respected eighteenth-century Quaker healers such as Susanna Wright, who likely obtained them from Native Americans. In the latter part of her second recipe book from the late 1810s, Waln's move to rural New Jersey is reflected in her record of recipes to cure veterinary diseases that are not present in her earlier manuscript. Waln, Logan, and other urban and rural women continued to keep medical recipe books and practice healing in their homes and communities.[41]

Sarah Logan's household manuscript includes recipes from Sarah Waln and others in her medical networks. The book dates from the 1810s to the mid-nineteenth century and was passed down among female family members. Logan cited a recipe for "an excellent salve for all kinds of sores recommended on long use by Margaret Marshall," the pharmacist Elizabeth Marshall's sister-in-law. The Moravian missionary John Heckewelder contributed "an Indian cure for a Felon or Whitlow [infected finger]." Reforming Quaker minister George Dillwyn shared his "Essence for the Headache," perhaps borrowed from his sister-in-law Margaret Hill Morris, whose headache powders won local acclaim. Logan also recorded an "Excellent" recipe from her cousin Gulielma Maria Morris Smith, Margaret Morris's daughter. By naming her daughter after the Quaker founding mother Gulielma Maria Springett Penn, Morris kept alive the legacy of an exemplary women healer and religious leader. As in the past, women healers like Morris passed down their knowledge to the next generations. Gulielma Smith and Morris's namesake granddaughter Margaret M. Smith both kept recipe manuscripts.[42]

The Quaker merchant's wife Margaret Burd Coxe, whose "Cook Book and Medicinal Recipes" date from 1817 to 1832, was also part of these networks. Like Sarah Logan, Coxe demonstrates the persistence of the classic Lady Bountiful healer exemplified by Gulielma Penn: an elite woman who provided medical care to her household and community. The large labor pool of domestic servants in the early nineteenth century allowed women such as Coxe to pursue idealized domestic womanhood while paying servants to do much of the actual work, including cooking and preparing medicines. Coxe collected recipes and advice from Philadelphia area physicians, including doctors Physick, Kuhn, and Hewson, but she more often recorded "approved" remedies from her female networks such as Samaritan's Balsam, "a certain cure" for wounds. Her fluency with apothecaries' terminology and the complexity of her herbal and chemical compounds demonstrate the depth of her medical knowledge. Like Elizabeth Paschall and Margaret Morris, Coxe cited the printed works of authoritative physicians such as William Buchan and the Swiss doctor Samuel-August Tissot. She also extracted remedies from newspapers, such as a Black healer's "cure for the [kidney] stone" taken from the *Alexandria Gazette* (Virginia). Her patent medicine recipes for Huxham's Tincture, Glauber's Salts, and Warner's Gout Cordial, as well as her remedies to cure dropsy, gangrenous wounds, or cancer, were similar to those of female healing entrepreneurs. Nonetheless, Coxe would have considered advertising paid medical services in newspapers or directories beneath her dignity. Still, when the Coxes faced financial difficulties in the1820s, Margaret's ability to home-manufacture pharmaceuticals and to provide health care for her household contributed to the family economy.[43]

Elite women's paid and unpaid medical work also provided important healing interventions for family and community members. Susanna Dillwyn Emlen's six-year battle with breast cancer demonstrates the ongoing importance of female medical networks in the face of incurable diseases. Emlen was particularly close to her cousin Deborah Logan and her Aunt Margaret Hill Morris. In 1798, Morris had advised her daughter, Gulielma, to counsel Susanna Emlen to take ginseng for a breast lump. That is, quipped Morris, unless Emlen was "so Modernizd as to neglect good medicine because it is recommended by an old woman." Emlen accepted Morris's remedy and the tumor resolved. However, in 1814, at age forty-four, Emlen detected another breast lump "the size of a partridge egg." It was diagnosed as cancer by her brother-in-law Dr. Philip Syng Physic. Emlen was in a quandary, because mastectomy without anesthesia was intensely painful and did not always eradicate the cancer.[44]

While Emlen awaited surgery, her cousin Deborah Logan wrote, advising her to try an Indigenous cure, a tea and a poultice both made from the herb pipsissewa. Deborah and her husband, Dr. George Logan, had prescribed it with success, and she hoped Emlen would "give it a Tryal." However, Deborah Logan realized, "in cases like this, different applications are posed by almost all with whom one converses." Emlen had received medical advice and remedies from physicians, aunts, and female friends. "Yet," Logan continued, "as in a more important concern [the Christian gospel], the wisdom of the wise has been confounded by the weak and the simple; and as I believe infinite goodness has imparted powerful efficacy to many simples in medicine." Paraphrasing a New Testament verse, Logan invoked a long-standing tradition that God had placed in nature the cure for diseases in basic herbal preparations, known as "simples." Perhaps Logan was also intimating that at times the wisdom of laywomen healers, purportedly feminine "weaker vessels," might confound the learned knowledge of physicians. Dr. Physic excised the tumor in 1814 but Emlen's symptoms recurred. She died of breast cancer in 1819. Despite physicians' claims to be the arbiters of a new scientific medicine, it was clear that numerous illnesses confounded the expertise of doctors and women healers alike. Sufferers melded their ongoing search for effective medical therapeutics with reforming visions that generated hopes for bodily wellness and perfection.[45]

The emergence of the Thomsonian botanical movement in the 1820s heralded the beginning of a renewed popular health movement that provided women healers with additional venues to assert their healing legitimacy. The evangelical religious transformations of the Second Great Awakening introduced theological notions of spiritual perfectionism, which informed new medical theories. Moreover, a revived culture of populism during the 1820s and 1830s promoted individualism and fostered a backlash against elitist professional physicians' organizations, as exemplified by Samuel Thomson, the founder of the Thomsonian movement. Thomson emphasized that self-diagnosis and self-medication with a limited number of botanical "simples" were safer and more effective than physicians' therapeutics based on extensive bleeding and purging. Thomson revealed that he learned his herbal skills as a youth on botanical excursions in the countryside with his village's healer, the Widow Benton. He reprised earlier populist arguments regarding the issues of the accessibility and affordability of health care. Thomson protested physicians' exorbitant fees and noted that the most educated physicians congregated in cities, leaving rural areas underserved. Thomsonian practitioners were facilitators who educated people to perfect their own health. By the 1830s, Thomsonianism had attracted over one million adherents. The rise of a popular botanical medical movement based on a female village healer's medical knowledge validated women's continued role as herbal healers. As Samuel Thomson's son John asserted, "We cannot deny that women possess superior capacities for the science of medicine." Women practiced Thomsonian self-help medicine and served as botanical medicine practitioners.[46]

The Thomsonian movement was only the beginning of a wave of novel medical theories and practitioners that were popular in the greater Philadelphia area during the 1830s and 1840s. Some women healers took advantage of these new opportunities. In addition to challenges from the Thomsonians, physicians found their practices and incomes threatened by practitioners called Eclectics, homeopaths, and hydropaths. In response, physicians derisively deemed their medical competitors "sectarians," as opposed to the orthodoxy of the "regular" doctors or allopaths. The medical movement called Eclecticism emerged as another botanical medical challenge to "regular" physicians that more readily accepted women as physicians. For example, Sarah Adamson Dolley, a resident of Montgomery County, north of Philadelphia, was admitted to an Eclectic medical college in New York in 1849 after facing rejection from "regular" medical schools. Homeopaths shared the Eclectics' and Thomsonians' beliefs that health care providers should facilitate nature's healing powers. The movement's German founder, Samuel Hahnemann, argued that "like cured like" and he crafted cures for diseases in diluted doses that complemented patients' symptoms. In 1848, homeopathic physicians founded the Homeopathic Medical School in Philadelphia, later called Hahnemann Medical College. Like Thomsonians and Eclectics, homeopaths were more open to women as practitioners than "regulars."[47]

Women also worked as "water cure" providers and developed hydropathic institutions that were popular with female sufferers. Hydropathists asserted that water had healing powers when ingested and applied using various topical therapies. One fifth of water cure practitioners were women. Women hydropathists promoted a sexual health reform movement that educated women about their bodies and physiological functions. For women who practiced as apothecaries and druggists, the popularity of the sexual health movement provided additional opportunities to market herbal contraceptives, abortifacients, and contraceptive devices. Contraceptive products were increasingly sold in pharmacies and dry goods shops, and drug companies hired women to sell them door-to-door. Female healers found new ways to demonstrate their expertise in women's health, as well in as general medical practice.[48]

However, as in the past, patients had no assurances regarding health care providers' qualifications or the safety and efficacy of their remedies. The "regular" medical community only complicated the picture when for-profit "diploma mill" medical schools sprang up throughout the expanding United States during the late 1820s, churning out physicians with minimal education and experience in as short a time as three months. Amid uncertainties regarding "regular" physicians' qualifications, consumers continued to seek care from reputable women practitioners. Women and men's health care practices rested on providers' personal credibility and their ability to win patients' hearts and minds.[49]

As the renewed popular health movement took off, educated middle-class women of various ethnicities were poised to become authoritative lecturers in anatomy, physiology, childbearing, sexuality, and women's health. Nonphysician practitioners appropriated the emerging authority of anatomy despite doctors' attempt to control the diffusion of this knowledge by preventing women from attending dissections. Literate women educated themselves in anatomy. Ann Bartram Carr, the granddaughter of Philadelphia botanists and healers John and Ann Bartram, owned a well-worn copy of *The Anatomist's Vade Mecum*, a personal pocket handbook of anatomy. Patience Lovell Wright of New Jersey studied anatomy to create physiologically correct wax anatomical models.[50] In 1828, at age eighteen, Mary Gove (later Nichols) recalled, "I commenced reading on Pathology, and continued for several years reading Medical, Anatomical, Physiological, and Pathological works, as they came my way." Her self-education was the prelude to her careers as a hydropathist and women's health educator.[51]

The popular health movement fostered women's interest in bodily education by supporting public discussions of women's anatomy and sexual health. In 1839, Mary Gove explained to a friend, that unlike residents of other cities who found her public speeches scandalous, Philadelphians endorsed her health lectures on sensitive subjects to mixed male and female audiences. She emphasized that Philadelphia was "a city of *women*," with "*more* intelligent women here than I have ever found in any other city." Women's education in oratory and the sciences gave them the confidence to speak publicly. Health lectures also advertised women's healing practices and provided income. The Quaker healer Sarah Coates of West Chester, Pennsylvania, used anatomical models as tactile and visual aids in her publicized health education classes in the 1840s. A broadside detailed her "Course of Lectures to the Ladies" on "ANATOMY, PHYSIOLOGY, AND HYGIENE," enlivened by "the MODELLE DE FEMME, OR ATIFICIAL FEMALE FIGURE, and a set of life-size anatomical plates." The anatomical models exhibited body organs "in situ," but could be taken apart to "answer all the general purposes of an actual dissection." As a marketing tool, Coates advertised a free introductory lecture with a twenty-five-cent admission charge for subsequent single lectures or one dollar for the entire course. There is evidence that she provided medical consultations after her lectures. After relocating to Salem, Ohio, Coates would later serve as the secretary of the Ohio Convention for Women's Rights. For Coates and Gove, women's health education was integral to their feminist activism.[52]

According to health reformers, self-improvement fostered social and moral progress. Health teaching allowed educated middle-class women to reconfigure female healers' traditional private health promotion practices into public endeavors. In turn, health education would ostensibly improve the body politic. As a member of Philadelphia's Black middle class, Sarah Mapps

Douglass taught anatomy and physiological health education as part of a program of "social uplift" and to contribute to the general health of the African American community. Douglass was the granddaughter of Cyrus Bustill, a founding member of the Free African Society. She continued her family's activist legacy. Organizations such as the Ladies' Physiological Society, founded in 1837, also supported women as health lecturers. Despite facing backlash among those who believed women's place was in the home, activist women lectured publicly on physiology, sexual health, abolition, and women's rights. For women such as Douglass and the Quaker healer Hannah Longshore, the public health and hygiene lecture circuit was a prelude to their formal academic medical education. The early nineteenth-century popular health movement provided new opportunities for women to provide public health education, serve as leaders in reform organizations, and to practice as healers and pharmaceutical vendors in new medical movements.[53]

The rhetoric of domesticity and male physicians' and pharmacists' attempts to control medical practice helped to create the historical amnesia surrounding women's early nineteenth-century health care practices. If Elizabeth Marshall's public accomplishments as an apothecary, druggist, and pharmaceutical manufacturer were forgotten by the late twentieth century, it follows that eighteenth and early nineteenth-century women's healing practices were also obscured. In their own time, white women healers such as Elizabeth Coates Paschall, Margaret Hill Morris, Mary Watters, and Martha Brand were so ubiquitous that they were unremarkable. Women practitioners of color such as Hannah Freeman and Sarah Bass Allen were also well known in their communities. Although women healers' work is poorly documented in the historical record, their recovered narratives trace a vibrant culture of women doctresses, nurses, apothecaries, druggists, herb sellers, Thomsonian practitioners, homeopathic physicians, health educators, and water cure providers who practiced well into the mid-nineteenth century. The special environment in the greater Philadelphia area catalyzed women's healing roles, with its Quaker values of social activism, female education, and egalitarianism. It is not surprising that homeopathic Quaker physicians, who participated in the abolition, women rights, and health reform movements, supported the Quaker healer Hannah Longshore's efforts to create the Female Medical College of Pennsylvania in 1850. Women healers built on their foremothers' skills and authority to establish the world's first medical school for women in Philadelphia.[54]

A Well-Trodden Path

In 1851, the Female Medical College of Pennsylvania's first women graduates listened avidly while their commencement speaker, Dr. Joseph Longshore, celebrated their achievements as a "new and momentous enterprise" and "an eventful epoch in the history of your lives, in the history of woman." As Longshore emphasized, the graduates demonstrated that "woman's intellect is fully capable of grasping and comprehending, in a pre-eminent degree, all the various branches comprised in a thorough medical education." He explained that their achievements defied the long-standing belief that women were "intellectually and physically inferior to man." According to Longshore, after treading "the rugged paths of science," the women graduates could look "from behind the impenetrable fortress of scientific attainment" with "well founded confidence." As she listened to her brother-in-law's speech, Dr. Hannah Myers Longshore likely reflected on her early interest in medicine and science as a girl growing up in a progressive Quaker family in the 1820s.[1]

Hannah Longshore began her healing career teaching public physiology and hygiene classes. After her marriage to Thomas Longshore in 1844, and following the birth of her two children, Longshore apprenticed with the homeopathist Dr. Joseph Longshore in Attleboro, Pennsylvania, northeast of Philadelphia. Joseph Longshore and other Quakers supported Hannah's efforts to create an institution that would provide professional legitimacy for women health care practitioners. Her classmate Ann Preston was also raised in an activist Quaker family in Chester County, Pennsylvania, and worked as teacher in Quaker schools. Both women's commitment to health reform was interwoven with their activism for women's rights, female education, abolition, and temperance. Preston also apprenticed with a physician for two years. Perhaps inspired by Elizabeth Blackwell's graduation from Geneva Medical College in New York in 1849, Preston applied to three Philadelphia-area medical schools. However, Preston became acutely aware of the barriers to women's academic medical education when all three schools rejected her application. With the support of Joseph Longshore, Quaker philanthropists, and five other male doctors who served as professors, the Female Medical College opened in Philadelphia in 1850. Preston and Hannah Longshore were among the college's first forty female medical students to matriculate at the first medical school for women. Within a few years after graduation, Preston was appointed professor of physiology at the college, and Hannah Longshore taught anatomy. Preston also supervised the creation of a nurses' training school. Longshore's and Preston's passage from women's health care activists to medical students and then to professors demonstrates the increasing importance of professionalization in women's battles for medical authority.[2]

In 1855, it was Dr. Ann Preston's turn to address the Female Medical College's incoming class embarking on what Preston described as a "new and untried course." However, Preston and Longshore had precedents in other women who had expanded gendered boundaries in health care. Female Medical College professors and students were indebted to innumerable Delaware Valley women who had practiced as healers and apothecaries, as well as Quaker ministers who had pioneered spaces for women's authoritative presence in public. Preston recognized women's long-standing and vital healing roles. She explained, "The scattered records that have come down to us upon the page of history" demonstrate "that women were, quite commonly, the physicians of the household" and their "insight and natural fitness best adapted them to the office." Preston and the female medical students would have known women healers with public practices in their communities, as well as remembered healers in the past.[3]

The obstacles that the Female Medical College graduates faced, as delineated by Drs. Ann Preston and Joseph Longshore, would have been familiar to female healers of previous generations. During Longshore's commencement speech, crowds of male medical students gathered outside the auditorium to ridicule and intimidate the women students. In her later address, Preston referred to ongoing hostility from the male medical community when she advised women students to "look with quiet pity on those self-elected arbiters, who, gratuitously, have taken upon themselves the labor of marking out for us [the medical profession's] boundaries." Amid this opposition, Preston underscored the continued need for supportive female health care networks for women physicians. Joseph Longshore's address also highlighted the importance of scientific study as a means of legitimizing women's medical

Figure 12. Women's Medical College students studying the human skeleton, ca. late nineteenth century. Courtesy Legacy Center Archives, Drexel University College of Medicine, Philadelphia. Women medical students understood that proficiency in anatomy was the essential mark of an educated physician. Although it was disrespectful to human remains, this type of pose was a ubiquitous rite of passage among male and female medical students.

work, just as Elizabeth Coates Paschall had enhanced her mid-eighteenth-century healing practice with botanical, chemical, and anatomical information from printed works and medical networks. Paschall had witnessed the emergence of the authority of anatomy along with the controversies over the dissection of human corpses. A century later, knowledge of anatomy through dissection was the definitive skill that differentiated professional physicians from nonphysicians. Dr. Hannah Longshore recognized the importance of her post as professor of anatomy and braced for the backlash from male physicians in this "unfeminine" pursuit. Her brother-in-law advised women students to ignore "the thousand tongues of calumny . . . ever busy to blast your reputations." Although Joseph Longshore's commencement speech situated the women physicians within a bastion of "scientific attainment," he recognized that critics would continue to challenge women's intellectual and scientific capabilities.[4]

Joseph Longshore also spoke to the problematic relationship between health care as an art that benefited humankind and the business of medicine. He exhorted the graduating women physicians to "be attentive and charitable to the poor everywhere" and "refuse them not your services, because of their inability to compensate you." However, he delineated limits to their roles as benevolent healers. He continued, "But when the competent and wealthy require your services, let a full and fair compensation be demanded. . . . You are as justly entitled to full fees as are your brethren of the profession." Joseph Longshore even launched into a discourse on the injustice of unequal pay for women. Margaret Hill Morris would have recognized the fine points of establishing a financially remunerative medical and apothecary practice while maintaining humanitarian values.[5]

However, Longshore's comments reflected the evolving distinctions between medicine and pharmacy as physicians sought to distinguish themselves from apothecaries and eschew advertising. Aggressive personal or pharmaceutical marketing was beneath the dignity of a professional physician. Those who resorted to overt commercialism risked being criticized as a mere "empiric" or "sectarian." As Longshore cautioned graduates, "Resort to no flaming or pretending advertisements." He advised the women to rely only on a simple business card to promote their practice, because blatant publicity was "evidence of empiricism and will bring upon you the odium and opposition of the profession." However, women pharmaceutical entrepreneurs could not yet aspire to become professional pharmacists, because the Philadelphia College of Pharmacy excluded women. Lydia Pinkham exemplifies alternative possibilities for women who wanted to follow in the footsteps of apothecaries like Elizabeth Weed. Pinkham, a respected Quaker healer, melded the knowledge in her manuscript recipe book with information in *The American Dispensatory* to create her Lydia Pinkham's Vegetable Compound. Like Elizabeth Weed and Mary Watters, Pinkham was adept at marketing. Her motherly face, which adorned her Vegetable Compound packages, invited women to purchase her product to cure "female complaints." Pinkham's "pink pills" became one of the best-selling patent medicines in the nineteenth and early twentieth centuries. Savvy businesswomen continued to have a respected voice in the consumer medical market. However, it was not until 1883 that the Quaker Susan Hayhurst became the first woman graduate of the Philadelphia College of Pharmacy, after receiving her degree from the Female

Medical College in 1857 and presiding over its Department of Pharmacy for a quarter century.[6]

Professional medicine also created barriers between doctors and nurses. Joseph Longshore encouraged female medical students to avoid placing themselves in the role of handmaidens to physicians. In their relationships with male doctors, he advised, "Do not, because you are women, regard yourselves as inferior, or your judgment of less value." He exhorted, "Have nothing to do with the duties of the nurse . . . further than to exercise supervision, give directions and require obedience." As Longshore explained, women physicians were "directed towards a higher and more responsible position than a performer of the mere drudgery of the invalid's chamber." Women graduates like Ann Preston imbibed values that created boundaries between diagnostics, prescribing, and personal nursing care that Margaret Hill Morris and Mary Watters would not have recognized. In their attempts to gain a foothold in the medical profession, women physicians reified hierarchies of medical authority that placed doctors' expertise as preeminent. The subsequent professionalization of nursing created new conflicts over the authority of nurses and physicians.[7]

Nonetheless, as a Quaker and an abolitionist, Ann Preston recognized African American women's rights to professional education. Sarah Mapps Douglass became the first African American student to attend the Female Medical College. After listening to several of Preston's medical lectures, Douglass wrote, "I cannot describe the pure intellect and enjoyment they give me." Like Sarah Bass Allen, Douglass intertwined health care, education, and abolitionist politics as part of her civil rights agenda. Dean Preston also mentored Rebecca J. Cole, who was the first Black woman to obtain a degree from the college in 1867 and the second African American woman to receive a medical degree in the United States. Decades later, in 1889, Susan La Flesche Picotte would become the first Native American woman to graduate from the renamed Woman's Medical College of Pennsylvania.[8]

Although women's entry into the professional fields of medicine and nursing are important narratives, they should not obscure women's ongoing roles as lay healers in their communities. The Lenape healer Elizabeth Harker Elmer exemplifies Native American women who practiced their healing craft throughout the nineteenth century and passed down their medical knowledge to female relatives. Elmer was remembered as a skilled healer who was an asset to her Lenape community in Bridgeton, New Jersey. The Quaker healer Elizabeth Neff Bowman continued her work as a respected "doctress" in her town west of Philadelphia through the mid-nineteenth century. A woman called "Granny Tribble" represents Pennsylvania German healers called *braucherei* who recorded their knowledge in manuscripts and practiced in rural areas into the 1870s. Many *braucherei* continue their healing work into the present day. Amid the increasing professionalization of medicine, pharmacy, and nursing in the mid-nineteenth century, laywomen healers continued their important but often unrecorded healing practices.[9]

Women's professional and lay healing work in the greater Philadelphia area has deep roots. Longshore, Preston, Cole, Elmer, and other mid-nineteenth-century healers built on the foundations established by women in the past. As the British North American colonies' "first city" of medicine and science, Philadelphia provided women healers with a nurturing environment enriched by diverse healing cultures and the Quaker values of gender equality and women's education. When English Quaker immigrants sailed to Philadelphia in the late seventeenth century, they transmitted a culture of skilled healers exemplified by their Quaker founding mother, Gulielma Springett Penn. Early Euro-American women practitioners of various social classes provided the bulk of health care in their communities. They exchanged medical knowledge with Lenape women healers and African American practitioners who were recognized for their healing expertise. Women healers of various ethnicities found ways to navigate the new challenges posed by Enlightenment science, capitalism, medical professionalization, and a constraining culture of domesticity. Some women developed science-based practices within networks of healers and natural philosophers, while others established apothecary businesses or sold medicines and healing advice in an unregulated consumer health care marketplace. Although Black women healers faced racial and gender discrimination, some used their healing expertise as a platform to demonstrate reforming benevolence and to promote Black civil equality. Other healers appropriated the authority of manuscript authorship, female education in the sciences, medical print media, and the health reform movement. All these women represent a bridge connecting the skilled women healers of the seventeenth century to the female health care professionals of the nineteenth century. The Female Medical College graduates' "new and untried course" was just a more obvious signpost on a well-trodden path.

Recovering women healers' authoritative work is more than a mere antiquarian pastime. Their narratives speak to issues that reverberate into the twenty-first century. Considering women healers' legacies, it is not surprising that women hold 76 percent of all health care jobs in the United States.

Nurses form the largest segment of health care professionals, and over 90 percent are women. However, studies demonstrate ongoing racial barriers within the nursing profession, as evidenced by increased attrition among Black nurses and nursing students, which leads to lower percentages of Black nurses in faculty and health care leadership positions. In view of her struggles to advance women in medicine, Ann Preston would be pleased to know that currently over half of the students in medical schools are women. Nonetheless, men still dominate the most lucrative medical specialties and earn 25 percent more than women in comparable fields. Minority women are underrepresented in all medical specialties. Women also dominate the field of pharmacy, but the percentages of minority women continue to lag behind their ratios in the US population. Moreover, the ongoing gender gap in science, technology, engineering, and mathematics (STEM) fields reflects the long history of women's marginalization in disciplines that form the basis for health care–related jobs. What Joseph Longshore called the "fortress of scientific attainment" can still be daunting for young women, particularly for women of color. The complex causes can be traced to systemic educational and social inequalities. However, several studies suggest that the paucity of educational curriculum highlighting women's past engagement in medicine and the sciences exacerbates the problem of attracting white women and women of color into these fields. Researchers underscored the importance of diverse historical role models for women and stressed the need to accentuate the history of women in health care and the sciences at all educational levels. Telling stories that enliven the struggles and successes of women of the past provides students and health care professionals with role models and strategies to navigate contemporary cultural barriers. This book contributes to these conversations by writing women healers back into the narratives of early American history.[10]

GLOSSARY

ague   Sudden and recurring attacks of chills and fever.

alchemy   An ancient practice that sought to transform metals through chemical processes, particularly to transmute base metals into gold and to discover the philosopher's stone that would confer healing and eternal life. Precursor to the fields of chemistry and metallurgy.

anodyne   Pain-relieving medicine.

apothecary   An individual or business that compounds and dispenses medicines.

bloodletting   Therapeutic removal of a portion of a patient's blood, often performed by incising a large vein in the arm or neck and draining blood into a cup. Used in Galenic medicine to balance a patient's bodily humors.

brank   Cage-like iron device that encircled the head. It featured a bridle bit that projected into the victim's mouth and pressed down on the tongue, interfering with speaking, eating, and drinking. Used to punish women speaking or preaching in public and was later used in the Atlantic slave trade to punish enslaved Africans.

chincough   Whooping cough.

cinchona bark (Peruvian bark or Jesuit's bark)   Bark from several species of a South American flowering shrub that yields the compound quinine used to treat a variety of fevers. We now understand that it is active against malaria.

classical republicanism   Although classical republicanism or civic humanism originated in the ancient Greco-Roman world, it was reprised during the Renaissance and the Enlightenment. This ideology argued that virtuous, male property-holding citizens should be active in public life and should subordinate their self-interest for the common good of the republic. This rhetoric was popular during the American Revolution and it was reintroduced during the 1793 Philadelphia yellow fever epidemic.

consumption   A variety of serious wasting illnesses, often associated with lung diseases that we would identify as tuberculosis or lung cancer.

culture of domesticity or "cult of true womanhood"   Nineteenth-century culture that sought to relegate women to the private household sphere, where they served as homemakers and mothers, safe from the perils of the business domain.

culture of sensibility   An emphasis on markers of refinement and civility as well as a rhetoric of feeling benevolence that promoted social reform.

distillation   Process of creating a concentrated extract through dissolving and then boiling off water.

dropsy   A life-threatening ailment characterized by swelling of the lower extremities, which we now understand can be caused by heart or kidney failure.

emmenagogue   Medication that stimulates menstrual flow.

empiricism   Method of accumulating knowledge through observation, measurement, and experiment.

felon   Infected fingertip.

flux, bloody flux   Diarrhea, bloody diarrhea.

Galenic medicine   See humoral medicine.

glister or clister   Enema: the injection of a liquid into the rectum for therapeutic purposes.

gout   An inflamed joint, most commonly on the foot, now understood to be caused by an accumulation of crystals in the joint fluid.

green sickness   A condition that may have been related to iron deficiency in young menstruating women or to the medicalization of female puberty.

homeopathy   A medical system developed by Samuel Hahnemann in 1796 that used small amounts of natural substances to help the body to heal itself. Practitioners assisted the body in curing itself.

humoral medicine   Medical theories established by the second-century Roman physician Galen. According to Galenic principles, the four humors—phlegm, black bile, yellow bile, and blood—were linked to the corresponding elements of water, earth, fire, and air, as well as qualities of warmth, wetness, coolness, and dryness. Wellness was achieved by balancing these bodily humors.

hydropathy or water cure   A therapeutic system popularized in the early nineteenth century that uses water treatments to cure illnesses. Therapies include prescribing large quantities of drinking water, water immersion, and water showers.

king's evil or scrofula   A common illness in the early modern period. It is understood today as tuberculosis of the lymph nodes in the neck.

Lady Bountiful   A character in George Farquhar's popular Restoration comedy *The Beaux-Stratagem*; a benevolent, elite English healer who cured her family, neighbors, and tenants gratis.

leeches   Bloodsucking worms used in humoral therapies to evacuate blood and maladaptive humors from the body.

man-midwife   Male physician who assisted women in childbirth; later known as an obstetrician.

natural philosopher   Student of the natural world and the physical sciences.

natural philosophy   Study of the natural world. This predated and encompassed many of the modern scientific disciplines including biology, chemistry, physics, and astronomy.

old wives   A derogative term applied to elderly and poor female healers who charged or bartered for their services.

Paracelsian medicine   A style of medicine contrary to humoral medicine, based on the theories of Paracelsus, a sixteenth-century Swiss physician. It links bodily disease to chemical imbalances, which could be cured by mineral-based remedies targeting particular symptoms and diseases. Paracelsus's chemically mediated paradigm argued that specific remedies for particular illnesses could be generalized across populations, as opposed to a more personalized Galenic analysis of an individual's bodily constitution.

pharmacopoeia   A listing of compounded medications usually published by an authoritative source such as a city or medical society. The *Pharmacopoeia Londinensis* or *London Pharmacopoeia* was first published in the early seventeenth century.

philosopher's stone   A mythical alchemical substance which could transmute base metals into precious gold and confer immortality and healing.

phthisis A wasting pulmonary disease.

physic or physick An early term for the practice of medical healing; also used in humoral practice to describe medicines that evacuated maladaptive humors from the body.

poultice A medication-coated cloth applied to the skin.

quinsy A pustular swelling around the tonsils, which might have been related to diphtheria or another infection. In severe cases, quinsy could lead to suffocation.

rheumatism Joint pain, usually chronic, that in humoral medicine was considered to be caused by maladaptive humors invading a joint or body part.

scald head Tinea capitis or ringworm. A fungal infection that caused hair loss and peeling skin on the scalp. Could become inflamed and infected. Although the problem was common, infected persons carried the stigma of poverty.

sciatica Back pain that radiates down the leg caused by irritation or injury to the sciatic nerve.

scurvy A disease now understood to be caused by a deficiency of vitamin C, which causes fatigue, aches, inflamed limbs, bleeding gums, tooth loss, anemia, and hemorrhages.

sensibility See *culture of sensibility*.

simples, simpling Medicinal herbs, the act of gathering those herbs. Also medications that used only one main herbal ingredient to treat an illness.

smallpox inoculation The act of exposing a patient to smallpox in a controlled, limited way in order to induce a mild case of the disease and to confer lifelong immunity. This was done by placing smallpox-infected pus into an incision on the patient's arm.

Society of Friends or Quakers A reforming religious sect that originated in the mid-seventeenth century. The sect challenged political, social, and gender hierarchies as well as the theological status quo. Friends sought a lifestyle that testified to their equality, simplicity, and integrity, and emphasized literacy for both women and men.

St. Anthony's fire, St. Antony's fire, or erysipelas Characterized by a red, swollen, weeping, and intensely burning rash associated with fever, chills, and vomiting, usually on the face or extremities. It could be deadly, particularly for women and infants following childbirth. We now understand that this disease is caused by a virulent strain of streptococcus.

Thomsonian botanical healing A health movement that began in the 1820s that emphasized that self-diagnosis and self-medication with a limited number of botanical "simples" were safer and more effective than physicians' interventionist bleeding and purging treatments.

tincture Concentrated medicinal extract that uses alcohol as a solvent, concentrated through heat distillation.

whitlow A synonym for *felon*, an infected finger.

worms Intestinal worms were a persistent and debilitating problem for children and adults in the late eighteenth century. Hookworms cause blood loss and anemia, tapeworms invade human tissues and organs, and roundworms migrate throughout the body and can infest the lungs.

ABBREVIATIONS

Frequently Cited Historical Archives

APS	American Philosophical Society, Philadelphia, PA
CCHS	Chester County Historical Society, West Chester, PA
CPP	College of Physicians Philadelphia, Philadelphia, PA
DCHS	Delaware County Historical Society, Chester, PA
HQSC	Haverford College Quaker Special Collections, Haverford, PA
HSP	Historical Society of Pennsylvania, Philadelphia, PA
LCP	Library Company of Philadelphia, Philadelphia, PA
NLM	National Library of Medicine, Washington, DC
UPRBM	University of Pennsylvania Rare Book and Manuscript Library, Philadelphia, PA
WL	Wellcome Library, London, UK
WML	Winterthur Museum and Library, Wilmington, DE

Journals

PMHB	*Pennsylvania Magazine of History and Biography*
WMQ	*William and Mary Quarterly*

NOTES

Introduction

1. Ann Preston, "Introductory Lecture to the Course of Instruction," Female Medical College of Pennsylvania, 1855, 13, Drexel University College of Medicine, Archives and Special Collections; Steven J. Peitzman, *A New and Untried Course: Woman's Medical College and Medical College of Pennsylvania, 1850–1998* (New Brunswick, NJ: Rutgers University Press, 2000), 5–13.

2. H. Macaulay Fitzgibbon, ed., *The Beaux-Stratagem: A Comedy Written by George Farquhar* (London: J. M. Dent and Co., 1898), xii–xvi, 2–3.

3. George Farquhar, *The Beaux-Stratagem: A Comedy* (London: Bernard Lintott, 1707), 3, 41–44, 99; Heather S. Nathans, *Early American Theatre from the Revolution to Thomas Jefferson* (New York: Cambridge University Press, 2003), 14–18; Jason Shaffer, *Performing Patriotism: National Identity in the Colonial and Revolutionary American Theater* (Philadelphia: University of Pennsylvania Press, 2007), 69–78; Paul Kuritz, *The Making of Theatre History* (Englewood Cliffs, NJ: Prentice-Hall, 1988), 241; George Overcash Seilhamer, *History of the American Theatre: Before the Revolution, 1749–1774* (Philadelphia: Globe Printing House, 1888; repr., 1968), 1–11, 49–50, 248–51; Thomas Clark Pollock, *The Philadelphia Theatre in the Eighteenth Century* (Westport, CT: Greenwood Press, 1968), 7; *Rivington's Gazette*, June 3, 1773; *New York Mercury*, June 7, 1773. In his popular 1678 allegory *Pilgrim's Progress*, John Bunyan included a character named Bountiful who showed "kindness to the poor." See J. M. Hare, ed., *Pilgrim's Progress by John Bunyan* (London: Simpkin, Marshall, and Co., 1856), 255.

4. John Gerard, William Rogers, and Rembert Dodoens, *The Herball or Generall Historie of Plantes* (London: Edm. Bollifant for [Bonham Norton and] John Norton, 1597), 288, 315, 351; Rebecca Laroche, *Medical Authority and Englishwomen's Herbal Texts, 1550–1650* (Burlington, VT: Ashgate, 2009), 21–23; Adam Fox, "Old Wives Tales and Nursery Lore," in *Oral and Literate Culture in England, 1500–1700* (New York: Oxford University Press, 2003), 174–77; Mary E. Lamb, "Old Wives' Tales, George Peele, and Narrative Abjection," *Critical Survey* 1, no. 1 (2002): 29–33; M. A. Katritzky, *Women, Medicine and Theatre, 1500–1750: Literary Mountebanks and Performing Quacks* (Burlington, VT: Ashgate, 2007), 135–50; Steven Shapin, *A Social History of Truth: Civility and Science in Seventeenth Century England* (Chicago: University of Chicago Press, 1994), 87–92, 200–201; George Peele, *The Old Wives Tale: A Pleasant Conceited Comedie* (London: John Danter, 1596); *The Old Wives Tales: A Poem* (London: J. Morphew, 1712); Thomas Bridges, *Homer Travestie: Being a New Burlesque Translation* (London: S. Hooper, 1767), 54.

5. See, for example, Wendy Wall, *Recipes for Thought: Knowledge and Taste in the Early Modern English Kitchen* (Philadelphia: University of Pennsylvania Press, 2016), 4; Lamar Murphy, *Enter the Physician: The Transformation of Domestic Medicine, 1760–1860* (Tuscaloosa: University of Alabama Press, 1991), 51–59; Regina Morantz-Sanchez, *Sympathy and Science: Women*

Physicians in American Medicine (Chapel Hill: University of North Carolina Press, 2000), 16–19; Paul Starr, *The Social Transformation of American Medicine* (New York: Basic Books, 1982), 49; Joseph Kett, *The Formation of the American Medical Profession* (Santa Barbara, CA: Greenwood Press, 1980); Sylvia D. Hoffert, *Private Matters: American Attitudes Toward Childbearing and Infant Nurture in the Urban North, 1800–1860* (Urbana: University of Illinois Press, 1989).

6. Charlotte Charke, *A Narrative of the Life of Mrs. Charlotte Charke, Youngest Daughter of Colley Cibber, Esq.* (London: Whittaker, Treacher, and Arnot, 1829), 9–10, 22–26; Kathryn Shevelow, *Charlotte: Being a True Account of an Actress's Flamboyant Adventures in Eighteenth-Century London's Wild and Wicked Theatrical World* (New York: Picador, 2005), 73–75, 352–55; William Salmon, *Pharmacopoeia Londinensis; or, The New London Dispensatory* (London: T. Dawns, 1678), UPRBM; and Nicholas Culpeper, *The Practice of Physick: Wherein is Plainly Set For the . . . Cure of All Diseases in the Body of Man* (London: P. Cole, 1664), UPRBM.

7. Charke, *Narrative*, 22–26. For similar examples, see Amanda Vickery, *The Gentleman's Daughter: Women's Lives in Georgian England* (New Haven, CT: Yale University Press, 1998), 154–56.

8. Anne Parrish, Visitations of the Sick, 1796, Parrish Collection, box 5, bound volumes, #1653, HSP, 4–5; Elizabeth Coates Paschall, Manuscript Recipe Book, ca. 1745–67, 4, 11, 10, CPP.

9. Moses Marshall, "The Examination &c of Indian Hannah," July 28, 1797, in Hannah Freeman file, CCHS; J. Smith Futhey and Gilbert Cope, *History of Chester County, Pennsylvania*, vol. 2 (Philadelphia: L. H. Everts and Co., 1881), 189–91; Kathleen M. Brown, *Good Wives, Nasty Wenches, and Anxious Patriarchs: Gender, Race, and Power in Colonial Virginia* (Chapel Hill: University of North Carolina Press, 1996), 1–6, 107–36; Sharla Fett, *Working Cures: Healing, Health, and Power on Southern Slave Plantations* (Chapel Hill: University of North Carolina Press, 2002), 111–68.

10. Gary B. Nash, *First City: Philadelphia and the Forging of Historical Memory* (Philadelphia: University of Pennsylvania Press, 2006), 45–78; Evan Haefeli, "The Pennsylvania Difference: Religious Diversity on the Delaware Before 1683," *Early American Studies* 1, no. 1 (2003): 28–60; Susan E. Klepp, "Encounter and Experiment: The Colonial Period," in *Pennsylvania: A History of the Commonwealth*, ed. Randall M. Miller and William Pencak (University Park: Pennsylvania State University Press, 2002), 47–100.

11. Monica H. Green, "Documenting Medieval Women's Medical Practice," in *Practical Medicine from Salerno to the Black Death*, ed. Luis García-Ballester et al. (New York: Cambridge University Press, 1994), 352; Rebecca Tannenbaum, *The Healer's Calling: Women and Medicine in Early New England* (Ithaca, NY: Cornell University Press, 2002), 118–27. For *doctress* or *doctoress*, see these popular reference books: John Kersey, *Dictionarium Anglo-Britannicum, or A General English Dictionary* (London: J. Wilde, 1708); John Quincy, *Pharmacopoeia Officinalis & Extemporanea*, 5th ed. (London: E. Bell, 1724), 101; Nathan Bailey, *An Universal Etymological English Dictionary* (London: R. Ware, 1751); Abel Boyer, *The Royal Dictionary of English and French* (London: J. M. Bruyset, 1756), 177; "Some nouns distinguish their feminine by ending in *ess*," William Perry, *A General Dictionary of the English Language* (London: John Stockdale, 1795); *Oxford English Dictionary*.

12. Laurel Thatcher Ulrich, *A Midwife's Tale: The Life of Martha Ballard, Based on Her Diary, 1785–1812* (New York: Vintage, 1990), 342, 28–33, 47; Barbara Ehrenreich and Deirdre English, *Witches, Midwives, and Nurses: A History of Women Healers* (New York: Feminist Press, 1973); John Duffy, *From Humors to Medical Science: A History of American Medicine*

(Urbana: University of Illinois Press, 1993), 284–86; Richard W. Wertz and Dorothy C. Wertz, *Lying-In: A History of Childbirth in America* (New York: Free Press, 1977); Jane B. Donegan, *Women and Men Midwives: Medicine, Morality, and Misogyny in Early America* (Westport, CT: Greenwood Press, 1978); Catherine M. Scholten, *Childbearing in American Society, 1650–1850* (New York: New York University Press, 1985); Judith Walzer Leavitt, *Brought to Bed: Childbearing in America, 1750 to 1950* (New York: Oxford University Press, 1986).

13. Tannenbaum, *Healer's Calling*; Susan E. Klepp, *Revolutionary Conceptions: Women, Fertility, and Family Limitation in America, 1760–1820* (Chapel Hill: University of North Carolina Press, 2009); Kathleen M. Brown, *Foul Bodies: Cleanliness in Early America* (New Haven, CT: Yale University Press, 2009); Susan Mosher Stuard, "Dame Trot," *Signs* 1, no. 2 (1975): 537–42; Mary Fissell, *Vernacular Bodies: The Politics of Reproduction in Early Modern England* (New York: Oxford University Press, 2004); Mary Fissell, "Introduction: Women, Health, and Healing in Early Modern Europe," *Bulletin of the History of Medicine* 82 (2008): 1–17; Monica H. Green, *The Trotula: A Medieval Compendium of Women's Medicine* (Philadelphia: University of Pennsylvania Press, 2001); Monica H. Green, *Women's Healthcare in the Medieval West: Texts and Contexts* (Burlington, VT: Ashgate, 2000); Monica H. Green, *Making Women's Medicine Masculine: The Rise of Male Authority in Pre-modern Gynaecology* (New York: Oxford University Press, 2008); Susan Broomhall, *Women's Medical Work in Early Modern France* (Manchester, UK: Manchester University Press, 2004); Barbara Duden, *The Woman Beneath the Skin: A Doctor's Patients in Eighteenth-Century Germany*, trans. Thomas Dunlap (Cambridge, MA: Harvard University Press, 1998); Laroche, *Medical Authority*; Elaine Leong, *Recipes and Everyday Knowledge: Medicine, Science, and the Household in Early Modern England* (Chicago: University of Chicago Press, 2018); Michelle DiMeo and Sara Pennell, eds., *Reading and Writing Recipe Books, 1550–1800* (Manchester, UK: Manchester University Press, 2013).

14. Ellen Hartigan-O'Connor, *The Ties That Buy: Women and Commerce in Revolutionary America* (Philadelphia: University of Pennsylvania Press, 2009); Mark S. R. Jenner and Patrick Wallis, *Medicine and the Market in England and Its Colonies, c. 1450–c. 1850* (Basingstoke, UK: Palgrave Macmillan, 2007), 1–23; Dorothy Porter and Roy Porter, *Patient's Progress: Doctors and Doctoring in Eighteenth-Century England* (Stanford, CA: Stanford University Press, 1989); Harold Cook, *Decline of the Old Medical Regime in Stuart London* (Ithaca, NY: Cornell University Press, 1986); Roy Porter, ed., *Patients and Practitioners: Lay Perceptions of Medicine in Pre-industrial Society* (Cambridge: Cambridge University Press, 1985); Roy Porter, *Health for Sale: Quackery in England, 1660–1850* (Manchester, UK: Manchester University Press, 1989); Charles Rosenberg, William Helfand, and James Green, *"Every Man His Own Doctor": Popular Medicine in Early America* (Philadelphia: Library Company of Philadelphia, 1998), 26; John Ball, *The Female Physician: or, Every Woman her Own Doctress* (London: L. David 1770).

15. Samuel Johnson, *A Dictionary of the English Language* (London: W. Strahan, 1755), LCP; Fett, *Working Cures*, 1–8; Perry, *A General Dictionary*; Michel Foucault, *The Birth of the Clinic: An Archaeology of Medical Perception*, trans. A. M. Sheridan Smith (New York: Pantheon Books, 1973); and Michel Foucault, *Discipline and Punish: The Birth of the Prison*, trans. Alan Sheridan (New York: Pantheon Books, 1977).

16. Kersey, *Dictionarium Anglo-Britannicum*. Bailey's definition of authority in his *Etymological English Dictionary* includes "A passage of a book quoted." See also Patrick Wallis, "Consumption, Retailing, and Medicine in Early Modern London," *Economic History Review* 61, no.1 (2008): 26–53; Lisa Forman Cody, "'No Cure No Money,' or the Invisible Hand of

Quackery: The Language of Commerce, Credit, and Cash in Eighteenth-Century British Medical Advertisements," *Studies in Eighteenth-Century Culture* 28 (1999): 103–30.

17. Tannenbaum, *Healer's Calling*, 3–8; Roy Porter, *Disease, Medicine and Society in England, 1550–1860* (Cambridge: Cambridge University Press, 1999), 1–17; Andrew Cunningham and Roger French, eds., *The Medical Enlightenment of the Eighteenth Century* (Cambridge: Cambridge University Press, 1990).

18. Walter Pagel, *Paracelsus: An Introduction to Philosophical Medicine in the Era of the Renaissance*, 2nd ed. (New York: Karger, 1982); Charles Webster, *From Paracelsus to Newton: Magic and the Making of Modern Science* (Cambridge: Cambridge University Press, 1982).

19. See, for example, Fett, *Working Cures*; Gladys Tantaquidgeon, *Folk Medicine of the Delaware and Related Algonkian Indians* (Harrisburg: Pennsylvania Historical and Museum Commission, 1971); Klepp, "Encounter and Experiment," 47–100.

20. George Farquhar, *The Beaux' Stratagem, Thornton Wilder and Ken Ludwig's Adaptation* (New York: Samuel French, 2006), 26–27.

Chapter 1

1. Gulielma Springett Penn (1644–94), My Mother's Recaipts for Cookerys Presarving and Cyrugery, copied by Edward Blackfan, 1702, Penn Family Recipes, Penn Papers, vol. 6, 1674–1716, flyleaf, 57, HSP; Gulielma Springett Penn, *Penn Family Recipes: Cooking Recipes of Wm. Penn's Wife, Gulielma*, ed. Evelyn Abraham Benson (York, PA: George Shumway, 1966), 1–5. The term *receipt* was used more often than *recipe* during the seventeenth and eighteenth centuries. However, to differentiate between culinary/medical recipe books and business receipt books, I will use the term *recipe*.

2. Penn, *Penn Family Recipes*, 1, 17; Elaine Leong, *Recipes and Everyday Knowledge: Medicine, Science, and the Household in Early Modern England* (Chicago: University of Chicago Press, 2018), 1–41; Louis A. Meier, *Early Pennsylvania Medicine* (Boyertown, PA: Gilbert, 1976), 1–24. See Chapter 1 for a discussion of Lady Bountiful and George Farquhar's *Beaux-Stratagem*.

3. L. V. Hodgkin, *Gulielma: Wife of William Penn* (New York: Longmans, Green and Co.), 1947, 2–32.

4. For Mary Proude Springett Penington (ca. 1625–82) and Catherine Partridge Springett, see Mary Penington, *Some Account of Circumstances in the Life of Mary Penington from Her Manuscript Left for Her Family* (London: Harvey and Darnton, 1821); Mary Penington, *A Brief Account of My Exercises from Childhood Left with My Dear Daughter Gulielma Maria Penn*, (Philadelphia: n.p., 1848); and David Booy, *Autobiographical Writings by Early Quaker Women* (Burlington, VT: Ashgate, 2004), 73–107. Penington's original manuscript is not extant.

5. Penington, *Some Account*, 40–54, 61–90; Hodgkin, *Gulielma*, 3–32; Andrew Bradstock, *Radical Religion in Cromwell's England* (London: Tauris, 2010); Richard Sherlock, *The Quakers Wilde Questions Objected against the Ministers of the Gospel* (London: E. Cotes, 1656).

6. 1 Tim. 2:12–15, King James Version; Rebecca Larson, *Daughters of Light: Quaker Women Preaching and Prophesying in the Colonies and Abroad, 1700–1775* (Chapel Hill: University of North Carolina Press, 2000), 68–78; Phyllis Mack, *Visionary Women: Ecstatic Prophesy in Seventeenth-Century England* (Berkeley: University of California Press, 1992), 1–11, 283–88; Karin Wulf, *Not All Wives: Women of Colonial Philadelphia* (Philadelphia: University of Pennsylvania Press, 2000), 55–66.

7. Margaret Askew Fell (1614–1702), *Women Speaking Justified, Proved, and Allowed by the Scriptures* (London: n.p., 1666), 8; Teresa Feroli, *Political Speaking Justified: Women Prophets*

and the English Revolution (Newark, DE: University of Delaware Press, 2006), 148–95; Margaret Spufford, "First Steps in Literacy: The Reading and Writing Experiences of the Humblest Seventeenth-Century Spiritual Autobiographers," *Social History* 4, no. 3 (1979): 407–35; Kristianna Polder, "Margaret Fell, Mother of the New Jerusalem," in *New Critical Studies of Early Quaker Women, 1650–1800*, ed. Michele Lise Tarter and Catie Gill (New York: Oxford University Press, 2018), 186–201; Bonnelyn Kunze, "The Friendship of Margaret Fell, George Fox, and William Penn," *Church History* 57, no. 2 (1998): 170–86; T. H. S. Wallace, ed., *A Sincere and Constant Love: An Introduction to the Work of Margaret Fell* (Richmond, IN: Friends United Press, 2009); William J. Scheick, *Authority and Female Authorship in Colonial America* (Lexington: University Press of Kentucky, 1998), 82–106.

8. Joseph Besse, *A Collection of the Sufferings Of the People call'd Quakers*, vol. 1 (London: printed and sold by Luke Hinde, 1753), 128; Meg Lota Brown and Kari Boyd McBride, *Women's Roles in the Renaissance* (Westport, CT: Greenwood Press, 2005), 67–70; Catie Gill, *Women in the Seventeenth-Century Quaker Community: A Literary Study of Political Identities, 1650–1700* (Burlington, VT: Ashgate, 2005), 1–10, 142; Booy, *Autobiographical Writings*, 11–19; Isaac Penington, *The Works of the Long-Mournful and Sorely-Distressed Isaac Penington*, vol. 2, 2nd ed. (London: Samuel Clark, 1761), 32, 499–505, 647–53; Mary Penington, *Experiences in the Life of Mary Penington*, ed. Norman Penney (Philadelphia: Biddle Press, 1911), 37–42, 55–59.

9. John Aubrey, *Aubrey's Brief Lives*, ed. Oliver Lawson Dick (London: Secker and Warburg, 1680; repr., 1949), 235; Thomas Ellwood, *History of the Life of Thomas Ellwood*, ed. C. G. Crump (London: Methuen & Co., 1900), 9–10, 145–60; Hodgkin, *Guleilma*, 40–45; Gulielma Springett and Mary Penington to William Penn, 5 mo. [July] 16, 1670, in *Papers of William Penn*, ed. Mary Maples Dunn and Richard S. Dunn (Philadelphia: University of Pennsylvania Press, 1981), 1:156–57; Penington, *Some Account*, 45–52.

10. Penn, Mother's Receipts, 43; William Penn to Gulielma Springett, 1668 [dictated to a servant] and Gulielma Springett and Mary Penington to William Penn, 5 mo. [July] 16, 1670, in Dunn and Dunn, *Papers of William Penn*, 1:85–86, 156–58, Marriage Certificate, 237–38; Kristianna Polder, *Matrimony in the True Church: The Seventeenth-Century Quaker Marriage Approbation Discipline* (New York: Routledge, 2015), 87–88; Wulf, *Not All Wives*, 57–60; Alison Duncan Hirsch, "A Tale of Two Wives: Mythmaking and the Lives of Gulielma and Hannah Penn," *Pennsylvania History* 61, no. 4 (1994): 429; Dunn and Dunn, *Papers of William Penn*, 1:238–39, 287, 646–48; Hodgkin, *Gulielma*, 157–63.

11. William Penn to Gulielma Penn, August 4, 1682, and Penn's "Frame of the Government of Pennsylvania, in Dunn and Dunn, *Papers of William Penn*, 2:269, 140–53; Andrew R. Murphy, *William Penn: A Life* (New York: Oxford University Press, 2019), 87–93; Jean R. Soderlund, ed., *William Penn and the Founding of Pennsylvania, 1680–1684* (Philadelphia: University of Pennsylvania Press and Historical Society of Pennsylvania, 1983), 3–10; Hodgkin, *Gulielma*, 164–74.

12. William Penn to My dear wife and Children, Sixth Month [August] 4, 1682, Transcript, Etting Papers, HSP; Edward Parrish, *An Essay on Education in the Society of Friends* (Philadelphia: J. B. Lippincott, 1866), 22; William Penn, *Fruits of Solitude in Reflections and Maxims Relating to the Conduct of Human Life* (London: William Elliot, 1807), 2–5; Dunn and Dunn, *Papers of William Penn*, 2:269–72. The Quaker schoolmaster Thomas Lawson, who tutored Margaret Fell Fox's daughters, concurred with Penn, advising instruction in botany, zoology, chemistry, "Medicine," "Chyrugery," and "Inoculating" for the "Benefit and Advantage of others." Ronald H. Peterson, *New World Botany: Columbus to Darwin* (Königstein, Germany:

Koeltz Scientific Books, 2001), 196, 228–89; and E. Jean Whittaker, *Thomas Lawson, 1630–1691: North Country Botanist, Quaker, and Schoolmaster* (York, England: Sessions Book Trust, 1986).

13. Gulielma Penn to Margaret Fox, 6 mo. [August] 21, 1683, in Dunn and Dunn, *Papers of William Penn*, 2:460–61; Gulielma Penn to Margaret Fox, 6 mo. [August] 16, 1683, CCHS; Henry J. Cadbury, "Another Child to William and Gulielma Penn," *PMHB* 74, no. 1 (1950): 110–12; Mary J. Dobson, *Contours of Death and Disease in Early Modern England* (Cambridge: Cambridge University Press, 2003), 184, 323–24. The Penns had eight children, including one set of twins: Gulielma Maria (January–March 1673); William (February 28–May 1764); Mary Margaret (February 1764–February 1765), Springett (January 1676–April 1696), Letitia (1679–1746), William Jr. (1681–1720), daughter (March 1683–March or April 1683), and Gulielma Maria (November 1685–November 1689).

14. William Penn, *An Account of the Blessed End of Gulielma Springett Penn and of Springett Penn, the Beloved Wife and Eldest Son of William Penn* ([London?]: printed for the benefit of his family,1699), 9–10; William Penn to Robert Turner, February 27, 1694, and William Penn to the Earl of Nottingham, November 21,1692, in Dunn and Dunn, *Papers of William Penn*, 3:388–89, 353; Aubrey, *Aubrey's Brief Lives*, 235; Murphy, *William Penn*, 215–25.

15. Leong, *Recipes and Everyday Knowledge*, 1–45; Sara Pennell and Michelle DiMeo, "Introduction," in *Reading and Writing Recipe Books, 1550–1800*, ed. Michelle DiMeo and Sara Pennell (Manchester, UK: Manchester University Press, 2013), 3–5, 9; Rebecca Laroche, *Medical Authority and Englishwomen's Herbal Texts, 1550–1650* (Burlington, VT: Ashgate, 2009), 104–13; Wendy Wall, *Recipes for Thought: Knowledge and Taste in the Early Modern English Kitchen* (Philadelphia: University of Pennsylvania Press, 2015), 112–65. In some cases, the life writings of an elite woman such as Margaret, Lady Hoby, may be the only evidence of a woman's healing practice when a recipe manuscript is not available. See Lucinda McCray Beier, "The Character of a Good Woman: Women and Illness," in *Sufferers and Healers: The Experience of Illness in Seventeenth-Century England* (London: Routledge, 1978), 211–41.

16. Wall, *Recipes for Thought*, 11–14; A. L. Wyman, "The Surgeoness: The Female Practitioner of Surgery, 1400–1800," *Medical History* 28 (1984): 30–34; Luella M. Wright, "William Penn and the Royal Society," *Bulletin of the Friends Historical Association* 30, no. 1 (1941): 8–10; John Ward, *The Lives of the Professors of Gresham College* (London: John Moore, 1740), 110; Aubrey, *Brief Lives*, 134–35. For Susanna Wren Holder (ca. 1627–88), see Aubrey, *Brief Lives*, 403–5. The life writings of elite women such as Margaret, Lady Hoby (1571–1633); Grace Sherrington, Lady Mildmay (1552–1620); and Anne, Lady Fanshawe (1625–80) evince their healing practices. See Linda A. Pollock, *With Faith and Physic: The Life of a Tudor Gentlewoman, Lady Grace Mildmay, 1552–1620* (New York: St. Martin's Press, 1995), introduction, 92–98.

17. Wyman, "The Surgeoness," 32; Amanda Vickery, *The Gentleman's Daughter: Women's Lives in Georgian England* (New Haven, CT: Yale University Press, 1998), 8–12. Elizabeth Walker, another rector's wife, was memorialized in print for her "holy life" and her medical and surgical practice. Walker treated those with "inward Sicknesses, and outward Wounds and Sores" with medicines from her well-stocked dispensary. See Anthony Walker, *The Vertuous Wife: or, the Holy Life of Mrs. Elizabeth Walker* (London: printed for N. R., 1694), 177–78.

18. Wall, *Recipes for Thought*, 112–18; Laroche, *Medical Authority*, 73–101; [Ann Charlotte] Lady Frescheville of Stavely, Recipe Book 1669, Fol. 164, Joseph Downs Coll., WML; Janet Theophano, *Eat My Words: Reading Women's Lives Through the Cookbooks They Wrote* (New York: Palgrave, 2002), 91–93.

19. Margaret Pelling, "Women of the Family? Speculations Around Early Modern British Physicians," *Social History of Medicine* 8, no. 3 (1995): 397.

20. Penn, Mother's Recaipts, 97, 208, 222, 224; Penn, *Penn Family Recipes*.

21. Mary Chantrell and others, Book of Cookery and Medical Receipts, ca. 1690s through early eighteenth century, MS 1548, 63R, WL, 30–32. For another example, see Anon., Recipe Book, English, ca. mid-eighteenth century, MS Codex 1038, UPRBM. See also Malcolm Thick, "Using Language to Investigate Ellen Chantrill's [*sic*] Recipe Book," in *Food and Language: Proceedings of the Oxford Symposium on Food and Cooking*, ed. Richard Hosking (London: Prospect Books, 2009), 350–59. For comparison with seventeenth-century New England, see Rebecca Tannenbaum, *The Healer's Calling: Women and Medicine in Early New England* (Ithaca, NY: Cornell University Press, 2002), 71–81.

22. Penn, Mother's Recaipts; Penn, *Penn Family Recipes*, 1–5. Scholars speculate that when William Penn Jr. returned to England, he may have left the book at Pennsbury Manor. It was likely sent in a cache of Hannah Penn's papers to England in the nineteenth century and was later accessioned by the HSP.

23. Maria Webb, *The Penns and Peningtons of the Seventeenth Century* (Philadelphia: Henry Longstreth, 1877), 61–63; Booy, *Autobiographical Writings*, 77; Penington, *Experiences*, 74–75. The king's evil, or scrofula, was a common illness in the seventeenth century. It is understood today as tuberculosis of the cervical lymph nodes.

24. Penington, *Some Account*, 64–65; Penington, *Experiences*, 75–76; Marvin L. Kwitko and Charles D. Kelman, *The History of Modern Cataract Surgery* (New York: Kugler Publications, 1998), 18–22.

25. Penn, Mother's Recaipts, 2; See, for example, a snail water recipe for consumption (wasting pulmonary disease) in Richard Morton, M.D., *Phthisiologia: Or, A Treatise of Consumptions* (London: W. and J. Innys, 1720), 168–69. Bruno Bonnemain notes ongoing interest in medical uses for snails in "Helix and Drugs: Snails for Western Health Care from Antiquity to the Present," *Evidence Based Complementary Alternative Medicine* 2, no. 1 (2005): 25–28, doi: 10.1093/ecam/neh057. See also Nicolas Culpeper, *Pharmacopœia Londinensis, or The London Dispensatory*, 6th ed. (London: Peter and Edward Cole, 1661), 33–34, 38. The first Latin edition was published in 1618. Culpeper translated it into English in 1649.

26. Penn, Mother's Recaipts, 4, 5–18; Roy Porter, *The Greatest Benefit to Mankind: A Medical History of Humanity* (New York: Norton, 1999), 37–38, 282.

27. E. Ashby, Recipe Book, early eighteenth century, MS B 1, ID 2931001R, loose note, NLM; Hannah Walker [letter] to Benjamin Franklin, June 16, 1768, Benjamin Franklin Papers, APS.

28. Penington, *Experiences*, 74–75; Penn, My Mothers Recaipts, 2, 5, 47, 55, 102. Leong, *Recipes and Everyday Knowledge*, 7; Wall, *Recipes for Thought*, 186.

29. Leong, *Recipes and Everyday Knowledge*, 1–12; Anne Stobart, *Household Medicine in Seventeenth-Century England* (London: Bloomsbury, 2016).

30. Leong, *Recipes and Everyday Knowledge*, 2. This historiography is extensive. See, for example, Steven Shapin, *The Scientific Revolution* (Chicago: University of Chicago Press, 1998), 1–14, 65–78; Michel Foucault, *The Order of Things* (New York: Routledge, 1989), 139–79; David C. Lindberg and Robert S. Westman, eds., *Reappraisals of the Scientific Revolution* (Cambridge: Cambridge University Press, 1990); Jan Golinski, *Science as Public Culture* (Cambridge: Cambridge University Press, 1992); Lorraine Daston and Elizabeth Lunbeck, eds., *Histories of Scientific Observation* (Chicago: University of Chicago Press, 2011); Bruce T. Moran, *Distilling Knowledge: Alchemy, Chemistry, and the Scientific Revolution* (Cambridge, MA: Harvard

University Press, 2006); Pamela H. Smith and Benjamin Schmidt, eds., *Making Knowledge in Early Modern Europe: Practices, Objects, and Texts, 1400–1800* (Chicago: University of Chicago Press, 2008).

31. Pamela H. Smith, *The Body of the Artisan: Art and Experience in the Scientific Revolution* (Chicago: University of Chicago Press, 2004), 1–28; Harold Cook, *The Decline of the Old Medical Regime in Stuart London* (Ithaca, NY: Cornell University Press, 1986), 28–29.

32. Sarah Hutton, *Anne Conway: A Woman Philosopher* (Cambridge: Cambridge University Press, 2004), 178–83; Patricia Fara, *Pandora's Breeches: Women, Science, and Power in the Enlightenment* (London: Pimlico, 2004), 74–87.

33. Zachary Dorner, *Merchants of Medicines: The Commerce and Coercion of Health in Britain's Long Eighteenth Century* (Chicago: University of Chicago Press, 2020), 3–12, 141; Harold J. Cook, *Matters of Exchange; Commerce Medicine, and Science in the Dutch Golden Age* (New Haven, CT: Yale University Press, 2007), 210–24; Londa Schiebinger, *Plants and Empire: Colonial Bioprospecting in the Atlantic* (Cambridge, MA: Harvard University Press, 2004), 73–89.

34. Porter, *Greatest Benefit*, 54–62, 174–75.

35. Penn, Mother's Recaipts, 25; John Hill, *A History of the Materia Medica, Containing Descriptions of All the Substances used in Medicine* (London: T. Longman, C. Hitch and L. Hawes, 1751), 815–22; William Eamon, "Corn, Cochineal, and Quina: The 'Zilsel Thesis' in a Colonial Iberian Setting," *Centaurus* 60 (2018): 141–58. This recipe may have been copied from a printed source, but I have not been able to locate it.

36. Penn, Mother's Recaipts, 25.

37. Mary Chantrell and others, Book of Cookery and Medical Receipts, 34; Penn, Mother's Recaipts, 7, 25; Kathleen M. Brown, *Foul Bodies: Cleanliness in Early America* (New Haven, CT: Yale University Press, 2009), 7–11.

38. *Oxford English Dictionary*, 2nd ed., 20 vols. (Oxford: Oxford University Press, 1989); Elizabeth Spiller, ed., *Seventeenth-Century English Recipe Books: Cooking, Physic and Chirurgery in the Works of Elizabeth Talbot Grey and Aletheia Talbot Howard*, The Early Modern Englishwoman: A Facsimile Library of Essential Works, ser. 3, vol. 3 (Burlington, VT: Ashgate, 2008), xvii–xxi; Louise Hill Curth, *English Almanacs, Astrology, and Popular Medicine: 1550–1700* (Manchester, UK: Manchester University Press, 2007), 135–44; Nicholas Culpeper, *Complete Herbal Consisting of a Comprehensive Description of nearly all Herbs with their Medicinal Properties* (London: W. Foulsham & Co., 1653; repr., Whitefish, MT: Kessinger Publishing, 2005), 58, 73.

39. Penn, Mother's Recaipts, 11, 29, 39; Ann, Lady Frescheville, Recipe Book, 1669, 93, WML; Mary Chantrell and others, Book of Cookery and Medical Receipts, 37–39; Wall, *Recipes for Thought*, 212–18. For another example, see Elizabeth Okeover (and others) Recipe Book, MS3712, 76, WL. See also Richard Aspin, "Who Was Elizabeth Okeover?," *Medical History* 44, no. 4 (2000): 532–40.

40. Walter Pagel, *Paracelsus: An Introduction to Philosophical Medicine in the Era of the Renaissance*, 2nd ed. (New York: Karger, 1982), 301–29; Charles Webster, *From Paracelsus to Newton: Magic and the Making of Modern Science* (Cambridge: Cambridge University Press, 1982), 1–14; Margaret Pelling, "Medical Practice in Early Modern England: Trade or Profession?," in *The Professions in Early Modern England*, ed. Wilfrid Prest (London: Croom Helm, 1987), 90–128; Harold J. Cook, "Markets and Cultures: Medical Specifics and the Reconfiguration of the Body in Early Modern Europe," *Transactions of the Royal Historical Society*, 6th ser., 21 (2011): 123–45.

41. William Russell (1634–96), *A Physical Treatise Grounded, not upon Tradition, nor Phancy, but Experience, Consisting of Three Parts . . . By William Russell, chymist in ordinary to His Majesty* (London: printed for John Williams at the Crown in St. Paul's Church-yard, 1684), 1, NLM.

42. Mary Trye, *Medicatrix, or The Woman-physician: Vindicating Thomas O Dowde . . . against the calumnies and abuseive reflections of Henry Stubbe . . .* (London: printed by T.R. & N.T. and sold by Henry Broome and John Leete, 1675), 2; Sara Read, "'My Method and Medicines: Mary Trye, Chemical Physician," *Early Modern Women: An Interdisciplinary Journal* 11, no. 1 (2016): 137–48; Leigh Whaley, *Women and the Practice of Medical Care in Early Modern Europe, 1400–1800* (New York: Palgrave Macmillan, 2011), 85–87. For Stubbe (1632–76), see James R. Jacob, *Henry Stubbe, Radical Protestantism and the Early Enlightenment* (Cambridge: Cambridge University Press, 2002).

43. Penn, Mother's Recaipts, 8, 12–14, 57; Elizabeth Okeover, Recipe Book, 191; Jennifer Munroe, *Making Gardens of Their Own: Advice for Women, 1550–1750*, Essential Works for the Study of Early Modern Women, ser. 3, vol. 1 (New York: Routledge, 2016), ix–xvi; J. H., *A Treatise of the Great Antidote of Van Helmont, Paracelsus and Crollius . . . called the Elixir Proprietatis* (London: printed for the author, 1667), 2–3. For quote, see Laroche, *Medical Authority*, 6.

44. Catalogue of Books Taken February 23, 1726, Penn Manuscripts, Misc., William Penn, 1674–1716, vol. 6, 51–52, HSP. The Penn family library in Pennsylvania included these and other alchemical, medical, and scientific volumes transported from Warminghurst Manor, England.

45. Allison Kavey, *Books of Secrets: Natural Philosophy in England, 1550–1600* (Champaign: University of Illinois Press, 2007), 60–71; William Eamon, *Science and the Secrets of Nature: Books of Secrets in Medieval and Early Modern Culture* (Princeton, NJ: Princeton University Press, 1996), 3–12; Cook, *Decline of the Old Medical Regime*, 28–29; Pennell and DiMeo, "Introduction," 1–22; Mary Fissell, "The Marketplace of Print," in *The Medical Marketplace and Its Colonies c. 1450–c. 1850*, ed. Mark Jenner and Patrick Wallis (Basingstoke: Palgrave Macmillan, 2007), 108–32; Elizabeth Lane Furdell, *Publishing and Medicine in Early Modern England* (Rochester, NY: University of Rochester Press, 2002).

46. Jayne E. Archer, "'The Quintessence of Wit': Poems and Recipes in Early Modern Women's Writing," in DiMeo and Pennell, *Reading and Writing*, 116–18; Wall, *Recipes for Thought*, 10, 20–32; John Partridge, *Treasurie of Commodious Conceits, & Hidden Secrets* (1573), title page; Wendy Wall, "Literacy and the Domestic Arts," *Huntington Library Quarterly* 73 (September 2010): 390. Partridge's *The Widdowes Treasure* was a retitled version of his *Treasurie of Commodious Conceits, and Hidden Secrets*. They were reprinted in sixteen editions between 1584 and 1689.

47. John Partridge, *The Widdowes Treasure Plentifully Furnished with Sundry Precious and Approoued Secretes in Phisicke and Chirurgery* (London: G. Robinson for E. White, 1586), preface. The 1653 edition was published by the female printer Jane Bell.

48. Nicholas Culpeper, *A Physicall Directory, or A Translation of the London Dispensatory* (London: Peter Cole, 1649), front matter, n.p.; [Patrick,] Lord Ruthven (1573–1651), *The Ladies Cabinet Enlarged and Opened: Containing Many Rare Secrets and Rich Ornaments of several kindes and different uses* (London: T.M. for G. Bedel and T. Collins, 1655), preface.

49. Abraham de la Pryme, *The Diary of Abraham de la Pryme*, ed. Charles Jackson (Durham, UK: Andrews and Co., 1870), 8 (quote); Elizabeth Talbot Grey, Countess of Kent, *A Choice Manual of Rare and Select Secrets in Physick and Chyrurgery* (London: printed by G. D.,

and are to be sold by William Shears, 1653); Countess of Kent, *A Choice Manual*, and Alethea Talbot, *Nature Unbowelled*, facsimile reproductions in Spiller, *Seventeenth-Century English Recipe Books*; Whaley, *Women and the Practice*, 68–90; Lynette Hunter, "Women and Domestic Medicine: Lady Experimenters, 1570–1620," in *Women, Science, and Medicine 1500–1700: Mothers and Sisters of the Royal Society*, ed. L. Hunter and Sarah Hutton (London: Sutton Publishers, 1997), 89–107. *A Choice Manual* was likely a transcription of Elizabeth Grey's recipe book and was reprinted twenty-two times.

50. Pennell and DiMeo, "Introduction," 11; Leong, *Recipes and Everyday Knowledge*, 167–69.

51. Grey, *Choice Manual*, 172–76; Penn, Mother's Recaipts, 8; Thomas Tegg, *London Encyclopaedia* (London: printed for Thomas Tegg, 1829), 648.The *Choice Manual* includes three recipes for Gascon's Powder, but the others use slightly different ingredients. Crabs' eyes are small stone-like concretions of limestone with antacid properties found in bags next to the stomachs and in the heads of crayfish. See John Quincy, *Lexicon Physico-medicum: Or, a New Medical Dictionary* (London: J. Osborn and T. Longman, 1730).

52. Johanna St. John Her Booke, 1680, n.p., MS4338, WL. According to the Wellcome Library catalogue, the compiler of this collection of medical receipts was the daughter of Oliver St. John (1598–1673), Lord Chief Justice.

53. Mrs Anne Brumwich her Booke of Receipts or Medicines for severall sores and other Infirmities (ca. 1625–1700), flyleaf, 115, MS 160, WL; Wall, *Recipes for Thought*, 209. In her 1704 will, Dame St. John bequeathed her recipe book to her daughter Anne Cholmondeley. See Frank T. Smallwood, "The Will of Dame Johanna St. John," *Notes and Queries* 16, no. 9 (1969): 344–47.

54. Wall, *Recipes for Thought*, 40, 41–44; Kate Campbell Hurd-Mead, *A History of Women in Medicine, from the Earliest Times to the Beginning of the Nineteenth Century* (Haddam, CT: Haddam Press, 1938), 400–406.

55. Hannah Woolley, *The Gentlewoman's Companion; or, A Guide to the Female Sex* (London: printed by A. Maxwell for Dorman Nowman at the Kings-Arms, 1673), Epistle Dedicatory, 161. This book is attributed to Woolley and may be a later compilation of her works. See Margaret J. M. Ezell, "Cooking the Books, or, The Three Faces of Hannah Woolley," in DiMeo and Pennell, *Reading and Writing*, 159–78; Elaine Hobby, *Virtue of Necessity: English Women's Writing, 1649–88* (Ann Arbor: University of Michigan Press, 1989).

56. Penn, Mother's Recaipts, 8; George B. Griffenhagen and Mary Bogard, *History of Drug Containers and Their Labels* (Madison, WI: American Institute of the History of Pharmacy, 1999), 72–73.

Chapter 2

1. Elizabeth Coates Paschall (1702–68), Recipe Book, ca. 1745–67, 28, CPP; Elizabeth Gartrell, "Women Healers and Domestic Remedies in 18th-Century America: The Recipe Book of Elizabeth Coates Paschall," *New York State Journal of Medicine* 87, no. 1 (1987): 23–29.

2. Abstract and Background Note, Collection 140, Coates and Reynell Family Papers, 1677–1930, HSP.

3. Paschall, Recipe Book, 28. For John Reynell (1708–84), see Thomas M. Doerflinger, *A Vigorous Spirit of Enterprise: Merchants and Economic Development in Revolutionary Philadelphia* (Chapel Hill: University of North Carolina Press, 2001), 19–55, 181–90. For the wasting lung diseases called phthisic or phthisis (or Tisick), see Benjamin Marten, *A New Theory of Consump-*

tions, More Especially of a Phthisis Or Consumption of the Lungs (London: R. Knaplock, 1720), 108–11. For Groth, see "Reynell Family," *Gentleman's Magazine* 136, part 2 (1824): 224.

4. Mary Coates, *Family Memorials and Recollections, or Aunt Mary's Patchwork* (Philadelphia: printed for the family, 1885), 13–14. For Beulah Jacques Coates (ca. 1659–1741) and Thomas Coates (1659–1719), see also Henry T. Coates, *Thomas Coates: Who Removed from England to the Province of Pennsylvania, 1683* (Philadelphia: privately printed, 1897), 1–22.

5. Laurel Thatcher Ulrich, *The Age of Homespun: Objects and Stories in the Creation of an American Myth* (New York: Alfred A. Knopf, 2001), 129–35; Thomas Allen Glenn, *Some Colonial Mansions and Those Who Lived in Them* (Philadelphia: Henry T. Coates and Company, 1899), 109; John Fanning Watson, *Annals of Philadelphia and Pennsylvania* (Philadelphia: Carey and Hart, 1830), 463. For the silver chocolate pot attributed to Boston silversmith Peter Oliver (ca. 1682–1712), see Jack L. Lindsay, ed., *Worldly Goods: The Arts of Early Pennsylvania* (Philadelphia: Philadelphia Museum of Art, 1999), 150, 195; Patricia E. Kane, ed., *Colonial Massachusetts Silversmiths and Jewelers: A Biographical Dictionary* (New Haven: Yale University Art Gallery, 1998), 741–42; Kathryn C. Buhler, *Colonial Silversmiths: Masters and Apprentices* (Boston: Museum of Fine Arts, 1956), cat. no. 111, illus. fig. 45; Elizabeth Coates Paschall, Will and Inventory, October 18, 1768, Philadelphia Will Book O, no. 210, 276, Philadelphia City Hall. Inscriptions on the pot that descend through the family line include Beulah Jacquett [Jacques] Coates, Elizabeth Coates Paschall, Beulah Paschall, Sarah Paschall Morris, and four subsequent generations. A silver chocolate pot is listed in Elizabeth Coates Paschall's will and inventory.

6. Coates and Reynell Family Papers, series 5, box 57, folder 6, HSP; Coates, *Thomas Coates*, 12; Carole Shammas, Marylynn Salmon, and Michael Dahlin, *Inheritance in America from Colonial Times to the Present* (New Brunswick, NJ: Rutgers University Press, 1987), 45–55; Karin Wulf, *Not All Wives: Women of Colonial Philadelphia* (Philadelphia: University of Pennsylvania Press, 2000), 3–13; Frederick B. Tolles, *Meeting House and Counting House: The Quaker Merchants of Colonial Philadelphia, 1682–1763* (New York: Norton, 1948; repr., 1963), 89; Thomas Coats [*sic*], Will, September 18, 1719, Abstracts of Wills, 1682–1726, Philadelphia, PA, HSP.

7. Paschall, Recipe Book, 37. For Joseph Paschall (1699–1742), Joseph's grandfather, Thomas Paschall Sr. (1634–1718), and his wife, Joanna Sloper Paschall (1634–1707), as well as his father, Thomas Paschall Jr., see Howard Williams Lloyd, *Lloyd Manuscripts* (Lancaster, PA: New Era Printing Company, 1912), 223–32; and "Account of the Paschall Family of England and Philadelphia, Presented June 7th 1894 by Miss Paschall," Fc Pa, HSP; Suzanne Parry Lamborn, *Thomas Paschall and Family* (Berwyn Heights, MD: privately published, 2003); Paschall Family Papers, Ann Paschall Jackson papers, RG 5/186, Friends Historical Library; Bible Records and Notes: Morris and Paschall families, BR MO LOC 104, HSP.

8. William H. Williams, *America's First Hospital: The Pennsylvania Hospital, 1751–1841* (Wayne, PA: Haverford House, 1976), 90–100; Theodore Thayer, *Israel Pemberton, King of the Quakers* (Philadelphia: Historical Society of Pennsylvania, 1943), 3–11; Benjamin Franklin, *Some Account of the Pennsylvania Hospital* (Philadelphia: B. Franklin, 1754), repr. in facsimile with an introduction by I. Bernard Cohen (Baltimore: Johns Hopkins Press, 1954), 29–30; Leonard W. Labaree, ed., *Papers of Benjamin Franklin*, vol. 5 (New Haven, CT: Yale University Press, 1962), 310–17; John Thomas Scharf and Thompson Westcott, *History of Philadelphia, 1609–1884*, vol. 2 (Philadelphia: L. H. Everts, 1884), 1584–85; Whitfield J. Bell Jr., *Patriot-Improvers: Biographical Sketches of Members of the American Philosophical Society* (Philadelphia: American Philosophical Society, 1999), 212–13, 290–91.

9. *Pennsylvania Gazette*, May 15, 1746; Benjamin L. Carp, *Rebels Rising: Cities and the American Revolution* (New York: Oxford University Press, 2007), 9–11; Paschall, Recipe Book, 9.

10. Paschall, Recipe Book, 21; Elizabeth Coates Paschall, Business Receipt Books, 1741–62 (2 vols.), William Henry Russell Collection of Morris Family Papers, 1684–1935, Hagley Museum and Library, Wilmington, Delaware.

11. For Elizabeth Whartnaby, see *American Weekly Mercury*, March 23–30, 1721, March 14–21, 1722/3, February 27–March 5, 1726/7, March 28–April 4, 1728, and January 28–February 4, 1734/5; John Richardson, ed., *The Friend: A Religious and Literary Journal*, vol. 29 (Philadelphia: Robb, Pile, and McElroy, 1856), 373–74; Rebecca Larson, *Daughters of Light: Quaker Women Preaching and Prophesying in the Colonies and Abroad, 1700–1775* (Chapel Hill: University of North Carolina Press, 2000), 68, 90–93. See also Wulf, *Not All Wives*, 13, 146; Patricia Cleary, "'She Will Be in the Shop': Women's Sphere of Trade in Eighteenth-Century Philadelphia and New York," *PMHB* 119, no. 3 (1995): 183.

12. *Pennsylvania Gazette*, May 15, 1746; Tolles, *Meeting House*, 89.

13. Rev. William Smith quoted in Carl Bridenbaugh, *Cities in Revolt: Urban Life in America, 1743–1776* (New York: Knopf, 1955), 14; Insurance Survey S00077, July 21, 1752, Primary Client Name: Paschall, Elizabeth, Philadelphia Contributorship Digital Archives online, http://www.philadelphiabuildings.org/contributionship/. See also Carole Shammas, "Changes in English and Anglo-American Consumption from 1550 to 1800," in *Consumption and the World of Goods*, ed. John Brewer and Roy Porter (New York: Routledge, 1993), 177–205; *Pennsylvania Gazette*, May 15, 1746; Tolles, *Meeting House*, 89, 130; Cedar Grove File, Fairmont Houses, Pennsylvania Museum of Art Archives, Philadelphia.

14. H. Macaulay Fitzgibbon, ed., *The Beaux-Stratagem, A Comedy, Written by George Farquhar* (London: J. M. Dent and Co., 1898), 7; *Pennsylvania Gazette*, March 6, 1750.

15. Paschall, Recipe Book; Henry Pemberton, "Directory of Friends," *PMHB* 16, no. 2 (1892): 231.

16. Paschall, Recipe Book, 8; Laurel Thatcher Ulrich, *A Midwife's Tale: The Life of Martha Ballard, Based on Her Diary, 1785–1812* (New York: Vintage, 1990), 36–71, 162–203; Janet Moore Lindman, "'To have a gradual weaning & be ready & wiling to resign all': Maternity, Piety, and Pain Among Quaker Women of the Early Mid-Atlantic," *Early American Studies* 17, no. 4 (2019): 498–518.

17. Paschall, Recipe Book, 29, 10; Susan E. Klepp, *Revolutionary Conceptions: Women, Fertility, and Family Limitation in America, 1760–1820* (Chapel Hill: University of North Carolina Press, 2009), 64–70, 104–9.

18. Paschall, Recipe Book, 42, 43, 34.

19. Paschall, Recipe Book, 18, 12, 14, 16.

20. Paschall, Recipe Book, 5, 34, 20; Dr. Robert James, *A Medicinal Dictionary; Including Physic, Surgery, Anatomy, Chymistry, and Botany, in All Their Branches Relative to Medicine* (London: T. Osborne, 1745), vol. 1 (headers) CHE, ICT, LEN; vol. 3 (headers) PEX, SAB, TAP. For "old wives," see Introduction. Butter made from cows grazing on spring grass had a different taste and presumably different components than that made at other times of year.

21. Paschall, Recipe Book, 9; Klepp, *Revolutionary Conceptions*, 196–97; Adele Pilliteri, *Maternal and Child Health Nursing: Care of the Childbearing and Childrearing Family*, 7th ed. (New York: Lippincott Williams & Wilkins, 2010), 557–59.

22. Paschall, Recipe Book, 13. Catherine Wistar (1703–86) and Richard Wistar (also spelled Wüster or Wister) and their children were part of a prominent Pennsylvania German mer-

chant family. Their son Caspar Wistar (1739–1811) became a well-known Philadelphia physician.

23. Patrick M. Erben, "Promoting Pennsylvania: Penn, Pastorius, and the Creation of a Transnational Community," *Resources for American Literary Study* 29 (2003–4): 25–65; Farley Grubb, *German Immigration and Servitude in America, 1709–1920* (New York: Routledge, 2011), 15–71; David W. Kriebel, *Pow Wowing Among the Pennsylvania Dutch: A Traditional Medical Practice in the Modern World* (University Park: Pennsylvania State University Press, 2008).

24. Paschall, Business Receipt Book, November 1749; Paschall, Recipe Book, 19, 21, 43; MS Recipe Book attributed to Beulah Paschall, 56, CPP; George B. Wood and Franklin Bache, *The Dispensatory of the United States of America*, 2nd ed. (Philadelphia: Grigg & Elliot, 1833), 809; Samuel Fitch Hotchkin, *Ancient and Modern Germantown, Mount Airy and Chestnut Hill* (Philadelphia: P. W. Ziegler and Co., 1889), 66–70; Townsend Ward, "The Germantown Road and Its Associations," *PMHB* 6 (1882): 141–45. Deshler's Salve was cited in Lowry Jones Wister, Medical Recipes MS, Eastwick Collection, 974.811.Ea 7, box 6, APS; an anonymously authored Recipe Book (ca. 1820), doc. 270, WML; and by Thomas Evans (1798–1868), a Philadelphia Quaker minister and druggist who married a descendant of Catharine Wistar. See Thomas Evans to Joel Evans, August 8, 1814, private collection. See also Elizabeth Ellicott Lea, *A Quaker Woman's Cookbook: The Domestic Cookery of Elizabeth Ellicott Lea*, ed. William Woys Weaver (Philadelphia: University of Pennsylvania Press, 1982), 260; General Medical Convention, *Pharmacopoeia of the United States of America* (Chicago: American Medical Association, 1909), 29; *Reading (PA) Times*, February 16, 1928; advertisement for "Deshler's Salve, 1 oz. jar, 15 cents," *The Mercury* (Pottstown, PA), November 1, 1945.

25. Paschall, Recipe Book, 3; Aya Homei and Michael Worboys, *Fungal Diseases in Britain and the United States, 1850–2000: Mycoses and Modernity* (Basingstoke, UK: Palgrave Macmillan, 2013), 17–20.

26. David Spencer, *The Early Baptists of Philadelphia* (Philadelphia: William Syckelmoore, 1877), 30–32, 63–66, 91, 130; Paschall, Recipe Book, 42, 12, 23; Paschall, Business Receipt Book, October 8, 1748; Gartrell, "Women Healers," 25–26; Fiske Kimball, "Cedar Grove," *Pennsylvania Museum Bulletin* 118 (1928): 5–24.

27. Paschall, Recipe Book, 47, 4; Beulah Paschall Recipe Book, 72.

28. David Brion Davis, *The Problem of Slavery in Western Culture* (Ithaca, NY: Cornell University Press, 1966), 222; Gary B. Nash, *Forging Freedom: The Formation of Philadelphia's Black Community, 1720–1840* (Cambridge, MA: Harvard University Press, 1988), 26–32; Bell, *Patriot-Improvers*, 192; Maurice Jackson, *Let This Voice Be Heard: Anthony Benezet, Father of Atlantic Abolitionism* (Philadelphia: University of Pennsylvania Press, 2011). Anthony Benezet was an executor of Paschall's will.

29. Paschall, Recipe Book, 7, 26, 25.

30. Paschall, Recipe Book, 21, 10, 43, 20; Wulf, *Not All Wives*, 122–30.

31. Paschall, Recipe Book, 11, 14, 17, 27; William S. Middleton, "The John Kearsleys," *Annals of Medical History* 3 (1921): 391–92; "The Case of Mr. T[homas] L[awrence] with regard to the method pursued therein by J[ohn] K[earsley], senior surgeon, with the uncommon treatment the said J.K. hath met with, in his procedure therein" (Philadelphia: William Dunlap, 1760), broadside, LCP; Thomas G. Morton and Frank Woodbury, *The History of the Pennsylvania Hospital, 1751–1895* (Philadelphia: Times Printing House, 1895), 347.

32. Fitzgibbon, *Beaux-Stratagem*, 2–3.

33. Tobias Smollett, *The Adventures of Ferdinand Count Fathom* (London: printed for W. Johnston, 1753), 310; Paschall, Recipe Book, 10, 11.

34. Arthur Kleinman, *Patients and Healers in the Context of Culture: An Exploration into the Borderland Between Anthropology, Medicine, and Psychiatry* (Berkeley: University of California Press, 1981), 187–94; Laurence Brockliss and Colin Jones, *The Medical World of Early Modern France* (Oxford: Clarendon Press, 1997), 19–20; David J. Hufford, "Contemporary Folk Medicine," in *Other Healers: Unorthodox Medicine in America*, ed. Norman Gevitz (Baltimore: Johns Hopkins University Press, 1988), 247–53; Paschall, Recipe Book, 4, 11; Kathleen M. Brown, *Foul Bodies: Cleanliness in Early America* (New Haven, CT: Yale University Press, 2009), 214–15.

35. Paschall, Recipe Book, 11, 19.

36. Paschall, Recipe Book, 2, 5, 6, 7, 11, 16, 20; Francisco Alonso-Almeida, "Genre Conventions in English Recipes, 1600–1800," in *Reading and Writing Recipe Books*, ed. Michelle DiMeo and Sara Pennell (Manchester, UK: Manchester University Press, 2013), 68–90.

37. Samuel Johnson, *A Dictionary of the English Language* (London: W. Strahan, 1755); Paschall, Recipe Book, 1, 5, 7, 10, 19; Josiah Leach and George Penrose, *History of the Penrose Family of Philadelphia* (Philadelphia: D. Biddle, 1903), 38–43. For additional dictionary references, see Chapter 1.

38. Mark S. Granovetter, "The Strength of Weak Ties," *American Journal of Sociology* 78, no. 6 (1973): 136–80; Richard Whitley, "Knowledge Producers and Knowledge Acquirers," *Sociology of the Sciences* 9 (1985): 3–28; Noah E. Friedkin and Eugene C. Johnsen, *Social Influence Network Theory: A Sociological Examination of Small Group Dynamics* (New York: Cambridge University Press, 2011), 28–52.

39. Granovetter, "The Strength of Weak Ties"; Paschall, Recipe Book, 14, 47, 45.

Chapter 3

1. J. Smith Futhey and Gilbert Cope, *History of Chester County Pennsylvania*, vol. 2 (Philadelphia: L. H. Everts and Co., 1881), 189–91; Henry Graham Ashmead, *History of Delaware County, Pennsylvania* (Philadelphia: L. H. Everts and Co., 1884), 314; Jane Levis Carter, *Edgmont: The Story of a Township* (Kennett Square, PA: KNA Press, 1976), 111–15; Jane T. Merritt, *At the Crossroads: Indians and Empires on a Mid-Atlantic Frontier, 1700–1763* (Chapel Hill: University of North Carolina Press, 2003), 1–18. Following the practice of scholars in this field, I use the terms "Native American" and "Indigenous" alternately and depending on context. Whenever possible I use the ethnonym recognized by the people themselves, e.g., Lenape rather than Delaware, Haudenosaunee rather than Iroquois. Settlers called Lenapes "Delawares."

2. Moses Marshall, "The Examination &c of Indian Hannah," July 28, 1797, in Hannah Freeman file, CCHS; Dawn Marsh Riggs, "She Considered Herself Queen of the Whole Neighborhood: Hannah Freeman, Lenape Sovereignty and Penn's Peaceable Kingdom," in *Place and Native American History and Culture*, ed. Joy Porter (Bern, Switzerland: Peter Lang, 2007), 243–62; Dawn G. Marsh, *A Lenape Among the Quakers: The Life of Hannah Freeman* (Lincoln: University of Nebraska Press, 2014); Marshall Becker, "Hannah Freeman: An Eighteenth-Century Lenape Living and Working Among Colonial Farmers," *PMHB* 114, no. 2 (1990): 249–69; *Poulson's American Daily Advertiser* (Philadelphia), January 31, 1824; Sherman Day, *History of Chester County, Pennsylvania* (Laughlintown, PA: Southwest Pennsylvania Genealogical Services, 1843; repr., 1986), 206–8.

3. For healing borderlands, see Cheryl Mattingly, "Health Care as a Cultural Borderland," *Lancet* 391, no. 10117 (2018): 198–99. For the concept of a "middle ground" of power relations,

see Richard White, *The Middle Ground: Indians, Empires, and Republics in the Great Lakes Region* (New York: Cambridge University Press, 2011), 50–60. See also Nancy Shoemaker, "Introduction," and Kathleen M. Brown, "The Anglo-Algonquian Gender Frontier," in *Negotiators of Change: Historical Perspectives of Native American Women*, ed. Nancy Shoemaker (New York: Routledge, 1995), 1–25, 26–48.

4. Regula Trenkwalder Schöenenberger, *Lenape Women, Matriliny, and the Colonial Encounter: Resistance and Erosion of Power (c. 1600–1876)* (Bern, Switzerland: Peter Lang, 1991), 76–95.

5. John Russell Hayes, *The Collected Poems of John Russell Hayes* (Philadelphia: Biddle Press, 1916), 317–18; Marshall J. Becker, "Legends About Hannah Freeman ("Indian Hannah"): Squaring the Written Accounts with the Oral Traditions," *Keystone Folklore* 4, no. 2 (1992): 1–14; *Reading Eagle* (Reading, PA), September 2, 1928.

6. Clinton Alfred Weslager, *Red Men on the Brandywine* (Wilmington, DE: Hambleton Company, 1953), 1–3. Weslager later opposed the trope of the "vanishing Indian." See Weslager, *The Delaware Indians: A History* (New Brunswick, NJ: Rutgers University Press, 1972), 277–78.

7. Marshall, "Examination"; Marsh, *A Lenape Among the Quakers*, 86–97.

8. Marshall, "Examination"; John Thomas Scharf, *History of Delaware, 1609–1888*, vol. 2 (Philadelphia: L. F. Richards & Co., 1888), 611–17, 920; Amy C. Schutt, *Peoples of the River Valleys: The Odyssey of the Delaware Indians* (Philadelphia: University of Pennsylvania Press, 2007), 12–20, 81; Herbert Standing, "Quakers in Delaware at the Time of William Penn," *Delaware History* 20, no. 2 (1982): 127; Jean R. Soderlund, "Quaker Women in Lenape Country," in *New Critical Studies of Early Quaker Women, 1650–1800*, ed. Michele Lise Tarter and Catie Gill (New York: Oxford University Press, 2018), 221–39.

9. Marshall, "Examination"; Marshall Becker, "A New Jersey Haven for Some Acculturated Lenape of Pennsylvania During the Indian Wars of the 1760s," *Pennsylvania History* 60, no. 3 (1993): 326; Daniel K. Richter, *Facing East from Indian Country: A Native History of Early America* (Cambridge, MA: Harvard University Press, 2001), 206–8; Krista Camenzind, "Violence, Race, and the Paxton Boys," in *Friends and Enemies in Penn's Woods: Indians, Colonists, and the Racial Construction of Pennsylvania*, ed. William Pencak and Daniel K. Richter (University Park: University of Pennsylvania State Press, 2004), 201–20; Benjamin Franklin, *A Narrative of the Late Massacres, in Lancaster County, of a Number of Indians* (Philadelphia: Franklin and Hall, 1764); Kevin Kenny, *Peaceable Kingdom Lost: The Paxton Boys and the Destruction of William Penn's Holy Experiment* (New York: Oxford University Press, 2011).

10. Carter, *Edgmont*, 114; Marsh, *A Lenape Among the Quakers*, 94–95; Hannah Freeman file, CCHS.

11. Bunny McBride and Harald E. L. Prins, "Walking the Medicine Line: Molly Ockett, a Pigwacket Doctor," in *Northeastern Indian Lives, 1632–1816*, ed. Robert S. Grumet (Amherst: University of Massachusetts Press, 1996), 321–47, quotation, page 338; Laurel Thatcher Ulrich, *The Age of Homespun: Objects and Stories in the Creation of an American Myth* (New York: Vintage, 2001), 248–76. For another healer called "Indian Hannah" who provided abortifacient herbs to a Euro-American woman, see Ann Marie Plane, *Colonial Intimacies: Indian Marriage in Early New England* (Ithaca, NY: Cornell University Press, 2000), 125–26.

12. Henry Tufts, *A Narrative of the Life, Adventures, Travels, and Sufferings of Henry Tufts* (Dover, NH: Samuel Bragg, 1807), 70–77, 87. Although Tufts's rollicking narrative of his life as a rogue, thief, and self-styled "Indian doctor" presents a problematic source, some scholars

argue that his descriptions of his years in an Abenaki village provide useful ethnographic information. See, for example, Gordon M. Day, "Henry Tufts as a Source on the Eighteenth Century Abenakis," *Ethnohistory* 21, no. 3 (1974): 189–97.

13. Schöenenberger, *Lenape Women*, 93–94; Herbert C. Kraft and John T. Kraft, *The Indians of Lenapehoking*, 3rd ed. (South Orange, NJ: Seton Hall University Museum, 1988); Herbert C. Kraft, *The Lenape: Archaeology, History, and Ethnography* (Newark, NJ: New Jersey Historical Society, 1986), 178–82; Gunlög Fur, *A Nation of Women: Gender and Colonial Encounters Among the Delaware Indians* (Philadelphia: University of Pennsylvania Press, 2009), 1–10, 44–46. For comparison, see Barbara Alice Mann, *Iroquoian Women: The Gantowisas* (New York: Peter Lang, 2000), 215–16.

14. William Penn, unpublished holograph letter, Philadelphia, April 3, 1684, in William Penn, *William Penn's Own Account of the Lenni Lenape or Delaware Indians*, ed. Albert Cook Myers, rev. ed. (Wallingford, PA: Middle Atlantic Press), 1970, 49. See also Schutt, *Peoples of the River Valleys*, 26–48.

15. Jane T. Merritt, "Cultural Encounters Along a Gender Frontier: Mahican, Delaware, and German Women in Eighteenth-Century Pennsylvania," *Pennsylvania History* 67, no. 4 (2000): 508; Alison Duncan Hirsch, "Indian, Métis, and Euro-American Women on Multiple Frontiers," in Pencak and Richter, *Friends and Enemies*, 76–79; John Heckewelder, *History, Manners, and Customs of the Indian Nations Who Once Inhabited Pennsylvania and the Neighboring States* (New York: Arno Press, 1876; repr., 1971), 226, 229; Kathleen M. Brown, *Foul Bodies: Cleanliness in Early America* (New Haven, CT: Yale University Press, 2009), 15–57; Mikkel Aaland, *Sweat: The Illustrated History* (Santa Barbara, CA: Capra Press, 1978), 98–104.

16. See Chapters 2 and 4.

17. Andreas Hesselius (1677–1733) [letter] till Kengl Radet Greve Gustaf Cronhjelm, December 1, 1712, in Gunlog Fur, *A Nation of Women*, 44; Andreas Hesselius, "Observations on the Natural History of Delaware During the Years 1711–1724," translated and transcribed in *The Proceedings of the Delaware Valley Ornithological Club*, 21 (Philadelphia: published by the club, 1918), 13–14; Jean Soderlund, *Lenape Country: Delaware Valley Society Before William Penn* (Philadelphia: University of Pennsylvania Press, 2015), 1–55; Gregory Evans Dowd, *The Indians of New Jersey*, New Jersey History, 3 (Trenton: New Jersey Historical Commission, 2001), 42–43; Benjamin Ferris, *A History of the Original Settlements on the Delaware: From Its Discovery by Hudson to the Colonization Under William Penn* (Wilmington, DE: Wilson & Heald, 1846), 179–80. For a comparative example, see Experience Mayhew, *Indian Converts: or, Some Account of the Lives and Dying Speeches of a considerable number of the Christianized Indians of Martha's Vineyard, in New-England* (London: Samuel Gerrish, 1727), 140–41.

18. Soderlund, "Quaker Women," 232; Jeffery M. Dorwart and Elizabeth A. Lyons, *Elizabeth Haddon Estaugh, 1680–1762: Building the Quaker Community of Haddonfield, New Jersey, 1701–1762* (Haddonfied, NJ: Historical Society of Haddonfield, 2013).

19. William Penn to Committee of the Free Society of Traders, in *Narratives of Early Pennsylvania, West New Jersey and Delaware, 1630–1707*, ed. Albert Cook Myers (New York: Scribners, 1912), 229; Susan E. Klepp, "Encounter and Experiment: The Colonial Period," in *Pennsylvania: A History of the Commonwealth*, ed. Randall M. Miller and William Pencak (University Park: Pennsylvania State University, 2002), 47, 55–58; Alfred W. Crosby, *The Columbian Exchange: Biological and Cultural Consequences of 1492* (Westport, CT: Praeger, 2003), 42–60; Peter Kalm, *Travels into North America; Containing its Natural History*, 2nd ed., vol. 1 (London: T. Lowndes, 1772), 93–120, 165–89; Elizabeth Fenn, *Pox Americana* (New York: Hill

and Wang, 2001), 3–43; Israel Acrelius, *A History of New Sweden: or, The Settlements on the River Delaware* (Philadelphia: Historical Society of Pennsylvania, 1876), 99.

20. Peter Kalm, *The America of 1750: Peter Kalm's Travels in North America*, trans. Adolph B. Benson (New York: Wilson-Erickson, 1937), 181 (quote), 78–79; Gladys Tantaquidgeon, *Folk Medicine of the Delaware and Related Algonkian Indians* (Harrisburg: Pennsylvania Historical and Museum Commission, 1971), 33; Virgil J. Vogel, *American Indian Medicine* (Norman: University of Oklahoma Press, 1970), 269–399.

21. Zachary Dorner, *Merchants of Medicines: The Commerce and Coercion of Health in Britain's Long Eighteenth Century* (Chicago: University of Chicago Press, 2020), 26–39, 82, 167–72; *Pennsylvania Gazette*, July 27, 1738; Nicholas Culpeper, *Pharmacopœia Londinensis, or The London Dispensatory* (London: Peter Cole, 1653), 100; Kalm, *America of 1750*, 606; David Zeisberger, "History of the North American Indians," *Ohio Archaeological and Historical Quarterly* 19, nos. 1–2 (1910): 51; Martha Robinson, "New Worlds, New Medicines: Indian Remedies and English Medicine in Early America," *Early American Studies* 3, no. 1 (2005): 94–8; Tantaquidgeon, *Folk Medicine*, 29–39, 267–399; Constantine J. Skamarakas, "Peter Kalm's America: A Critical Analysis of His Journal" (PhD diss., Catholic University of America, Washington, DC, 2009), 69.

22. Kalm, *Travels*, 34–35, preface.

23. Kalm, *The America of 1750*, 78–79. See also Chapter 4.

24. Kathryn Holland Braund, "Guardians of Tradition and Handmaidens to Change: Women's Roles in Creek Economic and Social Life During the Eighteenth Century," *American Indian Quarterly* 14, no. 3 (1990): 239–58.

25. Futhey and Cope, *History of Chester County*, 189–91; Schutt, *Peoples of the River Valleys*, 80; Dawn Marsh, "Old Friends in New Territories: Delawares and Quakers in the Old Northwest Territory," in *Contested Territories: Native Americans and Non-Natives in the Lower Great Lakes, 1700–1850*, ed. Charles Beatty-Medina and Melissa Rinehart (East Lansing: Michigan State University Press, 2012), 87–90; Weslager, *Delaware Indians*, 186–93.

26. Steven Craig Harper, *Promised Land: Penn's Holy Experiment, the Walking Purchase, and the Dispossession of Delawares, 1600–1763* (Bethlehem, PA: Lehigh University Press, 2006), 21–85. As their client state, the Lenapes appealed to the Iroquois League to mediate Pennsylvania's claims in the Walking Purchase, but it was in the Iroquois' best interest to allow the dispossession of this Lenape group.

27. Marshall, "Examination"; James H. Merrell, *Into the American Woods: Negotiators on the Pennsylvania Frontier* (New York: W. W. Norton, 1999), 54–56, 225–36; Marsh, *A Lenape Among the Quakers*, 104–11; Peter C. Mancall, *Valley of Opportunity: Economic Culture Along the Upper Susquehanna, 1700–1800* (Ithaca, NY: Cornell University Press, 1991), 29–36.

28. "Memorandum of Madame Montour," Peters MSS, II, 16, quoted in D. Graeff, *Conrad Weiser: Pennsylvania Peacemaker*, Pennsylvania German Folklore Society, vol. 8 (Allentown, PA: Schlechter, 1945), 144. See also Paul A. W. Wallace, *Conrad Weiser, 1696–1760: Friend of Colonist and Mohawk* (Philadelphia: University of Pennsylvania Press, 1945), 196; Charles A. Hanna, *The Wilderness Trail, or The Ventures and Adventures of the Pennsylvania Traders on the Allegheny Path*, vol. 1 (New York: G. P. Putnam's Sons, 1911), 200; and Alison Duncan Hirsch, "'The Celebrated Madame Montour': 'Interpretress' Across Early American Frontiers," *Explorations in Early American Culture* 4 (2000): 81–112; Hirsch, "Indian, Métis," 63–84.

29. John O. Freeze, "Madame Montour," *PMHB* 3 (1879): 85; Nancy Hagedorn, "'A Friend to Go Between Them': The Interpreter as Cultural Broker During Anglo-Iroquois Councils, 1740–70," *Ethnohistory* 35, no. 1 (1998): 60–80.

30. Sir William Johnson to Dr. Samuel Johnson (London) with an Acct. of an Indian plant for Dr. Gale of Killingworth, December 23, 1767, in *The Papers of Sir William Johnson*, vol. 6, ed. Alexander Flick (Albany: University of the State of New York, 1928), 31–32. Molly Brant (ca. 1736–96) became William Johnson's common-law wife in the 1750s. Elizabeth Simcoe recorded that Molly Brant "prescribed a Root—I believe it is calamus [sweet flag]" for her husband, Upper Canada's governor John Simcoe, which cured his cough. See Lois M. Feister and Bonnie Pulis, "Molly Brant: Her Domestic and Political Roles in Eighteenth-Century New York," in *Northeastern Indian Lives, 1632–1816*, ed. Robert S. Grumet (Amherst: University of Massachusetts Press, 1996), 318. See also James Taylor Carson, "Molly Brant: From Clan Mother to Loyalist Chief," in *Sifters: Native American Women's Lives*, ed. Theda Perdue (New York: Oxford University Press, 2001), 48–59.

31. Conrad Weiser to Richard Peters, [Provincial] Secretary in Philadelphia, September 27, 1747, and Conrad Weiser to Richard Peters, Esq., Secretary of the Province of Penna, transcribed in Clement Zwingli Weiser, *The Life of Conrad Weiser, the German Pioneer, Patriot, and Patron of Two Races* (Reading, PA: Daniel Miller, 1876), 155–59.

32. David Brainerd, diary entry, September 13, 1745, in Jonathan Edwards, ed., *An Account of the Life of the Late Reverend Mr. David Brainerd, Minister of the Gospel, Missionary to the Indians . . . Chiefly Taken from his Own Diary, and Other Private Writings* (Boston: D. Henchman, 1749), 352. See also John A. Grigg, *The Lives of David Brainerd: The Making of an American Evangelical Icon* (New York: Oxford University Press, 2009), 80–84; Schutt, *Peoples of the River Valleys*, 152–56, 360; David Brainerd, *Mirabilia Dei inter Indicos, or the Rise and Progress of a Remarkable Work of Grace amongst a Number of Indians in the Provinces of New Jersey and Pennsylvania* (Philadelphia: William Bradford, 1746).

33. William Henry Egle, ed., *Notes and Queries: Chiefly Relating to the History of Dauphin County*, vol. 1 (Harrisburg, PA: Harrisburg Publishing Company 1887), 74; Merritt, *At the Crossroads*, 70–86; Katherine Carte Engel, *Religion and Profit: Moravians in Early America* (Philadelphia: University of Pennsylvania Press, 2013), 1–2; Nancy L. Hagedorn, "'Faithful, Knowing, and Prudent': Andrew Montour as Interpreter and Cultural Broker, 1740–1772," in *Between Indian and White Worlds: The Cultural Broker*, ed. Margaret Connell Szasz (Norman: University of Oklahoma Press, 2001), 44–45.

34. Zeisberger on August Gottlieb Spangenberg (1704–1792), quoted in Vogel, *American Indian Medicine*, 293; Simone Vincens, *Madame Montour and the Fur Trade (1667–1752)*, trans. Ruth Bernstein (Bloomington, IN: Xlibris Corporation, 2011), 231–32; Hanna, *The Wilderness Trail*, 204–5.

35. John W. Jordan, ed., "Spangenberg's Notes of Travel to Onondaga in 1745," *PMHB* 3 (1879): 56, 60. Spangenberg had also learned Native American remedies during his 1752–53 travels in North Carolina. See August Gottlieb Spangenberg, *Journal of August Gottlieb Spangenberg's Voyage to North Carolina to Establish a Moravian Settlement, September 13, 1752–January 08, 1753*, vol. 5, 1–14, trans. Rev. R. P. Lineback, Archives of the Moravian Church, Salem, NC, Documenting the American South (Chapel Hill: University Library, The University of North Carolina at Chapel Hill, 2004), https://docsouth.unc.edu/csr/index.html /document/csr05-0001; Gregory Evans Dowd, *A Spirited Resistance: The North American Indian Struggle for Unity, 1745–1815* (Baltimore: Johns Hopkins University Press, 1992), 1–22.

36. John W. Jordan, ed., "Bishop J. C. F. Cammerhoff's Narrative of a Journey to Shamokin, Penna, in the Winter of 1748," *PMHB* 29, no. 2 (1905): 172–73; Schutt, *Peoples of the River Valleys*, 100, 98–105; Hirsch, "Indian, Métis," 79; Katherine Faull, *Moravian Women's Memoirs:*

Their Related Lives, 1750–1820 (Syracuse, NY: Syracuse University Press, 1997), xxvi–xxxi, 42–43; Alexander Henry (1739–1824), *Travels and Adventures in Canada and the Indian Territories Between the Years 1760 and 1776*, ed. Milton M. Quaife (Chicago: R. R. Donnelley and Sons, 1921), 75, 177. European Moravians forged intercultural ties through marriages with Moravians of Native American and African descent.

37. Henry, *Travels*, 177; Heckewelder, *History, Manners, and Customs*, 228–29; White, *Middle Ground*, 328–29; Merritt, *At the Crossroads*, 169–81; Merritt, "Cultural Encounters," 509–12. David Zeisberger, quoted in Vogel, *American Indian Medicine*, 61. The Moravian missionary George Henry Loskiel was also struck by Native Americans' acumen in wound management. See George Henry Loskiel, *History of the Mission of the United Brethren [Moravians] among the Indians of North America*, vol. 1, trans. Christian Latrobe (London: Brethren's Society, 1794), 112–13.

38. Renate Wilson, *Pious Traders in Medicine: A German Pharmaceutical Network in Eighteenth-Century North America* (University Park: Pennsylvania State University Press, 2008), 129–63; Lisa Minardi, *Pastors and Patriots: The Muhlenberg Family of Pennsylvania* (Kutztown: Pennsylvania German Society, 2011), 23.

39. Ann Whitall, Diary, pg. 4, 3rd mo. (March) 16, 1760, copied from a Library of Congress transcript, Gloucester County Historical Society Library, Woodbury, New Jersey; Virginia M. Lyttle, ed., *Ladies at the Crossroads: Eighteenth-Century Women of New Jersey* (Morristown, NJ: Compton Press, 1978), 131–32; Fred Anderson, *Crucible of War: The Seven Years' War and the Fate of Empire in British North America, 1754–1766* (New York: Random House, 2007), 86–107.

40. See Paschall, Recipe Book, 45. She cites Sarah Pyle Way (1708–74), who married Joseph Way (1697–1755); her granddaughter Mary (Polly) Webb Updergraff (1747–1833), who was related to William Webb; and Dr. John Pyle (1723–1804). See Lela L. Livingston, *Pyle Family History, 1594–1954* (Bethany, MO: H. Pyle, 1954).

41. Theodore Thayer, "The Friendly Association," *PMHB* 67, no. 4 (1943): 356–76. Signers of a Quaker Petition against War with the Indians (1756) included John Reynell and Israel Pemberton. See *Minutes of the Provincial Council of Pennsylvania: From the Organization to the Termination of the Proprietary Government*, vol. 7 (Harrisburg, PA: Theo. Fenn & Co., 1851), 86; "List of Goods Delivered to the Indians at Easton," July 30, 1756, Friendly Association Records, Philadelphia Yearly Meeting Coll., HQSC.

42. Paschall, Recipe Book, 7.

43. Paschall, Recipe Book, 26; Ann Whitall, Diary, 42, 9th mo. (September) 1762.

44. Paschall, Recipe Book, 13; Heckewelder, *History, Manners, and Customs*, 224; Vogel, *American Indian Medicine*, 60. Twenty-first-century cases of necrotizing fasciitis or "flesh-eating bacteria" demonstrate how quickly an embedded thorn or minor wound can become life threatening.

45. Paschall, Recipe Book, 37. See also Anderson, *Crucible of War*, 160–65; Peter Silver, *Our Savage Neighbors: How Indian War Transformed Early America* (New York: Norton, 2009), 39–48.

46. Anderson, *Crucible of War*, 204–7.

47. Captain Jacob Orndt to Governor Denny, July 1757, in *Pennsylvania Archives: Selected and Arranged from Original Documents*, ed. Samuel Hazard (Philadelphia: Joseph Severns and Co., 1855), 3:209; Dr. John M. Otto to Timothy Horsfield, Bethlehem, July 27, 1757, and John Matthew Otto to Governor [William] Denny at East-Town, July 31, 1757, in Hazard,

Pennsylvania Archives, 3:209, 247. See also James E. Gibson, *Dr. Bodo Otto and the Medical Background of the American Revolution* (Springfield, IL: C. C. Thomas, 1937); W. P. Walker, ed., *Lehigh Valley Medical Magazine* 10, no. 4 (1899), 55–56; Joseph M. Levering, *A History of Bethlehem, Pennsylvania, 1741–1892* (Bethlehem, PA: Times Publishing Co., 1903), 533–34; Merrell, *Into the American Woods*, 143–45.

48. "At A Meeting in Easton, Wednesday, July 27, 1757," reprinted in *Indian Treaties Printed by Benjamin Franklin, 1736–1762*, ed. Julian P. Boyd (Philadelphia: Historical Society of Pennsylvania, 1938), 195. For Tunda Moses Tatamy (ca. 1690–1760) and his son, William, see Merrell, *Into the American Woods*, 143–45, 293–94; [Moses] Tetamy's [Tatamy's] Account of the Indian Complaints, ca. 1750s, The [Quaker] Friendly Association Papers, vol. 1, 65A–658, HQSC. In another example, in November 1758, after the Treaty of Easton, an "Indian Man" named Captain Henry Quamash sought medical care for his chronic lameness at Bethlehem, Pennsylvania, from Mr. Horsfield, Dr. John Otto's partner, and he convalesced at a Moravian home. His "great Obligations to the Moravians," "during his Cure," led Quamash to divulge information to Pennsylvania officials regarding New Englanders' claims to contested lands in Wyoming, Pennsylvania. See Henry Quamash, an Indian to Gov. Hamilton, 1760, and Lewis Grodon to R.[Richard] Peters at Easton, July 29, 1761, in Hazard, *Pennsylvania Archives*, 4:66.

49. Kathryn Derounian-Stodola, *Women's Indian Captivity Narratives* (New York: Penguin, 1998), x–xv, 119–21; Daniel K. Richter, *The Ordeal of the Longhouse: The Peoples of the Iroquois League in the Era of European Colonization* (Chapel Hill: University of North Carolina Press, 1992), 39–60; James Seaver, *A Narrative of the Life of Mrs. Mary Jemison* (Howden, England: R. Parking, 1826).

50. For Margaret Frantz Wotring [or Woodring] (1745–83), who married John Nicholas Wotring (1745–1818) in 1769, see James J. Hauser, *A History of Lehigh County Pennsylvania from the Earliest Settlements to the Present Time* (Allentown, PA: Jacks, 1902), 19; Kae Tienstra, "Margaret Frantz Wotring," in *Our Hidden Heritage: Pennsylvania Women in History*, ed. Janice McElroy (Washington, DC: American Association of University Women, 1983), 115; Gladys M. Lutz, *The Early History of North Whitehall Township* (n.p.: North Whitehall Bicentennial Historical Committee, 1976), 4.

51. Marshall, "Examination."

52. Marshall, "Examination"; Becker, "Legends About Hannah Freeman," 16.

53. Tantaquidgeon, *Folk Medicine*, 1–12. The anthropologist Gladys Tantaquidgeon, a Mohegan, collected oral histories to recover Lenape healing practices for her 1942 book *Folk Medicine of the Delaware*. Minnie Fouts (Wèmeehëlèxkwe, 1871–1949) and Nora Thompson Dean (Weenjipahkihelexkwe, 1907–1984) exemplify Lenape women who were recognized as skilled healers and community leaders.

54. Dorner, *Merchants of Medicines*, 26–39, 82, 167–72; Thomas Short, *Medicina Britannica, with Mr. Bartram's Appendix containing Descriptions, Virtues and Uses of Sundry Plants of These Northern Parts of America; and Particularly of the Newly Discovered Indian Cure for the Venereal Disease*, 3rd. ed. (Philadelphia: B. Franklin and D. Hall, 1751), 5; Vogel, *American Indian Medicine*, ix.

55. Elizabeth Sarah Logan, "Receipts for Pickling, Preserving, Cooking, and Quacking," ca. 1810s, 68.2.50, n.p., Stenton Archives, Germantown, PA. For Paschall and her daughter, see Chapter 2.

Chapter 4

1. Elizabeth Coates Paschall (1702–68), Recipe Book, ca. 1745–67, 6, CPP; Carl von Linné [Linnaeus], *Species Plantarum: Exhibentes Plantas rite Cognitas*, vol. 2 (Stockholm, 1753), 800. Quinsy is a peritonsillar abscess. See J. E. Gordon and D. C. Young, "The Hazard of Incision for Apparent Quinsy in Diphtheria," *Archives of Internal Medicine* 46, no. 3 (1930): 402–9.

2. Paschall, Recipe Book, 6; Robert James, *A Medicinal Dictionary; Including Physic, Surgery, Anatomy, Chymistry, and Botany, in All Their Branches Relative to Medicine*, vol. 1 (London: T. Osborne, 1745), (header) ANA.

3. Immanuel Kant, *An Answer to the Question: "What Is Enlightenment?,"* trans. H. B. Nisbet (London: Penguin, 2013), 1.

4. Patricia Fara, *Pandora's Breeches: Women, Science, and Power in the Enlightenment* (London: Pimlico, 2004), 19 (quotation), 3–31; Peter Elmer, ed., *The Healing Arts: Health, Disease and Society in Europe 1500–1800* (Manchester, UK: Manchester University Press, 2004); Harold Cook, *The Decline of the Old Medical Regime in Stuart London* (Ithaca, NY: Cornell University Press, 1986), 19–64, 210–53; Leigh Ann Whaley, *Women's History as Scientists: A Guide to the Debates* (Santa Barbara, CA: ABC-Clio, 2003), 103; Londa Schiebinger, *The Mind Has No Sex? Women in the Origins of Modern Science* (Cambridge, MA: Harvard University Press, 1989), 220–39, 270–72; Barbara Taylor and Sarah Knott, eds., *Women, Gender, and Enlightenment* (New York: Palgrave Macmillan, 2007), 2–18; Karen O'Brien, *Women and Enlightenment in Eighteenth-Century Britain* (Cambridge: Cambridge University Press, 2009), 1–34; Eileen Pollack, *The Only Woman in the Room: Why Science Is Still a Boy's Club* (Boston: Beacon Press, 2015).

5. Fara, *Pandora's Breeches*, 24; Pamela H. Smith, *The Body of the Artisan: Art and Experience in the Scientific Revolution* (Chicago: University of Chicago Press, 2004), 1–28.

6. Susan Scott Parrish, *American Curiosity: Cultures of Natural History in the Colonial British Atlantic World* (Chapel Hill: University of North Carolina Press, 2006), 103–35.

7. Joyce Chaplin, *The First Scientific American: Benjamin Franklin and the Pursuit of Genius* (New York: Basic Books, 2007), 3–8; Lorraine Daston, "Framing the History of Scientific Observation," and "The Empire of Observation, 1600–1800," in *Histories of Scientific Observation*, ed. Lorraine Daston and Elizabeth Lunbeck (Chicago: University of Chicago Press, 2011), 1–10, 16–45; Thomas Kuhn, *The Structure of Scientific Revolutions*, 50th anniversary edition, 4th ed. (Chicago: University of Chicago Press, 2012).

8. Michelle DiMeo, "'Such a sister became such a brother': Lady Ranelagh's Influence on Robert Boyle," *Intellectual History Review* 25, no. 1 (2015): 21–36; Lynette Hunter, "The Circle of Katherine Jones, Lady Ranelagh," in *Women, Science, and Medicine 1500–1700: Mothers and Sisters of the Royal Society*, ed. Lynette Hunter and Sarah Hutton (London: Sutton Publishers, 1997), 178–97; Sarah Hutton, "Anne Conway, Margaret Cavendish and Seventeenth-Century Scientific Thought," in Hunter and Hutton, *Women, Science, and Medicine*, 218–33; Fara, *Pandora's Breeches*, 74–87.

9. Lady Damaris Masham (1659–1708), *Occasional Thoughts in Reference to a Vertuous or Christian Life* (London: printed for A. and J. Churchil, 1705), 44; O'Brien, *Women and Enlightenment*, 40–45; Jacqueline Broad and Karen Green, *A History of Women's Political Thought in Europe, 1400–1700* (Cambridge: Cambridge University Press, 2009), 199–220, 265–80; Margaret Atherton, ed., *Women Philosophers of the Early Modern Period* (Indianapolis: Hackett Publishing Company, 1994), 22–28, 96–105.

10. Karin Wulf, "Introduction," in *Milcah Martha Moore's Book*, ed. Catherine Blecki and Karin Wulf (University Park: Pennsylvania State University Press, 1997), 8–10; Gary B. Nash, *First City: Philadelphia and the Forging of Historical Memory* (Philadelphia: University of Pennsylvania Press, 2006), 45–78.

11. Benjamin Franklin, *A Proposal for Promoting Useful Knowledge Among the British Plantations in America* (Philadelphia: printed by Benjamin Franklin, 1743); William H. Williams, *America's First Hospital: the Pennsylvania Hospital, 1751–1841* (Wayne, PA: Haverford House, 1976), 90–100; Benjamin Franklin, *Some Account of the Pennsylvania Hospital*, facsimile, with an introduction by I. Bernard Cohen (Baltimore: Johns Hopkins Press, 1954; first published 1754, Philadelphia: B. Franklin), 29–30; Leonard W. Labaree, ed., *Papers of Benjamin Franklin*, vol. 5 (New Haven, CT: Yale University Press, 1962), 310–17; John Thomas Scharf and Thompson Westcott, *History of Philadelphia, 1609–1884*, vol. 2 (Philadelphia: L. H. Everts, 1884), 1584–85; Whitfield J. Bell Jr., *Patriot-Improvers: Biographical Sketches of Members of the American Philosophical Society* (Philadelphia: American Philosophical Society, 1999), 212–13, 226, 290–91.

12. Sarah Fatherly, *Gentlewomen and Learned Ladies: Women and Elite Formation in Eighteenth-Century Philadelphia* (Bethlehem, PA: Lehigh University Press, 2008), 105–6; *A Short Account of the Charter, Laws, and Catalogue of Books of the Library Company of Philadelphia With a Short Account of the Library Prefixed* (Philadelphia: Joseph Crukshank, 1770).

13. *Pennsylvania Gazette*, July 29, 1747; Parrish, *American Curiosity*, 103–33, 183–200.

14. *Short Account of the . . . Library Company of Philadelphia*, 4–5; *Pennsylvania Gazette*, December 6, 1750, January 29, 1751, and regular advertisements for Isaac Greenwood's "Course of Philosophical Lectures and Experiments" from January 3 through December 25, 1740; Ebenezer Kinnersley, "A Course of Experiments on the Newly Discovered Electrical Fire," (1752), MS Am.098, HSP; J. A. L. Lemay, "Franklin and Kinnersley," in *Early American Science*, ed. Brooke Hindle (New York: Science History Publications, 1976), 51–57; Parrish, *American Curiosity*, 185–86; Fatherly, *Gentlewomen*, 82–83.

15. Elizabeth Byles to Peggy, December 3, 1759, Elizabeth Byles, Letter Book, 1750–83, Ball Family Papers, HSP; Elizabeth Byles, Recipe Book, n.p., William Ball Collection, Col. 612, box 1, WML; Horatio Gates Jones, "The First Baptist Church of Philadelphia: List of Constituents and other Early Members," in *Miscellaneous Americana: A Collection of History, Biography and Genealogy*, ed. Horace Wemyss Smith (Philadelphia: Dando Printing and Publishing, 1889), 8–11; Janet Moore Lindman, *Bodies of Belief: Baptist Community in Early America* (Philadelphia: University of Pennsylvania Press, 2011), 27–30; James Delbourgo, *A Most Amazing Scene of Wonders: Electricity and Enlightenment in Early America* (Cambridge, MA: Harvard University Press, 2006), 87–101; Steven Shapin and Simon Schaffer, *Leviathan and the Air-Pump: Hobbes, Boyle and the Experimental Life* (Princeton, NJ: Princeton University Press, 1985), 22–79; Chaplin, *First Scientific American*, 53–55, 106–12; Stanley Finger, *Doctor Franklin's Medicine* (Philadelphia: University of Pennsylvania Press, 2011), 66–100.

16. Paschall, Recipe Book, 4.

17. Sir Hans Sloane to Dr. John Bartram, MS 4069, British Library; Ann B. Shteir, *Cultivating Women, Cultivating Science: Flora's Daughters and Botany in England, 1760 to 1860* (Baltimore: Johns Hopkins University Press, 1996), 33–47, 197; James Delbourgo, *Collecting the World: Hans Sloane and the Origins of the British Museum* (Cambridge, MA: Belknap Press, 2017); Thomas P. Slaughter, *The Natures of John and William Bartram* (Philadelphia: University of Pennsylvania Press, 2005), 1–22, 104–10; Lindsay O'Neill, *The Opened Letter: Network-*

ing in the Early Modern British World (Philadelphia: University of Pennsylvania Press, 2015), 1–15.

18. Whitfield J. Bell Jr., "John Bartram: A Biographical Sketch," in *America's Curious Botanist: A Tercentennial Reappraisal of John Bartram*, ed. Nancy Hoffman and John Van Horne (Philadelphia: American Philosophical Society, 2004), 3–22.

19. "A Copy of the Subscription Paper, for the Encouragement of Mr. John Bartram," *Pennsylvania Gazette*, March 10 and 17, 1742; Thomas Short [and John Bartram (1699–1777)], *Medicina Britannica, with Mr. Bartram's Appendix containing Descriptions, Virtues and Uses of Sundry Plants of These Northern Parts of America; and Particularly of the Newly Discovered Indian cure for the Venereal Disease*, 3rd ed. (Philadelphia: B. Franklin and D. Hall, 1751), 5, 46.

20. John Bartram to Doctor [John] Fothergill, July 24, 1744, in *Memorials of John Bartram and Humphry Marshall*, ed. William Darlington (Philadelphia: Lindsay and Blakiston, 1849), 22–23; William H. Goetzmann, "John Bartram's Journey to Onondaga in Context," in Hoffman and Van Horne, *America's Curious Botanist*, 97–106; Joel T. Fry, "John Bartram and His Garden," in Hoffman and Van Horne, *America's Curious Botanist*, 155–84; Alan W. Armstrong, "John Bartram and Peter Collinson: A Correspondence of Science and Friendship," in Hoffman and Van Horne, *America's Curious Botanist*, 23–42.

21. Parrish, *American Curiosity*, 104–13; Richard Drayton, *Nature's Government: Science, Imperial Britain, and the "Improvement" of the World* (New Haven, CT: Yale University Press, 2000); Londa Schiebinger, *Plants and Empire: Colonial Bioprospecting in the Atlantic World* (Cambridge, MA: Harvard University Press, 2004); Harold J. Cook, *Matters of Exchange: Commerce, Medicine, and Science in the Dutch Golden Age* (New Haven, CT: Yale University Press, 2007); Daniela Bleichmar and Peter C. Mancall, eds., *Collecting Across Cultures: Material Exchanges in the Early Modern Atlantic World* (Philadelphia: University of Pennsylvania Press, 2011), 1–11.

22. Paschall, Recipe Book, 7, 4; *Pennsylvania Gazette*, November 1, 1764.

23. Paschall, Recipe Book, 45; Steven Foster and Roger A. Caras, *A Field Guide to Venomous Animals and Poisonous Plants* (Boston: Houghton Mifflin, 1994), 86; Michael S. DeFelice, *Weeds of the South* (Athens: University of Georgia Press, 2009), 302. Sarah Pyle Way (1708–74) married Joseph Way (1697–1755). Her granddaughter was Mary (Polly) Webb Updegraff (1747–1833). John Pyle (1723–1804) was a loyalist physician during the American Revolution. See Lela L. Livingston, *Pyle Family History, 1594–1954* (Bethany, MO: H. Pyle, 1954).

24. Paschall, Recipe Book, 35; Merril Smith, "The Bartram Women: Farm Wives, Artists, Botanists, and Entrepreneurs," *Bartram Broadside* (Winter 2001): 1–4; J. Smith Futhey and Gilbert Cope, *History of Chester County, Pennsylvania*, vol. 2 (Philadelphia: L. H. Everts and Co., 1881), 477, 774–75.

25. Martha Logan (1704–79) to Ann Bartram, October 18, 1761, and John Bartram to Ann Bartram, Savannah, September 4, 1756, in Darlington, *Memorials*, 415–16, 425–26.

26. Martha Logan to Ann Bartram, October 18, 1761, and John Bartram to Ann Bartram, Savannah, September 4, 1756, in Darlington, *Memorials*, 415–16, 425–26. See also Mary Barbot Prior, "Letters of Martha Logan to John Bartram, 1760–1763," *South Carolina Historical Magazine* 59, no. 1 (1958): 38–46. Originals in Bartram Family Papers, HSP. Martha Logan was the daughter of the deputy governor of South Carolina. When widowed, she supported her family by opening a school and a plant nursery business in Charleston. In his southern travels, John Bartram met Logan and Dr. Alexander Garden. See Alex.[ander] Garden, M.D.,

"An Account of the Indian Pink . . . presented by Dr. Hope [to the Edinburgh Society]," later published in *Essays and Observations, Physical and Literary*, vol. 3 (Edinburgh: John Balfour, 1771), 145–50; Parrish, *American Curiosity*, 163–67; Virgil J. Vogel, *American Indian Medicine* (Norman: University of Oklahoma Press, 1990), 56–58.

27. Edmund Berkeley and Dorothy Smith Berkeley, *The Life and Travels of John Bartram: From Lake Ontario to the River St. John* (Tallahassee: University Presses of Florida, 1982), 57–81; John Bartram to Miss Jane Colden, January 24, 1757, and note on Jane Colden, in Darlington, *Memorials*, 20, 400–401; Cadwallader Colden to Peter Collinson, ca. October 1755, quoted in Kevin Hayes, *A Colonial Woman's Bookshelf* (Knoxville: University of Tennessee Press, 1996), 125–26; for Byrd, see 123–25. See also Beatrice Scheer Smith, "Jane Colden (1724–1766) and Her Botanic Manuscript," *American Journal of Botany* 75, no. 7 (1988): 1090–96.

28. Paschall, Recipe Book, 2, 5; Howard Atwood Kelly, *A Cyclopedia of American Medical Biography*, vol. 1 (Philadelphia: W. B. Saunders, 1912), 521; Joel T. Fry, "America's Ancient Garden: The Bartram Botanic Garden, 1728–1850," in *Knowing Nature: Art and Science in Philadelphia, 1740–1840*, ed. Amy R. W. Myers (New Haven, CT: Yale University Press, 2011), 60–95.

29. Paschall, Recipe Book, 14, 39; John Bartram to Peter Collinson, June 12, 1756, in Darlington, *Memorials*, 209–10; Bell, *Patriot-Improvers*, 286–93, 94–99; Victoria Johnson, *American Eden: David Hosack, Botany, and Medicine in the Garden of the Early Republic* (New York: Liveright, 2018), 94–99, 245–87.

30. Paschall, Recipe Book, 5.

31. For alchemists as "philosophers by fire," see Herman Boerhaave, *A New Method of Chemistry; Including the Theory and Practice of that Art*, trans. P. Shaw, M.D., and E. Chambers, Gent. (London: J. Osborn and T. Longman, 1721), 9; John Paschall, Commonplace Book, Paschall Family Papers, 1705–70, HSP. Stephen Paschall (1714–1800) founded Paschall's Steel Furnace and practiced lay healing. See *Pennsylvania Gazette*, September 24, 1767; Stephen Paschall, Business Receipt Book, 1760–71, doc. 657, Joseph Downs Collection, WML; Stephen Paschall, Commonplace Book, Paschall and Hollingsworth papers, HSP; Bell, *Patriot-Improvers*, 226; John W. Jordan, *A History of Delaware County and Its People*, vol. 2 (New York: Lewis Historical Publishing Company, 1914), 502.

32. Paracelsus, *Paracelsus: Essential Readings*, trans. and ed. Nicholas Goodrick-Clarke (Berkeley, CA: North Atlantic Books, 1999), 15, 74; Walter Pagel, *Paracelsus: An Introduction to Philosophical Medicine in the Era of the Renaissance*, 2nd ed. (New York: Karger, 1982), 50–62, 148–72; Allen G. Debus, *The Chemical Philosophy: Paracelsian Science and Medicine in the Sixteenth Century* (New York: Dover, 2002), 191–92, 285–90, 479.

33. Paschall, Recipe Book, 22; Sir Kenelm Digby, *A Late Discourse made in Solemne Assembly of Nobles and Learned Men Touching the Cure of Wounds by the Powder of Sympathy* (London: R. Lowdes, 1658); Paul Kleber Monod, *Solomon's Secret Arts: The Occult in the Age of Enlightenment* (New Haven, CT: Yale University Press, 2013), 97–98; E. Hedrick, "Romancing the Salve: Sir Kenelm Digby and the Powder of Sympathy," *British Journal of the History of Science* 41 (2008): 161–85; Betty Jo Dobbs, "Digby and Alchemy," *Ambix* 20 (1973): 143–54. For another woman's recipe for weapon salve, see E. Ashby, Recipe Book, ca. early eighteenth century, 49, MS B 1, NLM.

34. Paschall, Recipe Book, 22, 3; Renate Wilson, *Pious Traders in Medicine: A German Pharmaceutical Network in Eighteenth-Century North America* (University Park: Pennsylvania State University Press, 2000), 1–14, 55–57. For Dr. John Diemer (1720–57) and Catherine Diemer, see Letter of Mr. Boehm and the Consistory at Philadelphia to Deputy Velingius, Oc-

tober 28, 1734, "Letters and Reports of Rev. John Philip Boehm," *Journal of the Presbyterian Historical Society* 7 (1913–14): 128–31; Louis A. Meier, *Early Pennsylvania Medicine: A Representative Early American Medical History* (Philadelphia: Gilbert Print Company, 1976), 121; *Pennsylvania Gazette*, September 5, 1751, and July 4, 1754; Aya Homei and Michael Worboys, *Fungal Diseases in Britain and the United States, 1850–2000: Mycoses and Modernity* (Basingstoke, UK: Palgrave Macmillan, 2013), 17–20.

35. Paschall, Recipe Book, 22. For Catherina Sprogell and Lodowick Christian Sprogell (1683–1729), see Samuel W. Pennypacker, "Bebbers Township and the Dutch Patroons of Pennsylvania," *PMHB* 31 (1907): 13–15; Samuel W. Pennypacker, *The Settlement of Germantown Pennsylvania and the Beginning of German Emigration to North America* (Philadelphia: William J. Campbell, 1899), 139; John W. Jordan, *Colonial and Revolutionary Families of Pennsylvania* (New York: Lewis Publishing, 1911), 481. Scrofula, or king's evil, would now be recognized as cervical lymphadenitis caused by tuberculosis or other mycobacterium.

36. Paschall, Recipe Book, 42. For Christopher Witt (1675–1765), see *Germantauner Zeitung* (Germantown, PA), March 1, 1791; "Dr. Witt's Medicines," *Germantown Crier* 22, no. 3 (1970): 107–8; *Pennsylvania Gazette*, February 7, 1765; Pennypacker, *The Settlement of Germantown*, 224–27; Thomas A. Horrocks, *Popular Print and Popular Medicine: Almanacs and Health Advice in Early America* (Amherst: University of Massachusetts Press, 2008), 17–41; Bell, *Patriot-Improvers*, 226; Collinson Read, et al., *The American Pleader's Assistant* (Sunbury, PA: William M'Carty, 1853), 123, 224–27; William Woys Weaver, *Sauer's Herbal Cures: America's First Book of Botanic Healing, 1762–1778* (New York: Routledge, 2001), 22, 295.

37. Broadside advertisement for [Dr. John] "Paschall's Golden Drops," early nineteenth century, box C 10 #3, DCHS. Subsequent vendors included his son Dr. Henry Paschall and druggist Alice Pearson; A. L. Donovan, *Philosophical Chemistry in the Scottish Enlightenment: The Doctrines and Discoveries of William Cullen and Joseph Black* (Edinburgh: Edinburgh University Press, 1975), 3–90; Monod, *Solomon's Secret Arts*, 227–35, 263–67.

38. *Spectator* (London), no. 5, March 6, 1711; Fatherly, *Gentlewomen*, 69–79.

39. *London Gazette*, June 16–June 19, 1739, and March 22–March 25, 1740; John Rutty, M.D., *An Account of some New Experiments and Observations on Joanna Stephens's Medicine for the Stone* (London: R. Manby, 1742); Benjamin Franklin to Josiah and Abiah Franklin, September 6, 1744, in *The Works of Benjamin Franklin*, vol. 7, ed. Jared Sparks (London: Benjamin Franklin Stevens, 1882), 14–15; Fatherly, *Gentlewomen*, 69–73; Eliza Haywood, ed., *The Female Spectator* (London: T. Gardner, 1744–46); *The Spectator*, April 12, 1711; Sylvanus Urban, ed., *The Gentleman's Magazine* (London: Cave, 1739), 297–98.

40. Paschall, Recipe Book, 38, 42; Roy Porter, "Lay Medical Knowledge in the Eighteenth Century: The Evidence of the Gentleman's Magazine," *Medical History* 29, no. 2 (1985): 138–68.

41. Frederick Tolles, "Susannah Wright," in *Notable American Women, 1607–1950*, ed. Edward T. James, Janet Wilson James, and Paul S. Boyer (Cambridge, MA: Harvard University Press, 1971), 689; Elizabeth Meg Schaefer, *Wright's Ferry Mansion: The House* (Columbia, PA: Von Hess Foundation, 2005), 25–30; Karin Wulf, *Not All Wives: Women of Colonial Philadelphia* (Philadelphia: University of Pennsylvania Press, 2000), 55–66, 63–66; Susan Stabile, *Memory's Daughters* (Ithaca, NY: Cornell University Press, 2004), 10; Mrs. S. Wright, "Directions for the Management of Silk-Worms," *Philadelphia Medical and Physical Journal* 1 (1804): 103–7; Elizabeth Coultas, Recipe Book, ca. 1749, n.p., WML; Catherine Blecki, "Reading Moore's Book," in Blecki and Wulf, *Milcah Martha Moore's Book*, xvi, 27–67; Angela Vietto, *Women and Authorship in Revolutionary America* (Burlington, VT: Ashgate, 2005), 4–6.

42. Paschall, Recipe Book, 29; Rebecca Laroche, *Medical Authority and Englishwomen's Herbal Texts, 1550–1650* (Burlington, VT: Ashgate, 2009), 6–10.

43. Robert James, *Medicinal Dictionary*, vols. 1 and 3 (London: T. Osborne, 1745), preface; Robert James, *Dr. Robert James's Powder for Fevers: And All Inflammatory Disorders* (London: Published by Virtue of His Majesty's Royal Letters Patent, 1780); Lulu Stine, "Dr. Robert James," *Bulletin of the History of the Medical Library Association* 29, no. 4 (1941): 187–98; Roderick McConchie, *Discovery in Haste: English Medical Dictionaries and Lexicographers 1547 to 1796* (Boston: Walter de Gruyter, 2019), 140–70.

44. James, *Medicinal Dictionary*, vol. 3; Paschall, Recipe Book, 33; Laroche, *Medical Authority*, 6; Kathryn Shevelow, *Women and Print Culture: The Construction of Femininity in the Early Periodical* (London: Routledge, 1989), 16. Shevelow uses the term "resisting reader" to describe women who refused to be molded by prescriptive writers' restrictive notions of women's sphere. Paschall might rather be called a "synthesizing reader."

45. Paschall, Recipe Book, 30; James, *Medicinal Dictionary*, vol. 1.

46. Paschall, Recipe Book, 30; Boerhaave, *A New Method of Chemistry*, vi, 133.

47. Mary Pemberton to Israel Pemberton, Fifth Month [May] 23, 1759, Pemberton Papers, vol. 33, 71, HSP; Richard Russell, *Dissertation on the Use of Sea-water*, 3rd ed. (London: W. Owen, 1755); Paschall, Recipe Book, 8; Fatherly, *Gentlewomen*, 83; Theodore Thayer, *Israel Pemberton* (Philadelphia: Historical Society of Pennsylvania, 1943), 37–38, 197. See Library Company of Philadelphia, *A Catalogue of the Books, Belonging to the Library Company of Philadelphia; to which is Prefixed, A Short Account of the Institution* (Philadelphia: Zachariah Poulson, 1789). Mary Pemberton is listed as a member.

48. Richard Saunders [Benjamin Franklin], *Poor Richard Improved: Being an Almanak . . . for the Year of our Lord 1761* (Philadelphia: B. Franklin and D. Hall, 1760), 4, and *Poor Richard Improved* (D. Hall and W. Sellers, 1767); Robert Boyle, *The Philosophical Works of the Honourable Robert Bolye, Esq.*, vol. 3, ed. Peter Shaw (London: W. and J. Innys, 1738), 50, 446, 576–79, 582; Lawrence M. Principe, *The Aspiring Adept: Robert Boyle and His Alchemical Quest* (Princeton, NJ: Princeton University Press, 1998), 281–83, 304.

49. Boyle, *Philosophical Works*, 14–16; DiMeo, "'Such a sister,'" 21–36; Hunter, "Circle of Katherine Jones," 178–97.

50. John Hill to John Bartram, December 6, 1766, in Darlington, *Memorials*, 442; John Hill, *A History of the Materia Medica* (London: Longman, 1751), ii, 373, 886; Paschall Recipe Book, 27; George S. Rousseau, *The Notorious Sir John Hill: The Man Destroyed by Ambition in the Era of Celebrity* (Bethlehem, PA: Lehigh University Press, 2012).

51. John Quincy, *Pharmacopoeia Officinalis & Extemporanea, or A Complete English Dispensatory*, 6th ed. (London: J. Osborn and T. Longman, 1726), 35, 524; N. Howard-Jones, "John Quincy, M.D. Apothecary and Iatrophysical Writer," *Journal of the History of Medicine and Allied Sciences* 6 (1951): 149–75; Paschall, Recipe Book, 35.

52. Betsy Copping Corner, *William Shippen, Jr., Pioneer in American Medical Education* (Philadelphia: American Philosophical Society, 1951); *A Catalogue of the Medical Library, Belonging to the Pennsylvania Hospital . . . Also, a List of Articles Contained in the Anatomical Museum* (Philadelphia: Archibald Bartram, 1806), 121–27; William Pepper, *Descriptive Catalogue of the Pathological Museum of the Pennsylvania Hospital* (Philadelphia: Collins, 1869), iii; *Pennsylvania Gazette*, September 26, 1765, November 11, 1762, and May 19, 1763; Scharf and Westcott, *History of Philadelphia*, 1585–87; Michael Sappol, *A Traffic of Dead Bodies: Anatomy and Embodied Social Identity in Nineteenth-Century America* (Princeton, NJ: Princeton

University Press, 2002), 44–53, 76–77, 100–114; Sarah Knott, *Sensibility and the American Revolution* (Chapel Hill: University of North Carolina Press, 2009), 74–87.

53. Marie Catherine Biheron (1719–86) to Benjamin Franklin, September 10, 1772, June 26, 1773, October 10, 1774, Papers of Benjamin Franklin Part 1, APS; Lucia Dacome, "Women, Wax, and Anatomy in the 'Century of Things,'" *Renaissance Studies* 21, no. 4 (2007): 522–50; Danica Marković and B. Marković-Živković, "Development of Anatomical Models," *Acta Medica Medianae* 49, no. 2 (2010): 56; William Shippen [Philadelphia] to Benjamin Franklin, Craven Street, London, May 14, 1767, Benjamin Franklin Papers, APS; John Fothergill to James Pemberton, Philadelphia 1762, Pemberton Papers, Etting Collection, II, 47, HSP; *Pennsylvania Gazette*, September 26, 1765, and April 12, 1764; W. F. Bynum and Roy Porter, eds., *William Hunter and the Eighteenth-Century Medical World* (New York: Cambridge University Press, 1985). For Rachel Lovell Wells (ca. 1735–96), see Women's Project of New Jersey, Joan N. Burstyn, ed., *Past and Promise: Lives of New Jersey Women* (Syracuse, NY: University of Syracuse Press, 1990), 38–39; Charles Coleman Sellers, *Patience Wright: American Artist and Spy in George III's London* (Middletown, CT: Wesleyan University Press, 1976), 21–41; Catherine E. Kelly, *Republic of Taste: Art, Politics, and Everyday Life in Early America* (Philadelphia: University of Pennsylvania Press, 2016), 170–72.

54. James, *Medicinal Dictionary*, vol. 1, (header) ANA. James's term "bronchocele" in twenty-first-century terminology may refer to a brachial plexus tumor.

55. Paschall, Recipe Book, 53.

56. Fara, *Pandora's Breeches*, 19.

57. "Non-Importation Agreement Signed by the Merchants of Philadelphia," October 25, 1765, Am 340, HSP; Isaac Paschall to George Paschall, November 9, 1763, Morris and Paschall Families, Bible Records, Letters, and Notes, BR MO LOC 104, HSP; Paschall, Recipe Book, 83, 85.

Chapter 5

1. Margaret Hill Morris (hereafter MHM) to Hannah Hill Moore, April 1779, G. M. Howland MS Coll. 1000, box 4, HQSC; Roy Porter, *Bodies Politic: Disease, Death, and Doctors in Britain, 1650–1900* (Ithaca, NY: Cornell University Press, 2001), 139–42; Robert Campbell, *The London Tradesman*, 3rd ed. (London: T. Gardner, 1747), 41. A self-presentation of gravitas was more important than medical skill for physicians applying to the elite London College of Physicians.

2. Susan Hanket Brandt, "'Getting into a Little Business': Margaret Hill Morris and Women's Medical Entrepreneurship During the American Revolution," *Early American Studies* 13, no. 4 (2015): 774–807; Harold J. Cook, "Good Advice and a Little Medicine: The Professional Authority of Early Modern English Physicians," *Journal of British Studies* 33, no. 1 (1994): 1–31; MHM to Hannah Hill Moore, March 23, 1779, G. M. Howland MS Coll. 1000, box 4, HQSC.

3. Ellen Hartigan-O'Connor, *The Ties That Buy: Women and Commerce in Revolutionary America* (Philadelphia: University of Pennsylvania Press, 2009), 2; Cathy Matson, ed., "Special Forum: Women's Economies in North America Before 1820," *Early American Studies* 4, no. 2 (2006); Serena R. Zabin, *Dangerous Economies: Status and Commerce in Imperial New York* (Philadelphia: University of Pennsylvania Press, 2009), 32–62; Jeanne Boydston, "The Woman Who Wasn't There: Women's Market Labor and the Transition to Capitalism in the United States," *Journal of the Early Republic* 16, no. 2 (1996): 183–206; Laurel Thatcher Ulrich, *A Midwife's Tale: The Life of Martha Ballard, Based on Her Diary, 1785–1812* (New York: Knopf,

1990), 72–101; Lucy Simler, "'She Came to Work': The Female Labor Force in Chester County, 1750–1820," *Early American Studies* 5, no. 2 (2007): 427–53; Joan M. Jensen, *Loosening the Bonds: Mid-Atlantic Farm Women, 1750–1850* (New Haven, CT: Yale University Press, 1986).

4. John Duffy, *From Humors to Medical Science*, 2nd ed. (Chicago: University of Illinois Press, 1993), 284–86; Lamar Murphy, *Enter the Physician* (Tuscaloosa: University of Alabama Press, 1991), 51–59; Paul Starr, *The Social Transformation of American Medicine* (New York: Basic Books, 1982), 49; and Sylvia Hoffert, *Private Matters* (Urbana: University of Illinois Press, 1989), introduction.

5. Ann Dillwyn to Grace Buchanan (d. 1801), ca. 1781, G. M. Howland MS Coll. 1000, box 1, HQSC; William W. Hinshaw and Thomas W. Marshall, *Encyclopedia of American Quaker Genealogy*, vol. 2 (An Arbor, MI: Edwards Brothers, Inc., 1938), 167; John Jay Smith, *Recollections of John Jay Smith* (Philadelphia: Lippincott, 1892), 240; Joan Burstyn, *Lives of New Jersey Women* (Syracuse, NY: Syracuse University Press, 1997), 32–33; *American Weekly Mercury*, March 23–30, 1721; John Richardson, ed., *The Friend: A Religious and Literary Journal*, vol. 29 (Philadelphia: Robb, Pile, and McElroy, 1856), 373–74; Rebecca Larson, *Daughters of Light: Quaker Women Preaching and Prophesying in the Colonies and Abroad, 1700–1775* (Chapel Hill: University of North Carolina Press, 2000), 68, 90–93.

6. *American Weekly Mercury*, March 23–30, 1721; "Memoirs of Mrs. Hannah Hodge," *General Assembly's Missionary Magazine; or, Evangelical Intelligencer* 2, no. 2 (1806): 94; *Pennsylvania Gazette*, August 19, 1731, October 6, 1739, and September 17, 1747; Susan E. Klepp, "Benjamin Franklin and Women," in *A Companion to Benjamin Franklin*, ed. David Waldstreicher (Malden, MA: Wiley-Blackwell, 2011), 237–51; *Pennsylvania Gazette*, February 2, 1764, January 17, 1765, and October 31, 1766; *Der Wochentliche Pennsylvanische Staatsbote* (Philadelphia), January 19, 1773.

7. E. P. Thompson, *The Making of the English Working Class* (New York: Pantheon Books, 1964), 62–68; Amanda Vickery, *The Gentleman's Daughter: Women's Lives in Georgian England* (New Haven, CT: Yale University Press, 1998), 153–55; Elaine Leong and Sara Pennell, "Recipe Collections and the Currency of Medical Knowledge in the Early Modern 'Medical Marketplace,'" in *Medicine and the Market in England and Its Colonies, c. 1450–c. 1850*, ed. Mark S. R. Jenner and Patrick Wallis (Basingstoke, England: Palgrave Macmillan, 2007), 134; Craig Muldrew, *The Economy of Obligation: The Culture of Credit and Social Relations in Early Modern England*, 2nd ed. (London: Palgrave, 2016), 6.

8. Sara Pennell and Michelle DiMeo, "Introduction," in *Reading and Writing Recipe Books, 1550–1800*, ed. Michelle DiMeo and Sara Pennell (Manchester, UK: Manchester University Press, 2013), 3–5, 9–10; *Oxford English Dictionary*, 2nd ed., 20 vols. (Oxford: Oxford University Press, 1989); Samuel Johnson, *A Dictionary of the English Language* (London: W. Strahan, 1755), LCP; Clare Haru Crowston, *Credit, Fashion, Sex: Economies of Regard in Old Regime France* (Durham, NC: Duke University Press, 2013), 1–23; Zabin, *Dangerous Economies*, 10–31; Ben Mutschler, *The Province of Affliction: Illness and the Making of Early New England* (Chicago: University of Chicago Press, 2020), 49–65.

9. *Pennsylvania Gazette*, December 1, 1768; Laurence Brockliss and Colin Jones, *The Medical World of Early Modern France* (Oxford: Clarendon Press, 1997), 19; James Harvey Young, *The Toadstool Millionaires: A Social History of Patent Medicines in America Before Federal Regulation* (Princeton, NJ: Princeton University Press, 1961), 16–30; Charles Rosenberg, William Helfand, and James Green, *"Every Man His Own Doctor": Popular Medicine in Early America* (Philadelphia: Library Company of Philadelphia, 1998), 26; Mark S. R. Jenner and

Patrick Wallis, "The Medical Marketplace," in Jenner and Wallis, *Medicine and the Market*, 1–23.

10. John Tennent [authorship debated], *Every Man his Own Doctor*, 4th ed. (repr., Philadelphia: B. Franklin, 1736), LCP; William Buchan, *Domestic Medicine; or The Family Physician* (Philadelphia: John Dunlap, 1772); Rosenberg, Helfand, and Green, *"Every Man His Own Doctor,"* 26; John Ball, *The Female Physician: or, Every Woman Her Own Doctress* (London: L. Davis, 1770); Mary E. Fissell, "The Marketplace of Print," in Jenner and Wallis, *Medicine and the Market*, 108–132.

11. Anita Schorsch, "A Library in America" (PhD diss., Princeton University, 1986), 52–71; Sarah Fatherly, *Gentlewomen and Learned Ladies: Women and Elite Formation in Eighteenth-Century Philadelphia* (Bethlehem PA: Lehigh University Press, 2008), 105–7; Mary Poovey, *Genres of the Credit Economy: Mediating Value in Eighteenth- and Nineteenth-Century Britain* (Chicago: University of Chicago Press, 2008), 91–125.

12. Eliza Smith, *The Compleat Housewife* (London: J. Buckland, 1766), preface; "Account of Books Lent," Library Company of Burlington Archives, Microfilm Reel #3, LCP.

13. Patrick Wallis, "Consumption, Retailing, and Medicine in Early Modern London," *Economic History Review* 61, no. 1 (2008): 26–53.

14. John Morris Jr. to MHM, September 17, 1782, G. M. Howland MS Coll. 1000, box 7, folder 4, HQSC.

15. John Jay Smith, ed., *Letters of Doctor Richard Hill and His Children* (Philadelphia: T. K. Collins, 1854), vi–xxi; Margaret Hill Morris, Recipe Book, HC.MC-975-11-024, HQSC; Toby Ditz, "Shipwrecked; or, Masculinity Imperiled: Mercantile Representations of Failure and the Gendered Self in Eighteenth-Century Philadelphia," *Journal of American History* 81, no. 1 (1994): 51–80; Toby L. Ditz, "Secret Selves, Credible Personas: The Problematics of Trust and Public Display in the Writing of Eighteenth-Century Philadelphia Merchants," in *Possible Pasts: Becoming Colonial in Early America*, ed. Robert Blair St. George (Ithaca, NY: Cornell University Press, 2000), 219–44; David Hancock, "'A Revolution in the Trade': Wine Distribution and the Development of the Infrastructure of the Atlantic Market Economy," in *The Early Modern Atlantic Economy*, ed. John McCusker and Kenneth Morgan (Cambridge: Cambridge University Press, 2000), 105–41; Peter Mathias, "Risk, Credit and Kinship in Early Modern Enterprise," in McCusker and Morgan, *The Early Modern Atlantic Economy*, 16–31; David Hancock, *Oceans of Wine: Madeira and the Emergence of American Trade and Taste* (New Haven, CT: Yale University Press, 2009); MHM to Hannah H. Moore, August 12, 1769, June 6, 1772, G. M. Howland MS Coll. 1000, box 7, folder 1, HQSC.

16. Deborah Hill to Richard Hill Jr., May 16, 1743, and Deborah Hill (Madeira) to Hannah Hill Moore (Philadelphia), December 2, 1749, in Smith, *Letters of Doctor Richard Hill*, 30–32, 53. Deborah Hill may have used tansy as a contraceptive; see Susan Klepp, *Revolutionary Conceptions: Women, Fertility, and Family Limitation in America, 1760–1820* (Chapel Hill: University of North Carolina Press, 2009), 179–80.

17. Karin Wulf, *Not All Wives: Women of Colonial Philadelphia* (Philadelphia: University of Pennsylvania Press, 2000), 12; Gary B. Nash, *First City: Philadelphia and the Forging of Historical Memory* (Philadelphia: University of Pennsylvania Press, 2011), 1–8, 14–18, 69–76. See, for example, Hannah Hill Moore to Richard Hill Sr., January 27, 1757, in Smith, *Letters of Doctor Richard Hill*, 139.

18. Wulf, *Not All Wives*, 27, 41–43, 62–66; Rebecca Jones (1739–1818), Journal, Coll. 986, box 12, Diaries and MS Books G–Z, HQSC; and Mary Howell Swett (ca. 1739–1821), Memorandum

Book and Medicinal Remedies, 975 C, Diaries and Certificates, HQSC; Larson, *Daughters of Light*, 5–12, 98–104; Amanda E. Herbert, "Companions in Preaching and Suffering: Itinerant Female Quaker in the Seventeenth- and Eighteenth-Century British Atlantic World," *Early American Studies* 9, no. 1 (2011): 73–133; Susan Stabile, *Memory's Daughters: The Material Culture of Remembrance in Eighteenth-Century America* (Ithaca, NY: Cornell University Press, 2004), 10.

19. Patricia Cleary, "'She Will Be in the Shop': Women's Sphere of Trade in Eighteenth-Century Philadelphia and New York," *PMHB* 119, no. 3 (1995): 181–201, 183; Rebecca Jones (1739–1817), Manuscript Arithmetic Book [for her School], 1766, Diaries and Manuscript Books 968, box 12, HQSC; "Rebecca Jones," *Dictionary of Quaker Biography* [looseleaf, n.p.], HQSC; Thomas Scharf and Thompson Westcott, *A History of Philadelphia*, 2 vols. (Philadelphia: L. H. Everts & Co., 1884), 2:1250–51; Wulf, *Not All Wives*, 13; Fatherly, *Gentlewomen*, 85–88; MHM to Dr. Samuel Preston Moore, March 23, 1779, G. M. Howland MS Coll. 1000, box 7, folder 1, HQSC.

20. Catherine L. Blecki and Karin A. Wulf, eds., *Milcah Martha Moore's Book: A Commonplace Book from Revolutionary America* (University Park: Pennsylvania State University Press, 1997), 60–76; C. Dallett Hemphill, *Siblings: Brothers and Sisters in American History* (New York: Oxford University Press, 2011), 32–46.

21. MHM to William Morris, n.d., ca. 1758 and January 1759, G. M. Howland MS Coll. 1000, box 7, folder 1, HQSC.

22. "Non-Importation Agreement Signed by the Merchants of Philadelphia," October 25, 1765, Am 340, HSP; *Pennsylvania Gazette*, November 1, 1764; Edmund and Helen Morgan, *The Stamp Act Crisis* (Chapel Hill: University of North Carolina Press, 1962); Benjamin Carp, *Rebels Rising: Cities and the American Revolution* (New York: Oxford University Press, 2007), 172–212; Mary Beth Norton, *Liberty's Daughters: The Revolutionary Experience of American Women, 1750–1800* (Ithaca, NY: Cornell University Press, 1996), 160–69, 195–208; Linda K. Kerber, *Women of the Republic: Intellect and Ideology in Revolutionary America* (Chapel Hill: University of North Carolina Press, 1980), 37–39, 86–96; T. H. Breen, *The Marketplace of Revolution: How Consumer Politics Shaped American Independence* (New York: Oxford University Press, 2004), 57–58; Thomas Doerflinger, *A Vigorous Spirit of Enterprise: Merchants and Economic Development in Revolutionary Pennsylvania* (Chapel Hill: University of North Carolina Press, 1986), 181–94.

23. MHM to Hannah Hill Moore, February 8, 1768, and MHM to Hannah H. Moore, November 27, 1777, G. M. Howland MS Coll. 1000, box 7, folder 1, HQSC; "Wrote on the Death of Willm. Morris Junr.," in Blecki and Wulf, *Milcah Martha*, 168–69; Jack Marietta, *The Reformation of American Quakerism, 1748–1783* (Philadelphia: University of Pennsylvania Press, 2007), 170–79, 276.

24. MHM to Hannah Hill Moore, 11 Month [November] 27, 1777, G. M. Howland MS Coll. 1000, box 4, folder 1, HQSC; Stephen Wickes, *Medicine in New Jersey* (Newark, NJ: Martin Dennis, 1879), 63–69; Elizabeth Fenn, *Pox Americana: The Great Smallpox Epidemic of 1775–82* (New York: Hill and Wang, 2001); Emma Hart, *Trading Spaces: The Colonial Marketplace and the Foundations of American Capitalism* (Chicago: University of Chicago Press, 2019), 137–65; Bruce H. Mann, *Republic of Debtors: Bankruptcy in the Age of American Independence* (Cambridge, MA: Harvard University Press, 2009), 6–34; Carla Pestana and Sharon Salinger, eds., *Inequality in Early America* (Hanover, NH: University Press of New England, 1999); Anne Bezanson, *Prices and Inflation During the American Revolution: Pennsylvania, 1770–1790* (Phil-

adelphia: University of Pennsylvania Press, 1951), 5–33; Marc Egnal, "The Pennsylvania Economy, 1748–1762" (PhD diss., University of Wisconsin, 1974); J. Smith Futhey and Gilbert Cope, *History of Chester County, Pennsylvania, with Genealogical and Biographical Sketches*, 2 vols. (Philadelphia: Louis H. Everts, 1881), 1:101–8; George Griffenhagen, *Drug Supplies in the American Revolution* (Washington, DC: Smithsonian Institution, 1961).

25. Philadelphia Committee of Public Safety, April 9, 1776, in Peter Force, *American Archives: Consisting of a Collection of Authentick Records*, ser. 4, vol. 5, 1776 (Washington, DC: M. St. Clair Clarke and Peter Force, 1843), 828; Thomas Fleming, "Crossroads of the American Revolution," in *New Jersey in the American Revolution*, ed. Barbara J. Mitnick (New Brunswick, NJ: Rutgers University Press, 2005), 1–13; David J. Fowler, "'These Were Troublesome Times Indeed': Social and Economic Conditions in Revolutionary New Jersey," in Mitnick, *New Jersey in the American Revolution*, 15–30; Delight W. Dodyk, "'Troublesome Times a-Coming': The American Revolution and New Jersey Women," in Mitnick, *New Jersey in the American Revolution*, 140–50; Arthur J. Mekell, *The Relation of Quakers to the American Revolution* (Washington, DC: University Press of America, 1979), 173–88, 208–16; Larry R. Gerlach, *Prologue to Independence: New Jersey in the Coming of the American Revolution* (New Brunswick, NJ: Rutgers University Press, 1976).

26. John Pemberton to Sarah Zane, February 14, 1778, George Vaux Collection 1167, box 2, Parrish-Quary folder, HQSC; James D. Anderson, "Thomas Wharton, Exile in Virginia, 1777–1778," *Virginia Magazine of History and Biography* 89, no. 4 (1981): 425–47.

27. Margaret Morris, *Private Journal Kept During a Portion of the Revolutionary War, for the Amusement of a Sister*, ed. John J. Smith (Philadelphia: privately printed, 1836), 23–25, 30–31; and MHM to Hannah Moore, ca. 1777, G. M. Howland MS Coll. 1000, box 7, folder 2, HQSC.

28. Ann Cooper Whitall (1716–97), Diary, copied from a Library of Congress transcript owned by Miss Anne L. Nicholson of St. David's, PA, March 25, 1973, transcribed June 16, 2011, Frank H. Stewart Collection, Gloucester County Historical Society, Woodbury, NJ; Joan N. Burstyn, ed., *Past and Promise: Lives of New Jersey Women* (Syracuse, NY: Syracuse University Press, 1997), 38–40; Isabella George and Wallace McGeorge, *Ann Whitall: The Heroine of Red Bank* (Woodbury, NJ: Gloucester County Historical Society, 1917); Christopher Marshall, *Extracts from the Diary of Christopher Marshall, 1774–1781*, ed. William Duane (Albany, NY: Joel Munsell, 1877), 107–8, 157–58; Deborah Logan (1761–1839) to John Fanning Watson, September 20, 1822, Watson Family Papers, HSP.

29. For Lydia Darragh (1728–89), see Henry Darrach, *Lydia Darragh, One of the Heroines of the Revolution* (Philadelphia: Moyer and Lotter for the City History Society of Philadelphia, 1915), 383, HSP; John F. Watson, *Annals of Philadelphia: Being a Collection of Memoirs Anecdotes, and Incidents* (Philadelphia: E. L. Carey and A. Hart, 1830), 358, 613. For additional examples, see Shirley J. Horner, Sally S. Minshall, and Jeanne H. Watson, eds., *Ladies at the Crossroads: Eighteenth-Century Women of New Jersey* (Morristown, NJ: AAUW, 1978), 27, 30, 130.

30. John W. Jordan, "Extracts from the Journal of Rev. James Sproat, Hospital Chaplain of the Middle Department, 1778," *PMHB* 27, no. 4 (1903): 441–44; Kathleen Brown, *Foul Bodies: Cleanliness in Early America* (New Haven, CT: Yale University Press, 2009), 159–74; Alice Loxley, "Sustaining the Hospital: Food, Water, and Care During the American Revolution," in *Proceedings of the 2010 Association for Living History, Farm and Agricultural Museums*, ed. Carol Kennis Lopez (North Bloomfield, OH: ALHFAM, 2011), 88–91; Holly Mayer, *Belonging to the Army: Camp Followers and Community During the American Revolution* (Columbia: University of South Carolina Press, 1999), 137–43, 219–23.

31. Benjamin Rush, Letterbook, vol. 82, Yi 7262 F. vl, Rush Family Papers, HSP; James Hennessey, *A History of the Roman Catholic Community in the United States* (New York: Oxford University Press, 1983), 60.

32. Samuel Fothergill to Dr. Samuel Rutty, January 8, 1761, in John Kendall, *Letters on Religious Subjects, Written by Divers Friends, Deceased* (Burlington, NJ: J. Rakestraw, 1805), 21; Smith, *Letters of Doctor Richard Hill*, xv–xvi; David Hancock, "The Triumphs of Mercury: Connection and Control in the Emerging Atlantic Economy," in *Soundings in Atlantic History: Latent Structures and Intellectual Currents*, ed. Bernard Bailyn and Patricia L. Denault (Cambridge, MA: Harvard University Press, 2009), 112–40; John W. Jordan, ed., *Colonial and Revolutionary Families of Pennsylvania*, 3 vols. (Baltimore: Genealogical Publishing Co.; repr., 1978), 1:40–44.

33. MHM to Hannah Hill Moore, February 5, 1778, and MHM to Dr. Samuel Preston Moore, February 1, 1779, G. M. Howland MS Coll. 1000, box 1, folders 4 and 5, HQSC; MHM, Recipe Book, n.p., 975, Diaries and Certificates, HQSC.

34. Margaret Hill Morris to Samuel Preston Moore and Hannah Hill Moore, March 23, 1779, box 7, folder 1, G. M. Howland MS Coll. 1000, HQSC; Smith, *Recollections of John Jay Smith*, 242; John Lednum, *The Rise of Methodism in America: Sketches of Methodist Itinerant Preachers from 1736 to 1785* (Bedford, MA: Applewood Books, 1859), 214–15. For *heeltaps* and *down at heel*, see *Oxford English Dictionary. Heeltaps* could also refer to the final dregs of an alcoholic drink.

35. MHM to Hannah Hill Moore, ca. late 1770s, Edward Wanton Smith Coll. 95, box 6, folder 1, HQSC; MHM to Hannah Hill Moore ca. late 1770s, G. M. Howland MS Coll. 1000, box 7, folders 2 and 5, HQSC.

36. Thomas and Phineas Bond Co., Partnership Ledger, 1751–70, vol. 4, Z10/1, CPP; MHM to Milcah Martha, 1784, 955 Edward Wanton Smith Coll., box 6, HQSC; Ulrich, *Midwife's Tale*, 69–71, 197–99. Dr. John Morgan, founder of the medical school in Philadelphia, charged a guinea for a house call. See John Morgan, *Discourse upon the Institution of Medical Schools in America* (Philadelphia: William Bradford, 1765).

37. MHM to Hannah Hill Moore, n.d., ca. early 1780s, G. M. Howland MS Coll. 1000, box 7, folder 5, HQSC; Mutschler, *Province of Affliction*, 69–79. Men also watched over sickbeds. For inoculation, see Smith, *Recollections of John Jay Smith*, 242. Ellen Hartigan-O'Connor notes that female tavern keepers occasionally charged for nursing and medical care, often outsourced to local practitioners. See Hartigan-O'Connor, *Ties That Buy*, 44, 145, 192.

38. MHM to Hannah Hill Moore, June 2, 1787, box 7, G. M. Howland MS Coll. 1000, HQSC. Dropsy was a potentially fatal condition that was identified by severe swelling in the abdomen and extremities. Jones received his medical degree from Reims University in 1751. He served in the American Revolution and authored *Plain, Concise, Practical Remarks on the Treatment of Wounds and Fractures* (Philadelphia: Robert Bell, 1776).

39. Mary Burd Campbell, Memorandum Book, C1394, Princeton University Rare Books and Special Collections, Princeton, NJ.

40. Campbell, Memorandum Book. Medicines used to treat intestinal worms were also used for menstrual regulation or as abortifacients. See Klepp, *Revolutionary Conceptions*, 191–201. For quote, MHM to Hannah Hill Moore, February 5, 1778, G. M. Howland MS Coll. 1000, box 7, folder 4, HQSC. Martha Ballard charged one pound for her burn salve. See Ulrich, *Midwife's Tale*, 85, 362. For Hannah Freeman and Black healers, see Chapters 3 and 7.

41. MHM to Hannah Hill Moore, ca. 1780, and MHM to Hannah Hill Moore, May 16, 1782, G. M. Howland MS Coll. 1000, box 7, folder 4, HQSC; Margaret Morris, *Margaret Morris, Bur-*

lington, New Jersey, 1804 Gardening Memorandum, ed. Nancy V. Webster and Clarissa F. Dillon (Chillicothe, IL: American Botanist Booksellers, 1996); Buchan, *Domestic Medicine*, 711. Moore was one of a select group of Philadelphia area physicians who had trained at the prestigious Edinburgh University.

42. MHM to Samuel P. Moore, February 1, 1779, G. M. Howland MS Coll. 1000, box 1, folder 4, HQSC.

43. MHM to Hannah Hill Moore, ca. early1780s, G. M. Howland MS Coll. 1000, box 1, folder 5, HQSC; MHM to Hannah Hill Moore, June 2, 1787, G. M. Howland MS Coll. 1000, box 7, HQSC; MHM to Hannah Hill Moore, February 5, 1778; MHM to Hannah Hill Moore, May 7, 1781: "I enclose 7/6. Please to send me a pound & half of Glauber's Salt, from Speakmans, he sells for 5/—the others ask 6/"; MHM to Hannah Hill Moore, ca. 1780s, all in G. M. Howland MS Coll. 1000, box 1, folders 4 and 5, HQSC.

44. Thomas Corbyn, Business Ledger, MS 5443, WL; Roy Porter and Dorothy Porter, "The Rise of the English Drugs Industry: The Role of Thomas Corbyn," *Medical History* 33, no. 3 (1989): 277–95; Richard Palmer, "Thomas Corbyn, Quaker Merchant," *Medical History* 33, no. 3 (1989): 371–76; Jacob Price, "The Great Quaker Business Families of Eighteenth-Century London," in *The World of William Penn*, ed. Richard S. Dunn and Mary M. Dunn (Philadelphia: University of Pennsylvania Press, 1986), 363–90.

45. Renate Wilson, *Pious Traders in Medicine: A German Pharmaceutical Network in Eighteenth-Century North America* (University Park: Pennsylvania State University Press, 2000), 129–63; Lisa Minardi, *Pastors and Patriots: The Muhlenberg Family of Pennsylvania* (Kutztown, PA: Pennsylvania German Society, 2011), 23.

46. *Pennsylvania Gazette*, July 12, 1770, September 3, 1767, and December 23, 1772; *Pennsylvania Chronicle*, Philadelphia, July 4–11, 1768, June 25–July 2, 1770, and July 15–22, 1771; *New-York Journal; or, General Advertiser*, December 23, 1773. See also Susan Hanket Brandt, "Marketing Medicine: Apothecary Elizabeth Weed's Economic Independence During the American Revolution," in *Women in the American Revolution: Gender, Politics, and the Domestic World*, ed. Barbara B. Oberg (Charlottesville: University of Virginia Press, 2019), 60–82.

47. *Pennsylvania Packet* (Philadelphia), March 29, 1773; David Van Zwanberg, "The Suttons and the Business of Inoculation," *Medical History* 22 (1978): 71–82; Thomas Dimsdale, *The Present Method of Inoculating for the Small-pox*, 5th ed. (London: W. Owen, 1769). The "greensickness" was a condition that may have been related to iron deficiency in young menstruating women or to the medicalization of female puberty. See Helen King, "Green Sickness: Hippocrates, Galen and the Origins of the 'Disease of Virgins,'" *International Journal of the Classical Tradition* 2, no. 3 (1996): 372–87.

48. *Pennsylvania Evening Post* (Philadelphia), October 11, 1777; George Weed, Will, 1784, no. 66-1777, Philadelphia City Archives. Elizabeth Delaplaine Dickinson Weed Nevell's birthdate is unknown; she died in 1790.

49. Willard O. Mishoff, "Business in Philadelphia During the British Occupation, 1777–1778," *PMHB* 61, no. 2 (1937): 166.

50. *Pennsylvania Evening Post*, March 11, 1777; Rosenberg, Helfand, and Green, "*Every Man His Own Doctor*," 26; Roy Porter, *Health for Sale: Quackery in England, 1660–1850* (Manchester, UK: Manchester University Press, 1989), 43–63; Porter, *Bodies Politic*, 185, 244–51.

51. Dr. John Jones to a patient [Mr. Carey], April 19, 1781, G. M. Howland MS Coll. 1000, box 6, HQSC; MHM to Milcah Martha Hill Moore, February 7, 1797, and February 3,1797, Thomas Stewardson Coll., Letters, 1759–1844, (Phi) 631, HSP; Elizabeth Sandwith Drinker, *The*

Diary of Elizabeth Drinker, vol. 3, ed. Elaine Forman Crane (Boston: Northeastern University Press, 1991), 1630–39; Martha Winter Routh, *Memoir of the Life, Travels, and Religious Experience, of Martha Routh* (York, PA: W. Alexander, 1822).

52. MHM to Gulielma Morris Smith, December 11, 1795, G. M. Howland MS Coll. 1000, box 1, folder 7, HQSC. For Samuel Powel Griffitts (1759–1826), see Jordan, *Colonial and Revolutionary Families*, 112–13.

Chapter 6

1. *Weekly Magazine* 1 (February 3–April 28, 1798), bound edition, back cover; John Feather, *A History of British Publishing* (London: Routledge, 1988), 108. I appreciate the help of the librarians Connie King and Jim Green in discovering this information at the Library Company of Philadelphia.

2. Benjamin Rush, "Hints for the Life of Nurse Mary Waters [*sic*]," Benjamin Rush Letterbook, vol. 82, Yi2 7262 F.vl, ca. 1791, 146, HSP; Benjamin Rush, *The Autobiography of Benjamin Rush: His Travels Through Life Together with His Commonplace Book for 1789–1813*, ed. George W. Corner (Princeton, NJ: Princeton University Press, 1948), introduction, 200–202; Jane Austen, *Northanger Abbey and Persuasion*, vol. 1 (London: John Murray, 1818), 255.

3. Anne Hudson Jones, ed., *Images of Nurses: Perspectives from History, Art, and Literature* (Philadelphia: University of Pennsylvania Press, 1988), xix–xxii; *Pennsylvania Gazette*, October 19, 1769, August 19, 1762, and June 7, 1770; Rush, "Life of Nurse Mary Watters"; Sharon V. Salinger, "'Send No More Women': Female Servants in Eighteenth-Century Philadelphia," *PMHB* 107, no. 1 (1983): 45–46; Billy G. Smith, *The "Lower Sort": Philadelphia's Laboring People, 1750–1800* (Ithaca, NY: Cornell University Press, 1990), 42–62, 164–74; B. G. Smith, ed., *Life in Early Philadelphia: Documents from the Revolutionary and Early National Periods* (University Park: Pennsylvania State University, 2003), 3–28.

4. There is no documentation of a Mary or James Watters (or Waters) in early Philadelphia Catholic Church marriage or baptismal records. "Mary Waters" does appear in the 1780s as a godparent in St. Joseph's Church records. See American Catholic Historical Society of Philadelphia, *Records of the American Catholic Historical Society of Philadelphia*, vol. 4, 3rd. ser., Baptisms (Philadelphia: published by the Society, 1893), 57, 71. See also Kathleen M. Brown, *Foul Bodies: Cleanliness in Early America* (New Haven, CT: Yale University Press, 2009), 30–32; Jones, *Images of Nurses*, xix–xxii; Mary Peckham Magray, *The Transforming Power of the Nuns: Women, Religion, and Cultural Change in Ireland, 1750–1900* (New York: Oxford University Press, 1998), 1–21, 32–41, 74–7; Carol Helmstadter, "Old Nurses and New: Nursing in the London Teaching Hospitals Before and After the Mid-Nineteenth Century Reforms," *Nursing History Review* 1 (1993): 47–48; Leigh Whaley, *Women and the Practice of Medical Care in Early Modern Europe, 1400–1800* (New York: Palgrave Macmillan, 2011), 112–30.

5. Alice Loxley, "Sustaining the Hospital: Food, Water, and Care During the American Revolution," in *Proceedings of the 2010 Association for Living History, Farm and Agricultural Museums*, ed. Carol Kennis Lopez (North Bloomfield, OH: ALHFAM, 2011), 88–89. I have not located Mary Watters's service records. She is not listed in available Continental Hospital Returns or in pension rolls. Most records in War Department custody were destroyed by fire in 1800, and others were lost during the War of 1812.

6. Dr. John Morgan to Dr. Jonathan Potts, July 28, 1776, "Plan for Conducting the Hospital Department," Jonathan Potts Papers, HSP; *Pennsylvania Packet*, April 22, 1777; Brown, *Foul Bodies*, 179.

7. Frederic R. Kirkland, "Journal of a Physician on the Expedition Against Canada, 1776," *PMHB* 59, no. 4 (1935): 333, 337, 347; Richard L. Blanco, "American Army Hospitals in Pennsylvania During the Revolutionary War," *Pennsylvania History* 48, no. 4 (1981): 347–68; J. Smith Futhey and Gilbert Cope, *History of Chester County, Pennsylvania, with Genealogical and Biographical Sketches*, 2 vols. (Philadelphia: Louis H. Everts, 1881), 1:101–8.

8. Holly A. Mayer, *Belonging to the Army: Camp Followers and Community During the American Revolution* (Columbia: University of South Carolina Press, 1999), 67–68; 127–42; 220–22; Elizabeth Fenn, *Pox Americana: The Great Smallpox Epidemic of 1775–82* (New York: Hill and Wang, 2002), 80–103; Nancy K. Loane, *Following the Drum: Women at the Valley Forge Encampment* (Ann Arbor: University of Michigan Press, 2009), 121–25.

9. *Federal Galaxy*, October 30, 1797; "Plan of the Philadelphia Dispensary," *New-York Daily Gazette*, November 12, 1790; "City-Hospital [Philadelphia]," *New-York Gazette*, September 4, 1798, and September 7, 1798.

10. Thomas Rowlandson, *Humours of a Hired Nurse*, 1807, caricature, NLM; M. Patricia Donahue, *Nursing, the Finest Art: An Illustrated History* (New York: Mosby, 1985), 165; Lavinia L. Dock and Isabel Maitland Stewart, *A Short History of Nursing from the Earliest Times to the Present Day*, 4th ed. (New York: G. P. Putnam's Sons, 1938), 98; Margaret Pelling, "Nurses and Nursekeepers: Problems of Identification in the Early Modern Period," in *The Common Lot: Sickness, Medical Occupations and the Urban Poor in Early Modern England* (New York: Routledge, 1998), 179–80; Charles Dickens, *The Life and Adventures of Martin Chuzzlewit*, vols. 1–2 (London: Chapman and Hall, 1844), 307–19, 558–65; J. W. Hawkins, "Getting Rid of Sairy Gamp: Nursing and Feminism," *Imprint* 40 (1993): 7–9; Frances Ward, *On Duty: Power, Politics, and the History of Nursing in New Jersey* (New Brunswick, NJ: Rutgers University Press, 2009), 12–16. The term *nurse*, meaning a person who cared for the sick as opposed to a wet nurse or infant caregiver, emerged in the eighteenth century.

11. Rush, "Nurse Mary Waters." Fr. Ferdinand Farmer (1720–86) was a German-born Jesuit priest and a trustee of the College of Philadelphia. See Martin I. J. Griffin, *History of "Old St. Joseph's," Philadelphia* (Philadelphia: ICBU Journal Print, 1882), 3–5; James Hennessey, *A History of the Roman Catholic Community in the United States* (New York: Oxford, 1983), 60. See also Ann M. Little, "Cloistered Bodies: Convents in the Anglo-American Imagination in the British Conquest of Canada," *Eighteenth-Century Studies* 39, no. 2 (2006): 187–200; Owen Stanwood, "Catholics, Protestants, and the Clash of Civilization in Early America," in *The First Prejudice: Religious Tolerance and Intolerance in Early America*, ed. Chris Beneke and Christopher S. Grenada (Philadelphia: University of Pennsylvania Press, 2011), 218–40.

12. Deborah Norris Logan (1761–1839) to Sally Fisher Corbit, 1780, in John Sweeny, *The Norris-Fisher Correspondence: A Circle of Friends, 1779–1782* (Wilmington: Historical Society of Delaware, 1955), 46.

13. Constantia [Judith Sargent Murray], *The Gleaner: A Miscellaneous Production in Three Volumes*, vol. 1 (Boston: J. Thomas and E. T. Andrews, 1798), 220–21; Mary Wollstonecraft, *A Vindication of the Rights of Woman: With Strictures on Political and Moral Subjects*, 3rd. ed. (London: J. Johnson, 1796), 337, 2–17; Sheila L. Skemp, *First Lady of Letters: Judith Sargent Murray and the Struggle for Female Independence* (Philadelphia: University of Pennsylvania Press, 2009), 153–61; Syndy M. Conger, *Mary Wollstonecraft and the Language of Sensibility* (Rutherford, NJ: Fairleigh Dickinson University Press, 1994).

14. Rush, "Nurse Mary Waters."

15. Rush, "Nurse Mary Waters"; Benjamin Rush, *An Oration Delivered before the American Philosophical Society . . . Containing an Enquiry into the Influence of the Moral Faculty* (Philadelphia: APS, 1787); Sarah Knott, *Sensibility and the American Revolution* (Chapel Hill: University of North Carolina Press, 2009), 201–11; Brown, *Foul Bodies*, 159–83; Simon Finger, *The Contagious City: The Politics of Public Health in Early Philadelphia* (Ithaca, NY: Cornell University Press, 2012), 86–102; Marjorie Levine-Clark, *Beyond the Reproductive Body: The Politics of Women's Health and Work in Early Victorian England* (Columbus: Ohio State University Press, 2004), 170; 1 Pet. 3:7, King James Version.

16. John Morgan, *A Vindication of his Public Character in the Station of Director-General of the Military Hospitals, and Physician in Chief to the American Army* (Boston: printed by Powars and Willis, 1777), iv–v; John Morgan to John Jay, June 15, 1779, Continental Congress Papers, no. 63, f. 129, copy in Whitfield Bell–John Morgan Collection, CPP; Whitfield J. Bell Jr., *John Morgan: Continental Doctor* (Philadelphia: University of Pennsylvania Press, 1965), 70–75, 206–39; William Shippen to Nathaniel Greene, February 3, 1780, Edward Shippen Papers, original in Library of Congress, copy in Whitfield Bell–John Morgan Collection, CPP; *Pennsylvania Packet*, December 23, 1780; "Doctor Shippen's Vindication," *Pennsylvania Packet*, November 25, 1780.

17. *Federal Gazette*, September 9, 1793, and September 12, 1793; Benjamin Rush to Ashton Alexander, December 21, 1795, in *Letters of Benjamin Rush*, vol. 2, ed. L. H. Butterfield (Princeton, NJ: Princeton University Press), 766–67; Martin S. Pernick, "Politics, Parties, and Pestilence: Epidemic Yellow Fever in Philadelphia and the Rise of the First Party System," in *A Melancholy Scene of Devastation: The Public Response to the 1793 Yellow Fever Epidemic*, ed. J. Worth Estes and Billy G. Smith (Canton, MA: Science History Publications, 1997), 79–96.

18. Blanco, "American Army Hospitals," 347; Finger, *Contagious City*, 86–119; Stephen Wikes, *History of Medicine in New Jersey, and of Its Medical Men from the Settlement of the Province to A.D. 1800* (Newark, NJ: Martin R. Dennis & Co., 1879), 43–50; Benjamin Rush, *Transactions of the College of Physicians of Philadelphia* (Philadelphia: T. Dobson, 1793), vii; William Manning, *The Key of Libberty, Shewing the Causes Why a Free Government Has Always Failed*, ed. Samuel Eliot Morrison (Billerica, MA: Manning Association, 1922), 26; William Manning, *The Key of Liberty: The Life and Democratic Writings of William Manning, "a Laborer," 1747–1814*, ed. Michael Merrill and Sean Wilentz (Cambridge, MA: Harvard University Press, 1993), introduction, 26; Andrew John Lewis, *A Democracy of Facts: Natural History in the Early Republic* (Philadelphia: University of Pennsylvania Press, 2011), 1–12.

19. Rush, *Autobiography*, 201; Elizabeth S. Drinker, *The Diary of Elizabeth Drinker*, 3 vols., ed. Elaine Forman Crane (Boston: Northeastern University Press, 1991), 1: 544, 621, 521–36, 2: 720, 737. "Mary Waters" is listed as a doctress in Thomas Stephens, *Stephen's Philadelphia Directory, for 1796* (Philadelphia: Thomas Stephens, 1796), 193; as a doctress in Willing's Alley in Cornelius William Stafford, *Philadelphia Directory for 1798* (Philadelphia: William W. Woodward, 1798), 149, and again in 1799; and as an apothecary in Stafford's directories for 1797 (p. 190) and 1798 (p. 191). Other women were cited as nurses. For "Mary Brett, Widow, Nurses the Sick," see Edmund Hogan, *The Prospect of Philadelphia* (Philadelphia: printed by Francis and Robert Bailey, 1795), 62. For Kuhn and Redman, see Joseph M. Toner, *Annals of Medical Progress and Medical Education in the United States Before and During the War of Independence* (Washington, DC: Government Printing Office, 1874), 81–83.

20. Rush, *Autobiography*, 201.

21. Margaret Hill Morris to Hannah Hill Moore, n.d., ca. mid-1780s, G. M. Howland MS Coll. 1000, box 7, folder, 5, HQSC; Margaret Hill Morris to Hannah Hill Moore, January 7, 1794, in *Letters of Doctor Richard Hill and His Children*, ed. John Jay Smith (Philadelphia: privately printed, 1854), 424–25.

22. Lowry Wister, "On the Death of Her Infant Son William," October 23, 1781, and Lowry Wister (1743–1804), Medical Recipes, Eastwick Coll. MS 974.811. Ea7, Series I, APS; Lucia McMahon, "So Truly Afflicting and Distressing to Me His Sorrowing Mother": Expressions of Maternal Grief in Eighteenth-Century Philadelphia," *Journal of the Early Republic* 32, no. 1 (2012): 27–60.

23. Susan Hanket Brandt, "Marketing Medicine: Apothecary Elizabeth Weed's Economic Independence During the American Revolution," in *Women in the American Revolution: Gender, Politics, and the Domestic World*, ed. Barbara B. Oberg (Charlottesville: University of Virginia Press, 2019), 60–82; Hannah Benner Roach, "Thomas Nevel (1721–1797): Carpenter, Educator, Patriot," *Journal of the Society of Architectural Historians* 24, no. 2 (1965): 153–64; George Weed, Will, 1784, no. 66-1777, Philadelphia City Archives. Nevell (also Nevel or Nevill) sold his house for seven hundred dollars in 1775 to raise needed cash. Tax records cite Thomas Nevell as a carpenter with only one cow, no property, no servants, and a tax assessment of less than five pounds.

24. Francis White, *Philadelphia Directory* (Philadelphia: Young, Steward, & McCulloch, 1785), 52; *Pennsylvania Packet or The General Advertiser*, September 11, 1779; *Pennsylvania Gazette*, September 17, 1783, July 11, 1787, and August 1, 1787.

25. *Pennsylvania Gazette*, July 11, 1787, Charles J. S. Thompson, *The Quacks of Old London* (London: Brentanos Ltd., 1928), 253–58; Joseph M. Gabriel, *Medical Monopoly: Intellectual Property Rights and the Origins of the Modern Pharmaceutical Industry* (Chicago: University of Chicago Press, 2014), 1–41.

26. For debates on women's innate inferiority, see Chapter 4. See also *Philadelphia Gazette*, July 19, 1798; Ian Burn, *The Company of Barbers and Surgeons* (London: Farrand Press, 2000), 30–38, 196–98; *Pennsylvania Gazette*, August 1, 1787; Roach, "Thomas Nevel," 155–56; Marylynn Salmon, "The Court Records of Philadelphia, Buck, and Berks Counties in the Seventeenth and Eighteenth Centuries," *PMHB* 107, no. 2 (1983): 249–92; Philadelphia County Court of Common Pleas, Appearance Docket, December 1772–March 1789, 20.2, Philadelphia City Archives. An extant appearance docket lists Craft's countersuit initiated in September 1787 (*James Craft v. Thos. Neville & Eliza. His Wife*). Neither the appearance docket for the Nevell's initial suit nor the execution dockets are extant.

27. The Philadelphia Census, Middle District, 1790, http://us census.org/pub/usgenweb /census/pa/philadelphia/1790/pg0226.txt; Stafford, *Philadelphia Directory 1801*, 115; *Philadelphia Minerva*, December 3, 1796; W. A. Dorland, "The Second Troop Philadelphia City Cavalry," *PMHB* 46 (1922): 36, 74, 265, 350; John Scharf and Thomas Westcott, *History of Philadelphia, 1609–1884*, 3 vols. (Philadelphia: L. H. Everts & Co., 1884), 3:992; *American Daily Advertiser*, July 8, 1794; *The Casket: Flowers of Literature, Wit, and Sentiment* (Philadelphia: Samuel C. Atkinson, 1829), 75.

28. "Thomas Nevell's Day Book," 1762–1785, MS Codex 1049, UPRBM; Joseph W. England, ed., *The First Century of the Philadelphia College of Pharmacy, 1821–1921* (Philadelphia: Philadelphia College of Pharmacy and Science, 1922), 35–37; John W. Jordan, *Colonial and Revolutionary Families of Pennsylvania*, 3 vols. (New York, 1911; repr., Baltimore: Genealogical Publishing Co., 1978), 1:1022–23; Drinker, *Diary of Elizabeth Drinker*, 2:856; Philadelphia College of Pharmacy, *The Druggist's Manual* (Philadelphia: Solomon W. Conrad, 1826), 32.

29. American Catholic Historical Society, *Records*, 4:57, 71, and 16:204 (both Mary and James Waters [*sic*] were sponsors), and 17:477; Robert D. Arner, *Dobson's Encyclopaedia: The Publisher, Text, and Publication of America's First Britannica, 1789–1803* (Philadelphia: University of Pennsylvania Press, 1991), 112–14; James Watters, *Proposal of James Watters' for Publishing by subscription, a New Work, Entitled The Weekly Magazine* (Philadelphia: James Watters, 1798). For Charles Brocken Brown (1771–1810) and his literary circles, see Michael Cody, *Charles Brockden Brown and the Literary Magazine: Cultural Journalism in the Early American Republic* (Jefferson, NC: McFarland, 2004), 11–36.

30. Rush, *Transactions of the College of Physicians*, 191; *Weekly Magazine* 1 (February 3–April 28, 1798), bound edition, back cover.

31. *Weekly Magazine* 1 (February 3–April 28, 1798); Susan E. Klepp, *Revolutionary Conceptions: Women, Fertility, and Family Limitation in America, 1760–1820* (Chapel Hill: University of North Carolina Press, 2009), 185–87.

32. William Buchan, *Domestic Medicine, or, A Treatise on the Prevention and Cure of Diseases by Regimen and Simple Medicines*, Revised and Adapted to the Diseases and Climate of the United States of America, by Samuel Powel Griffitts, M.D. (Philadelphia: printed by Thomas Dobson, 1795), xii, 152–59.

33. Brian Waterman, *Republic of Intellect: The Friendly Club of New York City and the Making of American Literature* (Baltimore: Johns Hopkins University Press, 2007), 1–15, 189–230; A Lady, "Sensibility," *Weekly Magazine* 1, no. 4 (February 24, 1798): 126. Mary Watters signed her will with an *X*. She may not have been writing literate but may have been reading literate. She had the visual and tactile skills to run a medical and apothecary business and to administer the *Weekly Magazine* after James's death. Mary Watters, Will, #414-1799, Philadelphia City Hall. Thomas Dobson witnessed the will.

34. "The Rights of Women," *Weekly Magazine* 1, no. 7 (March 17, 1798): 198–200; *Weekly Magazine* 1, no. 8 (March 24, 1798): 231–35; *Weekly Magazine* 1, no. 9 (March 31, 1798): 271–74. See also Charles Brockden Brown, *Alcuin: A Dialog*, ed. Cynthia Kierner (New York: Rowman and Littlefield, 1995), introduction; Rosemaire Zagarri, *Revolutionary Backlash: Women and Politics in the Early American Republic* (Philadelphia: University of Pennsylvania Press, 2007), 11–13; Cathy N. Davidson, "The Matter and Manner of Charles Brockden Brown's Alcuin," in *Critical Essays on Charles Brockden Brown*, ed. Bernard Rosenthal (Boston: G. K. Hall, 1981), 74–86; Susan Branson, *These Fiery Frenchified Dames: Women and Political Culture in Early National Philadelphia* (Philadelphia: University of Pennsylvania Press, 2001), 141.

35. Elihu Hubbard Smith to Fanny Smith, 1796, quoted in *The Literary Utopias of Cultural Communities, 1790–1910*, ed. Marguérite Corporaal and Evert Jan van Leeuwen (New York: Rodopi, 2010), 27. Brown's close friend Elihu Hubbard Smith had studied medicine under Rush. See William L. Hedges, "Benjamin Rush, Charles Brockden Brown, and the American Plague Year," *Early American Literature* 7, no. 3 (1973): 295–311.

36. Ezekiel Forman, "James Watters," *Weekly Magazine* 3, no. 36 (February 1799): 3; Drinker, *Diary of Elizabeth Drinker*, 2:1079, 1109; Rush, *Autobiography*, 201.

37. Charles Brockden Brown, *Arthur Mervyn: Memoirs of the Year 1793* (Philadelphia: H. Maxwell, 1799), vi.

Chapter 7

1. Susan H. Brandt, "'We Shall Stand Justified': The Role of Free African Society Nurses in the 1793 Philadelphia Yellow Fever Epidemic," *Villanova University Undergraduate Student*

History Journal (Spring 2004): 1–18; Susan E. Klepp, "How Many Precious Souls Have Fled?," in *A Melancholy Scene of Devastation: The Public Response to the 1793 Philadelphia Yellow Fever Epidemic,* ed. J. Worth Estes and Billy G. Smith (Canton, MA: Science History Publications, 1997), 164–69; Simon Finger, *The Contagious City: The Politics of Public Health in Early Philadelphia* (Ithaca, NY: Cornell University Press, 2012), 120–34.

2. *Philadelphia Independent Gazetteer,* September 7, 1793; Absalom Jones and Richard Allen, *A Narrative of the Proceedings of the Black People, During the Late Awful Calamity in Philadelphia in the Year 1793 and a Refutation of Some Censures thrown Upon them in Some Late Publications* (Philadelphia: William W. Woodward, 1794), 14, 16. For similar contemporary accounts, see Mathew Carey, *A Short Account of the Malignant Fever,* 1st ed. (Philadelphia: printed by the author, 1793), 77; *Minutes of the Proceedings of the Committee appointed on the 14th September, 1793 . . . to alleviate the sufferings of the afflicted with the malignant fever* (Philadelphia: R. Aitken, 1794), 15–16; J. H. Powell, *Bring Out Your Dead* (1949; repr., Philadelphia: University of Pennsylvania Press, 1993), xx, 27.

3. Carey, *Short Account,* 3, 14; Jones and Allen, *Narrative,* 2.

4. Erica Armstrong Dunbar, *A Fragile Freedom: African American Women and the Emancipation in the Antebellum North* (New Haven, CT: Yale University Press, 2008); Gary Nash, *Forging Freedom: The Formation of Philadelphia's Black Community, 1720–1840* (Cambridge, MA: Harvard University Press, 1988); Julie Winch, *Philadelphia's Black Elite: Activism, Accommodation, and the Struggle for Autonomy, 1787–1848* (Philadelphia: Temple University Press, 1988); Julie Winch, *A Gentleman of Color: The Life of James Forten* (New York: Oxford University Press, 2002); Richard S. Newman, *Freedom's Prophet: Bishop Richard Allen, the AME Church, and the Black Founding Fathers* (New York: New York University Press, 2008), 78–104; Richard Newman, Patrick Rael, and Phillip Lapsansky, eds., *Pamphlets of Protest: An Anthology of Early African-American Protest Literature, 1790–1860* (New York: Routledge, 2001); Phillip Lapsansky, "'Abigail, A Negress': The Role and the Legacy of African Americans in the Yellow Fever Epidemic," in Estes and Smith, *Melancholy Scene,* 61–78; Mary Elizabeth Carnegie, *The Path We Tread: Blacks in Nursing, 1854–1984,* 2nd ed. (Washington, DC: National League for Nursing Press, 1991), ix–5.

5. Jones and Allen, *Narrative,* 12; Florence Nightingale, "Nursing Is an Art," *Macmillan's Magazine* (April 1867); Carol Helmstadter and Judith Godden, *Nursing Before Nightingale, 1815–1899* (Burlington, VT: Ashgate, 2011), 25–30.

6. William Douglass, *Annals of the First African Church* (Philadelphia: King and Baird Printers, 1862), 109; Edmund Hogan, *The Prospect of Philadelphia* (Philadelphia: Francis and Robert Bailey, 1795), 145; Janet R. Brittingham and Mildred C. Williams, *1790 Census for the City of Philadelphia* (Jamison, PA: Will-Britt Books, 1989), 249; Hallie Q. Brown, *Homespun Heroines and Other Women of Distinction* (Xenia, OH: Aldine Publishing Company, 1926), 11–12; J. Gordon Melton, *A Will to Choose: The Origins of African American Methodism* (Lanham, MD: Rowman & Littlefield, 2007), 91–94.

7. Sarah Bass Allen, death certificate, 1849, Philadelphia City Archives; Sarah Allen, Rent Book, Mother Bethel AME Church Archives, Philadelphia; Newman, *Freedom's Prophet,* 74–76; Darlene Clark Hine, *Black Women in America* (New York: Oxford University Press, 2005), 42–43; Daniel A. Payne, *History of the African Methodist Episcopal Church* (Nashville, TN: AME Sunday School Union, 1891), 86–88; conversations with Allen descendants and AME parishioners at the Founders of Philadelphia's African American Churches Conference, Old St. George's United Methodist Church, October 27, 2001.

8. Paul Heinegg, *Free African Americans of North Carolina, Virginia, and South Carolina*, 5th ed., vol. 1 (Baltimore: Clearfield Company by Genealogical Publishing Co., 2005), 111–30. "The Norfolk County Register of Free Negroes and Mulattoes, 1809–1852" lists free men and women with the surname Bass, many described as "mulatto," "Indian complexion," and "Indian descent." See also John H. Russell, *The Free Negro in Virginia, 1619–1865* (Baltimore: Johns Hopkins Press, 1913), 11, 61–62, 138, 159; John B. Boddie, *Seventeenth Century Isle of Wight County, Virginia: A History of the County of Isle of Wight, Virginia, During the Seventeenth Century* (Chicago: Chicago Law Print. Co, 1938; repr., Baltimore: Genealogical Publishing Co., 1973), 32, 88–90. Isle of Wight County had a population of between 250 and 450 free Blacks in 1790. See United States Census Office, *Ninth Census of the United States: Statistics of Population, Tables I to VIII Inclusive* (Washington, DC: Government Printing Office, 1872), 70, 72.

9. Sara Collini, "The Labors of Enslaved Midwives in Revolutionary Virginia," in *Women in the American Revolution: Gender, Politics, and the Domestic World*, ed. Barbara B. Oberg (Charlottesville: University of Virginia, 2019), 19, 20–38; Sharla M. Fett, *Working Cures: Healing, Health, and Power on Southern Slave Plantations* (Chapel Hill: University of North Carolina Press, 2002), 111–41; Deborah Gray White, *Ar'n't I a Woman? Female Slaves in the Planation South* (New York: W. W. Norton, 1990), 62–89; Jennifer L. Morgan, *Laboring Women: Reproduction and Gender in New World Slavery* (Philadelphia: University of Pennsylvania Press, 2004); Marie Jenkins Schwartz, *Birthing a Slave: Motherhood and Medicine in the Antebellum South* (Cambridge, MA: Harvard University Press, 2006).

10. Patricia M. Samford, *Subfloor Pits and the Archaeology of Slavery in Colonial Virginia* (Birmingham: University of Alabama Press, 2007), 209–31; Patricia M. Samford, "The Archaeology of African-American Slavery and Material Culture," *WMQ* 53, no. 1 (1996): 87–114; Fett, *Working Cures*, 41–56, 76–79, 101–6; Oyeronke Olajubu, *Women in the Yoruba Religious Sphere* (Albany: State University of New York Press, 2003), 110–18; Susan Scott Parrish, *American Curiosity: Cultures of Natural History in the Colonial British Atlantic World* (Chapel Hill: University of North Carolina Press, 2006), 259–89; Allan Kulikoff, "The Origins of Afro-American Society in Tidewater Maryland and Virginia," *WMQ* 35, no. 2 (1978): 226–59; Londa Schiebinger, *Secret Cures of Slaves: People, Plants, and Medicine in the Eighteenth-Century Atlantic World* (Stanford, CA: Stanford University Press, 2017), 1–17, 45–50.

11. Fett, *Working Cures*, 2–7, 53–82, 99–141; Katherine Paugh, *The Politics of Reproduction: Race, Medicine, and Fertility in the Age of Revolution* (New York: Oxford University Press, 2017), 100–138; Sarah Mitchell, "Bodies of Knowledge: The Influence of Slaves on the Antebellum Medical Community" (MA thesis, Virginia Polytechnic Institute and State University, Blacksburg, 1997). Lack of documentation makes it difficult to assess the persistence of African healing practices in the Delaware Valley. Bass and FAS nurses may have been familiar with vodou (or voodoo) healing practices from Black émigrés from Saint-Domingue. See Karol K. Weaver, *Medical Revolutionaries: The Enslaved Healers of Eighteenth-Century Saint Domingue* (Urbana: University of Illinois Press, 2006), 110–25; and Yvonne Chireau, *Black Magic: Religion and the African American Conjuring Tradition* (Berkeley: University of California Press, 2003), 8–10.

12. "The Negroe Caesar's Cure for Poison and Rattle Snake Bite," *Boston Newsletter* (from the *South Carolina Gazette*), January 23, 1751; *New York Evening Post*, January 24, 1751; *Pennsylvania Gazette*, August 30, 1764; Elizabeth Coates Paschall, Recipe Book, CPP; William Buchan, *Domestic Medicine; or, A Treatise on the Prevention and Cure of Diseases by Regimen and Simple Medicines* (London: printed for W. Strahan, 1784), 488; Herbert C. Covey, *African American Slave Medicine: Herbal and Non-herbal Treatments* (Lanham, MD: Lexington Books,

2007), 43–50, 78, 98–99; Fett, *Working Cures*, 112; Benjamin Breen, "The Flip Side of the Pharmacopoeia: Sub-Saharan African Medicines and Poisons in the Atlantic World," in *Drugs on the Page: Pharmacopoeias and Healing Knowledge in the Early Modern Atlantic World*, ed. Matthew James Crawford and Joseph M. Gabriel (Pittsburgh: University of Pittsburgh Press, 2019), 143–59. Caesar's Cure also circulated transatlantically. See reference from a British newspaper in *Carolina Gazette*, ca. early 1760s, in Samuel C. Reynardson [and family] of Holywell Hall Stamford, England, Manuscript Medical Recipe Book, 1765, HMD Coll., MS B 262, NLM.

13. Cassandra Pybus, "'One Militant Saint': The Much-Traveled Life of Mary Perth," *Journal of Colonialism and Colonial History* 9, no. 3 (2008): 1. Pybus cites "Singular Piety in an African Female," a letter from Rev. Clarke, dated July 29, 1796, published in *Evangelical Magazine* 4 (London, 1796), 464. See also Cassandra Pybus, "Mary Perth, Harry Washington, and Moses Wilkinson: Black Methodists Who Escaped from Slavery and Founded a Nation," in *Revolutionary Founders: Rebels, Radicals, and Reformers in the Making of the Nation*, ed. Alfred Young, Gary B. Nash, and Ray Raphael (New York: Alfred A. Knopf, 2011), 155–68; Dee E. Andrews, *The Methodists and Revolutionary America, 1760–1800: The Shaping of an Evangelical Culture* (Princeton, NJ: Princeton University Press, 2012), 44–45, 74–75.

14. *Virginia Gazette*, June 30, 1774; Emma L. Powers, "The Newsworthy Somerset Case: Repercussions in Virginia," *Colonial Williamsburg Interpreter* 23, no. 3 (2002): 1–6; David Waldstreicher, "The Mansfieldian Moment: Slavery, the Constitution, and American Political Tradition," *Rutgers Law Journal* 43 (2013): 471–85; Simon Schama, *Rough Crossings: Britain, the Slaves and the American Revolution* (New York: Harper Collins, 2006), 18, 44–57; Cassandra Pybus, *Epic Journeys of Freedom: Runaway Slaves of the American Revolution and Their Global Quest for Liberty* (Boston: Beacon Press, 2007), 81–85.

15. Payne, *History*, 86–88; Carol V. R. George, *Segregated Sabbaths: Richard Allen and the Emergence of Independent Black Churches, 1760–1840* (New York: Oxford University Press, 1973), 129–30; Brown, *Homespun Heroines*, 11–12; Wilma King, *The Essence of Liberty: Free Black Women During the Slave Era* (Columbia: University of Missouri Press, 2006), 21. Approximately 12 percent of runaways from Virginia between 1730 and 1740 were female. See Billy G. Smith, "Black Women Who Stole Themselves in Eighteenth-Century America," in *Inequality in Early America*, ed. Carla Gardina Pestana and Sharon V. Salinger (Hanover, NH: University Press of New England, 1999), 134–59.

16. *Virginia Gazette*, November 12, 1772. This group was from Middlesex County, making it less likely that this was Sarah Bass. See also David Waldstreicher, "Reading the Runaways: Self-Fashioning, Print Culture, and Confidence in Slavery in the Eighteenth-Century Mid-Atlantic," *WMQ*, 3rd ser., 56, no. 2 (1999): 243–72, *Pennsylvania Gazette*, November 2, 1770; Dee E. Andrews, "Reconsidering the First Emancipation: Evidence from the Pennsylvania Abolition Society Correspondence, 1785–1810," *Pennsylvania History* 64 (Special Supplemental Issue 1997), 230–49.

17. Richard Allen, *The Life, Experience, and Gospel Labours of the Rt. Rev. Richard Allen* (Philadelphia: Martin and Boden Printers, 1833), 8; Payne, *History*, 86–88; Brown, *Homespun Heroines*, 11–12; Edward Needles, *An Historical Memoir of the Pennsylvania Society for Promoting the Abolition of Slavery* (Philadelphia: Merrihew and Thompson, Printers, 1848; repr., New York: Arno Press, 1969), 29; Gary B. Nash and Jean R. Soderlund, *Freedom by Degrees: Emancipation in Pennsylvania and Its Aftermath* (New York: Oxford University Press, 1991), 137–93. David Waldstreicher, *Slavery's Constitution: From Revolution to Ratification* (New York: Hill and Wang, 2009), 87–89, 90–99; Nash, *Forging Freedom*, 100–161.

18. James Hardie, *Philadelphia Directory and Register: Containing the Names, Occupations and Places of Abode of the Citizens* (Philadelphia: T. Dobson, 1793), 2, 23, 55, 199; Hogan, *Prospect of Philadelphia*, 37, 79, 146; Clement Biddle, *Philadelphia Directory* (Philadelphia: James and Johnson, 1791), 3; Dunbar, *Fragile Freedom*, 43–48; Nash, *Forging Freedom*, 102–3; Billy G. Smith, *The "Lower Sort": Philadelphia's Laboring People, 1750–1800* (Ithaca, NY: Cornell University Press, 1990), 193–96; Joe Trotter and Eric Ledell Smith, eds., *African Americans in Pennsylvania: Shifting Historical Perspectives* (University Park: Pennsylvania State University Press, 1997), 81–84.

19. Anne Parrish, Visitations of the Sick, 1796, Parrish Collection, box 5, bound volumes, #1653, HSP, 4–5; Laurel Thatcher Ulrich, *A Midwife's Tale: The Life of Martha Ballard, Based on Her Diary, 1785–1812* (New York: Knopf, 1990), 49.

20. Allen, *Life, Experience*, 12–14; *African Methodist Episcopal Church, Class Leader's Book of Members of the Bethel African Methodist Church* (Baltimore, 1852), 16; Jualynne E. Dodson, *Engendering Church: Women, Power, and the AME Church* (Lanham, MD: Rowman & Littlefield, 2002), 10–11, 22; George, *Segregated Sabbaths*, 40–51; Melton, *A Will to Choose*, 94; Albert J. Raboteau, *A Fire in the Bones: Reflections on African American Religious History* (Boston: Beacon Press, 1995), 79–88.

21. Allen, "To the People of Colour," in *Narrative*, 27; Dunbar, *Fragile Freedom*, 48–53; Joanne Pope Melish, *Disowning Slavery: Gradual Emancipation and "Race" in New England, 1780–1860* (Ithaca, NY: Cornell University Press, 1998), 122–31; Newman, *Freedom's Prophet*, 57–58; James Oliver Horton, "Freedom's Yoke: Gender Conventions Among Antebellum Free Blacks," *Feminist Studies* 12, no. 1 (1986): 51–76.

22. The only extant FAS minutes were recorded in Douglass, *Annals*, 15. See also Robert Ulle, "A History of St. Thomas's African Episcopal Church, 1794–1865" (PhD diss., University of Pennsylvania, Philadelphia, 1986), 30–32. See also Carey, *Short Account*, 105; *Independent Gazetteer* (Philadelphia), October 5, 1793; *Federal Gazette*, August 20, 1793; Winch, *Gentleman of Color*, 210; Winch, *Philadelphia's Black Elite*, 4.

23. Benjamin Rush, *The Autobiography of Benjamin Rush: His "Travels Through Life" Together with His Commonplace Book for 1789–1813*, ed. George W. Corner (Westport, CT: Greenwood Press, 1948), 228; Benjamin Rush to Julia Rush, August 22, 1793, in *Letters of Benjamin Rush, 1793–1813*, ed. L. H. Butterfield, vol. 2 (Princeton, NJ: Princeton University Press, 1951), 639; Nash, *Forging Freedom*, 1–2, 121; Luke 14:16–24, Matt. 22:1–4, King James Version; John Wesley, ed., *The New Testament with Explanatory Notes* (Halifax, Nova Scotia: William Nicholson and Sons, 1869), 180–82.

24. Jones and Allen, *Narrative*, 11–12; Powell, *Bring Out Your Dead*, x, xvii; Klepp, "How Many Precious Souls?," 164–69; Philip Gould, *Barbaric Traffic: Commerce and Antislavery in the Eighteenth-Century Atlantic World* (Cambridge, MA: Harvard University Press, 2003), 152–89; Jacquelyn C. Miller, "The Wages of Blackness: African-American Workers and the Meanings of Race During Philadelphia's Yellow Fever Epidemic," *PMHB* 129 (2005): 163–94.

25. Jones and Allen, *Narrative*, 8.

26. Jones and Allen, *Narrative*, 4, 11; Sarah Knott, "Benjamin Rush's Ferment: Enlightenment Medicine and Female Citizenship in Revolutionary America," in *Women, Gender, and Enlightenment*, ed. Sarah Knott and Barbara Taylor (New York: Palgrave, 2005), 649–66.

27. Allen, *Life, Experience*, 6–17; Anna L. Barbauld, "Blest is the Man," in *A Selection of Hymns for Social Worship*, ed. William Enfield (Norwich: J. March, 1795), 171; Charles Wesley, *Short Hymns on Select Passages of the Holy Scriptures*, vol. 2 (Bristol, England: F. Farley, 1762),

94–95; Sylvia Frey and Betty Wood, *Come Shouting to Zion: African American Protestantism in the American South and British Caribbean to 1830* (Chapel Hill: University of North Carolina Press, 1998), xii, 104–10, 127–37, 165; G. J. Barker-Benfield, *The Culture of Sensibility: Sex and Society in Eighteenth-Century Britain* (Chicago: University of Chicago Press, 1995), 266–70.

28. John Wesley, *Thoughts Upon Slavery* (Philadelphia: Reprinted by Joseph Crukshank, 1774); Brycchan Carey, *British Abolitionism and the Rhetoric of Sensibility: Writing, Sentiment, and Slavery, 1760–1807* (New York: Palgrave Macmillan, 2005), 150–51, 1–21.

29. According to one popular hymn, "In Sickness will I make his Bed / The Cordial Draught prepare." See Charles Wesley, *Hymns and Sacred Poems*, vol. 1 (Bristol, England: Felix Farley, 1749), 215. See also John Wesley, *Primitive Physic: or An Easy and Natural Method of Curing most Diseases* (Philadelphia: Prichard & Hall, 1789); Deborah Madden, *A Cheap, Safe and Natural Medicine: Religion, Medicine, and Culture in John Wesley's Primitive Physic* (New York: Rodopi, 2007); John 15:13, King James Version. For "charge," see "A Charge to Keep," in Charles Wesley, *A Collection of Hymns* (London: J. Paramore, 1786), 306.

30. Benjamin Rush to Granville Sharp (ca. 1790s), in *The Selected Writings of Benjamin Rush*, ed. Dagobert D. Runes (New York: Philosophical Library, 1947), 24–25; Helen Thomas, *Romanticism and Slave Narratives: Transatlantic Testimonies* (New York: Cambridge University Press, 2000), 5–6; Newman, *Freedom's Prophet*, 32; Newman, Rael, and Lapsansky, *Pamphlets of Protest*, 2–28, 181–85; Carey, *British Abolitionism*, 19, 39, 132–42.

31. Jones and Allen, *Narrative*, 29–30, 4; Carey, *British Abolitionism*, 2, 39–48; Colin Kidd, *The Forging of Races: Race and Scripture in the Protestant Atlantic World, 1600–2000* (New York: Cambridge University Press, 2006), 40–48, 76–84; Acts 17:26; 1 Cor. 12:1–31.

32. Although the historiography on classical republicanism is extensive, a classic study is J. G. A. Pocock, *The Machiavellian Moment: Florentine Political Thought and the Atlantic Republican Tradition* (Princeton, NJ: Princeton University Press, 1975).

33. *Independent Gazetteer*, September 21, 1793; *National Gazette*, October 26, 1793; *General Advertiser*, September 23, 1793; *Columbian Gazetteer* (New York), September 23, 1793; Carey, *Short Account*, 90; *Mayor Clarkson Committee Minutes*, 35, LCP; Joseph Addison, *Cato: A Tragedy* (London: Chiswick Press, 1815), 187–92; Julie Ellison, *Cato's Tears and the Making of Anglo-American Emotion* (Chicago: University of Chicago Press, 2000), 18, 48–56; Sarah Knott, *Sensibility and the American Revolution* (Chapel Hill: University of North Carolina Press, 2009), 195–250; Susan Branson, *These Fiery Frenchified Dames: Women and Political Culture in Early National Philadelphia* (Philadelphia: University of Pennsylvania Press, 2001), 4–5.

34. Benjamin Rush, "An Enquiry into the Influence of Physical Causes on the Moral Faculty, Delivered Before the American Philosophical Society . . . on the 27th of Feb. 1786," in *Medical Inquiries and Observations* (Philadelphia: T. Dobson, 1793), 44–45; Rush to Allen (?), n.d., MSS Corr. B. Rush, vol. 38, 32, cited in Winch, *Philadelphia's Black Elite*, 15; Jones and Allen, *Narrative*, 18; Bruce Dorsey, *Reforming Men and Women: Gender in the Antebellum City* (Ithaca, NY: Cornell University Press, 2006), 31–32, 83.

35. Carey, *Short Account*, 90; *Minutes of the Proceedings*, 35, 3, 14, LCP; Carey, *Desultory Account*, 6–7. Carey missed the September 15 meeting of the mayor's emergency committee so did not know that the committee chose to pay Bush Hill hospital nurses from two to four dollars per day, which was comparable to the two to five dollars per day allegedly received by some home care nurses.

36. Powell, *Bring Out Your Dead*, 27; Jones and Allen, *Narrative*, 5, 13, 15; T. P. Monath and A. D. Barrett, "Pathogenesis and Pathophysiology of Yellow Fever," *Advances in Virus Research*, 60 (2003): 343–95; Jones and Allen, *Narrative*, 13; *Philadelphia Independent Gazetteer*, August 31, 1793; Butterfield, *Letters of Benjamin Rush*, 2:738–39.

37. *Independent Gazetteer* (Philadelphia), September 14, 1793; Jones and Allen, *Narrative*, 15; Benjamin Rush to Julia Rush, September 10, 1793, in Butterfield, *Letters of Benjamin Rush*, 2:657.

38. Bush Hill Hospital records in *Minutes of the Proceedings*, appendix 185–204; Benjamin Rush to Julia Rush, September 25, 1793, in Butterfield, *Letters of Benjamin Rush*, 2:684; Carey, *Short Account*, 79, 89–90; Thomas A. Apel, *Feverish Bodies, Enlightened Minds: Science and the Yellow Fever Controversy in the Early American Republic* (Stanford, CA: Stanford University Press, 2016), 1–34; Klepp, "How Many Precious Souls?," 167–68.

39. *Federal Gazette* (Philadelphia), September 13, 1793; Miller, "Wages of Blackness," 163–94; Letter to Caspar Wistar regarding Margaret Wister Haines (1735–93), September 29, 1793, Wyck Papers, series 3, box 87, APS; Milton Rubincam, "The Wistar-Wister Family: A Pennsylvania Family's Contributions Toward American Cultural Development," *Pennsylvania History* 20, no. 2 (1953): 142–64.

40. Margaret Hill Morris to My Patty [Milcah Martha Hill Moore], September 25, 1793, and Margaret Hill Morris to Richard Hill Morris, October 15, 1793, G. M. Howland MS Coll. 1000, box 7, folder 2, HQSC.

41. White, *Ar'n't I a Woman*, 27–62. Anne M. Boylan, "Benevolence and Antislavery Activity Among African American Women in New York and Boston, 1820–1840," in *The Abolitionist Sisterhood: Women's Political Culture in Antebellum America*, ed. Jean F. Yellin and John Van Horne (Ithaca, NY: Cornell University Press, 1994), 120; Kathleen M. Brown, *Good Wives, Nasty Wenches, and Anxious Patriarchs: Gender, Race, and Power in Colonial Virginia* (Chapel Hill: University of North Carolina Press, 1996), 110–28; Jennifer L. Morgan, *Laboring Women: Reproduction and Gender in New World Slavery* (Philadelphia: University of Pennsylvania Press, 2004), 1–48.

42. Samuel Johnson, *Dictionary of the English Language* (Boston: Benjamin Perkins, 1828), 94, 370, 376. Johnson defines *vile* as "sordid, wicked, worthless." In his *General Dictionary of the English Language* (London: John Stockdale, 1795), William Perry defined *prostitution* as "the life of a vile strumpet." The phrase "vile strumpet" to connote prostitution and murderous criminality appears frequently in popular eighteenth-century sources. See, for example, Aphra Behn, *The Dutch Lover*, in *The Plays, Histories, and Novels of the Ingenious Mrs. Aphra Behn*, vol. 1 (London: Mary Poulson, 1724), 204; Oliver Goldsmith, *The Vicar of Wakefield*, in *Miscellaneous Works of Oliver Goldsmith*, vol. 2 (Edinburgh, Scotland: W. & R. Chambers, 1833), 72, 98; Henry Fielding, *The History of Tom Jones* (Paris: Fr. Ambrose Didot, 1780), 19. For "vile nurse" see Alexander Thomson, *Pictures of Poetry: Historical, Biographical, and Critical* (London: Mundell & Son, 1799), 170.

43. Susan E. Klepp, *Revolutionary Conceptions: Women, Fertility, and Family Limitation in America, 1760–1820* (Chapel Hill: University of North Carolina Press, 2009), 90–132; Claire Lyons, *Sex Among the Rabble: An Intimate History of Gender and Power in the Age of Revolution, Philadelphia, 1730–1830* (Chapel Hill: University of North Carolina Press, 2006), 1–9, 289–92; Carey, *Short Account*, 61; Jones and Allen, *Narrative*, 9–10.

44. *Independent Gazetteer*, August 31, 1793; David Brion Davis, "Impact of the French and Haitian Revolutions," in *The Impact of the Haitian Revolution in the Atlantic World*, ed. David

Geggus (Columbia: University of South Carolina Press, 2001), 3–9; Simon P. Newman, "American Political Culture and the French and Haitian Revolutions," in Geggus, *The Impact of the Haitian Revolution*, 72–89; Susan Branson and Leslie Patrick, "Étrangers dans un Pays Étranger," in Geggus, *The Impact of the Haitian Revolution*, 193–208; Carey, *British Abolitionism*, 186–90; Nash, *Forging Freedom*, 3–4, 6; Jones and Allen, *Narrative*, 11, 20.

45. Mathew Carey, *A Desultory Account of the Yellow Fever, Prevalent in Philadelphia, and of the Present State of the City* (Philadelphia: M. Carey, 1793), 6–7. For "God and a Soldier" see Jones and Allen, *Narrative*, 21. I am uncertain of the origin of this oft-cited verse. It is quoted in a 1770 broadside, signed by the British "16th Regiment of Foot" expressing bitterness regarding the New York Sons of Liberty's lack of appreciation for their service in the Seven Years' War. See *Pennsylvania Gazette*, February 15, 1770.

46. Jones and Allen, *Narrative*, 11; Michael Brown, "Like a Devoted Army: Medicine, Heroic Masculinity, and the Military Paradigm in Victorian Britain," *Journal of British Studies* 49, no. 3 (2010): 592–622; Judith Rowbotham, "'Soldiers of Christ'? Images of Female Missionaries in Late Nineteenth-Century Britain: Issues of Heroism and Martyrdom," *Gender and History* 12, no. 1 (2000): 84.

47. See, for example, Benjamin Rush to Granville Sharp, in Runes, *Selected Writings*, 24; Wesley, *Thoughts upon Slavery*, 10; Carey, *British Abolitionism*, 134–35; Ellison, *Cato's Tears*, 6–8; Jones and Allen, *Narrative*, 29, 3.

48. *Philadelphia Gazette and Universal Daily Advertiser*, August 25, 1797; "Eulogium in Honour of Absalom Jones and Richard Allen, two of the Elders of the African Church, who furnished Nurses to the Sick, during the late pestilential Fever in Philadelphia," *Massachusetts Magazine* (December 1793); Heather Nathans, "Trampling Native Genius: John Murdock Versus the Chestnut Street Theatre," *Journal of American Drama and Theatre* 14 (Winter 2002): 29–43; John Murdock, *The Triumphs of Love, or Happy Reconciliation* (Philadelphia: printed by R. Folwell, 1795). Benjamin Rush purchased six copies.

49. Robert Purvis, *Appeal of Forty Thousand Citizens, Threatened with Disfranchisement, to the People of Pennsylvania* (Philadelphia: Merrihew and Gunn, 1838), 13–14, HSP; William Douglass, *Annals of the First African Church in the United States of America* (Philadelphia: King and Baird, 1862), 11.

50. Allen, *Life, Experience*, 1, 3, 40; Brown, *Homespun Heroines*, 10–12; James Oliver Horton and Lois E. Horton, *In Hope of Liberty: Culture, Community and Protest Among Northern Free Blacks, 1700–1860* (New York: Oxford University Press, 1997), 125–49; W. E. B. DuBois, *The Philadelphia Negro* (Philadelphia: University of Pennsylvania Press, 1899; repr., 1996), 19; Nash, *Forging Freedom*, 121–30; Charles H. Wesley, *Richard Allen: Apostle of Freedom* (Washington, DC: Associated Publishers, 1935; repr., 1969), 159, 197–99.

51. Mother Bethel AME Church Museum, Philadelphia; Marriage record of Richard Allen to Sarah Bass, 1801, *Marriage Records, 1789–1817*, St. George's Methodist Episcopal Church, Philadelphia; Benjamin Rush, *A Memorial Containing Travels Through Life or Sundry Incidents in the Life of Dr. Benjamin Rush*, ed. Louis Alexander Biddle (Philadelphia: Lanoraie, 1905), 153, 162.

52. Jarena Lee (1783–?), *Religious Experience and Journal of Mrs. Jarena Lee, Giving an Account of Her Call to Preach the Gospel* (Philadelphia: printed and published for the author, 1849), 11, 61; William L. Andrews, ed., *Sisters of the Spirit: Three Black Women's Autobiographies of the Nineteenth Century* (Bloomington: University of Indiana Press, 1986), introduction; Anna M. Lawrence, *One Family Under God: Love, Belonging, and Authority in Early*

Transatlantic Methodism (Philadelphia: University of Pennsylvania Press, 2011), 86–87, 214; Payne, *History*, 86–88.

53. Douglass, *Annals*, 11; Jones and Allen, *Narrative*, 12–13; Death certificate of Sarah Allen (dated 1849), Philadelphia City Hall, Register of Wills.

Chapter 8

1. May 1805 Philadelphia Monthly Meeting, quoted in John W. Jordan, *Colonial and Revolutionary Families of Pennsylvania*, vol. 1 (New York: Lewis Publishing Company, 1911), 1028. For Charles Marshall (1744–1826) and Elizabeth Marshall (1768–1836), see George M. Beringer, "The Centenary of Pharmaceutical Education in America," *American Journal of Pharmacy* 93, no. 2 (1921): 89; and Evan T. Ellis, "The Story of a Very Old Philadelphia Drug Store," *American Journal of Pharmacy* 75 (1903): 57–71.

2. M. I. Wilbert, "Elizabeth Marshall: The First Woman Pharmacist in America," *American Journal of Pharmacy and the Sciences* 76, no. 6 (1904): 271; Beringer, "Pharmaceutical Education," 89; Edward Kremers and Glenn Sonnedecker, *Kremers and Urdang's History of Pharmacy* (Madison, WI: American Institute of Pharmacy, 1985), 326; Kathleen M. Brown, *Foul Bodies: Cleanliness in Early America* (New Haven, CT: Yale University Press, 2009), 191–93, 212–32; H. V. Arny, "Pharmacy, 100 Years Ago," *American Journal of Pharmacy* 93, no. 3 (1921): 189. The popular early twentieth-century cartoonist Gene Carr reprised George Farquhar's Lady Bountiful as an elite philanthropist (not a healer) in newspaper comics, children's books, and magazines. See Judith O'Sullivan, *The Art of the Comic Strip* (Baltimore: University of Maryland Press, 1971), 65–66; Gene Carr, *Lady Bountiful and Phyllis: A Picture Book to Amuse Children* (New York: Cupples & Leon, 1903).

3. Margaret Morris Haviland, "Beyond Women's Sphere: Young Quaker Women and the Veil of Charity in Philadelphia, 1790–1810," *WMQ*, 3rd ser., 51, no. 3 (1994): 419–46; Martha H. Verbrugge, *Able-Bodied Womanhood: Personal Health and Social Change in Nineteenth-Century Boston* (New York: Oxford University Press, 1988), 28–35; Joan M. Jensen, *Loosening the Bonds: Mid-Atlantic Farm Women, 1750–1850* (New Haven, CT: Yale University Press, 1986), 38–46; Hannah Garrett, Recipe Book, Small MS 237, DCHS.

4. Wilbert, "Elizabeth Marshall," 274–76; E. Anthony Rotundo, *American Manhood: Transformations in Masculinity from the Revolution to the Modern Era* (New York: Basic Books, 1993), 167–93; Toby L. Ditz, "Shipwrecked; or, Masculinity Imperiled: Mercantile Representations of Failure and the Gendered Self in Eighteenth-Century Philadelphia," *Journal of American History* 81, no. 1 (1994): 51–80.

5. *The Pharmacopoeia of the United States of America*, 6th ed. (New York: William Wood & Company, 1883), 171; John U. Lloyd, *King's American Dispensatory*, 19th ed., vol. 2 (Cincinnati: Ohio Valley Company, 1905), 1269; Whitfield J. Bell Jr., "Benjamin Smith Barton, M.D.," *Journal of the History of Medicine and Allied Sciences* 26, no. 2 (1971): 197–203; Wilbert, "Elizabeth Marshall," 274–76; Simon Finger, *The Contagious City: The Politics of Public Health in Early Philadelphia* (Ithaca, NY: Cornell University Press, 2012), 103–19.

6. Wilbert, "Elizabeth Marshall," 274–76; John F. Watson, *Annals of Philadelphia: Being a Collection of Memoirs, Anecdotes, and Incidents of the City* (Philadelphia: E. L. Carey and A. Hart, 1830), 608; Ellis, "Story," 63; Jordan, *Colonial and Revolutionary*, 1029–30. For Isaac Paschall Morris (1803–69), see Jordan, *Colonial and Revolutionary*, 67–68.

7. "Paschall's Golden Drops," broadside, early nineteenth century, box C, 10, #3, DCHS; Thomas Wilson, *The Philadelphia Directory and Stranger's Guide for 1825* (Philadelphia:

Thomas Wilson & Wm. D. Vanbaun, 1825), xvii; Abraham Ernest Helffenstein, *Pierre Fauconnier and His Descendants* (Philadelphia: S. H. Burbank and Co., 1911), 69–70; Cornelius William Stafford, *The Philadelphia Directory for 1801* (Philadelphia: William W. Woodward, 1801), 91.

8. Hannah Lee, *Evening Amusement: Maxims on the Preservation of Health; An Account of Patent and Family Medicines* (New York, 1817), LCP; Lee family, *Maxims on the Preservation of Health* (?Baltimore, ca. 1801), LCP. Like Elizabeth Marshall, Hannah Lee came from a long line of Lee family druggists. For MS example, Sarah Richardson Waln (1746–1825), Recipe Book, ca. 1810–20, n.p., private collection.

9. Kremers and Urdang, *History of Pharmacy*, 181, 326, 471. See also Dennis B. Worthen, "The Pharmaceutical Industry, 1853–1902," in *American Pharmacy (1852–2002)*, ed. Elaine Condouris Stroud and Gregory Highby (Madison, WI: American Institute for the History of Pharmacy, 2005), 55. Worthen cites Christopher Marshall Jr. and Charles Marshall (not Elizabeth) for their roles in making Philadelphia the "cradle of pharmacy."

10. Carla Mulford, "Benjamin Franklin, Traditions of Liberalism, and Women's Learning in Eighteenth-Century Philadelphia," in *"The Good Education of Youth": Worlds of Learning in the Age of Franklin*, ed. John Pollack (New Castle, DE: Oak Knoll, 2009), 109–10; Ann D. Gordon, "The Young Ladies Academy of Philadelphia," in *Women of America*, ed. Carol Ruth Berkin and Mary Beth Norton (Boston: Houghton Mifflin, 1979), 68–91; Bruce Dorsey, *Reforming Men and Women: Gender in the Antebellum City* (Ithaca, NY: Cornell University Press, 2002), 1–89.

11. Milcah Martha Moore (1740–1829), *Miscellanies, Moral and Instructive, in Prose and Verse* (Philadelphia: Joseph Cruikshank, 1793); Catherine La Courreye Blecki and Karin A. Wulf, *Milcah Martha Moore's Book: A Commonplace Book from Revolutionary America* (University Park: Pennsylvania State University Press, 1997), 59–64; Haviland, "Beyond Women's Sphere," 420–24; Aimwell School Records, 1797–1935, MS 1183, boxes 1 and 4, HQSC; Female Society of Philadelphia for the Relief and Employment of the Poor subscriber list and constitution, 1812, Female Society of Philadelphia for the Relief and Employment of the Poor Records, HC.MC-1234, HQSC; *Some Account of the Aimwell School Instituted by the Society for the Free Instruction of Female Children, Now Incorporated Under the Title of "The Aimwell School Association"* (Philadelphia: Pile and M'Elroy, Printers, 1861); Philadelphia Religious Society of Friends Tracts and Annual Reports, 529.525.52, HSP; Rebecca Jones (1739–1817), "Manuscript Arithmetic Book [for Her School]," 1766, Diaries and Manuscript Books, 968, box 12, HQSC.

12. Maurice Jackson, *Let This Voice Be Heard: Anthony Benezet, Father of Atlantic Abolitionism* (Philadelphia: University of Pennsylvania Press, 2011), 20–25; Margaret Hill Morris to Margaret [Peggy] Smith, December 12, 1807, and November 18, 1800, G. M. Howland MS Coll. 1000, box 6, folder 4, HQSC; Helen Hole, *Westtown Through the Years* (Westtown, PA: Alumni Association, 1943), 1–14; Mary Kelley, *Learning to Stand and Speak: Women, Education, and Public Life* (Chapel Hill: University of North Carolina Press, 2006), 21–37; Jessica C. Linker, "The Fruits of Their Labor: Women's Scientific Practice in Early America, 1750–1860" (PhD diss., University of Connecticut, 2017); Kimberly Tolley, *The Science Education of American Girls: A Historical Perspective* (New York: Routledge Falmer, 2003), 1–12, 35–45. Van Dyke quoted in *To Read My Heart: The Journal of Rachel Van Dyke, 1810–1811*, ed. Lucia McMahon and Deborah Schriver (Philadelphia: University of Pennsylvania Press, 2000), 141.

13. Priscilla Wakefield, *Reflection on the Present Condition of the Female Sex with Suggestions for Its Improvement* (London: J. Johnson [etc.], 1798); Charles Jones Wister, *The Labour*

of a Long Life: A Memoir of Charles J. Wister by C. W. J., Jr. (Germantown, PA: privately printed, 1866), 55; Charles Jones Wister, Memoranda 1820, Eastwick Collection, MS 974.811/Ea 7, series 1, box 6, APS; Waln, Recipe Book, ca. 1810–20, n.p.

14. For Anne Parrish (1760–1800) and the Female Society of Philadelphia, see Visitations of the Sick, 1796, Parrish Collection, box 5, bound volumes, #1653, Parrish Family Papers, 1614–1874, HSP. See also Dorsey, *Reforming Men and Women*, 11–35; Elizabeth Marshall, "An Account of Anne Parrish," copybook, HQSC, Kathleen D. McCarthy, *American Creed: Philanthropy and the Rise of Civil Society, 1700–1865* (Chicago: University of Chicago Press, 2005), 30–35.

15. Elizabeth W. [Jones] Levick, *Recollections of Her Early Days* (Philadelphia: For her children, 1881), 23–24, 40.

16. Anne Parrish, Visitations of the Sick, 1796, 12, 23, HSP; John Scharf and Thompson Westcott, *History of Philadelphia, 1609–1884* (Philadelphia: L. H. Everts, 1884), 1449–50; Billy G. Smith, "The Institutional Poor: The Almshouse Daily Occurrence Docket," in *Life in Early Philadelphia: Documents from the Revolutionary and Early National Periods*, ed. Billy G. Smith (University Park: Pennsylvania State University Press, 1995), 29–56; Monique Bourque, "Populating the Poorhouse: A Reassessment of Poor Relief in the Antebellum Delaware Valley," *Pennsylvania History* 70, no. 3 (2003): 235–67; Simon Newman, *Embodied History: The Lives of the Poor in Early Philadelphia* (Philadelphia: University of Pennsylvania Press, 2003), 16–39.

17. Kristen A. Graham, *A History of the Pennsylvania Hospital* (Charleston, SC: History Press, 2008), 62.

18. Jeanne Boydston, *Home and Work: Housework, Wages, and the Ideology of Labor in the Early Republic* (New York: Oxford University Press, 1990); Barbara Welter, "The Cult of True Womanhood: 1820–1860," *American Quarterly* 18, no. 2 (1996): 151–74; Nancy F. Cott, *The Bonds of Womanhood: "Woman's Sphere" in New England, 1780–1835* (New Haven, CT: Yale University Press, 1997); Regina Morantz-Sanchez, *Sympathy and Science: Women Physicians in American Medicine* (New York: Oxford University Press, 1985), 19–24.

19. Erica Armstrong Dunbar, *A Fragile Freedom: African American Women and Emancipation in the Antebellum City* (New Haven, CT: Yale University Press, 2008), 48–69; Shirley J. Yee, *Black Women Abolitionists: A Study in Activism, 1828–1860* (Knoxville: University of Tennessee Press, 1992), 40–85.

20. Kathleen M. Brown, "The Maternal Physician: Teaching Mothers to Put the Baby in the Bathwater," in *Right Living: An Anglo-American Tradition of Self-Help Medicine and Hygiene*, ed. Charles Rosenberg (Baltimore: Johns Hopkins University Press, 2003), 88–11; Brown, *Foul Bodies*, 215–30; An American Matron [Mary Hunt Palmer Tyler], *The Maternal Physician: A Treatise on the Nurture and Management of Infants, from the Birth until Two Years Old* (New York: Isaac Riley, 1811); An American Matron [Tyler], *The Maternal Physician* (Philadelphia: Lewis Adams, Clark, and Raser, Printers; repr., 1818), LCP; Cornelia S. King, "Right Living by the Book: A Gift of Mother's Manuals from Charles E. Rosenberg," *Annual Report of the Library Company of Philadelphia for the Year 2010* (Philadelphia: Library Company of Philadelphia, 2011), 59–63; Lamar R. Murphy, *Enter the Physician: The Transformation of Domestic Medicine, 1760–1860* (Tuscaloosa: University of Alabama Press, 1991), 1–32.

21. Edward Potts Cheyney, *History of the University of Pennsylvania* (Philadelphia: University of Pennsylvania Press, 1940), 207–16; Judith Walzer Leavitt, *Brought to Bed: Childbearing in America, 1750–1950* (New York: Oxford University Press, 1986), 3–13; John C. Burnham, *Health Care in America: A History* (Baltimore: Johns Hopkins University Press, 2015), 53–67;

Charles E. Rosenberg, "Health in the Home: A Tradition of Print and Practice," in Rosenberg, *Right Living*, 1–21.

22. Burnham, *Health Care*, 62–75.

23. Watson, *Annals*, 608; Simon Baatz, "A Very Diffused Disposition": Dissecting Schools in Philadelphia, 1823–1825," *PMHB* 108, no. 2 (1984): 203–15; Caroline de Costa and Francesca Miller, "American Resurrection and the 1788 New York Doctor's Riot," *Lancet* 377, no. 9762 (2011): 292–93.

24. Pliny Earle, *The Memoirs of Pliny Earle, M.D.*, ed. F. B. Sanborn (Boston: Damrell & Upham, 1898), 56; Michael Sappol, *A Traffic of Dead Bodies: Anatomy and Embodied Social Identity in Nineteenth-Century America* (Princeton, NJ: Princeton University Press, 2002), 98–109; Jubilee Marshall, "Race, Death, and Public Health in Early Philadelphia, 1750–1793," *Pennsylvania History* 87, no. 2 (2020): 364–89; Ruth Richardson, *Death, Dissection, and the Destitute* (New York: Routledge, 1987), 76–90.

25. Henry Drinker Biddle, ed., *Extracts from the Journal of Elizabeth Drinker, From 1759 to 1807, A.D.* (Philadelphia: J. B. Lippincott Company, 1899), 410, 378, 380–85.

26. Whitfield J. Bell Jr., "Martha Brand (1755?—1814): An Early American Physician," *Journal of the History of Medicine* 33, no. 2 (1978): 218–19; *New Trade Directory for Philadelphia, Anno 1800* (Philadelphia: Way and Groff, 1799), 130.

27. Elizabeth Drinker, Diary, entries for June 11–June 15 and June 23, 1806, in *The Diary of Elizabeth Drinker*, vol. 3, ed. Elaine Forman Crane (Boston: Northeastern University Press, 1991), 1936–40. Martha Brand, Will, January 28, 1809, Philadelphia Will Book, no. 5, 233, Philadelphia City Hall; Mary Fayssoux, Will, June 12, 1804, Philadelphia Will Book, no. 1, 228; *New Trade Directory*, 130; Stafford, *Philadelphia Directory* (1801), 142, 149, James Robinson, *Philadelphia Directory for 1806* (Philadelphia: James Robinson, 1806), n.p., *American Daily Advertiser* (Philadelphia), March 26, 1814. For the Cathralls, see Scharf and Westcott, *History of Philadelphia*, 1166, 1615. Susannah Swett was Henry Drinker's first wife's mother, who died in March 1807. See Richard Goodbear, *World of Trouble: A Philadelphia Quaker Family's Journey Through the American Revolution* (New Haven, CT: Yale University Press, 2019), 355; Esther White, Will, January 20, 1791, Philadelphia Will Book, no. 27, 58, Philadelphia City Hall.

28. Ann Booth to Dr. Benjamin H. Coates (1797–1881), January 1819, Coates and Reynell Family Papers, ser. 3, box 50, folder 6, HSP.

29. For example, Catherine Heyler is listed as a bleeder at 148 Sassafras St. in Robinson, *Philadelphia Directory for 1806*, 134, and under "Dentists and Bleeders" as a "cupper, bleeder & layer out of the dead" in John A. Paxton, *Philadelphia Directory 1819* (Philadelphia: John A. Paxton, 1819), 42, 188. See also Lisa Rosner, "Thistle on the Delaware: Edinburgh Medical Education and Philadelphia Practice, 1800–1825," *Social History of Medicine* 5, no. 1 (1992): 19–42; John Adems Paxton and Edward Whitely, eds., *Paxton's Annual Advertiser*, 1818–19, *Whitely's Philadelphia Annual Advertiser*, 1820, *Whitely's Philadelphia Register*, 1820–21, and *Whitely's Annual Philadelphia Directory*, 1822 (Philadelphia: published for the editor, by E. & R. Parker, 1818–22); Stafford, *Philadelphia Directory* (1801), 142, 149; Robinson, *Philadelphia Directory* (1816), n.p.

30. Crane, *Diary of Elizabeth Drinker*, 134, 147, 154, 155, 231, 236, 671; Patricia D'Antonio, *American Nursing: A History of Knowledge, Authority, and the Meaning of Work* (Baltimore: Johns Hopkins University Press, 2010), 4–10.

31. MS Recipe Book Darlington Family, MS 1982, CCHS; Garrett, Recipe Book, DCHS; Samuel Fitch Hotchkin, *Rural Pennsylvania in the Vicinity of Philadelphia* (Philadelphia:

G. W. Jacobs and Company, 1897), 422–24. For Elizabeth Neff Bowman (1807–68), see Franklin Ellis, *History of Lancaster County, Pennsylvania* (Philadelphia: Everts and Peck, 1883), 281. See also Rappe Family Recipe Book, ca. 1810–40, Doc. 512, Joseph Downs Coll., WML; L[etticia] Billmeyer, "Medical Cookery and Other Recipes," ca. 1800–1810, private collection; Pennock Family Recipe Book and Eliza Pennock, Commonplace Book with Medical and Cooking Recipes, MS 31832–33, MS 1113, CCHS; Clymer Family, Account Book and Recipe Book, 1788–1854, MS Coll. 387, UPRBM. Women in other states also practiced into the early nineteenth century. For example, Silence Wilcox Ranney (1726–1811) "traveled on horseback with her stock of herbs, being a doctress of considerable reputation." See Charles C. Adams, *A History of the North Society of Middletown, Connecticut, from 1650 to 1800* (New York: Grafton Press, 1908), 174.

32. *Gazette of the United States* (Philadelphia), November 30, 1798, and December 4, 1798. For example, Stafford, *Philadelphia Directory* (1800) lists four midwives; Robinson, *Philadelphia Directory* (1806) lists twenty-two, Robinson, *Philadelphia Directory* (1816) lists eighteen.

33. Martha Austin Reeves (1760–1832), "Martha Reeves Record Book of Births, 1801–1831," *Vineland Historical Magazine* 24 (1939): 247–67, and 25 (1940): 27–35, 57–63, 90–103; Joan N. Burstyn, ed., *Past and Promise: Lives of New Jersey Women* (Syracuse, NY: Syracuse University Press, 1997), 81–82.

34. For Susanna Rohrer Müller (1756–1815) and quotations, see M. D. Learned and C. F. Brede, "An Old German Midwife's Record," in *The American Ethnological Survey: Conestoga Expedition, 1902*, vol. 12, ed. Marion D. Learned (New York: D. Appleton and Company, 1911), 3–4; "Susannah Müller," *German American Annals* 1, no. 2 (1903): 73–117; Manuscript Memorandum kept by Mrs. Joseph Sarber, Midwife at the Falls of the Schuylkill, from 1814 to 1831, Am 9235, HSP.

35. For Anna Maria Jung (ca. 1749–1819), see David W. Kriebel, *Powwowing Among the Pennsylvania Dutch: A Traditional Medical Practice* (University Park: Pennsylvania State University Press, 2007), 100–102. See also John George Hohman, *The Long Lost Friend: A Collection of Mysterious and Invaluable Arts and Remedies, for Man as Well as Animals with Many Proofs* (Harrisburg, PA: T. F. Scheffer, 1856).

36. Hohman, *Long Lost Friend*, 20; Don Yoder, "Hohman and Romanus: Origins and Diffusion of the Pennsylvania German Powwow Manual," in *American Folk Medicine: A Symposium*, ed. Wayland D. Hand (Berkeley: University of California Press, 1976), 235–48.

37. Priscilla Homespun [pseud.], *The Universal Receipt Book; Being a Compendious Repository of Practical Information . . . [in] All the Branches of Domestic Economy* (Philadelphia: published by Isaac Riley, J. Maxwell, printer, 1818); Laurel Thatcher Ulrich, *The Age of Homespun: Objects and Stories in the Creation of an American Myth* (New York: Vintage Books, 2001), 3–10.

38. Homespun, *Universal Receipt*, 82, 89, 90, 94, 113; Charles E. Rosenberg, "Medical Text and Social Context: Explaining William Buchan's Domestic Medicine," *Bulletin of the History of Medicine* 57, no. 1 (1983): 22–42.

39. Sarah Richardson Waln (1746–1825), Recipe Book, ca. 1800, (Phi) Am. 1743, HSP, 3, 18; S. R. Waln, Recipe Book, ca. 1810–20, n.p., private collection; Jackson, *Let This Voice Be Heard*, 124–25, 219–20; Richard S. Newman, *Freedom's Prophet: Bishop Richard Allen, the AME Church, and the Black Founding Fathers* (New York: New York University Press, 2008), 147–48. For Sarah Bass Allen, see Chapter 5.

40. Sarah Waln to Nicholas Waln, July 5, 1784, July 23, 1784, September 4, 1784, and October 25, 1784, Letters of Sarah Richardson Waln, 1784–86, box 1, folder 27, and Jacob S. Waln [her son] to Sarah Richardson Waln, February 10, 1807, box 1, folder 17, all in Nicholas Waln

Family Papers, MS Coll. 966, HQSC. See also Mary Harrison, *Annals of the Ancestors of Charles Custis Harrison and Ellen Waln Harrison* (Philadelphia: privately printed by J. B. Lippincott, 1932), 79–100; Leonard Snowden to Rebecca Jones, August 18, 1797, Hoskins-Warder Scrapbook of Letters and Documents, HQSC.

41. Waln, Recipe Book, 1810–20, n.p.; Waln, Recipe Book, ca. 1800, (Phi) Am. 1743, HSP, 3, 18; Jordan, *Colonial and Revolutionary*, 212; Philadelphia Monthly Meeting, *Quaker Biographies*, vol. 4 (Philadelphia: Friends' Book Store, 1916), 89–98; Hannah Logan Fisher Smith, *A Collection of Religious Memoirs and Extracts* (Philadelphia: E. G. Dorsey, 1839), 104–48.

42. Sarah Elizabeth Logan, Receipts for Picking, Preserving, Cooking, and Quacking, MS ca. 1810s–mid-nineteenth century, n.p., Stenton Archives, Germantown, PA; John Jay Smith, *Recollections of John Jay Smith* (Philadelphia: J. B. Lippincott Company, 1892), 14–17; Gulielma M. Smith, Recipe MS, and Margaret M. Smith, Recipe MS, Edward Wanton Smith Coll., 955, box 11, HQSC. See also Edward Wanton Smith Coll., 955, miscellaneous recipes, box 2b.

43. Mrs. Daniel W. [Margaret Burd] Coxe (1781–1845), Cook Book and Medicinal Recipes, 1817–1832, Am. 912339, vol. 1, HSP, 28, 36, 44, 49, 51, 55, 57; Burd Family Papers, MS Coll. 379, series 5, Coxe Family, folders 49, 50, 52, University of Delaware Special Collections; Faye E. Dudden, *Serving Women: Household Service in Nineteenth-Century America* (Middletown, CT: Wesleyan University Press, 1985), introduction; Eliza Cope Harrison, *Best Companions: Letters of Eliza Middleton Fisher and Her Mother* (Columbia: University of South Carolina Press, 2001), 82–83, 152, 255.

44. Margaret Hill Morris to Gulielma Morris Smith, January 9, 1798, G. M. Howland MS Coll. 100, box 7, folder 2, HQSC; for Susanna Dillwyn Emlen (1769–1819), see Susan Garfinkle, "This Trial Was Sent in Love and Mercy for My Refinement: A Quaker Woman's Experience of Breast Cancer Surgery in 1814," in *Women and Health in America*, 2nd ed., ed. Judith Walzer Leavitt (Madison: University of Wisconsin Press, 1999), 68–90.

45. Deborah Norris Logan to Susanna Dillwyn Emlen, May 29, 1814, G. M. Howland MS Coll. 100, box 6, folder 20, HQSC. Logan paraphrased 1 Cor. 27, King James Version, "But God hath chosen the foolish things of the world, to confound the wise: and God hath chosen the weak things of the world, to confound the things which are mighty."

46. For Samuel Thomson (1769–1842), see John S. Haller Jr., *The People's Doctors: Samuel Thomson and the American Botanical Movement* (Carbondale: Southern Illinois University Press, 2001); Martha M. Libster, *Herbal Diplomats: The Contribution of Early American Nurses to Nineteenth-Century Health Care Reform and the Botanical Movement* (West Lafayette, IN: Golden Apple Publications, 2004), 40–49; William G. Rothstein, "The Botanical Movements and Orthodox Medicine," in *Other Healers: Unorthodox Medicine in America*, ed. Norman Gevitz (Baltimore: Johns Hopkins University Press, 1988), 42–46. John Thomson, cited in Barbara Ehrenreich and Deirdre English, *For Her Own Good: Two Centuries of the Expert's Advice to Women* (New York: Anchor, 2005), 58–61, quote on 60.

47. Ronald L. Numbers, "Do-It-Yourself the Sectarian Way," in *Send Us a Lady Physician: Women Doctors in America, 1835–1920*, ed. Ruth J. Abram (New York: W. W. Norton, 1985), 43–54; Steven J. Peitzman, *A New and Untried Course: Women's Medical College and Medical College of Philadelphia, 1850–1998* (New Brunswick, NJ: Rutgers University Press, 2000); Anne Taylor Kirschmann, *A Vital Force: Women in American Homeopathy* (New Brunswick, NJ: Rutgers University Press, 2004), 8–26; Ellen S. More, *Restoring the Balance: Women Physicians and the Profession of Medicine, 1850–1995* (Cambridge, MA: Harvard University Press, 2001), 13–39.

48. Susan Cayleff, *Wash and Be Healed: The Water-Cure Movement and Women's Health* (Philadelphia: Temple University Press, 1991); Jane B. Donegan, *"Hydropathic Highway to Health": Women and Water-Cure in Antebellum America* (Westport, CT: Praeger, 1986); Morantz-Sanchez, *Sympathy and Science*, 28–47; Susan Klepp, *Revolutionary Conceptions: Women, Fertility, and Family Limitation in America, 1760–1820* (Chapel Hill: University of North Carolina Press), 276–78; Andrea Tone, *Devices and Desires: A History of Contraceptives in America* (New York: Hill and Wang, 2001), 13–16; Janet Farrell Brodie, *Contraception and Abortion in Nineteenth-Century America* (Ithaca, NY: Cornell University Press, 1994).

49. Paul Starr, *The Social Transformation of American Medicine* (New York: Basic Books, 1982), 40–59, 88–102; Burnham, *Health Care*, 74–90, 129–31.

50. [Walter Channing], *Remarks on the Employment of Females as Practitioners in Midwifery* (Boston: Cummings and Hilliard, 1820), 7; Laurel Thatcher Ulrich, *A Midwife's Tale: The Life of Martha Ballard, Based on Her Diary, 1785–1812* (New York: Vintage Books, 1991), 251; Charles Coleman Sellers, *Patience Wright, American Artist and Spy in George III's London* (Middletown, CT: Wesleyan University Press, 1976), 18–45; Robert Hooper, *The Anatomist's Vade-Mecum* [portable handbook], *Containing the Anatomy and Physiology of the Human Body*, 1st [American] ed. (Boston: David Carlisle, 1801), LCP, inscribed by James Bartram, John M. Bartram, and Ann Bartram [Carr] (1779–1858). See also Merril Smith, "The Bartram Women: Farm Wives, Artists, Botanists, and Entrepreneurs," *Bartram Broadside* (Winter 2001): 1–4.

51. For May Gove Nichols (1810–84), see Mrs. Mary S. Gove, *Lectures to Ladies on Anatomy and Physiology* (Boston: Saxton and Peirce, 1842), v.

52. Gove quoted in Jean Silver-Insenstadt, *Shameless: The Visionary Life of Mary Gove Nichols* (Baltimore: Johns Hopkins University Press, 2002), 42, 1–44. Broadside held by New York Historical Society, reproduced in Sally Gregory Kohlstedt, "Physiological Lectures for Women: Sarah Coates in Ohio, 1850," *Journal of the History of Medicine* 33 (1978): 75–81; Elizabeth Cady Stanton, Susan B. Anthony, and Matilda Joslyn Gage, eds., *History of Woman Suffrage, 1848–1861*, vol. 1 (New York: Fowler and Wells, 1881), 101–4; Brodie, *Contraception and Abortion*, 108.

53. Jean Soderlund, "Priorities and Power: The Philadelphia Female Anti-Slavery Society," in *The Abolitionist Sisterhood: Women's Political Culture in Antebellum America*, ed. Jean Fagan Yellin and John C. Van Horne (Ithaca, NY: Cornell University Press, 1994), 67–88; Carla L. Peterson, *"Doers of the Word": African-American Women Speakers and Writers in the North, 1830–1880* (New York: Oxford University Press, 1995), 15–16; Dorothy Sterling, ed., *We Are Your Sisters: Black Women in the Nineteenth Century* (New York: Norton, 1984), 129; Marie Lindhorst, "Politics in a Box: Sarah Mapps Douglass and the Female Literary Association, 1831–1833," *Pennsylvania History: A Journal of Mid-Atlantic Studies* 65 (1998): 263–78; April R. Haynes, *Riotous Flesh: Women, Physiology, and the Solitary Vice in Nineteenth-Century America* (Chicago: University of Chicago Press, 2015), 81–90.

54. Peitzman, *New and Untried Course*, 5–19.

Epilogue

1. Joseph S. Longshore, *Valedictory Address Delivered Before the Graduating Class at the First Annual Commencement of the Female Medical College of Pennsylvania* (Philadelphia: published by the graduates, 1852), 3, 5, 7; Steven J. Peitzman, *A New and Untried Course: Woman's Medical College and Medical College of Pennsylvania, 1850–1998* (New Brunswick, NJ: Rutgers University Press, 2000), 5–22, 45–55.

2. For Ann Preston (1813–72) and Hannah E. Myers Longshore (1819–1901), see Peitzman, *New and Untried Course*, 8–17, 45–55; Regina Morantz-Sanchez, "The Female Student Has Arrived," in *Send Us a Lady Physician: Women Doctors in America, 1835–1920*, ed. Ruth J. Abram (New York: W. W. Norton, 1985), 59–69; and Ruth J. Abram, "Will There Be a Monument?," in Abram, *Send Us a Lady Physician*, 71–84; Susan Wells, *Out of the Dead House: Nineteenth-Century Women Physicians and the Writing of Medicine* (Madison: University of Wisconsin Press, 2001), 57–79, 122–45; Ellen S. More, *Restoring the Balance: Women Physicians and the Profession of Medicine, 1850–1995* (Cambridge, MA: Harvard University Press, 2001), 15–18, 79. Ann Preston helped to establish the Woman's Hospital of Philadelphia in 1861. In 1863, she instituted the first chartered school of nursing in the United States. The Ann Preston, M.D., Papers, 1831–1880, and the Longshore Family Papers, 1819–1902, are held at Drexel University College of Medicine, Legacy Center: Archives and Special Collections on Women in Medicine and Homeopathy.

3. Ann Preston, "Introductory Lecture to the Course of Instruction," Female Medical College of Pennsylvania, 1855, 13, 6, Drexel University College of Medicine, Archives and Special Collections.

4. Preston, "Introductory Lecture," 8; J. Longshore, *Valedictory Address*, 9. See also Michael Sappol, *A Traffic of Dead Bodies: Anatomy and Embodied Social Identity in Nineteenth-Century America* (Princeton, NJ: Princeton University Press, 2002), 2–7, 74–97; Regina Markell Morantz-Sanchez, *Sympathy and Science: Women Physicians in American Medicine* (New York: Oxford University Press, 1985), 47–68; John Harley Warner, *The Therapeutic Perspective: Medical Practice, Knowledge, and Identity in America, 1820–1885* (Princeton, NJ: Princeton University Press, 1997); John Harley Warner and James M. Edmonson, *Dissection: Photographs of a Rite of Passage in American Medicine 1880–1930* (Jackson, TN: Blast Books, 2009).

5. Longshore, *Valedictory Address*, 12.

6. Longshore, *Valedictory Address*, 14; Autumn Stanley, *Mothers and Daughters of Invention: Notes for a Revised History of Technology* (New Brunswick, NJ: Rutgers University Press, 1995), 117–19; Sarah Stage, *Female Complaints: Lydia Pinkham and the Business of Women's Medicine* (New York: Norton, 1979); "Susan Hayhurst," *American Journal of Pharmacy*, ed. Henry Kraemer, 83 (Philadelphia: Philadelphia College of Pharmacy, 1911): 32–39. Hayhurst grew up in a Quaker community in Bucks County, PA.

7. Longshore, *Valedictory Address*, 13, 8; Patricia D'Antonio, "The Legacy of Domesticity," *Nursing History Review* 1 (1993): 229–46; Patricia D'Antonio, *American Nursing: A History of Knowledge, Authority, and the Meaning of Work* (Baltimore: Johns Hopkins University Press, 2010), 1–27.

8. Sarah Mapps Douglass to Hannah White Richardson, ca. 1850s, quoted in Wells, *Out of the Dead House*, 58; Darlene Clark Hine, "Co-laborers in the Work of the Lord: Nineteenth-Century Black Women Physicians," in Ruth J. Abram, *Send Us a Lady Physician: Women Doctors in America, 1835–1920* (New York: W. W. Norton, 1985), 107–20; Benson Tong, *Susan La Flesche Picotte, M.D.: Omaha Indian Leader and Reformer* (Norman: University of Oklahoma Press, 1999).

9. For Elizabeth Harker Elmer (1832–1915), see Joan N. Burstyn, ed., *Past and Promise: Lives of New Jersey Women* (Syracuse, NY: Syracuse University Press, 1997), 135; Evelyn Stryker Lewis, *Neptune and Shark River Hills* (Charleston, SC: Arcadia Publishing, 1998), 20. For Elizabeth Neff Bowman (1807–68), see Franklin Ellis, *History of Lancaster County, Pennsylvania* (Philadelphia: Everts and Peck, 1883), 281. See also *Lancaster Examiner and Herald* (Pennsylvania), January 19, 1876.

10. Jennifer C. Day and Cheridan Christnacht, "Your Health Care Is in Women's Hands: Women Hold 76% of All Health Care Jobs," U.S. Census Bureau, August 2019, https://www .census.gov/library/stories/2019/08/your-health-care-in-womens-hands.html; Campbell Robertson and Robert Gebeloff, "How Millions of Women Became the Most Essential Workers in America," *New York Times*, April 18, 2020; Richard Smiley et al., "The 2017 National Nursing Workforce Study," *Journal of Nursing Regulation* 9, no. 3 (2018); Kechinyere C. Iheduru-Anderson, "The White/Black Hierarchy Institutionalizes White Supremacy in Nursing and Nursing Leadership in the United States," *Journal of Professional Nursing* 32, no. 2 (2021): 411–421, https://doi.org/10.1016/j.profnurs.2020.05.005; American Association of Colleges of Nursing, "Enhancing Diversity in the Workforce," updated April 1, 2019, https://www.aacnnursing .org/News-Information/Fact-Sheets/Enhancing-Diversity; Lisa S. Rotenstein and Jessica Dudley, "How to Close the Gender Pay Gap in U.S. Medicine," *Harvard Business Review*, November 4, 2019; Cherisse Berry, "A Call to Action: Black/African American Women Surgeon Scientists, Where Are They?," *Annals of Surgery* 272, no. 1 (2020): 24–29, doi: 10.1097/ SLA.0000000000003786; Brendan Murphy, "These Medical Specialties Have the Biggest Gender Imbalances," *AMA Connect*, October 1, 2019; Aislinn Antrim, "Study Finds Increased Gender and Racial Diversity in Pharmacy Field," *Pharmacy Times*, May 19, 2020; American Association of Colleges of Pharmacy, "Academic Pharmacy's Vital Statistics," https://www.aacp .org/article/academic-pharmacys-vital-statistics#:~:text; American Association of University Women, "The STEM Gap: Women and Girls in Science, Technology, Engineering, and Math," https://www.aauw.org/resources/research/the-stem-gap/; Carole Bennett, Ellen K. Hamilton, Haresh Rochani, "Exploring Race in Nursing: Teaching Nursing Students About Racial Inequality Using the Historical Lens," *Online Journal of Issues in Nursing* 24, no. 2 (2019); Pamela M. Leggett-Robinson, "Celebrating Transformations Through STEM Storytelling," in *Overcoming Barriers for Women of Color in STEM Fields: Emerging Research and Opportunities*, ed. P. M. Leggett-Robinson and Brandi Campbell Villa (Hershey, PA: IGI Global, 2020), 54–81; Pamela M. Leggett-Robinson and Pamela E. Scott-Johnson, "A Journey Worth Traveling: Mentoring and Role Models Matter," in Leggett-Robinson and Campbell Villa, *Overcoming Barriers for Women of Color in STEM Fields*, 116–40; Heidi Reeder et al., "Perceptions About Women in Science and Engineering History," *Proceedings of the 2012 American Society for Engineering Education Annual Conference* (2012), http://www.asee.org/public/conferences/8 /papers/3444/view; Kim Tolley, *The Science Education of Girls: A Historical Perspective* (New York: Routledge, 2003). Since the mid-twentieth century, scholars have continued to ask why there are so few women in science. See Alice S. Rossi, "Women in Science: Why So Few?," *Science* 148, no. 3674 (1965): 1196–202; Catherine Hill et al., *Why So Few? Women in Science, Technology, Engineering, and Mathematics* (Washington, DC: AAUW, 2010); Eileen Pollack, "Why Are There Still So Few Women in Science?," *New York Times*, October 3, 2013.

INDEX

Page numbers in italic type indicate illustrations.

ACKNOWLEDGMENTS

I did not intend to write my PhD dissertation on women healers. When I embarked on a second career in history after my first profession as a nurse practitioner, I was interested in studying the intersections of politics and women's history. However, I was captivated when Susan Klepp, my dissertation advisor, introduced me to Elizabeth Coates Paschall's eighteenth-century medical recipe book. As I read Paschall's descriptions of her medical remedies and her patient encounters, my mind strayed back to the 1980s, when I worked in a clinic in a medically underserved area in the mountains of North Carolina. I recalled meeting lay healers and granny midwives who shared their vibrant and long-standing cultures of lay healing and self-help medicine. These healers described their family medical recipe books full of remedies that had been collected, curated, and passed down from mother to daughter through generations. Although I was ostensibly the health care expert, these respected practitioners offered me medical advice along with instructions for woodchuck oil poultices and recipes for yellowroot and ginseng tea. I knew that I should be recording these important oral histories, but I was distracted by the demands of work and family. Opening Paschall's medical recipe book revived my exchanges with the skilled North Carolina healers. I had lost the opportunity to collect their oral histories, but I realized that I could honor them by writing a history of women healers.

As I began my dissertation research, I remembered reading Laurel Thatcher Ulrich's compelling Pulitzer Prize–winning book, *A Midwife's Tale: The Life of Martha Ballard, Based on Her Diary, 1785–1812.* Through painstaking archival investigations, Ulrich brought Ballard's midwifery practice to life and wove her experiences into broader social, cultural, political, and economic histories. Susan Klepp's *Revolutionary Conceptions: Women, Fertility, and Family Limitation in America, 1760–1820* and Rebecca Tannenbaum's *The Healer's Calling: Women and Medicine in Early New England* provided me with additional strategies for unearthing the vernacular healing cultures of women who left only scarce documentary traces. I was puzzled that few scholars had followed in these historians' trail. However, as I began my own archival work, I appreciated just how difficult it was to recover women's historical health care practices.

In the process of researching and writing my dissertation on webs of healing information exchanges, I was supported by extensive networks of generous scholars, librarians, and archivists. I owe a profound debt of gratitude to my dissertation adviser, Susan Klepp, whose unstinting guidance and support sustained me through the long archival search to recover women healers and to compile their stories into a manuscript. David Waldstreicher's ongoing encouragement, humor, and insightful comments helped me to refine my ideas and develop the dissertation. Travis Glasson was always available to assist me with the British context for the work. My outside reader, Kathy Brown, encouraged me to embark on my odyssey into the history field, and her advice and support on this project have been vital from the beginning.

I visited more than twenty archives and special collections libraries to conduct my research, and the assistance of the staff members at these institutions contributed significantly to this project. Although there is not space to thank each of these individuals, I am in their debt. I am also grateful to the institutions that granted me fellowships to pursue my research. Jim Green, Connie King, and the staff at the Library Company of Philadelphia generously shared their expertise throughout the project and during my residence as a Helfand Fellow in Early American Medicine, Science, and Society. I also benefited from a fellowship at the American Philosophical Society under the guidance of Earle Spamer and numerous others. John Anderies, Ann Upton, and Diana Peterson helped me to explore the Haverford College Quaker and Special Collections Library during my tenure as a Gest Fellow. A Neville Thompson Research Fellowship at Winterthur enriched my project under the guidance of staff who helped me to explore their recipe books and medical material culture. Babak Ashrafi and Simon Joseph at the Consortium for History of Science, Technology, and Medicine (CHSTM) connected me to a scholarly community of historians of science and medicine, and their fellowship allowed me to conduct research at a variety of institutions. I would also like to thank Laura Keim (Stenton), John Pollack (Penn Rare Books and Special Collections), Stacey Peeples (Pennsylvania Hospital Archives), Rev. Mark Tyler and Margaret Jerrido (Mother Bethel AME Church), and Joel Fry (Bartram's Garden).

The McNeil Center for Early American Studies, under the direction of Dan Richter, has been a supportive scholarly home since I began my pursuit of history. My MCEAS Consortium Fellowship at the center provided me with a collegial community of scholars too numerous to name, whose insights added to my dissertation immeasurably. A Dissertation Completion Fellowship granted by the American Council of Learned Societies allowed me to focus on writing during the final year. The professors and graduate students in the Temple Department of History were indispensable.

I am grateful to Bob Lockhart and Kathy Brown at Penn Press, who offered careful edits and suggestions that improved the manuscript substantially. My thanks to the University of Pennsylvania Press and the University of Virginia Press for permission to reproduce portions of material that have appeared previously. Innumerable colleagues provided invaluable advice on the conference papers that provided the groundwork for this book. I have delivered portions of this monograph to the McNeil Center, the Society for Historians of the Early American Republic, CHSTM, the Omohundro Institute, the Program in Early American Economy and Society annual conference, the Front Range Early Americanist Consortium, the History of Women's Health Conference at the Pennsylvania Hospital, and the American Association for the History of Nursing.

This book was also inspired by the legacy of my grandmother Charlotte Browning Murphree, who corresponded with the poet Robert Frost to complete her MA in English Literature in 1927. She was a lifelong educator who my grandfather nicknamed "Fess," short for Professor. My parents and my extended family have supported me throughout the writing process. I appreciate my daughters, Laura and Christie, who offered their substantive editing and artistic skills for this project. Special thanks to my husband, Sam, for his constant support, tireless manuscript readings, and invaluable editorial comments.